THE LOGIC OF
LITERATURE

Käte Hamburger

THE LOGIC OF LITERATURE

Second, Revised Edition

Translated by

Marilynn J. Rose

Indiana University Press

Bloomington *London*

Originally published as *Die Logik der Dichtung*

Copyright © Ernst Klett Verlag, Stuttgart, Germany

English language edition copyright © 1973 by Indiana University Press

Published in Canada by Fitzhenry & Whiteside Limited, Don Mills, Ontario

Library of Congress catalog card number: 72–79906

ISBN: 0–253–33605–8

MANUFACTURED IN THE UNITED STATES OF AMERICA

CONTENTS

Foreword

This translation of the second edition of my book *Die Logik der Dichtung*, done by Miss Marilynn Rose, has been critically read in manuscript form by both myself and Reginald St. Leon, Associate Professor of German at the University of Sydney, Australia. I am responsible for all deletions of words, sentences, and paragraphs which appeared unnecessary for the American edition. We have omitted the final chapter of the German edition because the problems broached there on the symbolic structure of literature are no longer directly germane to the theme of the book and require further elaboration.

I would like to thank Miss Rose for her difficult and painstaking work in translating the book, Professor St. Leon for his valuable assistance, and Indiana University Press for the publication of the English edition.

Käte Hamburger

STUTTGART
AUGUST, 1971

TRANSLATOR'S PREFACE

A few words are in order about the standard translation procedures that have been followed throughout this book. With regard
to specific terms, the following deserve special comment: although
a final consensus was not reached on the translation of the German
word *Sachverhalt*, I have tried to render it consistently as "state of
affairs," which appears to be the standard translation in phenomenological discourse. Secondly, the term *Vorstellung* has been
translated as "mental representation" (a rendering I owe to Professor Kurt Müller-Vollmer), since "representation" alone is ambiguous, and often it is not clear from the English context what
kind of representation is intended. Third, the English term "poetological," which appears often throughout, corresponds to the
German *dichtungstheoretisch:* "of or pertaining to the theory of
literature." And, related to this, the English term "poet" has been
applied also to literary artists outside the medium of lyric poetry,
and therefore is not employed as a term of generic distinction.
Context will always make it clear whether the epic, the dramatic,
or the lyric poet is meant.

For reasons of uniformity, as well as for those of pure textual
accuracy, prose renditions are appended for all poems cited in
German in the body of the text.

As a reference tool incorporated into the text itself, the following procedure has been used regarding the titles of primary and secondary works cited: in all chapters except those dealing with lyric poetry, the English title of a work is given only in those cases where the particular work already exists in translation. Otherwise the German titles have been retained. In the chapter on the lyrical genre, as well as in that dealing with the special forms, English renderings are given for the titles of all poems cited, regardless of whether the poem exists in translation, because in many instances a knowledge of what the title means is pertinent to the discussion. In the footnotes, both English and German references are given for those works already in translation.

Finally, I would like to express my gratitude to those people who have consulted with me throughout the various stages of the preparation of the translation: to Professor James S. Churchill of Purdue University for his preliminary assistance; to Dr. Liselotte Gumpel of the University of Minnesota for her willingness to discuss issues of translation in the chapter dealing with the lyrical genre, and for her translation of some of the poems appearing there; and to Professor Reginald St.Leon of the University of Sydney, Australia, for his valuable stylistic criticism of the final draft. Special thanks are extended to Professor Kurt Müller-Vollmer of Stanford University for his continued generous support and advice on intricacies of translation, and, not least of all, to Professor Käte Hamburger herself, for her eagerness to read and critically appraise the manuscript throughout the entire course of its preparation.

M.J.R.

STANFORD, CALIFORNIA
NOVEMBER, 1971

THE LOGIC OF
LITERATURE

1

INTRODUCTION

THE CONCEPT AND OBJECTIVES OF A LOGIC OF LITERATURE

What follows is an attempt to extrapolate from the realm of general literary aesthetics a more specific logic of literature. This undertaking must be so particularly designated because every theoretical discussion of literature, regardless of what special aspects of the latter it might consider, can be included within the realm of literary aesthetics. Indeed, insofar as art is the object of enquiry of aesthetics and not of logic, and insofar as its province is the processes of creative shaping and not those of thought, any talk of a logic of literature might appear to be superfluous, or even misleading. However, the fact that this differentiation can be made, that there is nevertheless a logic, or a logical system, of literature, has its foundation in the special position which literature occupies within the realm of art.

In this respect the concept of a logic of literature is to be understood, so to speak, in an indirect sense. It is meaningful and legitimate because there exists a logic of language, or more precisely, because there is a concept of a logic of language which has entered into the modern notion of the logic of thought processes.[1] Thus used, the term "logic of language" can express the relation of language as "one of the principal instruments or helps of thought," as John Stuart Mill formulates it, to the logic of thought, or even to that of its objective content.[2] It is on these grounds that Edmund Husserl establishes the necessity that "we should begin logic with linguistic discussions."[3] In a still more comprehensive sense, one can understand the problem Ludwig Wittgenstein deals with as that of assessing the ability of language to render thought utterly undisguised, so that in effect he traces philosophy (and not merely logic in the narrower sense) back to a "critique of language," which as such is, then, a logic of language. In the course of such a procedure, Wittgenstein emphasizes, the logic of language is not to be directly extracted from colloquial speech, since the latter obscures pure thought.[4]

In all these instances, then, the logic of language is conceived of as a critical analysis of language with respect to its—grammatical or linguistic—function of expression, i.e., with respect to its capacity to express "thoughts" as well as the laws of thought processes. Were we to speak of a linguistic logic of literature in *this* sense, then the problem of literature would doubtless be misconceived from the very outset. The logic of literature does, of course, intend a relation between literature and language, but it is a different relation from that meant in the theories cited above. It does not consider language in its descriptive and expressive function, and therefore neither does it concern itself with that more or less banal truism that literature is linguistic art in the sense of word artistry. Instead, it develops out of the fact that language, being the formative material of literature, is at the same time that medium in which human life takes place. This is no new insight. Wilhelm Schlegel, for example, formulates it when he says that "the medium of literature is precisely that same medium through which alone the human mind attains self-aware-ness, and therewith mastery in the voluntary combination of its own mental representations: language."[5] But this proposition it-self already suggests that this medium does not exhaust itself in the mere fact that it consists of signs imbued with meaning, that is of words, but that, far more decisively, this medium designates literature in its specific ontic status: as art. A logic, or more spe-cifically, a linguistic logic of literature, therefore, does not signify a critique of language in Wittgenstein's sense, but rather can be more concisely designated as *a theory of language,* which investi-gates whether that language which produces the forms of literature (letting general terms suffice for the present) differs *functionally* from the language of thought and communication, and, if so, to what extent. *The logic of literature* qua *linguistic theory of litera-ture has as its object the relation of literature to the general system of language.* The logic of literature is therefore to be understood in the sense of a theory of language. In what follows, this theory of language shall be developed into what we will call a theory of statement, which, in the course of its elucidation, may replace the term "logic."

It appears to me that the numerous earlier and more recent theories of literature have not arrived at completely satisfactory results because this fact, namely the relation of literature to the general system of language, as such has not been penetrated sharply enough.—Or in any case the ultimate conclusions have not been drawn from it. Only once this is done will that specific phenomenon which is peculiar to literature come to light: that literature is an art form whose lines of demarcation cannot easily be drawn, that it is, as Hegel recognized, "that particular art in which art itself begins to break down." We shall presently see what Hegel's insight is grounded in, and, contrary to Hegel himself, we shall enquire after those conclusions which can be drawn from such an insight. For only when we pursue it consistently will we realize its methodological value. It will illuminate the concealed logical texture of literature, a texture which is both connected to and yet different from that of everyday thought and speech processes. In the disclosure of this structure, however, unique and often surprising phenomena shall emerge. Primarily, we shall see that the central problem of poetics, that of genre, reveals itself under a different aspect and ordering principle than any of those hitherto familiar to us, notwithstanding how diverse these may be. Since the time when Goethe, in emancipation from the constraint of classical poetics, designated lyric, epic, and drama as the only three "natural forms" (in the notes and commentary to his *West-East Divan*)—envisaging these as by no means bound to traditional genres, but as mutually operative "often in even the shortest poem"—literary critics, especially more recent ones, have been adopting this scheme. Thus Emil Staiger arrived at new ways of construing literature by distilling from the traditional formal concepts of lyric, epic, and drama the lyrical, the epic, and the dramatic, understood as consolidations of existential attitudes: as recollection, representation and tension. And even before him Robert Hartl had reduced literary genres to forms of experience, to the "mental and emotive faculties" of feeling, cognition and desire.

It is evident that all these definitions, no matter how well they may grasp fine nuances of literature as such, are nevertheless ultimately merely interpretations of the generic phenomenon in question, interpretations which themselves only became possible in that fixed, formal classifications were resolved into modes of both experience and expression. However, literary genres remain fixed forms, which as such ultimately resist all interpretation in the sense of an explication of meaning. We experience this directly whenever we read a poem, a novel or a drama. A novel may strike us as being ever so lyrical, a play may have a plot of ever so "epic" breadth, a poem may be ever so "unlyrical"—still it is respectively a piece of narrative fiction, a drama, or a poem which channels and contours our reading experience. It is this presentational form which orients and directs our experience—even as a historical work, for example, or a scientific textbook is apprehended by us in different fashion from a novel. We experience the lyric poem in a way completely different from that in which we experience a novel or a play—so differently that our direct experience of these latter two as literature is not made in the same sense as with a lyric poem, and conversely. Thus, even these pre-logical observations indicate that, with respect to our experience, narrative and dramatic literature conjoin over against lyric poetry, so that the latter presents itself to us on an entirely different level of our imaginative life from the former.

Hitherto neither the genre analysis of poetics nor the interpretation of individual literary works has taken into account the fact that narrative and dramatic literature afford us the experience of fiction or of non-reality, whereas this is not the case with lyric poetry. However, that which is mediated as experience has its cause in the mediating phenomenon itself. The phenomena are lyric, epic, and drama, and also every single representative of each of these types. That epic and drama impart the experience of non-reality, while the lyric imparts that of reality, is alone due to the logical and hence the linguistic structure which underlies them. For this reason the logic of literature is also the phenomenology of literature. This concept as it is applied here is laden with the specialized meaning of neither the Hegelian nor the Husserlian schools of phenomenology. It denotes simply the description of the phenomena themselves—not, however, in the sense of a superficially descriptive, but in the sense of a method of constitutive description, i.e., in Goethe's terms the theory which the very phenomena are. When Goethe rejected and prohibited investigating behind the phenomena—". . . One should not seek for things behind phenomena; they are themselves the theory" (*Maxims and Reflexions,* no. 993)—he meant by that the investing of phenomena with a meaning which cannot be directly derived from them, for example, any kind of metaphysical significance which would turn natural phenomena into a philosophy of nature, of those of history into a philosophy of history instead of a science thereof, or as Goethe also puts it, instead of a theory. But there is a significance in which Goethe, too, acknowledged and applied the method of seeking behind phenomena, the significance of the very notion that the phenomena are themselves the theory. They are the theory, since *qua* phenomena they are at once symptoms; that is, their particular ontic quality or manner of appearance points back or beneath to those constitutive elements which are contained within them and which condition their ontic status. That these constitutive elements can be so concealed and therefore so unobtrusive that in the course of our description of phenomena we may not at all recognize their constitutive character—this Goethe also succinctly stated: "Quite correctly it is said that the phenomenon is a result without reason, an effect without cause. It is difficult for us to discover reason and cause because these are so simple that they conceal themselves from our sight" (no. 1103). The methodology of the natural sciences consists in nothing other than this procedure. It enquires after the constitutive elements of those symptoms which phenomenal reality displays, and is not content until it has structured these constitutive factors into some kind of regularity or law. Here is not the place to venture into the detailed and much debated question as to whether the humanities, or the cultural sciences, also can be regulatory sciences, and if so in what way. We shall restrict our enquiry to the phenomenon of literature, and shall attempt to show that to a great extent—to the same extent as language itself—it is one of those phenomena which are rich in symptomatic constitutive factors. It is not a phenomenon whose ontic quality or mode of being is vague and therefore needs only to be described in ambiguous terms; rather literature is a phenomenon which can be explained and elucidated in terms of that concealed logical structure which, by virtue of literature's being art through language, underlies it.

Creative artists themselves are not conscious of this logical structure or inherent order, just as we, when we are thinking and speaking, are little aware of those laws of logic which we must follow if we are to make ourselves understood. However, these laws, once disclosed, provide the literary interpreter with a key to many hidden doors, doors behind which the secrets of the creative process and therewith the forms of literature themselves lie concealed. Therefore, when in what follows we attempt to analyze literature as the art of language, it must again be stressed that we do not understand language in its relation to literature in that narrower, aesthetic sense of the "poetic" language [*dichterische Sprache*] of a "verbal art work," but instead quite literally as *creative* language [*dichtende Sprache*], i.e., language investigated with reference to the logico-linguistic functions which govern it as it produces the forms of imaginative literature.

Therein is implied—as should be especially emphasized to avoid all misunderstanding—that the concept of literature is also to be understood in its aesthetically broadest, i.e., in the positive and negative sense: language is also creative in the above-defined sense when its product is a serial novel in a newspaper, or an opera libretto, or the poem of a schoolboy. For the logical laws of the creative processes of language are operative irrespective of whether those literary forms which they generate realize the concept of literature as art in the aesthetic sense or not. The logical laws here are absolute, the aesthetic relative; the former are the objects of cognition and the latter those of valuation. However, this does not preclude the possibility that the investigation of logical structures might often be useful in aesthetic valuation. This would only make it more apparent that the position of literature within the realm of art is conditioned by its place within the system of language and hence within the system of thought.

2

FOUNDATIONS IN THEORY OF LANGUAGE

Definition of the Concepts "Literature" and "Reality"

The fundamental theme of the logic of literature is ultimately none other than the definition and establishment of the concepts "literature" and "reality," for our poetological observations are always, whether explicitly or implicitly, based upon this definition. These two terms have formed a familiar and more or less popular polarity, and for this reason it is necessary for us to examine the precise nature of their antithesis and fix it more sharply than is usually the case with its usage in practical critical vocabulary.

As regards the concept "reality," let us first make the precautionary and anticipatory remark that it has become problematic, especially from the standpoint of modern natural sciences and logistics; and from this standpoint it might be objected that the term is used in this study in the sense of an antiquated and naive realism. Against such potential objection we ought therefore to stress that the concept of reality is here treated exclusively in its interrelation, be this of a contrastive or of a comparative nature, with that of literature, and that consequently "reality" does not appear in this context as the object of epistemology. Hence neither is it to be understood in the sense of a naive realism. As will certainly become clear from the ensuing exposition, "reality" here means nothing other than the reality of human life (of nature, of history, of mind), in contradistinction to what we experience as the "content" of literary works; it designates the mode of being of human life as opposed to that mode of being which creative literature represents. And it seems not at all misleading to say that precisely in the exact determination of this difference the phenomenon of reality shall display itself quite significantly beyond all scientific and theoretical definitions.

Thus understood, what does the definition of the concepts "literature" and "reality" imply? It implies something twofold: first, that literature is something other than reality, but second the seemingly contradictory proposition that reality is the stuff of literature. The paradox is only an apparent contradiction: literature is of a different nature from reality precisely because the latter is its material. But even as we make these statements in the generality of preliminary conceptual definition, the first difficulties appear; obscurities and discrepancies inherent in the traditional methods of viewing literature proclaim themselves. If we disregard the purely biographical and sociological investigation of sources and background, which includes the *roman à clef* as well as poems about real persons, it appears that in the course of correlating literature and reality the reference is tacitly established to narrative and dramatic literature, and yet without our consciously and expressly having restricted the concept of literature to these forms. Nevertheless, the third sphere within that realm which both poetics and our general experience understand as literature, namely lyric poetry, is not, or at least not directly, included in the correlation of the concepts "literature" and "reality." For this correlation is in fact meaningful only with respect to the first two genres, whereas lyric poetry yields no evidence for its being relevant to such correlation. That this circumstance has not developed into a real problem is evidently due to the fact that the meaning of the concepts "literature" and "reality," as they occur together here, has not been subjected to a more rigorous analysis. The concept of literature, however, will establish itself in its anything but unequivocal meaning only once the concept of reality in its relation to literature—the subject of this enquiry—becomes clarified. Such clarification is the task of the following study.

At this point of departure in the posing of our problem, reference should be made, by way of a prelude, to a crown witness whose great discernment in this point has remained, as it were, unreflected upon and has thus hitherto been veiled, but is for that all the more illuminating: to Aristotle. Generally the fact that Aristotle in his *Poetics* dealt only with *epos* and *drama,* but not with the lyric, has been attributed to the fragmentary character of this work. Or it was assumed that Aristotle made no mention of the great Greek lyrics of the fifth and sixth centuries because these were supposed to have been "sung" poetry, that is poetry accompanied by instrumental music and thus reckoned as music.[6] Yet, as we shall presently see, Aristotle did mention sung poetry, namely the dithyramb, as well as purely instrumental music as such, but precisely the context in which this occurs indicates that he did not reckon these to the lyric, but rather to ποίησις, that precisely that which we denote as lyric poetry, as "poetry" in the strict sense, Aristotle did not consider to belong to "literature," namely to ποίησις, but rather to another realm of "linguistic works."

These relationships only come to light when one notes the fact that Aristotle used the concept μίμησις to define ποίησις and that accordingly ποίησις and μίμησις are identical in meaning for him. Consideration of this fact appears on the one hand to have been impeded because we have lost sight of the basic meaning of the concepts ποιεῖν and ποίησις, namely "to make, to produce," and on the other hand because μίμησις has been translated by *imitatio* and has become burdened with the sense of "copying." Erich Auerbach, in subtitling his famous work *Mimesis* with "Represented Reality,"* has restored the banished concept to an honorable position again and established it in its proper Aristotelian sense. For a more accurate examination of Aristotle's definitions reveals that for his concept of μίμησις the sense of imitation, which is certainly contained in this concept, is far less decisive than the fundamental sense of representing, making.[7] Not only the above-mentioned identity between ποίησις and μίμησις—which we shall now proceed to prove—sheds light on this point, but also, and predominantly so, does the precise meaning which Aristotle gives the concept of mimesis. Those works are designated as μιμήσεις which have as their subject-matter ποάττοντες, men in action, and therewith also ποάξεις, actions themselves. "Epic poetry, Tragedy and Comedy, as also Dithyrambic poetry, and most flute and lyre playing are μιμήσεις,"[8] and in addition also dance, since this, with the aid of rhythm and pantomime, "represents characters, passions and actions."[9] That these modes of art, which, by virtue of the inclusion of a part of instrumental music and the dance, extend beyond the narrower concept of the purely "verbal art work," are nevertheless ποίησις precisely because they are μίμησις,[10] is clearly substantiated only somewhat later, with the following deduction: "Since the mimes (μιμούμενοι) represent men in action, and since these men must necessarily be either noble or base . . . , then they must either be better or worse than we are, or they must be the same as we are."[11] The conclusion drawn in the main clause of this sentence confirms what we inferred from the identical meaning of ποίησις and μίμησις, namely that the tenor of μίμησις must not be dominated by *imitatio*, which is merely a nuance of meaning contained within this concept; or respectively that imitation enters into mimesis only insofar as human reality furnishes the stuff of literature, of that

---

* [Unfortunately the English translation bears the sub-title "The Representation of Reality," which is a misrepresentation of the original.—Tr.]

literature which represents and "makes" men in action. This is essentially epic and dramatic literature, the analysis of which also comprises the content of Aristotle's *Poetics*.

Two further passages, inconspicuous in themselves, throw still brighter light on the identity of ποίησις and μίμησις; and quite possibly they reveal the reason why what we designate as lyric poetry is not treated in the work entitled Περί Ποιητιχῆς. Aristotle is surprised that people reduce the concept of "poetic composition" (τὸ ποιεῖν) to meter, e.g. elegiac meter, even in cases where a verbal work composed in this meter is by no means μίμησις, as for example the nature poem of Empedocles. "Because people associate poetic composition with metrics, they call those who write elegies epic poets, they bestow the name 'poet' not after mimetic, but after metrical standards. . . . Homer and Empedocles, however, have nothing in common apart from metre (hexameter), wherefore one ought to call the former poet, but the latter rather physicist."[12] In the Greek word φυσιόλογος there is contained the concept λόγος, and if with reference to this we consult a further passage in the *Poetics*, the idea of a distinction between ποιεῖν and λέγειν (to state), between μίμησις and λόγος, presents itself; which in turn indicates that for Aristotle the concept "literature" was exhausted only in the representing, in the "making" of men in action, that this concept was not realized by a statement put to meter, no matter how "poetic" this might be. It is no coincidence that this problem becomes acute for him when he treats "narrative literature." He disapproved of an epic poet's speaking "in his own person" (αὐτόν) instead of mimetically fashioning men in action. "A poet should state as little as possible in his own person, for in doing this he is no μιμητής."[13] And he praises Homer as the only epic poet to have fulfilled the injunction of ποίησις that after a short introduction the poet immediately let a man or woman appear who then does the speaking.[14]

The exclusion of non-mimetic "literature" (which, with regard to Aristotle, we must express in quotation marks) from ποίησις can be interpreted as leading up to the insight that any form of literature which does not "make" ($\pi o \iota \epsilon \hat{\iota}$) any action or men in action—which, we may say, creates no fictive persons existing in the mode of $\mu \acute{\iota} \mu \eta \sigma \iota s$ as opposed to that of reality—has taken up residence in another sphere within what we today would designate as the total realm of literature. How significant this differentiation, which we shall term the difference between mimetic and lyric literature, is for the logical structure of the general realm of literature, and therefore also for the phenomenology of literary genres, will become apparent in the course of our investigation.

Though the conceptual definitions of "literature" and "reality" are latently contained in the notion of $\mu \acute{\iota} \mu \eta \sigma \iota s$, they nevertheless did not become programmatic for Aristotle. It lies in the very nature of this latent and unrealized state of affairs that later poetics, which did conceptualize this polarity, did also in the course of such conceptualization involuntarily conform to the Aristotelian definition of literature, which was restricted to the "mimetic genres." Only sporadically has it been expressly noted that one cannot speak of a relation of literature to reality with respect to lyric poetry in the same sense that one can speak of such a relation with respect to narrative or dramatic literature.[15] And because in the past we have not become conscious of this with full phenomenological clarity, neither have we considered how and in what sense it not only is possible for and intimately connected with narrative and dramatic literature, but indeed also essential to them. The traditional tripartite division of literature into genres juxtaposed to one another on the same plane has thwarted our becoming consciously aware of our primary experience of these phenomena (and thus of our giving it theoretical expression), namely that a novel or a drama can to a certain extent only artificially be classified together with lyric poetry under the general heading of literature.

Aristotle traced this artificiality back to that which in his day the *epos* and the elegy shared in common: meter and the couplet verse form of the distich. Later poetics and literary theories saw in the material, in language, that common denominator of all the various kinds of literature which would unite them into the general realm of literary art. In so doing modern poetics has proceeded more strictly and more generally, but on the other hand is less aware of the problem, than Aristotle. And precisely on that account it has been able to come to grips with neither the problem of reality nor that of literature. But from the the way in which we formulated the problem in the Introduction, it is evident that it is indeed the linguistic medium of literature which will ultimately clarify the establishment of the concepts "literature" and "reality," whereby the concept and general system of literature will itself become discernible.

Several significant attempts have already been undertaken to grasp the problem of literature from the point of view of language, i.e., of creative language in our sense and not merely poetic language. One of the first to have vigorously attacked this problem is Hegel. The sentence from his aesthetics, already mentioned in the Introduction and providing the most succinct expression of the problem, runs in its entirety as follows: "Poetry[16] is, then, that particular art in which at the same time art itself begins to break down and, for the philosophical consciousness, to obtain its point of transition to the prose of scientific thought."[17] This proposition puts us right within that realm of literary theory which we shall distinguish as the specifically logical in contradistinction to the aesthetic. With great acumen did Hegel penetrate this situation when he designated not language as such as the proper material of literature, but "the mental representation and intuition" [*geistige Vorstellung und Anschauung*], whereas "the material through which its constructive activity is asserted only retains for it the value of a means, however much this may be elaborated in an artistic sense, by which mind is expressed for mind."[18] Here Hegel clearly separates the logical from the aesthetic aspect of literature, even though he did not reflect on the problem of language *per se,* and consequently did not recognize the connection between its logico-grammatical function on the one hand, and its role as the constitutive factor of literature on the other. However, what is of primary relevance in this context is Hegel's recognition that literature is in danger of dissolving not only itself as art, but thereby also the whole edifice of art, by virtue of its belonging to the more comprehensive system of general representation and thought, or in other words "in that even outside the realm of art mental representation is the most common mode of consciousness."[19] In this discerning statement there emerges *that* concept of reality which alone contains the criterion for the form, as well as for the different forms, of literature: *that* reality which exists in the modus of "being thought," i.e., which exists as the object of representation and any kind of description. "Thought," Hegel states, "dematerializes the form of reality to that of pure concept, and even though it grasps and knows real things in their essential particularity and proper existence, it nevertheless elevates the particular to the level of the general and the ideal, in which alone thought is in its proper element."[20]

That reality "dematerialized to the form of pure concept" is the reality which can be construed by creative language as we understand this term, as well as by non-creative language, i.e., by the "prose of scientific thought."[21] What distinguishes a painted landscape from a real one is not difficult to specify. Not equally tangible, however, is the boundary which separates the description of a landscape in a work of literature from the description of a landscape in a work which is not literature (as we phrase it here, wishing still to remain with general, pre-logical terms). The representational world of literature is distinguished from that of extra-literary prose not through the categories of material and of geometrical shape (as the stuff or model of a painting is different from the painting itself). And Hegel realized it would in no way be an easy task "to isolate poetic from prosaic representation."[22] But even he made it altogether too easy for himself by positing "the artistic imagination" as the criterion for this differentiation.[23] For imagination is by no means that factor which would be capable of preventing art from dissolving and taking its point of transition into the prose of scientific, i.e., theoretical thought. Indeed it is also directly obvious that this vague psychological concept is unsuitable for fixing those strictly logical relationships which Hegel, in the important sentence cited above, did intimate, but without, to be sure, satisfactorily analyzing and explicating them. In his aesthetics he did not further develop the concept of reality which is set forth there, and to which the system of literature is to be oriented. Thus he did not draw the ultimate conclusions from the idea that the "mode of being" of literature is a part of the general system of both the realm of consciousness and language, an idea which in itself is correctly conceived.

But the beginning he made is important enough to justify our returning to him, behind the back of modern literary theories, so to speak, theories which have thought further along these lines and which treat literature as part of the general system of language. This is above all true of Hegel's modern pupil, Benedetto Croce. Without taking his departure from Hegel in this particular point, Croce, in his *Aesthetic as Science of Expression and General Linguistic,* through a dictum of his own to a certain extent disposed of the problem seen by Hegel. Croce eliminates all danger of literature's dissolution into the "prose of scientific thought" via the division which he makes in the realm of epistemology and its linguistic manifestation in general: the bifurcation into "intuitive" and "theoretical" (logical) knowledge. Intuitive cognition is the knowledge of individual entities, logical cognition the knowledge of the universal. The former expresses itself in or produces images, the latter concepts. Intuitive knowledge and that symbolic language concomitant to it (expression), is thereby understood in the broadest conceivable terms. Every sentence in which we describe an individual thing or occurrence is already an intuition, and, therefore, an expression. An intuition is present when we say "this glass of water," whereas the statement "water" is already a universal concept.[24] Croce, then, eliminates the conceptual character of a statement's meaning the moment the statement refers to an individual phenomenon rather than to a concept (under which individual phenomena fall). From this point of departure (whose ambiguities themselves are not the topic here), it is clear that Croce must designate all utterance in literature as intuitions, or expressions. For literature does not describe universal concepts, i.e., it is not theoretical knowledge; rather, it describes only unique, individual phenomena. Even "philosophical maxims in the mouths of characters in a tragedy or a comedy function in that context no longer as concepts, but as characterizing features of these persons: exactly as the red of a painted figure no longer emerges as the concept of the color red in the physicist's sense, but as a characterizing element of that figure. . . . A work of art can be full of philosophical concepts. . . . But the result of the work of art is nevertheless an intuition," i.e., not theoretical knowledge.[25]

As incontestable as this is for the example of dramatic literature which Croce chose—and it is in itself somewhat suspect that on the whole he prefers this example—nevertheless the aesthetic of expression is diminished in its applicability by the fact that the area in which the intuitive-expressive form of cognition can be applied is too broad. For if all those statements which intend single phenomena, and therefore even "history" in the sense of the science of history, are designated as intuition and aligned under the general concept of aesthetics, then there is no longer a specific theory of art, or here no specific theory of literature, and all possibility of distinguishing literary "expression" from extra-literary expression escapes us. If the statement "this glass of water," which I might make in a real context, is just as much an intuition as the same statement in a literary context, then the structure of literature is no longer recognizable. And conversely, so one ought at least to enquire, can the "theoretical" sense ever be eliminated from a concept, no matter how strongly the context indicates it to be intuitive? Rickert touches once upon this problem when (without reference to Croce), in the Introduction to his book on Goethe's *Faust*, he raises the question whether, "in works of art which consist of words and sentences, that aesthetically apprehensible meaning which they *qua* literature possess can be completely separated from the theoretical meaning which these words and sentences can express in addition."[26]

Indeed the problem of literature's place within the general system of language, so keenly discerned already by Hegel, but therewith also that problem of reality specific to literature, is not resolved if one, in such dictatorial and merely stipulative fashion as Croce, determines language, or more precisely the meaning-content of language, through the context in which statements and words appear. Certainly, as we shall see, context does have important and decisive significance for determining the forms and kinds of literature. But this significance cannot be simply "conferred" under any kind of arbitrary label such as the concept of expression: it first results from strict observation of linguistic functions.

Such a procedure is followed in Roman Ingarden's well-known book, *Das literarische Kunstwerk*, which, on the basis of Husserl's theory of judgment, i.e., on the basis of an ontological-phenomenological epistemology, seeks to isolate the mode of being of literature from that of the "prose" of statements in a real context. The Hegelian problem (to which Ingarden also makes no reference) emerges here more emphatically than with Croce, since here the representational system, i.e., the transcendental referring of the act of mental representation to an ("existentially autonomous") reality, is also the basis of the system of judgment. Nonetheless,

Ingarden does not go beyond a mere labelling of the phenomena of thought and language in question. If Croce's rubrics have too broad a conceptual basis, then Ingarden has defined the differentiating concept too narrowly. This is so notwithstanding the fact that the concept "literary work of art" is applied only to narrative and dramatic literature (as is all too tacitly assumed in the book—or in any event is evident in the approximation to English terminology). It is exclusively a matter of pointing out the phenomenon and the experience of "non-reality" in these kinds of literature. But for this demonstration Ingarden avails himself of an epistemological tool which, at the very least, proves itself to be not altogether effective. I refer to the concept of the "quasi-judgment," which stems from the phenomenological theory of "intentional objects." This theory distinguishes, though, between merely "intentional" and "purely intentional" objects. "Purely intentional" refers to the mental representation of a (real or ideal) object as such, or more precisely, to a mentally represented state of affairs which has not yet become the object of a "judgment." If it becomes the object of a judgment, this means it has been "transposed into the ontic sphere of reality,"[27] i.e., it has been referred to an object or state of affairs existing in reality. In this case we have an "authentic judgment," whose statement is verifiable and "lays claim to truth." This means that the "objective state determined" through the judgment "exists not as a purely intentional object, but rather as an object which is actually rooted in an ontic sphere which is existentially autonomous vis-a-vis the act of judgment."[28] So reads the phenomenological definition of that which, in what follows, we shall designate (and define in its proper place) as reality statement. Now, those sentences of which a work of literature (a novel or a drama) is composed, are, according to Ingarden, not genuine judgments, but rather "quasi-judgments," so defined because they do not entail any transposition into a sphere of real being. An object in literature has only a purely intentional existence. But this does not exhaustively describe the relation between literature and reality for Ingarden. That reality is nevertheless the stuff of literature is expressed as follows: "the sentence correlates are transposed, with respect to their content, into the real world."[29] But the character of pure intentionality is retained through the qualification that "the transposition . . . is not achieved in the mode of complete earnest, but rather in a unique way which only feigns this earnestness. Therefore the purely intentional contents and objects, respectively, are merely addressed as existing in reality without their . . . being imbued with the character of reality."[30] Ingarden maintains that it is these so-defined "quasi-judgmental assertions" which render it possible to "evoke . . . the illusion of reality," that these sentences "carry a suggestive power which allows us, in the act of reading, to become immersed in the feigned world and to live, as it were, in a world which is uniquely and distinctively non-real, but which nevertheless appears to be real."[31] This reduction of the character of non-reality inherent in a mimetic work of literature to the sentences of which the work is composed nevertheless does not seem to elucidate the phenomena satisfactorily. Indeed, in the final analysis it presents nothing but a circle. The sentences or assertions of a novel are first constituted as "quasi-assertions" by the very fact that they occur in a novel. Not the sentence *per se*, for example "Everything was topsy-turvy in the house of Oblonsky," with which Tolstoy's *Anna Karenina* begins, summons up the illusion of reality. For, as far as its form is concerned, it can, once released from the context of a novel, function to give information about a real situation: for example, should it occur in a letter. As we shall see, the non-reality of the novel's world is generated by totally different functions of language, namely, by exactly those legitimate functions which constitute the phenomena. The designation of the sentences in a novel or in a drama as quasi-judgments implies nothing but the tautological fact that whenever we read a novel or a play we know we are reading a novel or a play; in other words, we know we are not in a context of reality. Ingarden—and, to be sure, not he alone—has completely overlooked the decisive factor which evokes "the mysterious accomplishment of the literary work of art,"[32] and which Aristotle termed the mimesis of men in action. This misunderstanding is especially conspicuous in Ingarden's efforts to fix the phenomenon of the historical novel. He cannot quite make the concept of the quasi-judgment accord with this category of literature. Here, he maintains, "we approach yet a step nearer to authentic judgments,"[33] for direct reference is made to a reality identified as actual without this reality's being represented in its actuality, without "the intentionally projected situations' being made to coincide fully with actual situations."[34] The fictive nature of the historical novel, and therewith that of a novel in general, is already entirely misunderstood if, from the viewpoint of literary theory, one considers that which we know as historical reality, which is the stuff of these novels, to be of a different kind from all other reality formed in novels (as we shall further demonstrate below). This misconception becomes even more clearly evident when Ingarden maintains that only through the quasi-judgment can we differentiate a historical novel from a historical treatise, that between these two a transition from quasi- to authentic judgments could take place, and consequently that a historical novel could become an account in the sense of the science of history. "The past, long since disappeared and become void, arises again before our eyes (in the novel) through the purely intentional situations which now embody it. But it is not this past itself which is reviewed in the novel, because the final step separating the quasi-judgmental assertions from genuine judgments is still lacking: the identification with the respective historical reality in question, and therewith both the positing, performed in full earnest, and the anchoring of the intentional meaning content of the sentences within this reality. This final step would be accomplished only with the transition to scientific observation, or even to a mere recounting from memory. However, we would thereby also obtain sentences which are authentic judgments."[35] Following this description, it is indeed difficult to imagine a historical novel. But it does make it especially clear that the concept of the quasi-judgment by no means delineates the linguistic-literary structure and specific phenomenal form of the novel, but instead describes nothing other than a vague psychological attitude of the author and likewise of the reader: the modes of respectively complete or incomplete earnestness. In other words, the attitude we assume toward a historical novel or drama is different from the one we assume toward a historical account. Only the investigation of linguistic functions will show that a change from a historical novel into an account of historical reality can never happen, and that it is precisely those "embodying" situations that Ingarden disregards, namely the mimetic situations, which render such a transition impossible.[36]

In Croce's as well as in Ingarden's theories concerning the linguistic material of literature, and therewith concerning literature itself, it only *seems* that language is comprehended and portrayed in its nature as constitutive of literature. Consequently both theories dissolve into tautologies. We can perceive in what respects the language of literature is distinguished from that of reality by looking not only at language or at the "sentences" themselves, but also by looking behind and beneath them. Only that structure which then comes to light can indicate the way in which—indeed the diverse ways in which—literature is related to reality. Furthermore, only once this is done will we have fully and completely established the meaning of the concepts "literature" and "reality," will we see that these are relative not only to the mimetic types of literature, but are also inclusive of lyric poetry. The nexus between them is established in such a way that the phenomenology of literature and the phenomenology of reality reciprocally illuminate and contour one another. Thus it becomes apparent that precisely that

nuance of meaning contained in the multifarious conceptual polarity of "literature" and "reality," namely that of comparison, is of
importance for the present study. Because the "representational
activity" which manifests itself in language "is also the most common mode of consciousness outside of art (literary art)," as Hegel
has stated, the *continuous comparison of creative with non-creative
language* is the methodological means requisite to extracting the
structure of literature (as a collective phenomenon).

The Statement-System of Language

The Concept of Statement

If the criteria for creative language are to be made known in
comparison with non-creative language, then we ought properly
first to examine this non-creative language itself from the point of
view of its structure, which categorically separates it from the creative language which produces literature. The logic of literature
shall hence come to be exhibited as founded in *theory of language,*
as a linguistic logic of literature. For this reason we must now in-
terpolate an investigation of wider range which at first prescinds
from the specific realm of literature and concerns itself with the
structure of language, or, in other words, with what we term the
statement system of language.

In the first edition of this book the concept of statement was
presupposed to be all too self-evidently one belonging to the theory
of language. Only with subsequent investigations has it been revealed that as yet the phenomenon of statement has not really been
discerned and described for itself, and that in this respect at least
the theory of language shows a gap—no matter how closely here
or there it has approached the essence of statement. But on the
other hand it is completely understandable that this deficiency

still persists, that it has not been sensed within theory of language, nor even in logic and grammar. For the phenomenon of statement is indeed first exposed to view from the perspective of the lingua-logical structure of literature, specifically of narrative literature. That epic or fictional narration furnishes the decisive criterion for the entire system of literature, and why it does so, will become evident in the following exposition. Here we have the extraordinary instance that the analysis of the structure of literature helps us to recognize what is an essential part of the structure of language in general.

The recurrent use of the concept or, better, of the term "statement" [*Aussage*] in German schools of logic, grammar, and theory of language necessitates our examining its meaning as a technical term—at the risk of reviewing what is obvious and most likely has scarcely been misunderstood in the literature relevant to these topics. But because the usage of this term rests in great measure on established convention is the reason we must take careful note of it, in order to avoid the misunderstanding of terms and therefore of meaning.

In logic the concept of statement is used with the same meaning as that of judgment. And as early as in the translation of Aristotle's *Organon*, for example, those two terms interchange which are meant to render what Aristotle calls λόγος ἀποφαντχός, a discourse that can be either true or false (which, as Aristotle notes, is not the case with all discourse, for example with requests). In general, "stating discourse" [*aussagende Rede*] came to be designated later as predicative judgment having the form S is p. This is the "simple" judgment from which then the comprehensive theory and all the various forms of judgment developed. But I. M. Bocheński, for instance, in his book entitled *Formal Logic*, uses the term "statement" exclusively, and moreover in affiliation with the "vocabulary of contemporary formal logic."[37]

With respect to the following discussion I should like nevertheless to follow the older tradition and use the term "judgment" as belonging to logic, the concept "statement" as belonging to theory of language, and immediately affix and reserve the third concept to come, that of "proposition" [*Satz*], as belonging to grammar. My reasons for so doing are those of the unequivocalness and clarity resulting from the definitive meaning of these concepts in German usage. For although the word "judgment" (*iudicium*) originated in the language of jurisprudence and only became a term of logic via its usage in the determination of the truth or falsity of a statement, it is nevertheless as such clearer and more precise than the word "statement" would be in designating the same phenomenon. When we use the term predicative (or hypothetical, apodictive, etc.) judgment, none of the other, extra-logical meanings of the word "judgment" are suggested; the domain of logic remains self-enclosed. However, the situation is different with the term "statement." This word carries over into grammar, where the assertion or declarative sentence [*Behauptungssatz*] is also termed a statement sentence. And also as a logical term it retains a certain tinge of ambiguity in meaning. Bocheński must expressly stress that he understands "by statement an 'expression' (a materially apprehended sign), and not that which this sign signifies."[38]

Indeed, the nuance of meaning of the act of stating as well as of that which is stated plays into the concept of statement to a far greater and more disturbing extent than that of the act of judging and that which is judged enters into the concept of judgment. This is inadvertently expressed even in the definitions of the predicative judgment: "Discourse is either a simple statement, when it states something of something or when it denies something of something . . ."—so Kirchmann translates Aristotle's sentence . . . τούτων δέ ἡ μὲν ἁπλῆ ἐσιν ἀποφάνσις, οἷον τί χατὰ τίνος ἤ τὶ ἀπο τίνος . . . . It is clear that the translator who calls the *Hermeneia* "the theory of judgment" would not be able to insert here the verb "to judge."[39] In this expression only "discourse" is rendered active and referred to as being the act of stating. But it is striking and also symptomatic when Christoph Sigwart writes: "What happens when I form and articulate a judgment can initially and cursorily be described in that I state something of something."[40] This "psychological" formulation, which includes the act of statement, does not, however, play any further role in Sigwart's definition of the judgment. The "I state" is henceforth dropped, and only the logical factor of the judgment's structure, namely that something is stated of something, or in other words the relation between the subject and predicate of the judgment, is the object of his analysis. "There are in any case two elements present; the first is that which becomes stated, τὸ χατηγοεούμενον, the predicate, and the second is that of which something becomes stated, τὸ ὑποχείμενον, the subject."[41] Sigwart does, though, characterize this formula for the judgment as "only an external designation taken from the perspective of the speech act." But notwithstanding the fact that the procedure throughout the rest of his study is "psychological," which for him means that he considers the judgment as object-oriented language (to use the term of modern logic here), namely as "statement" which "concerns not the words themselves, but rather the mentally represented objects which these words designate,"[42] nevertheless his transformal considerations move within the framework of the S–p relation, which is established through the form of the judgment. For it is of no consequence for this form whether the variables S and p are represented by words themselves or by those states of affairs which come to be designated through these words.

But it is not our aim here to enter into critical debate with this older form of judgmental logic, which misinterprets itself as being psychological. We merely intend the example of Sigwart to show that the term "statement" used for the predicative judgment tends to abandon the domain of logic and, retaining the judgmental form S is p, to pass into the more comprehensive domain of language and speech in general.

The predicative judgment, S is p, has always been associated with the propositional sentence. That is, logic has always been brought into connection with grammar, because the proposition, particularly the assertive sentence as the basic form thereof, is the linguistic formulation of the judgment. If one used the term "statement" for the judgment, then the assertive sentence was also designated as a statement sentence and distinguished from all other sentence modalities: from questions, wishes, commands, and exclamations. In the assertive or statement sentence the judgment and the proposition amalgamate to the point of complete identity: the subject of the judgment is identical with the subject of the proposition, and the predicate of the judgment is identical with the predicate of the proposition. Once again Husserl formulated this unmistakably in the context of the bipartite character of the predicative judgment, hypokeimenon and kategoroumenon: "Every statement sentence must consist of these two parts."[43] There are also other views which are based on various interpretations of the judgment and the proposition. Thus H. Ammann will not have the statement sentence understood merely as the linguistic formulation of the judgment, whereby he implicitly dismisses the terminological equivalence between judgment and statement. For he defines the judgment not as being formally capable of bipartite division, but rather as being an act of conferring which pertains to a judging consciousness. But a proposition such as "the bird sings," as a linguistic formulation, is not a judgment because a judging consciousness is no longer taking part in it; rather, it is just an assertive sentence, "which can only simulate a judgment so long as one equates assertive sentences with judgments."[44] And Ammann states: "The relation between grammatical subject and predicate here, therefore, has nothing to do with the relation between the subject and predicate of a judgment, since here no judgments are under consideration, but rather simple linguistic formulations of encountered facts."[45]

However the interpretations and definitions of judgment and

proposition may differ, and to however great a degree terminology is also apt to blur the phenomena—for instance the equating or alternating use of "judgment" and "statement" and of "assertive" and "statement sentence"—we can nevertheless determine two facts which are untouched by these divergencies and which precisely on that account point the way to further problems and relations which, as far as I can see, as yet have not been examined.

The first of these facts is the less relevant. It concerns the already mentioned relation between grammar and judgmental logic: namely the simple fact that these two areas converge—if at all—only in *one* logico-grammatical moment, in the assertive or statement sentence. Beyond this one instance the theories of judgment and proposition immediately diverge again, and each pursues its own course. The theory of judgment concerns itself with the various kinds of judgment beyond the predicative judgment; the theory of proposition develops into syntax and is concerned with subject and predicate not as the form of the judgment, but as elements existing along with other elements in a sentence. This very fact calls to mind the question which Ammann raised in another context, as to whether the convergence of the predicative judgment and the proposition in the "statement sentence" is not merely an illusory one, i.e., whether the judgmental form S is p merely maintains the illusion of coinciding with the proposition by virtue of the names of its grammatical parts, subject and predicate.

The second factor is, to be sure, connected with the relation between judgment and statement sentence, but it is of far more decisive significance for our problem. In question is the gap which, pertaining to the problem of statement, exists between logic and grammar, and which can only be filled by a third discipline, i.e., a theory of language. Sigwart, in formulating the definition of the judgment in "that I state something of something," had unwittingly touched upon the problem which is pertinent to theory of language, but he immediately excluded it again by making no further reference to the "I state . . . ," and discussing only the traditional judgment-formula that "something becomes stated of something." Sigwart—who here stands as representative of the older school of logic in general—had no need to concern himself about the significance of this "I state," and likewise neither does grammar when it deals with the statement sentence. Similarly, neither do psychology and phenomenology have anything to do with this factor, for the significance of the "I state" in this pronouncement is not that of an act of consciousness, of a "subjective activity." The definition given this sentence concerns the judgment and not the act of judging. This must be especially stressed with respect to a remark which Husserl makes in his *Erfahrung und Urteil*. He reproaches traditional logic with not, "as it would have been necessary, placing judging as a subjective activity," as an "achievement of consciousness . . . in the center of its studies, instead of believing it could leave this to psychology."[46] Husserl poses the—as he claims, not psychological, but phenomenological—problem of judging construed as a subjective activity as the necessary alternative to the formal theory of judgment, where, as is expressly stated, the judgment as apophansis "is first presented to the logician in its linguistic expression as a statement sentence."[47] This alternative, or "the two-sided nature of the logical thematic," as Husserl proposes, makes it quite clear that with respect to the problem of statement there exists a gap between logic and grammar—a gap which, let us emphasize once more, was concealed in that the predicative judgment was designated as statement. The formal factor of being inclusive of a subject, which Sigwart instinctively accorded the definition of judgment *qua* statement, directs our attention to a structure which, certainly, was not intended in his formulation. It requires no proof that this subject has nothing in common with the logical subject, the hypokeimenon, nor with the grammatical subject, other than its name. It is not the subject of the statement, but the *statement-subject*. Again it would be incorrect to designate this as the stating subject, for example, as Husserl's "subjective activity" of judging or stating, which has the character of transcendental-intentional acts of consciousness. Rather there emerges here a concept of the subject which appertains neither to logic nor to psychology, nor to the theory of knowledge, but to the theory of language. For, as we shall endeavor to demonstrate in what follows, the problem of statement is the problem of language itself.

Nevertheless, as far as I can ascertain, the problem of statement has formerly not become an object of investigation within theory of language. This appears to be due to the fact that language theory has essentially directed its attention toward only two aspects: toward language as a grammatico-linguistic structure, and toward language as communication or speech. But let us dwell for a moment upon the theory of communication. For here there is a concept of the subject which likewise belongs only to language, to our speaking life, and does not appear within formal grammar and linguistics. It is the concept of that subject which, taken by analogy from the techniques of radio, is designated as the sender and whose opposite pole is the receiver. Thus Karl Bühler states in his *Sprachtheorie*: "The word 'I' names all possible senders of human communications, and the word 'you' the class of all recipients as such."[48] This formula for communication immediately indicates, or at least makes it ascertainable, both that and wherein the theory of communication differs from the theory of statement. Whereas the latter proves to be the theory of the structure, and moreover of the concealed structure of language in general, the theory of communication or speech is concerned only with the speech act. It becomes clear that the sender-I in communication is something different from the statement-subject of language, whose polar correlative, correspondingly, is not the receiver-you, but rather the *statement-object*. This means that neither the grammatical proposition, not even the so-called statement sentence, nor the verbal form of communication is the topic under discussion whenever a subject-object relation, or more precisely a subject-object structure appears within the realm of language. Rather, it is the concept of statement alone which presents itself here *as the subject-object structure of language*. Inasmuch as it embraces the system of *all* sentences, i.e., all sentence modalities, statement is a concept belonging neither to grammar nor even to judgmental logic, but rather to the theory of language. Not only the "statement" (i.e., assertive) sentence, but also sentences expressing questions, wishes, commands and exclamations are statements:[49] *statements of a statement-subject about a statement-object*. Thus the statement-object is the very content of the statement, in whatever sentence modality the statement may appear. Sigwart's "I state something of something" can be reduced to "I state something." In this form it is no longer the description (poorly formulated, incidentally) of the predicative judgment, but rather the expression for the statement *per se*. It means: statement is the statement of a subject about an object. Only this formula, which is a structural one, permits us to recognize that not only the single statement, but also the whole of life which manifests itself in language, is described by the concept "statement." And if already at this point we must allude to the sole instance in the realm of language for which the statement formula is not valid, namely to narration in narrative literature, this single exception then only confirms, as shall be demonstrated, the validity of the statement formula for the entire remaining domain of language, within which lyric poetry also belongs.

ANALYSIS OF THE STATEMENT-SUBJECT

The definition of statement as that of a statement-subject about a statement-object can be achieved only by an exact analysis of the statement-subject. Such analysis shall demonstrate why the statement-subject alone, and not the statement-object, is of consequence.

The concept of the statement-subject is an analogue to that of the subject in epistemology, the cognitive subject.[50] But it evinces differences from the latter, differences which, to be sure, are not disclosed at first glance. They are rooted in the fact that the statement *qua* verbal form, i.e., as one manifesting itself in the system of sentences, is more fixed and static than the processes of thought and cognition as such. Precisely on that account is the statement a phenomenon belonging to the theory of language and not to the theory of knowledge. This in turn means that the statement-subject—which, as noted above, is not to be construed as a "stating" subject—does not reflect those multiple aspects which attach to the cognitive subject (or, more generally, the subject of consciousness), and which attach to it because it is so to speak a factor within the free realm of personal life as a whole, one which is concealed in its structural abstractions and could be interpreted in a variety of ways: psychologically, transcendentally, intentionally. Indeed, although the concept of subject is thought correlatively to that of object, the latter can nevertheless subside into the background and the specific subjectivity of the subject be presented isolated as such, as is already the case in the everyday usage of the adjective "subjective." This is so to speak the non-relative, a-polaric meaning of the adjective when for example Husserl speaks of judgment as a subjective activity (without wishing this to be understood in a psychological sense), or when Roman Ingarden speaks of subjective, intentional operations of thought and consciousness whose result and correlate is the sentence.[51] Thus Whitehead utterly rejects the "technical phrase" subject-object, because it is too "reminiscent of the Aristotelian 'subject-predicate.'" He therefore gives the subject independence as the "ego-object among objects," as the "primary situation disclosed in cognitive experience."[52]

Naturally our concern here with the interpretations of the cognitive subject cited above, as examples from copious others, is not that of discussing them in the context of the various epistemological or metaphysical positions of the respective philosophers mentioned. They serve only as an indication of the breadth and wealth of aspects contained in the meaning of the concept of the subject of consciousness, and thus that now one, now another aspect will be accentuated, according to the interpretation of the respective epistemology in question. Confronted with the statement-subject we find ourselves in a more confined and fixed situation, a situation fixed in the structure of statement, where the statement-subject always states only in reference to its statement-object. *Statement structure is a fixed, clearly perceptible subject-object relation.* However, the analysis of this structure will show that the character and function of statement is based exclusively on the statement-subject, that indeed the concept of statement is identical with the statement-subject, while the statement-object is only intentionally implied therein. Concurrently we shall thereby bring into focus a phenomenon which at first sight seems somewhat astonishing: the fact that all statement is reality-statement, and that therewith is presented a foundation upon which we can fix precisely the relation of language, and therefore also that of literature, to reality.

We shall begin with a simple declarative sentence, e.g.: The student is writing. The statement-object, or the content expressed by this declarative sentence is the simple fact that the student is writing. But this state of affairs, i.e., the content of the statement, changes its denotative, ontically real character according to the kind of statement-subject the statement has; indeed it changes already according to the sense in which this subject speaks the sentence. If we encounter the sentence in a speaking situation, where for example a teacher says "The student is writing"—then the teacher is the statement-subject. The state of affairs designated by the statement-object can then be a real situation wherein the student is writing here and now. The statement-subject *qua* statement-subject becomes conspicuous when for example someone asking for quiet says: "Silence! The student is writing!" But this statement-subject can also articulate the sentence in another sense (or write it on the board, for example), as a grammatical example of the declarative sentence, or as a sentence submitted for translation into another language. In this instance the teacher-as-statement-subject will be less conspicuous; and the state of affairs expressed in the statement is not then a concrete situation, but rather a linguistic-grammatical example. If the statement-subject articulates the sentence in this sense it makes itself less "subjectively" noticeable than in the first case. And should the same sentence occur in a grammar textbook, then it appears that no statement-subject whatever is present or noticeable; or in any event the question as to its nature seems to be irrelevant.

The example of this simple declarative sentence is merely a preliminary indication of those problems contained in the concept of the statement-subject, which in turn is the statement itself. When we explain the meanings which the sentence-content "The student is writing" can assume semantically from the context in which the sentence stands or is spoken, our attention becomes directed to that structural element which, so to say, first produces the relations of context. Statement contents, and therefore contexts, are infinite in number, since everything which is, which can be mentally represented and thought, can become a statement-object. Therefore the structure of language cannot become known via the statement-object. The structuring element in language is the statement-subject. And as we are endeavoring to show, the analysis of the statement-subject reveals that the entire infinite realm of subject matter and thematic units for the statement is reducible to a *system*, which can be ordered with the help of few, namely three categories or types both of statement-subjects and therefore also of statements *per se*. The three categories which may be distinguished I shall designate as (1) the historical, (2) the theoretical, and (3) the pragmatic statement-subject.

The concept *historical statement-subject* is to be understood in a specific way. What is meant here is not the statement-subject who gives historical documentation in the narrow sense, for example the author of a historical treatise. Rather this term designates a statement-subject whose essential feature is its individuality. The nature of the historical statement-subject can be most clearly elucidated with the example of the letter as a document which is fixed in writing and which does not fluctuate as does oral communication in the light of various situations, moments and intents. The letter writer is a statement-subject whose individual self is always the most important factor because the letter is an expressly personal communication directed from one person to another, even in cases where this communication is predominantly objective in content. He is always a specific, individual, and therefore in the widest sense "historical" statement-subject in whose individual self we are interested, irrespective of whether this interest is only for private or for more general, more narrowly "historical" reasons. The letter is always a historical document which bears testimony to an individual self—and it requires no special mention that any letter, no matter how private it was originally intended to be, can be used as a historical document in the narrower sense, as a source of historical research of every kind; whereby again it is a matter of indifference whether this research pertains more to the letter writer as an individual person or to those circumstances of time and event which might be conveyed by him. The letter writer is only one example of the historical statement-subject. Other related examples are the statement-subjects of diaries, memoirs—in short, those of autobiographical documents of any kind. The individuality that is the essential determinant of the historical statement-subject makes its relevance clear in that it appears as an "I." But this does not mean that its statement must be one of marked "subjectivity." The subject-object relation of statement is not constituted in or even influenced by the first-person form, but is subject to other regulatory factors which lie in the essence of statement and which will be presented below. Indeed, we shall see that the statement of a theoretical statement-subject can be more subjective than that of a historical statement-subject presenting himself in the first-person form.

The *theoretical statement-subject* is distinguished from the historical precisely through the characterizing quality designated in its name. Here the individual self of the person making the statement is not any decisive factor. The teacher who says the sentence "The student is writing" as a grammatical illustration is a theoretical statement-subject, whereas, when his sentence intends an actual situation in which he is involved, he functions either as a historical statement-subject, or (depending upon what intonation he gives the sentence) as a pragmatic one—as we shall describe below. Instructive for the difference as well as for the possible borderline cases between the historical and the theoretical statement-subject is the example of the statement-subject of a historical account in the narrower sense, which account we will therefore characterize as historiographical [*geschichtlich*]. So applied the concept "historiographical" is itself to be understood in a relatively comprehensive sense: extending from a work of the scientific discipline of history to a newspaper report covering daily political events, and also all documents pertaining to the history of literature and the other arts. The authors of these reports or presentations are without doubt individual persons who affix their names to, and whose individuality is of significance for the character of that which is presented by them, i.e., a book pertaining to the disciplines of historical or literary studies. Nevertheless such authors are not historical statement-subjects, because their individual selves do not matter in this case and can be neglected: the reader assimilates only the objective content and does not refer this content to the respective author, as he would in the case of a letter. The author of the historiographical work is a theoretical statement-subject. Should the case arise where interest does become directed toward the author's individual self, as for example when his lifetime or his individual bias become important for the appraisal of the work, he nevertheless *qua* author of the work remains a theoretical statement-subject, even if this statement-subject is bound up with an individual person whose characteristics can exert a greater or a lesser influence upon the statement-object.—We encounter similar if somewhat modified conditions with the statement-subjects of philosophical works. The specific individuality of the philosopher is more directly connected with his work, with precisely *his* philosophy, than is the case with the author of a work of history. The distinctness of the philosopher is identical with that of his doctrine itself; his individual self is not detached from his philosophical doctrine, and therefore his name can also serve to designate his philosophy. By no means can one speak here of an influence of the personal circumstances of the statement-subject upon the statement-object, as one is able to in the case of the historiographical author.

The individuality of the theoretical statement-subject diminishes in proportion to the degree to which the statement-object is theoretical, namely, uninfluenced by its statement-subject. The purest instance of the theoretical statement is the statement of a law in logic, mathematics or the natural sciences. For example, the statement "Parallel lines intersect in infinity" is so "objectively" universal that no statement-subject seems to be present. For in the mathematical law the prime importance lies neither in the statement-subject who says or writes the proposition, nor in that statement-subject represented by the mathematician who first established the law. Nevertheless the statement-subject is present, not as an individual one, but rather—corresponding to the universality of the statement-object—as an inter-individual, general one, i.e., one intending all conceivable statement-subjects, of which then none is distinguished from the other.

The pragmatic statement-subject. The historical and the theoretical statement-subject share in common the characteristic that their statement-objects are states of affairs which appear in the mode of an account or an expository statement. These two forms or types of statement command by far the greatest portion of our stating lives: nearly all written material in the statement system, and also the greater part of verbal communication. They comprise that portion of the statement system which in the past has been designated as "statement" in the less inclusive sense: both in the sense of the assertion or declarative sentence as well as in the broader, non-grammatical sense of making a statement (e.g., before a court of law). The sentence modalities represented by the question, the command, the exclamation and the ellipsis are excluded from this more restricted meaning of the concept "statement." But when we understand statement in the broader, structural sense as the statement of a statement-subject, then these sentence modalities, too, become incorporated within the statement system. Indeed, it will further be revealed that only then will it become possible to delineate completely and exactly the particular structure of language which underlies all our thinking and speaking life: the subject-object structure.

It is now possible to combine within the category of the pragmatic statement-subject those several sentence modalities not belonging to the type of the expository statement, that is, those which are not declarative sentences—namely questions, commands, and wishes. Such a concept of the pragmatic statement-subject has its foundation in the fact that these statement modalities, each appearing in its own different grammatical sentence-form, are all oriented toward the attainment of some end, of some effect. The statement-subject who questions, commands, or pleads *wants* something with respect to the statement-object. It wants the state of affairs which is also virtually intended in the question, command, or wish to be respectively answered, carried out or fulfilled. That it is more-over necessarily essential of questions, commands, and wishes that they be directed toward some other person as recipient, whereas the expository statement is independent of this, is bound up with the communicative quality of language and not with its statement structure.

THE SUBJECT-OBJECT STRUCTURE OF STATEMENT

In the preceding section, by tracing the whole of all conceivable statements back to the three categories of the historical, theoretical, and pragmatic statement-subject, we were provided only with the fundamental tools with which to uncover not only the structure of the simple statement, but also that of the entire statement system, as being a subject-object structure. For from the mere categorization of statement-subjects in itself we cannot yet derive and obtain knowledge of this structure. More closely defined, this means that those concepts which emerge in connection with subject-object structure, namely the cognates "subjectivity" and "objectivity," as well as the corresponding adjectives "subjective" and "objective," are not given through the various types of the statement-subject. The historical statement-subject, because it appears mostly in the grammatical first-person form, need not on that account state or behave "more subjectively" than a theoretical statement-subject. But if we are correct in saying that the statement-subject, being fixed in language, is therefore the more precisely determinable analogue to the cognitive subject or subject of consciousness, so also can the relation of subjectivity and objectivity be more concisely fixed within theory of language than is possible in epistemology.

In order to test and observe these relations, let us select a series of random statements from all three categories:

1. I am a teacher.	historical statement-subject
2. How difficult life is!	
3. In 1806 Napoleon was victorious in Jena.	
4. Parallel lines intersect in infinity.	
5. "Do we have an answer nowadays to the question as to what we actually mean by the words 'in the act of being'? By no means." (Heidegger)	theoretical statement-subject
6. "Oh Duty, you sublime and great name . . . what is the cause commensurate with you, and where does one find the root of your noble lineage?" (Kant)	
7. Can you come see me tomorrow?	pragmatic statement-subject
8. Leave me in peace!	
9. Do not lean out of the window!	

As is indicated, these sentences are ordered according to their membership within the three categories of statement-subjects. But the type of subject-object polarity structuring each of these statements *qua* statement is not given by this membership. The first-person declarative sentence of a historical statement-subject, "I am a teacher" (1), seems more objective than the rhetorical question of the philosophical and therefore theoretical statement-subject whose name is Kant (6), and this in turn seems more subjective still than the question of the philosophical-theoretical statement-subject Heidegger (5). The exclamatory sentence of the historical statement-subject (2) is without doubt more subjective than the prohibitional sentence having an exclamation point (9), and the interrogative sentence (7) again more objective than the command. These examples may suffice to make it apparent that within the entire statement system—consisting of all sentence modalities—there is no statement which cannot be put to question as to the degree of its objectivity, and vice versa of its subjectivity. The polaric relation existing between subject and object is displayed precisely in the comparison of statements, wherein one proves itself to be more subjective or more objective than the other. Only in the linguistic manifestation, in the (formulated) sentence, does subjectivity appear in its polaric relation to objectivity and vice versa; only then does a subjective formulation really show itself as being less objective, and conversely an objective formulation as being less subjective—whereby the gradations of less and more can attain the limit of absolute objectivity, namely in the (sole) instance of that mathematical proposition which has the linguistic form of the assertion sentence. For as soon as the mathematical proposition is vested with the form of a question, perhaps as a teacher might ask: Do parallel lines intersect in infinity? or Where do parallel lines intersect?—the objectivity of the statement undergoes a subjective reduction which is precisely that of the question itself.

Two further moments are touched upon at the same time with this example. There is reason for the fact that only a limit of absolute objectivity, but not one of absolute subjectivity is attainable. The absolute objectivity of the mathematical statement (as a purely theoretical statement and thus here paradigmatic for objectivity) has as its subject pole the inter-individual universality of that statement-subject which does not appear *as* an observable subject precisely because it has subsided into the generality of all conceivable statement-subjects. Conversely, however, there is no statement-object which might disappear within an absolute statement subjectivity, since a statement-subject cannot make a statement without a statement-object. Therefore the statement-object always remains visible, no matter how subjectively the statement is formulated. This is the problem which is of consequence for the structure of the lyric poem.

Now, without question the polarity of subject-object structure is most explicitly perceptible in the declarative sentence, and conversely it is also only with respect to this sentence form that such polarity is relevant. In addition, the declarative sentence is that particular statement form whose subject-object polarity is least influenced by "expression," wherein emotional attitudes of the statement-subject emerge. It is just this factor which is significant for those types of statement-subjects—and that is types of statements—which we have summarily designated as pragmatic: those of questions, commands, and wishes. When Heidegger (example 5) vests the theoretical statement that "today we have no answer to the question as to what we actually mean by the words 'in the act of being'" with the form of a—however rhetorical—question, the statement-subject is nonetheless still a theoretical statement-subject—precisely because the question is a rhetorical one. But by means of the interrogative form the statement-subject gains a certain tenor of exigency, let us say, which introduces a pragmatic note to the theoretical character of the statement. In the example from Kant (6), taken from the *Critique of Practical Reason,* the aspect of urgency is stronger still; indeed, the theoretical statement-subject all but becomes a pragmatic one here, because the question "what is the cause commensurate with you . . . ?" is addressed to the personification Duty, and a reply is still expected of it, no matter how rhetorical the question might be. Precisely for this reason Kant's question appears to be more subjectively colored than does the one from Heidegger.—Both of these examples indicate that the structure of subject-object polarity specifies not only the declarative sentence where the theoretical and historical statement-subjects predominate, but also the category of the pragmatic. There are those questions, commands, and wishes which are more objective, and those which are more subjective. But the questioning, commanding, pleading or wishing statement-subject is *eo ipso* a subject who is more conspicuous as subject than is that of the assertion or declarative sentence.

THE CONCEPT OF STATEMENT AS REALITY STATEMENT

It is the structure of subject-object polarity which now opens up the horizons of the further structural elements of statement, and which at once brings us to the realization that all statement is reality statement. If this assertion appears problematic and even open to criticism, and if the concept of reality which here emerges at first seems confusing, nevertheless concise analysis of the relationships present here shall establish that indeed only the structure of statement will elucidate the much debated relation of language, and therewith that of literature, to reality. It will be seen that—and this is crucial for our topic—not the concept of reality itself, but rather that of reality statement furnishes the decisive criterion for the classification of literary genres. Therefore, it is now necessary to define the concept of reality statement.

We shall begin from a documented text, a passage from a letter of Rilke's to Lou, dated December 4, 1904:

Mitten im Geläute von zehn kleinen Glocken ging es durch eine lange Lindenallee—der Schlitten bog aus, und da war der Schloßplatz, eingefaßt von den kleinen Seitenflügeln des Schloßes. Dort aber, wo vier Treppen mühsam und schwer aus dem Schnee des Platzes zur Terrasse hinaufstiegen und wo diese Terrasse, von einem vasengeschmückten Geländer begrenzt, auf das Schloß vorzubereiten glaubte, dort war nichts, nichts als ein paar schneeversunkene Büsche, und Himmel, grauer, zitternder Himmel, aus dessen Dämmerung sich fallende Flocken auslösten. *

* Amidst the pealing of ten small bells we went through a long avenue of lindens—the sleigh turned off, and there was the courtyard, enclosed by the small sidewings of the castle. But there, where four steps wearily and heavily ascended from the snow in the yard to a terrace, and where this terrace, bordered by a balustrade adorned with vases, was intended to serve as a prelude

This passage consists of a group of objective declarative sentences in which no personal pronoun occurs; for it is above all with such a declarative sentence that the structure of statement can most lucidly be demonstrated. In addition, the letter is an especially well suited text for this demonstration because in such cases we are dealing with an individual (historical) statement-subject. Let us propose that—though it may seem tautological at first—those objects and natural phenomena described in the sentences above were "really" there and "really" so because they are described in a letter which is certified as genuine, and because the writer of this letter is describing them not as a fantasy or a dream, but rather as something so seen and "really" experienced by him. And conversely it is implied in this that the objects described existed and formed the respective circumstances *independently of whether they became described or not*. For example, Napoleon lived at such and such a time and waged such and such wars independently of whether any documents have given account of this or not. Conversely we, as posterity, know that Napoleon lived and waged wars because these documents are presented and authenticated as historical, as reality-documents, just as the sleigh ride described by Rilke is certified as really having taken place because it is described in a letter intended as a document of reality.

These examples analyzed from reality-documents might mislead us into designating a statement as a reality statement only *if* it is documenting reality, i.e., if the statement-object is one of empirical reality, or in the case of theoretical statement, if it is an abstract, "ideal" object. In this sense even a mathematical proposition would naturally be a reality statement. Indeed, we

---

to the castle proper, there was nothing, nothing but a few shrubs sunken in snow, and sky, grey, quivering sky, from whose twilight falling snowflakes were unloosed.

can say that in all cases where reality is ascribed to a given state of affairs—be this reality of a sensuous or a supra-sensuous, of a material or an intellectual nature—a statement concerning this state of affairs could be called a reality statement. However, the character of statement as being reality statement is not grounded in the reality of the statement-object. Were such the case, then difficulties would arise immediately, and our definition would be lost in inexactness. It would already be lost in that the concept "reality" is subject to all possible interpretations and definitions— physical, epistemological, ontological and metaphysical—and our definition of all statement as reality statement would meet with inconsistencies. Indeed, the definition would fail us the moment the statement-object were a demonstrably "unreal" one, for instance a dream, a fantasy or a lie. That even such an "unreality statement" is nonetheless still and under all circumstances a reality statement, is rooted in the fact that not the statement-object, but the statement-subject is the decisive factor in this regard. *Statement is always reality statement because the statement-subject is real, in other words, because statement is constituted only through a genuine, real statement-subject.* And the concept of reality which emerges in this context no longer admits of various epistemological interpretations, but is to be understood only in one, unambiguous sense, in a meaning which is grounded in that of the subject itself, or more precisely: which can be true of the subject only in an unambiguous way. Only once we have clarified that concept of reality which concerns the statement-subject can the structure of statement as reality statement be elucidated, and this means only then can the subject-object relation of statement, the already professed independence of the object from its being stated, be completely analyzed.

But ultimately there is only one criterion which establishes the reality of the statement-subject: this, that we *can pose the question as to its place in time*, even if, owing to the character of the respective statement, no specific answer can be given or if the question is irrelevant. This becomes apparent as soon as we glance at the three categories of statement-subjects, the historical, theoretical, and pragmatic. It is clear that the element of reality is already contained within these subject categories, and provides their constitutive foundation. That this has only been established now is because with its aid we shall now be able to ground the nature of statement as reality statement. Naturally the question as to its place in time is most easily and directly answered by the historical statement-subject, precisely because here we are dealing with an individual subject, whose statements—for example, those of the memoir or letter writer—can be dated, and these dates are then of interest and in some circumstances also of relevance for purposes of the individual existence of these statement-subjects. The various sorts of theoretical statement-subjects, and in other words also the various gradations of objectivity for theoretical statements, entail that the question as to the temporal designation of the statement-subject can indeed always be posed in principle, but is either relevant or answerable only to a relatively greater or lesser extent. For example, we consider the date of newspaper articles important, whereas the time when a textbook or any other kind of basic text was written only becomes relevant from the point of view of whether it has become outdated or has been written under the influence of the tide of events in any given period. That in the case of purely theoretical statements we are, so to speak, groping in a vacuum with the question of the statement-subject's designation in time is something which necessarily occurs in conjunction with this subject's absolute "non-personality," with its inter-individual universality, which intends every conceivable but no specific statement-subject. —As for the pragmatic statement-subject, that associated with questions, commands, and wishes, the question as to its place in time is for other, almost opposite reasons, indeed possible, but irrelevant. For the answer is always the respective point of present time, the Now and Here wherein someone asks, commands, or wishes, as in this case these sentence modalities occur predominantly, if not exclusively, in the spoken language and do not appear in the written language (exclusive of literature) other than in instances of rhetorical questions or wishes.

In having defined the reality of the statement-subject, and thereby the reality statement itself, via its place in time, we have singled out only one of the components of the spatial and temporal system of coordinates which describes reality as being spatio-temporal, and therefore conversely—which is conclusive here for our context—describes the spatio-temporal as reality. That time is bound up with space and vice versa requires no discussion here. But however interwoven space and time are from the physical perspective—for the designation of reality it is nevertheless time and the temporal experience which are the decisive components and which eclipse that of space. The experience of space is contingent upon the here and now of perception, as also it is contingent upon the here and now of mental representation when this either remembers or projects. Even all historical reality in the narrow sense is determined on a temporal scale, is chronologically and not topographically structured. Time as a factor of lived reality is to be sure more abstract, but more powerful and more determinant than is space, more existential, if you will. And clearly a structural element of language such as the statement-subject is determinable in its reality solely through the temporal coordinates of the system of time and space. In and precisely by the degree of its abstraction the statement-subject occupies a position mediate between the acting and the cognitive subject. For the actional subject space is just as necessary a condition of its reality as is time, the question as to the Where equally important as that of the When. On the other hand the cognitive subject directed toward abstract phenomena is independent of time and space, and when it appears as a theoretical *statement*-subject we do not pose the question as to its place in time; or, if we do, only under certain aspects.

The possibility of the question as to its place in time demonstrates the statement-subject as being real, and let us emphasize once more that this means nothing other than that all statement is reality statement. And precisely therein is grounded that subject-object structure which contours the statement, and in turn the whole of our linguistically stating life. Furthermore, subject-object structure implies that the subject is stating *about* the object, a formulation which means the same as that the object "exists" independently of whether it becomes stated about or not. And it was already shown in the above analysis that this independent existence of the object is not synonymous with the object's reality, or, better put, is not synonymous with any specifically determined kind of reality belonging to the object. That a mathematical law "exists" just as independently of whether or not it comes to be formulated in a proposition, as a real thing or event "exists" independently of whether it becomes stated about, requires no explanation. In this context there is only one instance which needs yet to be clarified, so that we might avoid all misunderstandings. This is the case where the statement-object is obviously not independent of its being stated, or at least does not appear to be so: in a fantasy, or for that matter also in a lie. In elucidating this instance we need no longer have recourse to the concept of reality or of unreality itself, since, as was already pointed out, this concept as a determination of being is problematic and can be interpreted in various ways. But then how do matters stand with a fantasized or a fabricated state of affairs, which obviously does not "exist" independently of the fantasizing or the lying statement-subject, but rather is so to speak produced by him? Here it is indeed not the nature of the statement-object *per se* which is our criterion. For this we can check, we can verify fantasized or fabricated things and events, i.e., these can be put to question as to their truth or falsity.

This is a process which pertains not to statement-structure, but rather to the content of the statement. But for the subject-object relation the point at issue is the sense in which the statement-subject is stating. For the unconsciously fantasizing statement-subject the fantasized object is equally independent of its having become stated as is the object which we can establish empirically as existing. The subject "believes" in its existence, one might say (as for example on the religious plane the believer does with respect to the existence of God and the Christian mysteries). The lying statement-subject is indeed consciously aware that those things and events which he is stating do not "correspond with the facts," that they are fabricated by him; but as a stating subject he "pretends" or "alleges" that the state of affairs fabricated by him "is" true, and that means in turn that it is structurally independent of its being stated.

That which grounds statement as reality statement, the subject-object structure, finds a certain analogue and confirmation in the ontology and ontological epistemology of Nicolai Hartmann, to which we shall therefore make brief reference. Hartmann, as is well known, was strongly opposed to idealistic epistemology, which is based upon that argument of subject-object correlation which says that that towards which cognition is directed, the existent as Hartmann terms it, is only an "object" [*Gegenstand*] of the cognitive subject, and therefore has a "mode of being" which is immanent within consciousness. But, Hartmann shows, cognition is distinguished from other acts of consciousness such as mental representation, thought, and fantasy precisely in that its orientation is transcendent of consciousness, in that "its object, in becoming an object of consciousness, does not cease being an object for itself." "There can only be cognition of that which 'is'—and 'is' independently of whether it becomes cognized or not."[53] Hartmann has the courage to trace the problem of cognition back to a natural realism, to the natural attitude of consciousness for which "the world in which we live and which we in the act of cognition make into our object, is not created by our cognition"—as idealism ultimately presupposes, and in its extreme form, the philosophy of Fichte, has overtly stated—"but rather is there and exists independently of us."[54] And Hartmann then expresses what to an unbiased view ought to be a self-evident discernment, namely that the existent existing independently of all cognition only becomes an object of cognition *if* and *when* it is made into an object of cognition—which is only tautological in its formulation. However, it is not tautological in fact but denotes a true epistemological condition.—We have already contended that a state of affairs in an epistemological context has its exactly perceptible manifestation in the structure of statement, and therewith in the statement-system of language. If with the process of cognition conditions are such that cognition, precisely because it involves "making the existent into an object,"[55] remains conscious of the ontic status of the existent as "being" independently of its being made into an object, or in other words if cognition remains conscious of the reality of the existent, so it is also the phenomenology of statement which illuminates just such conditions for us, and we can moreover directly infer them from it. For the independence of the statement-object—and to be exact and correspond with Hartmann's definitions we ought to speak of the independence of the existent now become statement-object—from its being stated is a less disputable fact than is the independence of the cognitive object from its being cognized. Cognition as such is a process which is problematic in itself, and has been a central problem in epistemology; for example to Hartmann's ontological realism one could always oppose transcendental or phenomenological theories of knowledge. The statement, however, is a formalized fact which is firmly embedded in the various sentence modalities, and, as is not so with cognition, poses no problems as to its origin and nature. It is a subject-object structure which in each single instance is exactly determinable with respect to its subjectivity or objectivity. To summarize, we can define the essence of reality statement thus: *that which is stated is the statement-subject's field of experience*,[56] which is merely another way of expressing the fact that there exists a polar reference, a relation between the statement-subject and the statement-object. Since the description of the sleigh ride in Rilke's letter presents itself to us in a historical document which is attested as being historical, it has the character of reality, i.e., we experience it as being the experience of the I which is here stating.

If we have been successful in demonstrating that all statement is reality statement, the statement of a real statement-subject, then we can venture the further contention that *the statement-system of language is the linguistic correlative to the system of reality itself*. Whenever we operate within the statement-system— whether actively or passively, speaking or writing, hearing or read-ing—we find ourselves in the system of reality. But if we make the transition from reality statement, i.e., from language to reality itself, then it does seem necessary to clarify once again the relation of language and reality established with this transition in that sense in which it is meant here. For although the reality statement as a phenomenon of the theory of language has not, until the pres-ent study, been discussed whenever this problem has been treated, still the relation of language and reality itself has long been—since antiquity—a frequent topic of discussion. However, as far as I can see it was always the word, the word-substance of language which has been set into a relation to reality, judged as being a relation of such and such a kind, and this in turn became limited to the nominal word, to "names" in the broader sense. A work as early as Plato's *Cratylos* treats of the "natural" accuracy of denomina-tions (ὀενότης τῶν ὀνοματικῶν), of the question whether things possess names befitting them by nature or whether these names are con-ventions, arbitrarily fixed designations which "a few have agreed upon among themselves" (383a). And even though in the thought of later epochs, and even already in Plato himself, words no longer signified mere names, but instead between word and object there was inserted the abstraction of the concept, this nevertheless did not represent any principal difference for the way in which language was related to and compared with reality. Between the elements of (material and spiritual) reality: things and states of affairs, and the elements of language: words and sentences, there resulted, according to whatever interpretation was given, a relation wherein on the one hand language either designated reality [*Bezeichnungsverhältnis*], or on the other hand even depicted it [*Abbildverhältnis*].

Language as a mirror or as a picture of reality—this at one time accepted, at another rejected relation—is yet also the problem of Ludwig Wittgenstein's very influential *Tractatus Logico-Philosophicus*. The elements of reality (or of world: "The sum-total of reality is the world") are designated as "facts" [*Tatsachen*], the elements of language as "propositions" [*Sätze*]. Via the concept of the "logical picture" the "proposition" comes to be designated as "a picture of reality" (4.021). And the proposition itself Wittgenstein construes, "like Frege and Russell, as a function of the expressions contained in it," and he grounds this pictorial theory with the following statements: "For I know the situation that it (the proposition) represents if I understand the proposition," and "A proposition communicates a situation to us, and so it must be *essentially* connected with the situation. And the connection is precisely that it is its logical picture."[57]

Our present concern with Wittgenstein is not one of discussing his concepts, for example the difficulties posed by his concept of the logical picture, which remains unclarified. We have referred to him only because there the theory of depiction is stated in extreme abstraction, and because with this theory it is again clear that language is understood, so to speak, in the manner of a substratum, as a "substance" existing just as much for and in itself as reality—or more precisely, it is only as so understood that language is brought into relation and confronted with reality. For it is a truism to state that the mode of being of language is a different one subject to different laws from that of reality, here understood as physical, spatio-temporal reality. Language shares as an intellectual mode of being that of thought and the "ideal objects" produced by thought, and hence also the manner in which these are customarily confronted with reality. But precisely because language for its part, as distinguished from constructs of thought and from thought processes, is an intellectual form which is "sensibly perceivable," i.e., writable and readable in letters and audible in sounds (qualities it shares with the products of art), and furthermore because above all it displays demonstrably historical structures far more precise and fixed than do thought and cognition, for these reasons it has been possible to investigate language as a special "substance" having, so to speak, an intellectual materiality, and thus to evolve a science of language including phonetics, linguistics, and grammar. Therein lies a possible reason why it has always been the purely lingual, i.e., the linguistic layer of language —and even this essentially only as word-substance—which was confronted to reality, such confrontation then being made under the aspect of the function of designation and the more or less problematic function of depiction. Wittgenstein even refers back to Egyptian hieroglyphics in order to support his depiction theory: "In order to understand the essential nature of a proposition, we should consider hieroglyphic script, which depicts the facts that it describes. And alphabetic script developed out of it without losing what was essential to depiction" (4.016).

The concept of statement such as we have endeavored to analyze it here places language in a different relation to reality. It is such that "language" is not understood as a composite of words or even of propositions which can then be compared with the concrete or intellectual reality which, so to speak, faces and is mirrored in it, but rather that language *qua* statement is understood as a subject-object structure that has become fixed and that "relates" to what is being stated. With that the concept of reality is rendered more precisely; i.e., it is freed from the indeterminateness in which it persists when it is applied to that to which the statement—be this as a word or as a sentence in any modality—refers. If it has been shown that all statement is reality statement, then, as we must again emphasize, reality here does not denote the statement-object, but the statement-subject, such that even an "unreal" statement-object does not impair the character of the statement as reality statement.

The description of non-creative language as the statement-system serves as the necessary basis of comparison for determining and describing the genres of creative literature, that is, the system of literature itself. For, to anticipate any possible misunderstandings (or to counter any that might already have arisen), let it be stressed again that this system, and thus the classification of genres, shall be traced to and founded upon the functions of creative language, i.e., the language which produces literature. This means that the position of literature both within and with regard to the statement system of language is to be investigated. And in the course of such investigation literature as "verbal art" shall be grounded by our tracing the relation of literature to reality, from which we originally set out, back to the relation of literature and reality statement, as we have defined the latter. According to the differentiations possible within this relation we shall then determine the fictional and the lyrical genres, as well as the special literary forms, the first-person narrative and the ballad.

3

THE FICTIONAL OR
MIMETIC GENRE

Preliminary Remarks on the Concept
of Literary Fiction[58]

Before applying theory of language in the founding of epic (narrative) and dramatic literature as fictional, we should first preface an excursus on the concept of literary fiction. For the concepts "fiction" and "fictive" are applied to the most diverse phenomena, and even within the discipline of literary studies they are commonly understood in a more or less imprecise sense, meaning roughly that which is invented or made up. In addition, the ambiguity of this concept, or of its application, has been increased by the English usage of "fiction" as a designation for the novel (instead of this latter, older term), yet not for the drama as well. Therefore it is all the more imperative to define fiction as an exact methodological concept of literary studies and to isolate it as such from the various meanings and uses to which it has been put.

"Fiction" is derived from the Latin *fingere*, which has the most radically differing meanings extending from that of shaping or inventing to that of deceitful fabrication. And precisely when we survey the meanings of the verb *fingere* and its cognates in the living western European languages do we approach a somewhat exact definition of what is understood by "literary fiction," and above all what is to be so understood in the context of the theory of literature developed in what follows. Corresponding to the Latin *fingere* we have *fingere* in Italian, *feindre* in French, *to feign* in English and *fingieren* in German—which means that the Latin verb, as it was carried over into the modern languages, has exclusively preserved the meaning of falsely alleging, simulating, imitating and the like. The corresponding substantives *Finta, feinte, feint,* and *Finte* were then developed from the verbal form. However, it is another matter with the substantive *fictio*. This indeed has retained both the pejorative and the meliorative meanings of *fingere* in the modern languages, but in such a way that the latter meaning, which denotes the function of creative forming, does in any case dominate over the pejorative meaning. At least in French, and also in German, which in this case conformed to French usage, a second adjective, *fictif* (*fiktiv*) was formed (accompanying *feint, fingiert*) to denote the positive meaning of *fingere,* and this adjectival form has become more practicable in the theory of fine art than the substantive "fiction" itself.

These developments, however, only complicate the situation. What significance does the difference between feigned and fictive have; why is it significant, for example, that we speak of the persons in a novel or in a drama as being not feigned, but fictive persons? How do matters stand with the imaginative figurations of art in general? To which of these figurations do the concepts "fiction" and "fictive" apply, and to what extent? Since H. Vaihinger's *Philosophy of the As-If* (1911), people have customarily explicated fiction as the form of the as-if, or in other words through the structure of the state of being feigned. This holds for the fictions of the sciences—of mathematics, the physical sciences, jurisprudence, etc. Mathematics calculates with non-spatial points, as does physics with empty space, as if there were such structures, just as jurisprudence deals with construed cases as if they had factually occurred. The definition of fiction as the as-if structure makes use, as it must, of the irreal subjunctive, which indicates the state of being feigned. And in linguistic usage the concepts of the feigned and the fictive probably do approximate one another. Mathematical points are, in their capacity as being feigned, also fictive. And in everyday usage "fictive" and "fiction" carry the meaning of the irreal, the merely imagined.

Our question, however, is whether the "aesthetic fictions," as Vaihinger terms them, the figurations of art, are also to be determined through the structure of the as-if. Let us examine those of the plastic arts. We might say of Terborch's paintings that for example taffeta is so painted to appear—in any case, according to the intentions of this great realistic movement in art—as if it were real taffeta. Notwithstanding such intentions, it would nevertheless be doubtful whether the ever-so-realistic figuration of art could be described by the as-if structure. The conception of art in antiquity praised the cherries of Zeuxis because the sparrows took them for actual cherries, whereas for the modern conception the pinnacle is reached when an element of deception is in play, where, for example, something inanimate shams being animate or is feigned as being so, as a collection of wax figures. The works of the plastic arts, or more precisely that which is represented in these works, is not fiction in the sense of the as-if. But the fictive is to be distinguished from the state of being feigned. This distinction will show that in the realm of art the fictive has validity only for literature and not for the plastic arts, and that the fictive, or literary fiction, moreover, does not have the structure of the as-if. What various relations are present here? Why do we not designate a portrait of Maria Stuart as a fictive figuration, i.e., the painted Maria as a fictive Maria, although we do designate the figure Maria Stuart in the tragedy by Schiller as fictive; whereas on the other hand the Scottish queen as the object of a historical presentation is the real queen herself, i.e., is intended as such? On what basis do we not designate a painted person, be he ever so realistically painted, as a fictive person, while we do designate as such every figure in either a novel or a drama, be these figures ever so surrealistically moulded? Vaihinger and his successors, for example E. Utitz among others, have erroneously spoken of the persons in a novel or a drama as being feigned; as, too, Vaihinger utterly fails in his definition of aesthetic fiction because he does not incorporate into his concept of fiction the difference in meaning between feigned and fictive, in other words, because he interprets fiction exclusively as an as-if structure. But Schiller did not form his character Maria Stuart as if she were the real Maria. If we nevertheless perceive her, or the world of any drama or novel, as fictive, this is based not on an as-if structure, but rather, so we might say, on an *as-structure*. Theodore Fontane unwittingly once gave this definition of literary fiction: "A novel . . . should tell us a story in which we believe," and he meant by that that it ought to "allow us a world of fiction to momentarily appear as a world of reality. . . ." In this unwitting, so to speak naive definition, arising entirely out of the spirit of naturalism (appearing in a review of Gustav Freytag's *Ahnen* in 1875),[59] there is nevertheless—and perhaps just on that account it is not fortuitous—precisely pinpointed the mode of being literary fiction, epic as well as dramatic. The expression "appear as reality" designates this mode of being through each of its three words. It means that the appearance or semblance [*Schein*] of reality is to be created, which in turn signifies (beyond the intentions of Fontane) the semblance of reality even in cases where the drama's or novel's world is ever so unreal. Even the fairy tale appears as reality as long as we, as we read it or watch it enacted, abide within it; but nevertheless it does not appear as if it were a reality. For inherent in the meaning of the as-if is the element of deception, and in turn the reference to a reality which is formulated in the irreal subjunctive precisely because as an as-if reality it *is* not that reality which it pretends to be. The as-reality, however, is semblance, the illusion of reality, which is called non-reality or fiction. But the concept of fiction in the sense of the as-structure is realized solely by dramatic and epic fiction (the third-person narrative), as well as by the film. Should we ask how here and only here the semblance, the as-structure of reality is produced, the answer is: in that the semblance of life is produced. And in art the semblance of life is produced only by the person as a living, thinking, feeling, and speaking subject. The figures of the third-person novel or drama are fictive persons because they are formed as fictive persons or subjects. Of all the creative materials in the arts, however, it is language alone which is capable of producing the semblance of life, i.e., living, feeling, thinking, speaking, or also silent persons. That language processes are much more complex in narrative literature than in dramatic is shown by the structure of epic narration, which we shall hence term fictional narration and proceed to describe below.

Epic Fiction (or the Third-Person Narrative)

FICTIONAL NARRATION AND ITS CHARACTERISTIC FEATURES

Our reasons for beginning the descriptive analysis of the system of literature with the third-person narrative, i.e., with epic fiction, lie within the theory of language. This definition, the equating of epic fiction with the third-person narrative, does not encompass the whole of narrative literature, to which the first-person narrative also belongs. But it will be shown that the latter is not fiction in the sense defined by us, in that sense which we believe is an exact one in the theory of language and in poetology. For, as we have concluded in the previous section, the concept of fiction is not realized by the invented, such that an invented and to that extent "fictive" first-person narrator would be sufficient to realize the concept of fiction. And it is therefore also not with the narrative structure of first-person narration, but with that of the third-person narrative, i.e., fictional narration in the exact sense, that the description of literature based on theory of language can commence at all. For it is fictional narration that occupies a decisive position within the system of literature and of language, that of a line of demarcation separating the fictional or the mimetic genre—epic fiction, and subsequent to it, dramatic fiction—from the *statement system of language.* Hence the structure of fictional narration can be elaborated only in constant comparison to the statement, which was explicated above in its basic characteristics as a subject-object structure.

We shall begin with a text suited to the purposes of our demonstration, the beginning of C. F. Meyer's novel *Jürg Jenatsch:*

> Die Mittagssonne stand über der kahlen, von Felshäuptern umragten Höhe des Julierpasses im Lande Bünden. Die Steinwände brannten und schimmerten unter den stechenden senkrechten Strahlen. Zuweilen wenn eine geballte Wetterwolke emporquoll und vorüberzog, schienen die Bergmauern näher heranzutreten und die Landschaft verengend, schroff und unheimlich zusammenzurücken. . . . In der Mitte der sich dehnenden Paßhöhe standen rechts und links vom Saumpfade zwei abgebrochene Säulen, die der Zeit schon länger als ein Jahrhundert trotzen mochten. *

This passage from the novel exhibits the same logico-linguistic structure as the excerpt from the Rilke letter (p. 43f). Its nature

---

* The noonday sun stood over the barren height of the Julian Pass, jutted with rocky peaks, in the canton of Bünden. The stone walls burnt and shimmered under the piercing, vertical rays. At times, when a billowing storm cloud welled up and passed over, the mountain walls seemed to draw nearer and the landscape, contracting, uncannily to compress. . . . In the middle of the extending height of the pass, to the left and right of the mule path, stood the ruins of two pillars which might well have been withstanding time for more than a century already.

is such that, once detached from its context, it would in no way be possible to recognize it as a passage from a novel, all the less so in this case because the Julian Pass in the Gresins belongs to geo-graphical reality, which is known to us. The passage is so con-structed that, as with the description of the sleigh ride in Rilke's letter, it could come from a historical document, a journal, a travel log, or a letter. Were we to be presented with this passage out of context, we would be able to view this barren height of the Julian Pass, lying there in the noonday sun in the canton of Bünden, as being the experience-field of the reporting subject, whom we would in turn take to be a historical statement-subject. However, when we read this passage with the knowledge that it is the beginning of a novel, i.e., knowing we have entered upon the scene of a novel, then our reading experience is one of a totally different kind. Now the most distinctive feature of our reading experience is that it lacks the character of reality. And this although the setting depicted is a geographical reality known as such to us, and although this reality is brought vividly before the mind's eye by means of poeti-cally illustrative depiction. But it is simply because we know that we have begun to read a novel that this description, despite the geographical actuality, does not impart to us the experience of reality. In turn, this statement might appear to be a tautology, differing in no way whatever from the above-criticized tautology of the quasi-judgments, which have the character of "not being made in full earnest." However, we believe we can say, and dem-onstrate with increasing detail in what follows, that precisely here we find ourselves confronted with one of the cardinal points of the genuine logic of literature. The experience of non-reality has its precise logical, and in a broader sense epistemological cause, which, as we shall demonstrate in detail in the next sections, finds its grammatical and semantic expression in quite precise phenom-ena of fictional narration. That also this beginning passage from the novel *Jürg Jenatsch*, which in a purely verbal sense is no differ-

ent from a possible historical or biographical description, evokes
the experience of non-reality, this has its cause not in the narrated
itself, but in the "narrator," as we shall phrase it in traditional manner for the present. For because we know we are reading a novel
and not a travel log, we do not—and this we do unconsciously—
refer the depicted landscape to the storyteller. We know that we
are not to take this as being his experience-field, but rather as the
experience-field of other persons, whose appearance we anticipate
because it is a novel we are reading: fictive persons, the figures of
the novel.

> Jetzt erscholl aus der Ferne . . . das Gebell eines Hundes. Hoch
> oben an dem . . . Hange hatte ein Bergamaskerhirt im Mittags-
> schlafe gelegen. Nun sprang er auf . . . zog seinen Mantel fest um
> die Schultern und warf sich in kühnen Schwüngen von einem
> vorragenden Felsturme hinunter zur Einholung seiner Schaf-
> herde, die sich in weißen beweglichen Punkten nach der Tiefe hin
> verlor. . . . Und immer schwüler und stiller glühte der Mittag. . . .
> Endlich tauchte ein Wanderer auf. . . . Jetzt erreichte er die zwei
> römischen Säulen. Hier entledigte er sich seines Ränzchens. . . .
> Schnell bedacht zog er eine lederne Brieftasche hervor und be-
> gann eifrig die beiden ehrwürdigen Trümmer auf ein weißes Blatt
> zu zeichnen. Nach einer Weile betrachtete er seiner Hände Werk
> mit Befriedigung . . . , ließ sich auf ein Knie nieder und nahm mit
> Genauigkeit das Maß der merkwürdigen Säulen, "Fünfthalb Fuß"
> sagte er vor sich hin. "Was treibt Ihr? Spionage?" ertönte neben
> ihm eine gewaltige Baßstimme. *

---

* Now there resounded out of the distance . . . the barking of a dog. High
above on the . . . slope, an Alpine shepherd had lain down in midday sleep.
Now he sprang up . . . drew his cape firmly around his shoulders and threw
himself in bold leaps down from a jutting stone tower to gather his heard of
sheep, which lost itself in white moving points into the lower depths. . . . And
the afternoon glowed more and more sultry and still. . . . Finally a wanderer
emerged. . . . Now he reached the two Roman pillars. Here he removed his
small satchel. . . . Quickly intent, he took out a leather portfolio and zeal-
ously began to draw the two venerable ruins on a white sheet of paper. After

We shall see below why in this passage the sentence "Quickly intent, he took out a leather portfolio" first supplies the actual proof that we are really dealing with a novel and not, for example, with a vivid eye-witness description, i.e., still a historical document. For this proof enters into the demonstration of those fundamental phenomena that bring to light the categorical difference separating fictional narration from statement.

That it is the persons of the novel, or more generally: epic persons, which render a piece of narrative literature just that, namely narrative literature, seems to have been taken as something so banal and self-evident, or even tautological, that no theory of epic literature has dwelled on this fact. But this fact proves to be no longer quite so banal and tautological once one takes into account the additional fact that the persons of a novel are *fictive* persons. For it is only this which first discloses the structure of literary fiction, the epic as well as the dramatic, which from the point of view of the logical structure of literature are taken together as the fictional genre and set opposite to lyric poetry, from which they manifest categorical differences. But only epic and not dramatic fiction exhibits all those phenomena which can demonstrate this with full and stringent conclusiveness. For only with the problem of narration can those logical and epistemological, grammatical and semantic relations be delineated which distinguish fiction from reality. Only in narrative and not in dramatic literature is language alive and at work in its totality, and only in the former can it be shown what it means when language produces the experience of fiction and not that of reality. In other words, only in the distinction between statement and fictional narration is the logical structure of literature to be elaborated.

---

a while he observed his hands' work with satisfaction . . . , went down on one knee, and with precision took the measurements of the remarkable columns. "Five and a half feet," he said to himself. "What are you doing? Spying?" sounded a powerful bass voice beside him.

The Epic Preterite

We said that in our example, the beginning of *Jürg Jenatsch,* it is the anticipation of the appearance of the persons of the novel which makes what is depicted appear to us as non-real, i.e., not as the experience-field of the narrator. But this only indicates the general experience we have in reading third-person narrative literature, in reading a work of Homer's as well as any serial novel in a newspaper. And one can also raise the objection that, still, there are very "subjectively" narrated novels, those kinds wherein the narrator steps forward using the words "I" and "we," turns to his "dear readers," and the like. These and other objections can only be answered once the essence and function of the "narrator" is fully elucidated in terms of both theory of language and grammar, which in turn means once the psychological reading experience of non-reality has been given its foundation.

For this purpose we must seek out a narrative phenomenon so obvious from the point of view of theory of language that it can offer this proof with greater stringency than any other aspect of narration. Indeed, it must be one so constituted that all other narrative phenomena can be explained and developed from it without objection. There is such a phenomenon, and we are not surprised that it is connected with the verb, with the tense of the verb, and therefore with the problem of time. In the sentence, in speech, it is the verb which decides the "mode of being" of persons and things, which indicates their place in time and therefore in reality, which states of their being and non-being, of their still, no longer, and not yet existing.

"In the midst of the pealing of ten small bells we went through a long avenue of lindens, the sleigh turned off, and there was the palace courtyard," so reports Rilke in the above-cited letter of the fourth of December, 1904, and we know that he took this sleigh ride before this date, that the winter excursion to Oby in Sweden is a past event for him: for he reports it in the simple past tense. "The noon sun stood over the barren heights of the Julian Pass, jutted with rocky peaks, in the canton of Bünden. The stone walls burnt and shimmered. . . ." This depiction, too, is narrated in the simple past. And therefore, say the grammarians and literary theorists, the epic writer reports his story as past, or at least as if it were past. They have not progressed essentially beyond the much-quoted interpretation made by Goethe in his famous discussion with Schiller in December of 1797 on the topic of epic and dramatic literature, where he said that "the dramatist (mime) presents an event as completely present, and the epic poet (rhapsodist) reports it as completely past." And even if the experience we have in reading a novel, as well as in reading Homer and the *Nibelungenlied,* made us aware that the situation is more problematic with the being-past, or even the being-thought-of-as-past of the epic action, nevertheless we still have not advanced far beyond the modification of Goethe's pronouncement undertaken already by Schiller: "that literary art compels even the epic poet to presentify, or present as present, that which has happened" And the frequent occurence of the historical present appeared as a welcome fulfillment of the meaning of this concept of presentification [*Vergegenwärtigung*]. And even Schiller, in using the term antithetically to "past," burdened the concept too significantly with the meaning which is attached to the German word for "present" [*Gegenwart*]. But particularly in connection with theories about the historical present has the concept of presentification been overestimated with respect to its temporal aspects, as we shall elaborate more closely below. And this overestimation originated in the assumption, which only endorsed it and which was never doubted, that the content of epic narration is thought of and presented as being past because it is narrated in the grammatical form of the past tense. For the possibility has never been discussed whether the preterite might occur in any use in language where it would not express a past action. For this reason epic narrative form could never be described satisfactorily, and linguistic and grammatical problems such as narrated monologue [*erlebte Rede*] remained unsolved. But it is indeed the change in meaning—which at first strikes us as being paradoxical—that is effected with the preterite of fictional narration which with full stringency identifies this as fictional, or in other words sheds light on the fact that the "epic I," as we are accustomed to say, is not a statement-subject. *The change in meaning, however, consists in that the preterite loses its grammatical function of designating what is past.*

In order to prove this we must first of all acquire a clear understanding of the grammatical function of the preterite. Not all definitions which have been established for this tense are illuminating for our purposes. It is not sufficient for our intent, for example, along with H. Paul and O. Behagel to determine the preterite, or simple past, through its relation or non-relation to the "present," nor through a "point of reference" which lies in the "past" and from which point time is to move forward within the past."[60] For in this definition of the (aoristic) past and of the tenses in general something essential is lacking, something which explicates them on a more profound level than the merely grammatical. As far as I have been able to ascertain in examining both German and foreign language grammars, the older German grammarian Christian August Heyse was the only one to have uncovered this essential moment. Heyse's *Deutsche Grammatik* generally excels in that as much as possible it derives grammatical laws and forms from logical meaning relations. It is his explication of the tenses which first made me aware of the real cause of the categorical difference between statement and fictional narration, although Heyse himself, like all other grammarians before and after him, by no means recognized this difference.

Whereas Paul and Behagel speak only of the relation of the tenses to the present, Heyse renders the concept of the present more profoundly by adding: "the present, or the present moment of the speaking subject."[61] By this means he arrives at much sharper distinctions among the major temporal designations of present, preterite, and future. These are designated as "subjective tempora" because "they set the action or events plainly—i.e., without inner limitation according to their sequential stages—within the present, past or future of the speaking subject." With the concept of the "speaking subject" Heyse thus introduced the statement-subject into the definition of the tenses, and therefore into the system of time, or (which is the same) the system of reality. Conversely, this means that the statement-subject is made known as existing in time, i.e., as real, which in turn implies nothing other than that talk of present, past and future is meaningful only in relation to a real, genuine statement-subject. In what follows we shall use as synonymous with the concept of the statement-subject a term having stronger epistemological overtones, namely the concept of the *I-Origo*, which we use in compliance with the terminology employed by Brugmann and Bühler. This concept designates the originary point occupied by the I (the experience- or statement-I), i.e., the *Origo* of the system of temporal and spatial coordinates which coincides or is identical with the Here and Now. The "Origo of the Here-Now-I system," which we shall abbreviate to "I-Origo," was employed by Brugmann and Bühler[62] in the description of the functions of demonstrative, i.e., deictic pronouns in speech, a problem which will serve as an important and convincing argument in connection with our own exposition.

We are substituting the epistemological concept of the I-Origo for the concept of the statement-subject—which has its origin in the logic of language—because the purely grammatical perspective does not suffice to elucidate those unique grammatical relations which are established, without the cognizance of the narrator, within fictional narration. No realm of language demonstrates more clearly than does literature that the system of syntax can be too constricting a vestment for the creative life of language, which as such has its source in the more comprehensive sphere of thought and mental representation. If the too narrow garb of syntax rips when processes of this sphere become noticeable—and the point is to notice them!—then there is no alternative but to enlarge upon such places with newly added pieces. We believe that the epic preterite can be looked upon as just such a piece. The expansion of the grammatical theory of tenses through this piece requires that we penetrate to those underlying epistemological relations where the reasons can ultimately be found as to why the preterite in fiction does not have the function of expressing what is past.

To this end we shall first consider the function of the preterite in the reality statement, with the aid of two simple examples of objective statements. 1. I report, either orally or in writing, of a person: Mr. X was on a trip (a sentence articulated perhaps in the course of a conversation, for example in answer to the question where Mr. X was at such and such a time). 2. A random sentence from any work of history, such as the history of Frederick the Great: "The king played the flute every evening." These statements about third-persons or objective facts are, according to Heyse's theory, "set into the past of the speaking subject," (i.e., the statement-subject); in our terminology: both statements contain a real I-Origo, with respect to the temporal coordinate of whose spatio-temporal system an undated interval exists between him and the events named. In the first example the I-Origo is clear. I report here and now that Mr. X was on a trip, I look from my Now back to the temporal point of Mr. X's travels and can then answer the question as to when he was on his trip. It follows from the past tense of my statement that his travels belong to the past and that now he is no longer traveling. In the second example, from the history text, the I-Origo is not as conspicuous, but nonetheless is just as present as in the first. The work of history, the totality of statements comprising it, seems to be suspended from the system of time (and space). Its statements possess "objective validity" and are not, or are no longer bound to the Here and Now of someone stating. This is the common way of determining the objectivity of statements, and it is here that we are to seek the real reason as to why the structure of literature has not been penetrated, and why literary genres have been falsely defined in such a way as to contrast epic and drama as objective to the lyric as a subjective genre.

The error lies in that the structural factor of reality, and therefore the I-Origo, has not been incorporated into the definition of statement—and moreover not only the I-Origo involved in the statement act, but also that of the statement's receiver. The statement from the historical text does not differ principally from our first example. It, too, is set into the past of the speaking subject, the I-Origo: it is in the past of the history text's author. For Kugler, who published his work on Frederick the Great in 1840, Frederick's lifetime lay some 70 years back in the past. But this work is also set into the past of the respective reader: for a reader in the year 1940 Frederick's life lies approximately 170 years back. The existential significance of time for both the experience and the phenomenon of historical reality consists in its uniting the "sender" and the "receiver" of the statement or information on *one* plane of reality and in *one* experience of reality. This is valid for the simultaneous as well as for the non-simultaneous existence of sender and receiver. In the last instance, should a reality-account survive its author in the form of a printed book or posthumous journals, etc., then the I-Origo of the respective reader always replaces that of the original giver of the information—to be sure, in respect to the temporal experience. Precisely the fact that the reader coming later in time has a different temporal relation to the content of the account than does the author demonstrates that this content is a reality-account, which is or can be subject to the question as to the temporal When. This "When?" can be asked only from the perspective of the I-Origo who at any given time is occupied with the account. Everything past (in the broadest sense, everything historical), just as everything which is contemporaneous and future, relates to "me," is set into my past, present, or future, even if these past, present, or future occurrences have nothing to do with my individual, personal self. The possibility of the question as to the When of an occurrence proves the reality of the occurrence, and the question itself proves the presence of an I-Origo, be this implicit or explicit. The preterite of a reality statement signifies that that which is being reported is past, which implies the same as that it is known by an I-Origo as past.

Let us now investigate the simple past tense of fiction. We assume that the sentence "Mr. X was on a trip" occurs in a novel. Instantaneously we sense that it has changed its character completely. We can no longer pose the question as to When, not even when perchance a date is named, for instance: summer, 1890. With or without any date's being given, I learn from this, as a sentence occurring in a novel, not that Mr. X *was* on a trip, but that he *is* on a trip. The situation is exactly the same with the sentence about Frederick the Great, should it occur in a novel about him. This is so even though here we are dealing with a historical personality whose existence in reality, a reality which for us today is a past lying some 200 years back, is something we know. Even the sentence in the novel, "The king played the flute every evening," does not inform us that at that time, 200 years ago, he *did* this, but that he *does* it now. The sentence in Kugler's *History of Frederick the Great* which follows after the story of Frederick's flute-playing at the evening concerts, namely: "At the appointed hour he entered the concert room, his music under his arm, and assigned the parts . . . ," lets it be clearly known that as a sentence occurring in a historical work it informs us of something past, and that as a sentence occurring in a novel it depicts a "present" situation. The grammatical past tense form loses its function of informing us about the past-ness of the facts reported.

These circumstances are not to be merely psychologically explained on the basis of our reading experience. This experience itself would not occur if it did not have its structurally fixed logical and epistemological causes. And if we are to gain a closer knowledge of these we cannot rely on a merely subjective symptom such as our reading experience. Rather, it is a genuine, objective symptom, the behavior of language itself, which furnishes a more exact elucidation of the relations present here. We can imagine the sentence "Mr. X was on a trip" as being followed in a novel by another having the form: "Today he roamed through the European port city for the last time, for tomorrow his ship sailed for America." The sentence about Frederick's flute-playing can have the following form in a novel: "This evening the king intended to play the flute again." Now, here we encounter the objective grammatical symptom which in all its inconspicuousness provides decisive proof that the past tense of fictional narration is no statement of past-ness: the fact that deictic temporal adverbs can occur conjointly with the past tense.

This phenomenon must be analyzed a bit more closely. It is directly obvious for the future adverbs used here: "tomorrow," "this evening," and so on, for in no real speaking situation is it possible for these to occur with the past tense. But this is also impossible for past adverbs in real speech, for these can be used with the past tense only in relation to the Now of the speaker: "yesterday this and that happened." But in the reality statement this combination is no longer possible for a temporal phase which, in relation to the Now of the person stating, is already past. If a person speaking here and now transposes himself to a point lying in the past, for example: "On July 15th such and such happened," then he can just as little designate something having occurred before this day with "yesterday" as he can designate something having occurred after it with "tomorrow." In such cases adverbial forms like "on the day before that" (or ". . . after that") are necessary. But we need only to open any random novel, be it of literary or non-literary aesthetic calibre, in order to see that these logico-grammatical laws, which are so to speak inherent within the reality statement, have lost their validity. Let us test some additional examples:

> Aber am Vormittag hatte sie den Baum zu putzen. Morgen war Weihnachten.
>> (Alice Berend, *Die Bräutigame der Babette Bomberling*)
> . . . and of course he was coming to her party to-night.
>> (Virginia Woolf, *Mrs. Dalloway*)
> Unter ihren Lidern sah sie noch heute die Miene vor sich. . . .
>> (Thomas Mann, *Lotte in Weimar*)
> Das Manöver gestern hatte acht Stunden gedauert.
>> (Bruno Frank, *Tage des Königs*)
> Man versammelte sich, und alle waren durch das gestrige Fest verstimmt.
>> (Goethe, *Wilhelm Meisters Lehrjahre*, 5. Buch, 13. Kap.)
> Er überdachte das Winterleben dieses guten Vaters, und dessen einsame bange Feier des heutigen Tages. . . .*
>> (Jean Paul, *Hesperus*, 7, Hundsposttag)

Whereas the combination of the deictic future adverb with the past tense in the sentence "Tomorrow was Christmas" immediately

---

* But in the morning she had to trim the tree. Tomorrow was Christmas.
>> (Alice Berend, *The Bridegrooms of Babette Bomberling*)
Still today, when she closed her eyes, she saw before her the expression on his face.
>> (Thomas Mann, *Lotte in Weimar*)
The maneuvers yesterday had lasted for eight hours.
>> (Bruno Frank, *Days of the King*)
They assembled, and everyone was out of humor because of yesterday's festivities.
>> (Goethe, *Wilhelm Meister's Apprenticeship*, Book 5, Ch. 13)
He pondered the winter life of this good father and his lonely, anxious celebration of the present occasion.
>> (Jean Paul, *Hesperus*, 7th Hundsposttag)

makes this known as a sentence occurring in a novel and only as such, the adverb "yesterday" seems, for so to speak natural reasons, not to function in semantic contradiction to the past tense. If we look a bit more closely, however, the past tense in a fictional text reacts still more sensitively and flexibly with a deictic past adverb than with a future adverb. For now it actually does disappear, and is replaced by another preterite form, the pluperfect. "The maneuvers yesterday had lasted eight hours" (example 4). The combination of "yesterday" with the pluperfect, though less conspicuously, nevertheless just as directly identifies this sentence as one appearing in a novel as does the combination of "tomorrow" with the simple past. For a reality statement—and in this case it would always be direct discourse—having the same wording would have to use either the simple past or the present perfect tense.† The pluperfect can indeed also appear in certain temporal constructions within the reality statement: The maneuvers had lasted exactly eight hours yesterday when a thunderstorm broke out; but conversely, if this sentence were to appear in a novel, the pluperfect would have to occur where we would otherwise have a simple past tense. In a novel we can indeed have a sentence like "Tomorrow was Christmas," but never one such as "Yesterday was Christmas."[63] We can only have "Yesterday had been Christmas." This pluperfect, the only tense possible in combination with the deictic past adverb, is equally as instructive for fictional narration as the combination of a future adverb with a simple past, which is possible only in fiction. And *constitutively underlying both these phenomena of tense is the same law: that that which is narrated is referred not to a real I-Origo, but rather to fictive I-Origines, and is therefore itself fictive.*[64] Epic fiction is defined solely in that it contains no real I-Origo, and secondly in that it therefore must contain fic-

† [In German one has the choice between the simple past and present perfect tense here, but under these same conditions English would require the simple past.—Tr.]

tive I-Origines, i.e., reference or orientational systems which epistemologically, and hence temporally, have nothing to do with a real I who experiences fiction in any way—in other words with the author or the reader.[65] And conversely, precisely this signifies that they are non-real, fictive. These two conditions, however, imply one and the same thing, and are explained in both a positive and a negative phrasing for the sake of clarity. For only the appearance, or respectively the anticipated appearance of the fictive I-Origines, the persons of the novel, is the reason why the real I-Origo disappears, and simultaneously, as a logical result, the preterite relinquishes its function of designating the past. Before we describe the structure of fiction more closely, we should like to enlist the aid of a particularly well-suited example, placed at our disposal by an in itself inconspicuous passage from German prose literature, in demonstrating both the poetological meaning of the concept "fictive person" and why it is that only his appearance in a narrative simultaneously gives this the character of non-reality, and relieves the past tense of its temporal meaning of referring to the past.

We find this passage at the beginning of Stifter's *Hochwald*. It is especially instructive for our problem because it is not only a description of a milieu, as is the beginning of *Jürg Jenatsch*, but also one in the first-person form, which later disappears from the novel. In the way in which this form appears in our example it serves, by way of a particularly clear contrast effect, that fact which we wish to demonstrate. It makes this passage a well of information for the literary theorist in that it fixes a juxtaposition of reality statement and fictional narration, which permits the logical difference between these two to emerge very nicely.

The narrative begins with a present tense description of the scene of the action:

An der Mitternachtseite des Ländchens Österreich zieht ein Wald an die dreißig Meilen lang seinen Dämmerstreifen westwärts ... Er beugt ... den Lauf der Bergeslinie ab, und sie geht dann mitternachtwärts viele Tagreisen weiter. Der Ort dieser Waldesschwenkung nun ist es, in dessen Revieren sich das begab, was wir uns vorgenommen haben, zu erzählen.*

In contradistinction to the opening passage of *Jürg Jenatsch,* this present tense milieu description, even though it begins a novel, is a genuine reality description. And what identifies it as such is not the geographical locale, but the present tense, which is not a historical present, but rather designates the (even if undated) Now in which the narrator is telling his story—for which reason we are not setting the concept of the narrator in quotation marks here. For here the narrator is a real I-Origo; he is thinking back to the time when he himself had wandered about in the region described, which is to be the scene of the coming action of the novel—and it matters not whether or to what extent this memory is genuine or non-genuine, i.e., feigned. What matters is only the form of the narrative act, which is that of a reality statement, the statement of a genuine statement-subject and therefore of a real I-Origo. And it is not accidental that the more general personal pronoun "we" used at the beginning (which, as we know, is often employed in theoretical presentations) is replaced by the first-person pronoun:

> Ein Gefühl der tiefsten Einsamkeit überkam mich jedesmal unbesieglich, so oft und gern ich zu dem märchenhaften See hinaufstieg.... Oft entstieg mir ein und derselbe Gedanke, wenn ich an diesen Gestaden saß.... Oft saß ich in vergangenen Tagen in dem alten Mauerwerke....†

* On the midnight side of the tiny land of Austria, a forest extends westward along the thirty mile length of its dusky strip. It branches . . . off from the course of the mountain line, which then continues many a day's journey westward. Now, it is in this place of the woods' turning in whose environs that came to pass which we have undertaken to tell.
† A feeling of deepest loneliness came over me, each time invincibly, however often and gladly I climbed up to the magical lake. . . . Often one and the same thought arose within me when I sat on this shore. . . . Often in days past I sat in the old masonry. . . .

The past tense used in this passage, too, like the present tense in the previous one, is referred to the Now of the narrator. It indicates a past time of his life, his youth, when he had roamed about in that region.—Then the description of what, with respect to this first-person narrator, is a present scene, is transformed into what for him is a historical account. That is, in his imagination he shifts into a more remote past, no longer one which was directly experienced by him:

> Und nun, lieber Leser, wenn du dich satt gesehen hast, so gehe jetzt mit mir um zwei Jahrhunderte zurück.†

The image of the castle, as the imagination constructs it from the familiar castle ruins, is brought before the eyes of the reader. But nevertheless the action of the novel still does not begin with this. Rather, we have here a literary example for the difference, both logical and based in theory of language, between fantasy and fiction, a difference we have already drawn attention to above:

> Denke weg aus dem Gemäuer die blauen Glocken und die Maßlieben und den Löwenzahn . . . streue dafür weißen Sand bis an die Vormauer, setze ein tüchtig Buchentor in den Eingang. . . .*

The sketch of this imaginary scene which is placed before the reader is a reality statement, even though its content is expressly made known as a fantasy. For it is referred to the "speaking subject," it is presented as a construct of the imagination, and moreover as one not quite unreal, since it is localized within what is for the narrator a specific past epoch. The fantasy statement, so characterized by the presence of the narrating I-Origo, continues fur-

† And now, dear reader, if you have seen your fill, then go back with me now some two hundred years.

* Imagine away out of the ruins the bluebells, daisies and dandelions . . . instead of these strew white sand up to the outer wall, and put a strong arch of birches at the entrance. . . .

ther, as now the figures who will be the coming heroines of the novel, the two daughters of Heinrich Wittinghauser, are introduced. For they do not "make their appearance" yet; they are introduced, like—indeed as—accessories belonging to the scene:

> ... die Türen fliegen auf — gefällt dir das holde Paar? ... Die jüngere sitzt am Fenster und stickt. ... Die ältere ist noch nicht angezogen. ...†

The present tense of this depiction, too, is not a historical present, even though we find ourselves in a historical past expressly designated as such by the narrator. But it is not this which is of importance here. What is decisive is the still-present I-Origo of the narrator, who in his imagination, which has set him back into a specific past, still holds the locality with the young girls like an image before his eyes, and who places it before the reader in a present tense which is designated as a *tabular* present.[66] And only once the mute images of the young girls become living figures— men in action, as Aristotle said—does the simple past tense set in, without the cognizance of the author and unnoticed by the reader:

> Die am Fenster stickt emsig fort und sieht nur manchmal auf die Schwester. Diese hat mit einmal ihr Suchen eingestellt und ihre Harfe ergriffen, aus der schon seit längerer Zeit einzelne Töne wie träumend fallen, die nicht zusammenhängen, oder Inselspitzen einer untergesunkenen Melodie sind. Plötzlich *sagte*[67] die jüngere: ....*

From this "said" on the story continues in the simple past tense, and in this context that means that only with it have we entered

† ... the doors fly open—does the charming pair please you? ... The younger one sits at the window and embroiders. ... The older girl is not yet dressed. ...
* The girl at the window continues to embroider industriously, and only occasionally looks up at her sister. The latter has suddenly ceased her searching and taken up her harp, from which for some time now isolated tones have been falling as though dreaming, tones which do not hang together, the island peaks of a submerged melody. Suddenly the younger girl *said*. ...[67]

the realm of fiction. For no text can elucidate more clearly the fact that with his simple past tense the I-Origo of the narrator disappears, withdraws, as it were, from the narrative; and in its place there appear the fictive I-Origines of the figures of the novel. Up until this "said" the time and setting of the story had still stood in the past of the narrator and were referred to his genuine I-Origo, to the real Now when he is telling his story. They were the object of a reality statement, even if this be a fantasized, indeed a feigned reality statement. Only with the simple past tense does the mute image become a live scene, a novel: fiction in the precise poetological sense. It is just this contrast between the simple past and the preceding present tense of scenic description, which here is not a historical present, that draws this boundary with complete clarity. From the sentence "The younger girl sits at the window and embroiders . . ." on, the scenic depiction does certainly form a transition to fiction, in that it shows the girls in their occupation with something. But the formative tendency present here governs grammatical meaning contents so exactly that this present tense would only then have taken on the meaning of a historical present if this depiction had appeared *after* the past tense "said." For then it would have already belonged to the realm of fiction. At this point it could be asked by way of objection whether it is then the simple past tense, the preterite as such, which demonstrates fictional narration as fictional, since, after all, in our cited text a present tense could have stood in its place without altering the fictional character of the passage. Precisely with this question we touch upon the actual nature and essence of the epic preterite. But before we disclose it completely, we should like to examine some further processes at work in this passage from *Hochwald,* not only in order to refute potential objections arising from it, but also because exactly these processes elucidate especially well the phenomenology of the epic preterite.

First, we shall adhere to the assertion that from the simple past tense "said" on, the figures in the novel first really "make their appearance" as living persons autonomously "in action," and, without yet becoming absorbed again in the meaning of this phenomenon, this signifies (and is directly sensed) that, from this point on, the action, and in turn the time of the action, is no longer referred to the narrator, but to these figures. A displacement of the I-Origo out of the system of reality and into another one, the system of fiction—or as we could also say, into the field of fiction—has taken place, where now "today," "yesterday," or "tomorrow" refer to the fictive Here and Now of the respective figures, and no longer to a real Here and Now of the narrator—and can therefore without further ceremony occur in combination with the grammatical past tense:

> Heute aber war der Tag gekommen, wo die Heerschar der Gräser und Blümlein dieses Rasens . . . zum ersten Male etwas anderes sehen sollten als Laubgrün und Himmelsblau. . . .*

so, also, reads a sentence occurring toward the beginning of the second chapter, entitled "A Forest Passage." And here our instructive text once more offers us the opportunity to make the law of fictional narration quite clear through a contrast with its opposite, the reality statement. For at the very beginning of this chapter the real I-Origo of the narrator enters upon the scene and intrudes into the fiction, supplanting it. Once again he depicts the landscape as it still is "nowadays," at his time, the time when he is telling his story:

> Es sind noch heutzutage ausgebreitete Wälder und Forste um das Quellengebiet der Moldau. . . . An dem Laufe des frischen Waldwassers . . . und in dem Tale geht heutzutage ein reinlicher

---

* But today the day had come when the host of grass and blossoms on this turf . . . were for the first time to see something other than the green of foliage and the blue of the heavens. . . .

Weg gegen das Holzdorf Hirschbergen. . . . Damals aber war
weder Dorf noch Weg sondern nur das Tal und der Bach . . . .†

In this portion of the text the present and simple past tenses
once again, just as in the beginning passage of the novel, fulfill
their natural function of designating the present and past of the
"speaking subject," and therefore the temporal adverbs "nowadays"
and "at that time" occur in grammatically correct or natural combination with their respective tenses. And, moreover, the "was"
of the last sentence proves itself to be a genuine simple past, the
past tense of a reality statement, only in that it occurs in contradistinction to the "nowadays" of the present-tense sentence, just as
for exactly the same reason the "at that time," too, proves itself to
be an adverb pointing back to a real past.

But immediately our text obliges us by contrasting to the real
"today" a fictive "today," to the genuine preterite a non-genuine,
fictional preterite, when, in the sentence from the passage already
quoted above, "Today the day had come . . . ," "today" occurs in
combination with the pluperfect. With this sentence, then, the
reality statement about a past time, standing at the very beginning
of the chapter, once again passes over into fictional narration; the
"today" no longer refers to the temporal standpoint of the narrator,
but rather to the fictive Here and Now of the figures of the novel:

Klare, liebliche Menschenstimmen — Mädchenstimmen —
drangen zwischen den Stämmen hervor, unterbrochen von dem
teilweisen Anschlage eines feinen Glöckleins. . . .*

---

† Nowadays there are still extensive forests and woods around the area where
the Moldau has its source . . . Along the course of the fresh sylvan water . . .
and in the valley runs a cleared path toward the logging village of Hirschbergen. . . . But at that time there was neither village nor path, but only the
valley and the stream. . . .
* Clear, lovely human voices—girls' voices—resounded between the boughs,
interrupted by the partial and subtle striking of a tiny bell. . . .

And, no longer interrupted by further intrusions of a real, narrator's I-Origo, by further present-tense descriptions (which in this narrative characterize such intrusions and never have the sense of a historical present), the fictive world of the novel now unfolds— in a preterite form which no longer makes the question as to a When possible.

Let us once more make it expressly clear that this example from Stifter is so particularly instructive for our problem only because its narrative form makes it possible to demonstrate the problem of the preterite in fictional narration directly in its genesis. This passage exhibits the seemingly paradoxical phenomenon that the present tense expresses consciousness of the past-ness of the time and locality depicted, whereas the preterite that appears thereafter, on the other hand, expresses consciousness of their "presence"; for in the same moment with its appearance the preterite is no longer perceived as stating the past. The figures and events now portrayed "are" here and now.

The Verbs of Inner Action

By no means, however, does this exhaustively elucidate the phenomenology of the epic fictional preterite, nor therefore the phenomenology of fictional narration. Thus far it has been demonstrated that the preterite relinquishes its function of designating past-ness, and that this arises from the fact that the temporal aspect of epic action, and therefore the epic action itself, is not referred to a real I-Origo, to a "speaking" or to a statement-subject, but to the fictive I-Origines of the figures in the novel. But now it is necessary to disclose the actual cause of our not experiencing an epic action as a past one, even though it is narrated in the past tense.

It may be true that Homer or the poet of the *Nibelungenlied* intended to tell those stories which lived in the minds of their audiences as having *occurred* "once upon a time." With far greater certainty, however, can it be established that they did not intend to narrate them as having happened "once upon a time," but rather as "happening now." What tells us this are the verbs of which the epic poet makes use. We shall differentiate verbs designating outer from those designating inner actions. "To go," "to sit," "to stand," "to laugh," etc., are verbs which designate external events or actions, things which we can ascertain about a person from without, things which we can perceive. They serve for all kinds of description, including non-epic description. However, the epic poet can never make do with just these. He requires verbs of inner action, such as to think, to reflect, to believe, to intend, to feel, to hope, and so forth. He makes use of these in a way such as no other giver of information or story-teller can do—be this orally or in writing. For when we draw upon our logico-psychological experience of ourselves and recall that we can never say of another real person: he thought or is thinking, felt or is feeling, believed or believes, etc., we realize that when these verbs appear in a narrative the preterite in which the story is narrated becomes a meaningless form, if one takes it to be the tense which designates the past. In other words, the use of these verbs constitutes the stringent epistemological proof that the preterite in epic literature does not have the function of designating past-ness, just as its combination with the deictic adverbs constitutes the grammatical proof thereof (and is for its part, of course, contingent upon the former).

At this point it could be objected that nevertheless verbs like "to believe," "to intend," "to think," and so on do come to be used in non-epic, in historical presentation. For example, I can say that Napoleon hoped or believed he would conquer Russia. The use of "believe" here is only a derived one, however, and in such a context it can function only as a verb which introduces indirect discourse. From those documents transmitted to us it is derived, or concluded, that Napoleon was of the belief that he would conquer Russia. In a historical, i.e., in a reality account, however, Napoleon cannot be portrayed as someone in the act of believing "here and now." That is, he cannot be portrayed in the subjectivity, in the I-originarity of his inner, mental processes, of his "existence." Should this occur, we would find ourselves in a novel about Napoleon, in a work of fiction. *Epic fiction is the sole epistemological instance where the I-originarity (or subjectivity) of a third-person* qua *third-person can be portrayed.* The verbs of inner action, which provide the stringent evidence to that effect, also provide the foundation for the preterite's losing its function of designating pastness, this preterite being the tense of verbs of inner action as well as of all other verbs in fiction. Here it is not a past experience being conveyed when it is said of a person that he thought, hoped, reflected upon, or even said this or that.

The verb "to say" requires particular discussion, for it occupies a kind of intermediate position between the verbs of outer and those of inner action. It signifies that an inner action is being articulated and in turn can then be perceived. Nevertheless, it has a different meaning from other verbs which designate perceivable sounds, like "to sing," "to scream," and so on. The verb "to say" does not refer, as these others do, to the acoustic material of that which is being articulated, but rather to its meaning. From the perspective of semantics it is therefore as much a verb of inner action as "to think," "to hope," etc., and I make use of it in an indirect account in exactly the same manner as I do of these others. Indeed, when I report of another person that he thought, hoped, or believed this or that, it is automatically implied that what was thought or hoped was also said, articulated. For this reason the verb "to say" in fiction also assumes a place on the same level with the verbs of inner action. And, as that verb which occurs the most frequently, it conveys the most striking impression of fiction just when it occurs in connection with direct discourse, as an introductory verb. In epic fiction "he . . ." or "she said" does not mean that someone, the "narrator," is reproducing in indirect form what the person "has said," but rather makes the figure concerned become experienceable as someone in the act of saying; just as through the other verbs of inner action the figure becomes one experienceable in the act of thinking, believing, hoping, etc. And therein lies the significance of the passage in our example from *Hochwald,* where the fictional preterite commences with the verb "to say"; and through it the seemingly paradoxical situation is established whereby the preterite produces the impression of "presentification." Before we pursue this significance further—and it has its source on a more profound level than that thus far disclosed—we must investigate the behavior of the fictional preterite still more thoroughly.

Narrated Monologue [erlebte Rede]

These verbs of inner action—and not least among them the verb "to say"—which are then the decisive indication of the disappearance of the preteritive meaning of the past tense, also anticipate that phenomenon of narrative literature which perhaps first of all caused linguistic and literary theory to become aware of the problem involved in the presumed past-ness (or being-thought-of-as-past) of epic action: namely, the so-called *erlebte Rede,* or narrated monologue. Precisely the past tense form for rendering unformulated stream of consciousness in the third person is what literary theory has found problematic.[68] And no solution has proven successful because the difference between reality statement and fictional narration, along with the change in the meaning of the preterite established therein, had not been noted. The narrated monologue is, however, the uttermost consequence of the verbs of inner action. Even more explicitly than these it elucidates the fact that in fiction a real I-Origo is replaced with fictive I-Origines, and the past tense form in phrases such as "How marvelous this blue sky was," or "Was he to have been so mistaken," does not vitiate the fictive Here and Now of the person who is thinking these things.

Narrated monologue, which in the course of the development of the novel had become the most ingenius means of fictionalization in epic narration (even if it is used nowadays in every serial novel in a newspaper), is, from the point of view of both the theory and the logic of literature, a particularly fruitful means of elucidating the a-preteritive, indeed as we shall see the completely a-temporal function of the epic preterite. So that we might experience this phenomenon directly in fictional texts, let us submit three such passages for consideration:

> Das konnte einfach nicht wahr sein—wenner nur allein an sie dachte! Aber wieviel würde sie verstehen? Würde er sie nicht schon nach den ersten drei Minuten verlieren? Und das sollte er wagen? Wer verlangte das von ihm, wer konnte es verlangen?
>
> > (Eduard Schaper, *Der letzte Advent*)
>
> He dropped her hand. Their marriage was over, he thought, with agony, with relief. The rope was cut; he mounted; he was free, as it was decreed that he, Septimus, the lord of men, should be free; alone . . . he, Septimus was alone. . . .
>
> > (Virginia Woolf, *Mrs. Dalloway*)
>
> Und er verglich in Gedanken den Kirchturm der Heimat mit dem Turm dort oben. Jener Turm, bestimmt, ohne Zögern gerade-wegs nach oben sich verjüngend, breitdachig, abschließend mit roten Ziegeln, ein irdisches Gebäude—was können wir anderes bauen?— . . . Der Turm hier oben, es war der einzig sichtbare—der Turm eines Wohnhauses, wie es sich jetzt zeigte, vielleicht des Hauptschlosses, war ein einförmiger Rundbau . . . mit kleinen Fenstern, die jetzt in der Sonne aufstrahlten—etwas Irrsinniges hatte das—und einem söllerartigen Abschluß. . . .*
>
> > (Franz Kafka, *Das Schloß*)

* That simply could not be true—he didn't dare even think of her! But how much would she understand? Would he not already lose her after the first three minutes? And he should risk that? Who demanded that of him, who could demand that?

> > (Eduard Schaper, *Der letze Advent*)

[For the passage from Virginia Woolf, cf. text above.]

And in his mind he compared the church tower at home with the tower there above him. The former, firm in line, soaring unfalteringly to its tapering point, its broad roof topped with red tiles, an earthly edifice—what else can

It does not promote the knowledge of the structure of literature when, even in the face of this now so common narrative form, one anxiously adheres to the original grammatical meaning of the past tense and will not abandon the interpretation of epic action as being past or "remembered." In this context it is necessary to subject precisely this concept of memory, which of late has been introduced into the theory of narrative literature, to a critical analysis. In the American philosopher Suzanne Langer's work entitled *Feeling and Form,* in many basic aspects a significant theory of art, it is stated that it is the aim of narrative literature not to give information about what has happened and when, "but to create the illusion of things past, the semblance of events lived and felt, like an abstracted and completed memory," or, as she also says, like "a semblance of memory," or "virtual memory."[69] Does this complicated admixture of concepts describe the phenomenon in question? Does it correspond with our reading experience, and, as we will not hesitate to add, with the author's own creative experience? What is the experience of remembrance in its autochthonous sense? Memory is primarily linked with our self-experience. I can remember only my own past. I can have only indirect experience and cognizance of the past of (real) third-persons, a past which I myself did not experience along with them; just as I can have only indirect experience of that historical past which extends back beyond my own lifetime. That historical consciousness, "the sense of history," constitutes itself as "memory," as Miss Langer maintains, is a metaphor which expresses a possible life-feeling, one out of several possible interpretations of historical experience.[70] But

---

we build?— . . . The tower above him here was the only one visible—the tower of a residential house, as was now evident, perhaps that of the main castle, was uniformly round . . . with small windows, which now glittered in the sun—there was something uncanny about that—and atop something like an attic. . . .

(Franz Kafka, *The Castle*)

such an interpretation becomes incorrect when, on the basis of the "past tense," it is applied to a novel. Such an attempt necessitated that Miss Langer form a new concept, namely that of "abstracted memory" or "semblance of memory," which now corresponds neither to any objective nor to any directly experienced phenomenon whatever. It was formulated to assimilate her definition that narrative literature creates not merely the semblance of life, but rather the semblance of past life, or "virtual past." It is quite correct, indeed tautological, to say that fiction creates an illusion of life, for which reason Aristotle called it mimesis. However, it is not correct to refer this quality of being semblance back to past-ness as such. Something can only be formed as semblance which itself is concrete, an object—or a quality which manifests itself in some way in objects (persons, things). Life can be portrayed in art, as semblance, but past life *qua* past cannot be transformed into semblance. For past-ness is a property which is not perceivable; it is conceptual, determined and known via dates. For example, when we see in a museum the objects of a past epoch: furniture, clothing, tools, we attach the concept of the historical to them only through our knowledge that they are historical objects, such knowledge being governed and specified by the data of time and place indicated. On the other hand, when we see such objects in one of Terborch's paintings, the knowledge that they belong to a past era disappears to a great extent, and we experience them as the artistic semblance of things which are suspended from all time. Even though S. Langer does wish to emphasize, through the concept of abstract, illusionary past, that here it is not a matter of "real" past, nevertheless she does not note that through this concept of abstract, illusionary past the concept of all past whatever is negated or eliminated. Fiction (not merely epic, but likewise dramatic and cinematic fiction), in producing the semblance of life, suspends this semblance from the past, suspends it from time; and this means nothing other than that the semblance of life is suspended from all reality. And precisely since this latter is one of the basic tenets of Miss Langer's theory of fine art, the concept of "virtual memory" must be retracted from her theory of literature. We shall see in what way the function of the epic preterite contributes toward proving this a-temporality.

We have looked at Miss Langer's theory in some detail in reference to the form of narrated monologue because it is just this narrative mode which is best suited to carry such a theory *ad absurdum*. For it indicates, more conspicuously than does any other narrative form, that error which has become part of all theories of epic literaure—and particularly of those interpreting epic action as being set in a temporal past. This error is that these theories have not taken into account the phenomenon which first renders a piece of epic literature epic: the fictive persons, the "mimesis of men in action," which only Aristotle has recognized as the phenomenon of central importance. And had he been acquainted with the narrated monologue, he would have been still more amazed at the fact that even his contemporaries ignored this factor. For only this form, whose sole grammatical locus is narrative literature, completely discloses the paradoxical law of tenses—which prevails as a "natural necessity" in all of narrative literature—in its grammatical paradox. "Who demanded that of him, who could demand that?"—"Since she had left him, he, Septimus, was alone."—"The tower there above him was the only one visible—. . . there was something uncanny about that—." The simple past or respectively the pluperfect tense of these verbs becomes as such unstressed, temporally meaningless. Only the semantic meaning-content of the verbs itself, which states about the thinking and feeling that is going on within the figures at this fictive moment in their fictive existence, is relevant. ". . . he, Septimus, was alone": not that he "at that time"—when, anyway?—*was* alone, but rather that he *is* alone in his poor, ravaged soul at the moment of his life being portrayed, is the experience we have in reading the novel. *It is the figure of the novel, the fictive person, which annuls the past-tense meaning of the depictional verbs.* Narrated monologue demonstrates this more clearly and comprehensibly than any other narrative form because it—unlike both dialogue and soliloquy, which in themselves have the same function—retains the form of epic reporting, and with that the past-tense form, and is therefore the most adequate means of presenting the figures in their I-originarity. (Thus the increased popularity of this device is no mere coincidence.) For narrated monologue yields direct evidence in uncovering the logico-semantic process which is the cause behind the extinction of the preterite's function of designating past-ness: the shifting of the spatio-temporal system of reference, i.e., of the orientational system of reality, into a fictive one, the replacement of a real I-Origo, which anyone doing the telling in a reality-report represents, by the fictive I-Origines of the figures in the novel. How the "narrator" of fiction (which we again intentionally set in quotation marks) is now to be logically explained—this is the really basic question in the elucidation not only of epic fiction, but also of the entire system of literature in general, and it shall be answered in the next main section (beginning p. 134). For this answer shall only then appear as a wholly discerning and reasonable one once these logical and linguistic processes which take place in epic fiction have been elucidated to the greatest possible degree.

The A-Temporality of Fiction

Let us return to the example at the beginning of our investigations, the passage from *Jürg Jenatsch*. The analysis of fictional narration, which for a while departed from our direct consideration of this passage, now enables us to answer the question as to why purely logically it is only the sentence "Quickly intent, he took out his leather portfolio," which first proves that the story being told is fiction, and why in turn we experience the action depicted in the preterite form not as a past, i.e., not as a real, but rather as a fictively "present," or non-real action. For all the preceding sentences in this opening passage are constructed with verbs which still could allow the depiction to appear as a reality-report, for example as an eye-witness account. Goethe's description of the St. Rochus Festival in *A Tour on the Rhine, Maine, and Neckar:*

> Zwischen Gestein und Gebüsch und Gestrüpp irrt eine aufgeregte, hin und wieder laufende Menge, rufend: Halt! hier! da! dort! . . . Ein flinker, derber Bursche läuft hervor, einen blutenden Dachs behaglich vorzuweisen. . . .*

bears no structural differences from the manner in which the persons are introduced in the opening of *Jürg Jenatsch:*

> Jetzt erscholl aus der Ferne das Gebell eines Hundes. Hoch oben an dem Hange . . . hatte ein Bergamaskerhirt im Mittagsschlafe gelegen. Nun sprang er auf . . . Endlich tauchte ein Wanderer auf. . . .†

It is only the sentence occurring somewhat later, "Quickly intent . . . ," which first alters the structure of the passage, which up until this point is constructed of verbs of outer action and is not distinguishable from a reality-report such as Goethe's travel record or Rilke's letter. Everything which is stated here can fall within the experience-field, the perceptual range, of a statement-subject. And the boundary here is so fine (but, as we shall see still more closely, for all its refinement nonetheless categorically separates the two realms of language from one another) that without the tiny word "intent" the content of this sentence could still fall

---

* Among stones, bushes, and underbrush roves an excited crowd, running to and fro and calling: Stop! Here! There! Over there! . . . A brisk, robust lad runs forth and, with pleasure, exhibits a bleeding badger. . . .

† Now there resounded out of the distance the barking of a dog. High above on a cliff . . . an Alpine shepherd had lain in midday sleep. Now he jumped up . . . Finally a wanderer emerged. . . .

within the domain of perception: for example, should the sentence read "Quickly he took out his leather portfolio." Whether someone does something quickly or slowly can be determined through observation. But whether a person deliberates quickly or slowly in doing something, this escapes observation. In effect, then, this sentence, even when taken out of its context, can be recognized immediately as fictional, as a sentence occurring in a novel. And, let us emphasize once more, this means that in this narrative work we find ourselves not in the past of the poet who is telling the story, but rather in the "present" of the characters Mr. Vasa and the other persons of the novel. " 'Five and a half feet,' he said to himself. 'What are you doing? Spying?' sounded a powerful bass voice beside him . . . ," and so on. A "present" which, to formulate it still more precisely, despite the past tenses "took out," "said," "sounded," does not stand in the past of the narrating poet, as the sleigh ride in the Rilke letter stands in the past of the letter writer, and the St. Rochus Festival (despite the genuine historical present tense here) in that of the travel-record keeper, Goethe.

Literary art, Schiller had replied to Goethe, necessitated that even the epic poet presentify that which has happened. Schiller uses the concept of "presentification" [*Vergegenwärtigung*] here exclusively in the sense—based on the temporal meaning of the German concept of "presence" [*Gegenwart*]—of the opposite of "past," on which the discussion between the two poets centered. That he uses the concept in its temporal meaning is also expressed in the participial formulation "that which has happened." But the temporal meaning contained in the German term as well as in the Romance language concepts *représenter, representation* by no means always appears as the dominant one whenever this concept is used. That is, the element of temporal opposition to a past thing or event subsides behind the more prominent meaning of mental representation [*Vorstellen*], which the German term, moreso than the Romance language terms, combines with the sense of plastic representation. This brief analysis of the meaning of the concept "presentification" is not without import for the problematic of fictional narration, and also, most intimately connected with the phenomenology of the preterite, for that of the historical present.

In order to make it clear that we do not experience the action narrated in a novel as a past action, we had designated it as "fictively present." Yet not without intention have we both times set the concept of "present" in quotation marks. For here we encounter relations which require closer investigation. If it is correct that the preterite form of a narrative does not signify that the narrated events and persons are past, or even thought of as past, can we then simply designate them as—even if fictively—present? When we said above that the sentence from a novel which reads "Mr. X was on a trip" did not mean that at thus and such a time he *was* away, but that he *is* now—does this present *eo ipso* have the meaning of what in the strict sense is the temporal present? Were we to answer this question affirmatively without restriction, we would indeed be guilty of a logical error, an error which would place the entire phenomenology of the epic preterite in question again— indeed, would invalidate it. Even the demonstration that the past tense of narration can be combined with deictic adverbs is no logically conclusive proof that the grammatical past tense assumes the meaning of the grammatical present. What is the logical error, although one not easily ascertainable, which we would thereby be committing? We would be moving on two different epistemological planes. We cannot equate the fictive present of the persons in the novel with the experience of not-being-past. In other words, we cannot introduce into the experience of the events in a novel a temporal moment designated as a fictive present because the action of a novel has no relation to any temporal experience of the reader (or of the author). That the events in the novel are not experienced as past does not imply that they are experienced—by us—as present. For the experience of past-ness is as such only meaningful in relation to an experience of present and future—and this implies nothing other than that the experience of the present, as well as that of past and future, is the experience of reality. The fictional preterite, to be sure, does not have the function of awakening an experience of past-ness, but neither does it therefore have the function of evoking an experience of the present: the a-temporal "was" of fictional narration does not mean "is," which itself is temporal. The concept of the "fictive present" is in itself just as erroneous as that of the "virtual past," which was criticized above. It is meaningful only in relation to the concepts of "fictional past" and "fictional future." And this means that it belongs to the fictive temporal system, which can be formed in narrative literature just like all other aspects of the formative material which reality in its various kinds and degrees supplies to creative literature. Fictive time, the present, past, and future of the persons in the novel, comes to be experienced when it is formed as such, when it is elaborated through those presentational means open to narration: just as space only then appears in the novel when it is narrated into it. But not every mention of temporal moments in narrative (and likewise in dramatic) literature may thereby be designated as a means of "portraying time." Since events, actions, life, occur in time, temporal designations can be given along with the course of action without their having to be on that account more significant or more thematic than, for example, are directional indicators for space. Fictive present certainly is marked by the deictic temporal adverbs "today," "tomorrow," etc., just as fictive past and future are marked by past and future adverbs, or also by other means of portrayal. But—what is crucial for our context—a great deal of narrative literature does not make any fictive time known. It "presentifies" without referring to any temporal present, past, or future of the epic figures. We can demonstrate this with the aid of a passage which precisely on account of the temporal indicator contained within it is especially instructive for such purposes. The story which provides the framework for Keller's *Züricher Novellen* begins with the following sentence:

> Gegen das Ende der achtzehnhundertzwanziger Jahre, als die Stadt Zürich mit weitläufigen Festungswerken umgeben war, erhob sich an einem hellen Sommermorgen mitten in derselben ein junger Mensch von seinem Lager, der von den Dienstboten des Hauses bereits Herr Jacques genannt und von den Hausfreunden einstweilen geihrzt wurde, da er für das Du sich als zu groß und für das Sie sich noch zu unbeträchtlich darstellte.*

Nothing seems to concur more than does this text with the notion that the action of a novel is thought of as being past and is therefore narrated in the past tense. When does it take place? At the close of the 'twenties in the nineteenth century. We ask further: what happened then? A young man arose from his bed. However, should we turn it around and ask: when did the young man arise from his bed?, then we would have to answer: toward the end of the 1820's, on a bright summer morning. As we give these answers, we notice that they are inadequate. The question "When did that happen?" somehow does not seem to fit with the verb in reference to which the temporal question is posed. Verbs such as "to get up" (from bed, from a chair), "to go," "to sit," "to have a restless night"

---

* Toward the end of the 1820's, when the city of Zurich was still surrounded with extensive fortifications, on a bright summer morning in the middle of the city there arose from his bed a young man, whom the house servants already called Mr. Jacques, and who was addressed by friends of the family with the informal "you" for the time being, since he was too old for the familiar "thou," and for the polite "you" still too unimportant. [These distinctions between modes of second-person address do not exist in modern English, and therefore they cannot be rendered here with precision. German itself no longer retains the *Ihr* form as a semi-formal address for one person, and uses only the familiar *du* and the polite *Sie* forms. The familiar "thou" expresses intimacy and is used with family members, close friends, with all children, and in prayer. The polite "you" is a formal address, and is used for all other occasions.—Tr.]

—"for he had spent a restless night," as our text reads immediately following the sentence cited above—and so forth, are verbs that we do not use when we make statements about points in time that are either indefinite or that lie far back within the distant past. We can say: yesterday, or a week ago, Peter cycled to the city, but we usually do not say something like: ten years ago, or at the start of this century, Peter cycled to the city, or got up from a chair. In the reality statement we use such *situation verbs* in the simple past tense only in reference to points in time lying in the near past. This is such because these verbs designate a concrete situation which I, the person here and now stating, can still survey and remember. A sentence such as the one cited from our text above could not occur in a reality statement. For in that context the continuity between a young man's getting up out of bed and the assertion that the city of Zürich, where this took place toward the close of the 1820's, was surrounded with extensive fortifications, would not be possible. Should we read the text without knowing what context it comes from, we would nevertheless know immediately that here we are not dealing with a reality-report. The first verb we encounter, "arose from his bed," lets us know we are dealing with a fictional narrative. And this verb does still something else: it *annuls* the temporal designation, the date given, in its property as a designation of past-ness, and it does so even though it is in the past tense. Moreover, it renders the indicated past time *present,* just as it also does the place, turning them into a fictive situation that is at hand here and now, where our "young man" did not arise, but is arising. But what happens with the dating of a time which even for the author of the *Züricher Novellen* is one lying in the past? It loses its function as a statement of a historical past, and merely sets the scene we have now entered upon as that of the coming story: the picture of the city of Zurich, which at this time was still surrounded with fortifications. The situation-verb annuls the character of past-ness which in a reality statement both a date and a past-tense form share, and establishes instead a fictive present, which thenceforth becomes more clearly and intensively underscored with each subsequent narrative moment. When we read further that:

> Herrn Jacques' Morgengemüt war nicht so lachend wie der Himmel, denn er hatte eine unruhige Nacht zugebracht, voll schwieriger Gedanken und Zweifel über seine eigene Person.*

we the reader, as well as the author who wrote it, experience this only in the sense that Mr. Jacques' morning disposition *is* not sunny—at this fictive moment in the existence of this fictive figure. The decisive fictionalizing element in this text is therefore the situation verb, which by itself has the power to dissolve the character of past-ness from verb tenses and temporal adverbs. Situation verbs will always expedite fictionalization; but from the point of view of language theory they still are not decisive for the character of epic fiction, since they also appear in the reality statement, in every description of a situation. They function as direct indications of fiction only in a text such as the one cited above, where the depiction of a situation conflicts with a designation of historical time.

Here and now, i.e., presentified, the action in narrative literature unfolds, but this Now, this presentification, must not necessarily have the sense of the temporal present, although it can assume this sense—rather easily, too—as a fictive present. But if literary art, as Schiller, in disagreement with Goethe, believed (and many shared this notion), necessitates that even the epic poet "presentify," this concept nevertheless becomes erroneous once one means, as did Schiller, that "something which has happened," something past,

---

* Mr. Jacques' morning disposition was not as sunny as the sky, for he had spent a restless night, filled with ponderous thoughts and doubts about his own self.

must be made present. The preterite in narrative literature no longer functions to designate past-ness solely because literature does not presentify in a temporal sense. The concept of presentification is in its ambiguity not only inexact, but, as a designation for the structure of fictional, mimetic literature, it is also incorrect and misleading. What it means here is fictionalization. And it does not stand in contradiction to this when we nevertheless say that the action of a novel unfolds "here and now." For "here and now"— and with this we close the circle of our proof of the preterite's loss of temporal function—means epistemologically, and therefore also in terms of theory of language, primarily the zero-point of the system of reality, which is determined through the coordinates of time and space. It means the I-Origo, in reference to which the Now has no precedence over the Here and vice versa. Rather, all three terms designate the originary point of experience. Even if a "present time" (which in the temporal sense is not a series of points, but rather a duration which is arbitrary, extended according to subjective experience) is not indicated at all, such as by the word "today" or a specific date, etc., we experience the action of the novel as being "here and now," as the experience of fictive persons, or, as Aristotle said, of men in action. In turn, this means nothing other than that we experience these fictive persons in their I-originarity, to which all representational particulars, including all possible temporal ones, are referred.

This is tantamount to saying that the preterite's losing its function of designating past-ness does not mean that instead it assumes the function of establishing a present. Even though the sentence "The noonday sun stood over the barren height of the Julier Pass," occurring in a novel, does convey the experience that the noonday sun *is standing* over the Julier Pass, since we have entered upon the scene of fictive persons, nevertheless this present form has just as little a meaning of temporal present as the preterite form has that of past-ness. This present quality is none other than that conveyed to us by a painting or a statue, the quality of being-there [Da-sein], of being-eternal, a "static Here and Now," which is the basic meaning of the German concept of *Gegenwart* as well as of the Romance language concept *representare,* with respect to which the temporal meaning is secondary and derived. The Now is contingent upon the Here, *être présent,* not the Here upon the Now.

Fictionalization, action presented as the Here and Now of the fictive persons, *nullifies the temporal meaning of the tense* in which a piece of narrative literature is narrated: the preteritive meaning of the grammatical past tense, as well as the present meaning of the historical present. Although this widely-discussed and problematic tense has in effect already been systematically explicated by the above demonstrations, we must nonetheless now insert a more precise description of it, with the aim of critically discussing this tense with reference to the function which both authors and interpreters are accustomed to ascribe to it.

The Historical Present

Almost throughout the historical present has served as the mainstay of the theory of presentification in epic narration. But its characterization was always obscured by the fact that no differentiation was made between its appearance in oral and written first-person accounts, in historical documents or presentations on the one hand, and in epic literature on the other. This is due to the fact that linguistics and grammar have always based their investigations of verb tenses and pronouns upon a single concept of narration. Hence almost without exception the relation to the past became the decisive factor in explicating this tense. The narrator, as Jespersen, for example, says, "steps outside the frame of history, visualizing and representing what happened in the past as if it were present before his eyes"[71]—whereby there is no material difference whether one thinks of the "event as having been simultaneously moved up to the present,"[72] or whether one "thinks oneself back into the past."[73] A more precise foundation of the historical present's function of presentifying past events, and, it seems to me, the decisive one which captures the essence of this phenomenon, is found in Wunderlich-Reis, where the genesis of the historical present is traced back to vividly narrated experiences which the person doing the telling has had himself, and where in this case he "lets himself see" these events, which are past for him, "again as present experiences."[74] But it remains an open question whether from the point of view of the history of language this explanation is a tenable one.[75] In any event, it does illustrate the experience of presentification which we have through present-tense depictions of past events. This can only occur in documentations of what a person has experienced himself, i.e., in any kind of autobiographical documents. Gerhart Hauptmann's travel depiction *Griechischer Frühling* (1907) provides a good example of this. It is narrated throughout in the present tense, such that not only situational descriptions, but also every step of the way in the journey is brought back to the moment of its occurrence, and is thus to a certain extent reproduced in the manner of a film:

> Die Wendung des Weges ist erreicht. Die Straße zieht sich in einem weiten Bogen unter mächtigen roten Felswänden hin. . . . Wir schreiten die weiße Straße langsam fort. Wir scheuchen eine anderthalb Fuß lang grüne Eidechse, die den Weg . . . überquert. Ein Esel, klein, mit einem Berge von Ginster bepackt, begegnet uns. . . .*

That this present tense, despite its undoubted presentifying effect, nonetheless retains the reference to past events, is due to the

---

* The turn of the road is reached. The street bends in a wide arc under mighty red stone walls. . . . Slowly we walk along the wide street. We chase away a foot and a half long green lizard, which . . . is crossing the road. A donkey, small, laden with a mountain of furze, meets us. . . .

fact that this portrayal is a first-person account. Indeed, the auto-biographical account is the only narrative instance whatsoever where the consciousness of past-ness is retained, and it is retained precisely because the present tense here presentifies in a genuine sense. Since the narrator cannot have written these events down while he was actually wandering about, etc., the historical character of the present tense emerges clearly, and we know that this journey is one which took place a more or less short time ago. But as far as the consciousness of past-ness in an autobiographical depiction is concerned, the effect created by the present tense prevailing here is nevertheless no different from cases where it is used interchangeably with the preterite. This is the case with Goethe's depiction of the St. Rochus Festival cited above, where the alternation between present and past tense is so arbitrary—for example "the procession climbs the mountain," "a red silk canopy tottered into sight"—that neither of these tenses in itself takes precedence over the other in rendering the events vivid, and moreover doing so without our losing consciousness of the fact that this travel experience was written down after it took place. For since the things depicted here are put forth as having been experienced by the writer himself, that is, since the first-person narrator portrays himself as being present at these goings-on (which is the essence of all first-person narration, genuine or feigned), we refer these experienced events to him and to that point in his past when they occurred. In an autobiographical account the consciousness of time is not altered by the historical present tense, however much it is indicated precisely here that—wherein it seems to me that Wunderlich-Reis are completely correct—the narrator vividly sets himself back into the past experience, thereby presentifying it both for himself and for those for whom the account is being given. For in personal memory vivid mental representation falls together with the feeling of the Then, of the Before, and when this image is reproduced from memory it in turn coincides with the temporal

Now of the act of remembering and re-living. The exclusively existential significance and function of memory (which at most can only in a metaphorical sense be applied to other mental processes like knowledge, for example) also becomes evident, then, in the elucidation of the historical present tense.

For the historical present undergoes quite a change when it appears in an objective historical document. Let us cite an example from a modern textbook of history (which as such meets all the requirements of modern history instruction for advanced levels), which is written almost throughout in the historical present:

> Mit Umsicht führt Barbarossa den erneuten Zusammenschluß mit der Reichskirche herbei. Er benützt jedes Recht, das ihm nach dem Wormser Konkordat zusteht, um die deutschen Kirchenfürsten wieder fest in die Hand zu bekommen. . . . Gleichzeitig erneuert der König das . . . Regalien- und Spolienrecht der Krone. . . . Nach dieser vorläufigen Festigung der deutschen Verhältnisse zieht Friedrich 1154 nach Rom, um sich die ihm im Vorjahr bereits zugesagte Kaiserkrone zu holen. Die Fahrt durch Ober- und Mittelitalien zeigt ihm den vollen Umfang der Schwierigkeiten, die. . . .*   (*Geschichte unserer Welt* II, 1947)

Wherein lies the difference between this historical present and that of the autobiographical example? Both are reality statements; in both there is a real I-Origo, a statement-subject present. But the objective, or objectively portrayed facts in the history text are (relatively) objective because they are presented as being independent of the statement-subject, as being not directly experienced by

---

* With caution Barbarossa brings about a renewed union with the official church. He utilizes every right which the Concordat of Wurms accords him, in order to get the princes of the church firmly in hand once more. . . . At the same time the king renews the crown's right of regalia and of spoils. . . . In 1154, after this preliminary consolidation of German domestic affairs, Friedrich goes to Rome, to get the imperial crown already promised him the previous year. The journey through upper and middle Italy shows him the full extent of the difficulties which. . . .

him himself. The statement-subject, the historian, does, to be sure, occupy a place in time, as does the I of the autobiographical account: the time of Barbarossa lies in his past. But we do not refer the narrated events to this temporal point, which, so to speak, is too far removed from that of the events themselves, and just for this reason, precisely because the historian does not remember the depicted events in the way that the autobiographer does, i.e., because he cannot "presentify them to himself," the historical present tense in his text has no function of presentification. In view of historical presentations of this type, Brugmann-Delbrück thus already interpreted the historical present not in the sense of presentification, i.e., of a temporal relation between past and present, but rather ascribes to it the function of dramatic visualization: "The speaker has the action before his eyes as in a drama, and his interest does not extend beyond this action to any temporal relation existing between himself and it."[76] If we replace the expression "as in a drama" by "in epic fiction," then we can say that Delbrück has viewed the matter here with complete correctness. The historical present here does not fulfill a function of temporal presentification, but rather one of fictional presentification. More powerfully than does the preterite, it allows the persons to appear as acting of themselves, shows them in the execution of their actions, whereas the past tense in a historical account designates far more the completed acts, the facts.

Even more consistently is this fictionalizing function of the historical present in an objective historical account revealed in many passages in F. Sengle's fine biography of Wieland (1949). We shall include an analysis of one such passage, since through its demonstration of rather concealed boundaries it is very instructive for the elucidation of the historical present in epic fiction:

So lagen die Dinge, als Wieland sich plötzlich zur evangelischen Heirat entschloß. Er wußte, daß es unter dieser Voraussetzung ganz ausgeschlossen war, die Zustimmung von Christines Mutter zu erhalten. . . . Sie wird alle Hebel gegen eine protestantische Verheiratung Christines in Bewegung setzen. Deshalb will Wieland das Mädchen möglichst rasch aus Augsburg holen lassen . . . und sie in seinem Haus verstecken. Die Fenster eines Zimmers sind bereits mit Papier verkleidet, damit die Nachbarn nichts merken, die alte Floriane hat allein Zutritt und sie ist bis in den Tod verschwiegen. . . . Dem guten Schmelz bleibt weiter nichts übrig als zu warten . . . und Vater und Tochter ins Kloster Rot zu begleiten . . . Wieland fährt nach Rot, er trifft Vater und Tochter nicht mehr an. . . . Jetzt ist er am Ende. Die Sehnsucht nach dem Tod überkommt ihn . . . In solcher Verfassung sitzt er nach der Rückkehr von Rot brütend zu Hause. . . . Er versteht Gott nicht mehr, wie er Menschen von solcher barbarischen Härte schaffen kann. Gibt es kein Mittel, ihnen zu entrinnen? (S. 133 f.)*

This present-tense passage comes very close to being a novelistic, a fictional narrative (whereas one naturally could not say this with respect to the historical example above). In this biographical presentation, whose past tense retains its natural function of designating past-ness, there are even verbs as well as other forms of presenting inner action employed, which have their only legitimate

---

* So stood matters when Wieland suddenly decided on a Protestant marriage. He knew that with this precondition it would be quite out of the question to obtain the permission of Christine's mother. . . . She will spare no effort against a Protestant marriage on the part of her daughter. For this reason Wieland wants to have her fetched out of Augsburg as quickly as possible . . . and hide her in his home. The windows of one room are already masked with paper, so that the neighbors will notice nothing; the elderly Floriane alone has access to the room, and she will remain silent to the death. . . . For everything to work out well there remains nothing further to do but to wait . . . and to escort father and daughter to the cloister in Rot. Wieland travels to Rot; he does not meet father and daughter. . . . Now he is at his wits' end. The longing for death takes hold of him. In such a disposition he sits brooding at home after the return from Rot. . . . He does not understand God anymore, how He could create people of such barbaric harshness. Is there no way of escaping them? (p. 133f.)

place in fictional narration. "He sits at home brooding" . . . "He does not understand God anymore" . . . "Is there no way of escaping them?"—and this, moreover, an interrogative form of narrated monologue. How are we to explain this "historical" form of narration? Does the biographer put himself back into Wieland's past, does he place it before our eyes as "present"? Here we are faced with the curious phenomenon that just such a fictionalizing presentification would have been effected precisely through the simple past tense; especially in passages such as these, which would then appear as follows: "In such a disposition he sat at home brooding. . . . He didn't understand God anymore. . . . Was there no way of escaping them?" Here the past tense would have had the effect—on the basis of the verbs of inner action—of making Wieland appear as a figure in a novel. That he no longer understood God, that he asked himself whether one could not escape barbaric mankind, would be interpreted as thoughts attributed to Wieland by the narrator. The narrator, in turn, would no longer be a historical one, but a fictional one—and the paradoxical behavior of the preterite in fiction would at once go into effect: all past-ness, and therewith historical reality, would be blurred, indeed abolished. It is precisely the present tense in this historical account, in the unique form of these sentences, which maintains the consciousness of the historical: it has a "documentary" function, it denotes the reproducing of the content of those letters from which the biographer reconstructed Wieland's outer and inner situation at that time. The awareness of historical documentation is strengthened by the present tense. For the documents exist and are still available, whereas the life portrayed by them is past, gone. The present tense in this presentation, therefore, combines the function of "presentifying" an external and an inner state with that of rendering the historical, and thus prevents the transition to a novelistic, fictionalizing account, such as can easily occur in depictions of this nature, and which in this case would have immediately ensued from the use of the past tense.

The Fictional or Mimetic Genre

The borderline case represented by the example from Sengle sheds light on the function of the historical present in narrative literature. Through the comparison with its appearance in the reality statement, in the objective historical account, it can now be shown very clearly that in epic fiction it has no genuine function: neither a temporal one nor one of fictional presentification. This results from and is conditioned by the fact that in fiction the preterite has no function of designating the past. So that we may have concrete insight into this phenomenon, too, we shall demonstrate it with the help of a single example, a passage from the only chapter in Thomas Mann's *Buddenbrooks* which has the present-tense form. It is clear that the intent in this section of the novel is that of making the bustle and excitement of the events depicted there especially concrete: Toni's wait in front of the city hall, where the senatorial elections are going on:

> Die Sache hat sich in die Länge gezogen. Es scheint, daß die Debatten in den Kammern sich nicht beruhigen wollen. . . . Steht dort drinnen Herr Kaspersen, . . . der sich selbst nie anders als »Staatsbeamter« nennt, und dirigiert was er erfährt . . . durch einen Mundwinkel nach draußen? . . . Es sind Leute aus allen Volksklassen, die hier stehen und warten. . . . Hinter zwei tabakkauenden Arbeitsleuten . . . steht eine Dame, die in großer Erregung den Kopf hin und her wendet, um zwischen den Schultern der beiden vierschrötigen Kerle hindurch auf das Rathaus sehen zu können. . . . »Hei het je woll 'ne Swester, die von twe Männern wedder affkamen is?« Die Dame im Abendmantel erbebt. . . . »Je, dat 's so 'n Saak. Öwer doa weiten wi nix von, und denn kann der Kunsel doar nix för«. . . . Nein, nicht wahr, denkt die Dame im Schleier, indem sie ihre Hände unter dem Mantel zusammenpreßt. . . . Nicht wahr? Oh, Gott sei Dank!*

---

* Things have become drawn out. It seems the debates in the chambers will not subside. . . . Is that Mr. Kaspersen standing inside there, who never calls himself anything but a "civil servant," telling what he hears out of the corner of his mouth? . . . There are people of all classes standing and waiting here. . . . Behind two workers chewing tobacco stands a woman, craning her head back and forth in great excitement, in order to be able to see between the shoulders

In the face of such a passage, like any other from a novel, the traditional temporal interpretation of the present tense collapses, according to which it presents events having occurred in the past "as if they were present before our eyes." For would the events depicted here be less present before our eyes if they were rendered in the past tense? Are they more present than other scenes in the same novel where this latter tense does occur?

> Eine große Unruhe ergriff ihn, ein Bedürfnis nach Bewegung, Raum und Licht. Er schob seinen Stuhl zurück, ging hinüber in den Salon und entzündete mehrere Gasflammen des Lüsters über dem Mitteltische. Er blieb stehen, drehte langsam und krampfhaft an der langen Spitze seines Schnurrbarts und blickte, ohne etwas zu sehen, in diesem luxuriösen Gemache umher. . . .*

Following all our demonstrations, it requires no further confirmation that neither the description in the past tense nor that in the present arouses the experience of past-ness. Neither of the two scenes produces a stronger temporal present than the other. In both it is a matter of the fictive Here and Now of the figures, which in both cases is not accentuated as a fictive present-time by the presence of particularly temporal concepts (time adverbs or other temporal attributes). The temporal interpretation of the historical present in epic fiction is already misconstrued in that even the past tense does not indicate any past.—But why is it that the present

---

of the two thick-set fellows and get a glimpse of the city hall. . . . "Don't he got a sister who's been through two men already?" The woman in the evening coat shudders. . . . "Yeah, one of those things. But we don't know nothin' about it, an' prob'ly the Consul can't do nothin' about it neither." . . . No, that's so, thinks the woman in the veil, pressing her hands together beneath her coat. . . . Isn't that so? Oh, thank God!

* A great uneasiness took hold of him, a need for movement, space, light. He pushed his chair back, went over into the salon and lit several of the gas flames in the chandelier over the middle table. He stood still, twisted the long tip of his mustache slowly and spasmodically and looked, without seeing anything, around this luxurious chamber. . . .

tense also does not have any particular function of fictional pre-sentification beyond that of the past tense? For it does have just such a function in the historical account, in the type represented by the passage from the history textbook as well as in the example from Sengle's *Wieland*. We can answer this with the metaphor that a patch of red on a blue surface will stand in relief against its sur-roundings, whereas it does not do so on a surface of the same color red. In historical statement the present tense is different from the past, which here has the function of portraying past-ness. In the epos, in the novel, on the other hand, it is no different from the past tense; that is, it is not functionally different. Since here the preterite does not infringe upon the experience of the fictive Here and Now, it need not be replaced by a tense which in a differently structured context, namely that of the reality statement, eventu-ally can have such a fictionalizing effect, an effect which here would not equally well be produced by the past tense itself. Thus, without exception, in every fictional context where the historical present appears, we can replace it with the preterite without notic-ing any change in our experience of fiction.[77] "Things had become drawn out. . . . There were people of all classes. . . . Behind two workers stood a woman. . . . No, that's so, the woman thought." In this passage, as we encounter the verbs "to think," "to shudder" ("The woman shudders"), we notice that the verbs of inner action avail themselves more readily to being replaced by the preterite than do other verbs. And of course it is they which are the most valid proof that the past tense in fiction is not a statement of past-ness, because it is precisely they which bring about the crucial I-origination, or fictionalization, of the figures in the novel. But fictionalization is not intensified by the fact that the verb is in the present tense. Indeed, precisely because a form such as "the woman thought" can never legitimately occur in a reality statement, that is, can never designate a past event, and because the past tense is completely unstressed here, is why the present-tense form has even a disquieting effect. To a certain extent it first draws attention to the fact that only in a novel, and nowhere else, can we experience what a person is thinking right now, and thereby it destroys in some measure the illusion of fictive life which the novel produces. But what in this particularly striking way applies to the verbs of inner action is ultimately valid for any use whatever of the historical present in fiction. With that we have arrived at the point where we can now totally elucidate the phenomenology of the epic preterite, or more generally, that of the tense of fictional narration.

That in narrative literature, in epic fiction, such liberties can be taken with the preterite as are impossible in the real statement, is, as we have repeatedly intimated, an indication that in narrative literature the finite verb loses its temporality. The union that exists[78] in the reality statement between the meaning-content of the verb as a word and its tense, no matter how much the one might recede into the background behind the other, to a certain degree is dissolved in fiction. The comparison with painting is very instructive here. Just as a painting cannot be painted in thin air, but rather must have a substratum, a wall or a canvas, so also must the act of narration in narrative literature proceed in a finite verb-form. Now the canvas, above and beyond the painting, has its own material value *qua* canvas. But as substratum of a painting, and therefore being subsumed within it, it loses this material value: as a painting, it is no longer a canvas as such. The same relationship applies to the tense of the finite verb. Outside of fiction, in the reality statement, the preterite has its genuine grammatical function: it expresses a relationship between the statement-subject and the temporal past; and likewise the present tense here either has its own temporal meaning of contemporaneity, or it functions as a historical present. Within fiction, as a narrative tense (i.e., not as fictive temporal statements occurring with reference to the fictive life of the persons in the novel, which might, for example, be expressed in their speech), the preterite (to which, semantically speaking, the historical present also belongs) is merely the sub-stratum in which the narrative must proceed. As a past tense *per se* it is just as unnoticed as the canvas in a painting; and of the verb wherein this past tense occurs, and which must appear in a finite form, there remains only the semantic content, that is, the act, state, etc., which is expressed by the respective verb, but not the fact that this act, state, etc., is past. When I read in *Anna Karenina* that "Everything was topsy-turvy in the house of Oblonsky," I do not experience that at some time in the past things *were* topsy-turvy, but that things were *topsy-turvy*; and should this sentence occur in the historical present tense, I would experience the very same thing: a given state of affairs, but not time.

As an indication of the a-temporal conditions in epic fiction we may cite that present tense which we use involuntarily, but with logical necessity, whenever we re-tell the content of a narrative, as well as that of a drama, and which we can therefore term the *reproducing present*. The function and significance of this present tense emerges clearly if, instead of it, we were to use the past tense. For this past would immediately give the piece of fiction the character of a reality-document—it being, as scarcely needs to be said, not identical with the epic preterite. Just for this reason the reproducing present is not a historical present either, but rather the a-temporal present tense of statements about ideal objects. When in the discussion of a work of fictional literature the re-counting of content is combined with reflective, evaluative inter-pretation—as, for example, when Schiller writes to Goethe about Wilhelm Meister: "From that unhappy expedition on, where he wants to put on a play without having given any thought to the content, to the moment where he chooses Therese as his wife, he has, as it were, traversed the entire circuit of humanity." (July 8, 1796)—the a-temporal meaning of the present tense is not at all altered. And if perhaps we did not know what Schiller's sentence refers to, the present tense would make it clear that he is speaking about a work of literature and not about a real situation, in which case he would have used the past tense of the reality statement.

The Problem of Time in the Historical Novel

The phenomenology of verb tenses in fiction still requires an explication of the problem of time in such novels where it plays a material role, and where it therefore creates opportunity for misinterpreting the conditions of fiction. In view of such an opening passage in a novel which, to be sure, leaves nothing to be desired as far as exact dating of a point in past time or historical preciseness is concerned, there could be objections raised against the temporal devaluation of the past tense:

> Der 2. März 1903 war ein schlechter Tag für den 30jährigen Handlungsgehilfen August Esch; er hatte mit seinem Chef Krach gehabt und war entlassen worden, ehe sich noch Gelegenheit ergeben hatte, selber zu kündigen. Und so ärgerte er sich weniger über die Tatsache der Entlassung als darüber, daß er nicht schlagfertiger gewesen war.* (Hermann Broch, *Esch oder die Anarchie*)

Does this date—which doubtless indicates a past time known to author and reader alike, a past which a good many of those persons alive at the time the novel appeared (1931) can personally remember—does the date March 2, 1903, evoke the experience that from 1931 it lies some 28 years back in the past? By no means. It merely names one day which is of importance in the life of the character, one which at the same time informs us that we are to imagine the turn of the century as his milieu, which is one of the conditions contributing to Esch's particular kind of experience and values in life. The date is a fictive Now, a Today even, in the life of a figure,

---

* The second of March, 1903, was a bad day for thirty-year-old sales assistant August Esch. He had had a disagreement with his boss, and had been dismissed before he had opportunity to give notice of his quitting. And so he was less annoyed over the fact of his dismissal than over the fact that he had not been more quick-witted.

for whom it signifies a turn in his life; it is not a Then in the directly or indirectly experienced past of the reader or the author, for this past is not a part of his experience of fiction. The date plays a role no different from that of any other characterization of a day in a novel. It is nothing other than a piece of the raw material furnished to literature by reality, and in fiction it is just as fictive as house and street, field and forest, as the cities Mannheim and Cologne, where the novel *Esch* takes place, as the Julian Pass and the mid-day of the fictive Here and Now with which *Jürg Jenatsch* begins. For as soon as time and place constitute the field of experience belonging to fictive persons, i.e., as soon as they render the field of fiction itself, they no longer possess any character of "reality," even though the field of fiction may exhibit some constituents that originate in a more or less familiar realm of reality. Indeed, it is true that our knowledge of geographical and historical reality is thoroughly relative. For a geographically uninformed reader, someone on another continent, let us say, the names "Cologne" and "Mannheim" can just as little refer to the reality of these cities as the generally unfamiliar name of some village existing somewhere, which indeed does have geographical reality for the author who chooses it as the scene of his novel. Here, once again, the significance of context for the problem of reality or respectively of non-reality becomes apparent. If an unfamiliar geographical name (as with any other name, too) crops up in a historical document, a reality-account, even those readers who do not know this name do not doubt the reality of the place named by it. But in fiction, on the contrary, even a well-known real locality is divested of any question as to its reality. And the same reasoning can be applied to temporal reality. In a novel, the date March 2, 1903, is just as fictive as the year 1984, in which Orwell's utopia of political havoc is set—and obviously not because this latter names a time not yet experienced by those living in the year the book appeared (which would no longer be valid for the following generation), but rather because it treats of time in a novel. And the fact that even this, like all other utopian visions of the future, is narrated in the past —and not in the future—tense, once again drastically discloses the a-temporal meaning of the epic preterite. The utopian novel, too, narrates its events in reference to its fictive persons, as their Here and Now, such that the conditions of fictional structure in it differ in no respect from the structure of "historical" and "present-day" novels.

For it no longer requires lengthy discussion to make it understood that even the past tense of the historical novel has nothing to do with the historical character of its material. The Franco-Russian War of 1812, to which, as a historical event, today's generation has a different temporal relation than did the generation of the 1870's, nonetheless, *qua* subject-matter of Tolstoy's *War and Peace*, is experienced by us in the same "present-ness" as by the reader of the 1870's, when the novel appeared. For even in such a novel, where the raw material provided by reality is known as belonging to history, to the temporal past, the I-Origo of the reader, and therefore also his consciousness of time and of reality, is not present. Thus he experiences the "there was" of this narrative mode in precisely the same way he does that of a novel whose subject-matter is invented, namely as the fictive Now of the figures: the Now of Napoleon portrayed at his morning toilet, as well as that of Prince Andrei Bolkonski, of whom we are not equally certain whether—and to what extent—the material used for characterizing him is contrived or, like that characterizing Napoleon, historical. As subject-matter of a historical work Napoleon is portrayed as an object, about whom things are being stated. As subject-matter of a historical novel, however, Napoleon becomes a fictive Napoleon. And he is so not because the historical novel can deviate from historical truth. Even those historical novels which adhere to historical truth just as exactly as an actual historical document does, nevertheless transform the historical person into a non-historical, fictive figure, transferring him out of a possible system of reality into a system of fiction. For the system of fiction is defined by the figure's not being presented as object, but as subject, portrayed in his I-originarity (or, as is also possible, as an object in the experience-field of other persons in the novel). These processes are the "embodying states of affairs" which are overlooked in Ingarden's theory of quasi-judgments; it is the process of fictionalization which renders non-historical all ever so historical raw material in a novel.

But these relations—which we have developed only by way of example in connection with the combining of fictive dates with the epic preterite—by no means apply only to historical novels, but to historical dramas as well. And this fact makes it quite unequivocal that the preterite in a narrative has nothing to do with fictional subject-matter that is historical or that is in any other way characterized by temporal description.—Should this be phrased in general terms, however, then objections can be raised, particularly with respect to a form of the novel belonging especially to modernity, a form which could serve proponents of theories interpreting epic action as past as a refutation of our demonstrations: such works in which the past quality of the events narrated is especially stressed, or is even made thematic. In German literature this type of novel is represented—albeit in respectively very different fashion—by Thomas Mann's Joseph novels and Robert Musil's *Man Without Qualities*. Thomas Mann's artistic strategy and methodical point of departure is what we may call a humoristic one: namely, to awaken the Joseph legend to unsuspected life and to give it an illusion of present-ness, but at the same time by means of constant commentary to make it an object of historical and psychological knowledge.[79] Musil, too, keeps us constantly aware through his particular narrative style that this novel of temporal satire is written in retrospection of the past epoch of "Kakanien" (the royal imperial Austro-Hungarian Empire), and that the year 1913, in which the novel is set, is to be considered as past. And precisely for this reason the center of the novel's action, namely the "parallel action" which prepares the jubilee celebration of the reign of Franz Joseph, due in the year 1918, is by itself also the central object of temporal satire. But in both works the awareness of the past-ness, indeed of the respectively historical or mythical having-taken-place is not to be ascribed to the past tense in which they, like all epic literature, are narrated. In a passage from Musil's novel such as the following: "Walter and he had been young in the time, now vanished, shortly after the last turn of the century, when many people were imagining that the century, too, was young. The century then just gone to its grave had not exactly distinguished itself in its latter half" (I, Ch. 15), the narrator *qua* author certainly does expressly maintain a temporal distance from the action of the novel. But this comes about through the literal meaning of the words themselves—"in the time, now vanished," "the century then just gone to its grave." The narrative act here assumes the appearance of a historical account, which in this work has the function of repeatedly allowing the sense of temporal satire in the material being narrated to be rekindled. Nevertheless this novel, too—is a novel, namely a work of fiction; and it forms fictive persons in the Here and Now of their fictive life, doing so with all the means which narration in its modern stage of development commands. In descriptions such as the following (taken at random from *The Man Without Qualities*): "As Ulrich and Clarissa were talking, neither of them noticed that the music behind them was occasionally interrupted. Walter then came to the window. He couldn't see the two, but he felt that they were standing just beyond the limit of his field of vision. Jealousy tormented him." (I, Ch. 17); the narrator's "historical" narrative distance disappears as in any other novel, and the past tense no longer has any trace of the character of past-ness about it. For in narrative literature conditions are such that the narrative act can indeed take on the appearance of borrowing its material from a temporal past, be this an actual historical or an invented, contrived past; but it is not the past tense which substantiates this, nor is it the criterion for judging whether in any given case the material being narrated is respectively past or thought of as past. Musil's novel as well as Thomas Mann's, and our example from *Hochwald*, too, demonstrate that this illusion is evoked through quite different means, irrespective of whether the narrative deals with a genuinely historical material or one which is invented, more or less feigned as being historical.[80]

But when both historical and invented material is "presentified" in the same novel, as in *War and Peace*, and where consciousness of the past-ness of events is by no means to be evoked, but rather just the opposite, i.e., forgotten, in such a novel the functioning of the fictional preterite in those parts known as containing historical material is especially suited to provide further elucidation of the phenomenology of the epic preterite. We shall again demonstrate this with an example from the text. When we read:

> Um halb sechs Uhr ritt Napoleon nach dem Dorfe Schewardino. Es wurde schon hell; der Himmel hatte sich aufgeklärt; eine einzige Wolke hing noch im Osten. Die verlassenen Wachtfeuer brannten im schwachen Morgenlicht herunter.*

it is only the meaning-content of the verbs which comes to be experienced, irrespective of what tense they are in. But the laws of language, that is, of context, function so strictly and unerringly that these relations would immediately present themselves differently were we to encounter the same sentence in a historical document, for example in a posthumous eye-witness account of this particular day in the war, of this early morning ride with Napoleon to the trenches of Schewardino, where the—historically authenticated—acts of war were going on. Surely even here the meaning-

---

* At 5:30 Napoleon rode to the village of Schewardino. It was getting light already; the sky had cleared up; a single cloud still hovered in the East. The abandoned fires from the night watch were burning out in the dim morning light.

content of those verbs carrying the action or describing a situation would stand in the foreground of consciousness as we read the text, but nevertheless the meaning of the Then, of the fighting day which then was but is now past, would not be altogether lost. For as a historical statement this depiction would stand in time: in the temporal standpoint of the statement-subject, and in turn in that of the reader. And should we make the test of the historical present with these sentences, considering them first as a description in a novel and then as historical statements, it will prove itself to be quite especially instructive for the substratum-quality of the tenses in epic narration, and it will do so precisely because of the historical faithfulness of the content of these sentences. In the historical statement: "At 5:30 Napoleon rides to the village of Schewardino. It is getting light already . . ." the historical present would have the above-described effect of a kind of fictionalizing and vivifying. But when this depiction appears in a novel it does not need this kind of fictionalization, since in this context it is *eo ipso* the Here and Now of Napoleon on this particular morning which is being narrated— moreover, narrated not by someone who was there as an eye- witness when he rode to Schewardino, but rather the Here and Now of the character Napoleon whom, so to speak, we encounter alone, which is produced by the narrative act. Thus we come upon a phenomenon which, though often enough noted, had never been given any foundation: we sense the preterite to be more adequate, more aesthetically pleasing than a historical present, which—as we already could observe in the example from *Buddenbrooks*— can easily call our attention in all too obtrusive a manner to the fact that we are dealing with fictional relations, and which pre- cisely in so doing disrupts that illusion, that semblance which it is the essence of epic fiction to produce. Prevailing here is an aes- thetic and stylistic law which is so directly conditioned by the logical laws of literature and of language, that we must therefore observe it more closely.

The Fictional or Mimetic Genre

Stylistic Aspects

There are two aspects to this law. The first, aesthetically more superficial one, is based on the fact that something practically superfluous is aesthetically superfluous, too. Because the historical present does not fulfill any bona fide function in fiction—neither a temporal one nor one of fictionalization—it can always be replaced with the preterite without infringing upon the experience of fiction, or indeed upon any particular point of emphasis in the fictive person's experience which a narrator might wish to express through the use of the historical present.[81] A phenomenon appearing periodically in German narrative literature of the eighteenth, and also in that of a good part of the nineteenth centuries, seems to me only to confirm this observation: the extreme interchanging of these two tenses, very often occurring in the same sentence. Even if we assume an influence from the French here, such that a historical present tense would correspond to the French *Imparfait,* and the German perfect tense to the French *passé défini*—therefore, in a very rough sense corresponding respectively to the static portrayal of a state and to the progression of the action[82]—nevertheless it appears to me to be impossible, for example, in Wieland's verse epics or in Mörike's *Maler Nolten,* to discover any meaningful sequence in the alternation of these tenses. As a concrete example of this, let us observe a sample passage from Mörike's novel:

> Er faßte sie schonend an beiden Schultern, und sanft rückwärts gebeugt lehnte sie den Kopf an ihn, so daß die offenen schwimmenden Augen unter seinem Kinn aufblickten. Freundlich gedankenlos schaut sie an ihm hinauf, freundlich senkt er die Lippen auf die klare Stirn nieder. Lang unterbrach die atmende Stille nichts. Endlich sagt er heiter . . . Konstanze schüttelte, als wollte sie sagen. . . . Abermals versagt ihm ein weiteres Wort. . . .*

* Tenderly he took her by the shoulders, and, gently leaning back, she rested her head against him, so that her open, drifting eyes gazed up beneath his chin. In cheerful absentmindedness she looks up at him, and graciously he

The stylistic problem posed by this phenomenon is the object of H. Brinkmann's careful study of Goethe's *Elective Affinities*.[83] But it seems to me that Brinkmann burdens Goethe's very frequent interchanging of the past and the present tenses too heavily with interpretative meaning when, in reference to the central chapters of *Elective Affinities* (Part II, Ch. 13–14), he interprets the present tense as having the significance of denoting demonic happenings.[84] Perhaps it is possible to come a bit farther in judging this phenomenon by applying to it a distinction made in modern linguistics, namely that between diachronic and synchronic perspectives. It is precisely the tenses which are a specific object of study of synchronic grammar,[85] because they are morphemes, whereas the verbs themselves, on the other hand, are semantemes. It seems to me not impossible that modern linguistics might be able to regard our demonstration of the loss of temporal meaning undergone by verbs in fictional narration as a confirmation of its method of study. But conversely modern linguistics, too, confirms the circumstances surrounding pure phenomena of fiction: namely that the "present-ification," and in turn also the semantic content of that which is narrated, rests not on morphemes, but rather on semantemes and their respective meaning-content. With reference to the historical present in epic fiction, this implies that eliciting interpretative meaning from it in texts, i.e., through diachronic study, cannot lead to very valid results. Brinkmann's interpretation of the historical present in certain parts of the *Elective Affinities* as expressing the meaning of demonic happenings is an interpretation which just on this account must remain subjective and more uncertain than interpretations of meaning based on the action, the characterization of the figures, and so forth, because the temporal morpheme is relatively "mute," i.e., carrying no meaning beyond a

---

touches his lips to her clear forehead. For a long time nothing broke their breath-filled silence. Finally he says cheerfully . . . Konstanze nodded, as if to say. . . . Again no more words will come to him. . . .

temporal one. Therefore it seems to me that one is going too far when one burdens the historical present in certain contexts with the function of carrying a deeper meaning, since when it appears in other chapters of the same novel, for example, in sections where Charlotte is the main figure in the action,[86] it by no means allows for such interpretation, and, secondly, since the pronounced alternation between the present and perfect tenses is also to be found in other writings of the period. Morphemes seem to me in great measure to be subject to trends in language, which in themselves are not illuminating as far as the interpretative meaning of any given work is concerned. It appears to me that Goethe's interchanging of tenses, not only in the novel, but also in the autobiographical writings, can be explained via synchronic study, but cannot be interpreted on the diachronic level. Included in such a synchronic explication would be, then, the demonstration attempted in the preceding discussion, the demonstration that the temporal function and meaning of verbs—which *qua* temporal is also existential, i.e., referring to the conditions of reality, but not to those of fiction—fades and disappears in fictional narration. Therefore the effect of a style such as the incessant alternation of present and perfect tenses, even in a novel by Goethe, is more a disturbing than a meaningful and significant one. This disturbing element has its systematic and logical explanation in the fact that the historical present in fiction is superfluous because the preterite has no function of designating past-ness, and therefore has no influence upon the effect of fiction; it neither disrupts nor underscores this effect (which in turn would only disrupt it again).

With this there unfold further aspects of that law of the pleasing aesthetic effect of a preterite narrative form unbroken by any present-tense intrusions. Inherent within the rudimentary grammatical meaning of the preterite as being a statement about the past is the *quality of facticity*. From a semantic point of view, it is distinguished from all other tenses in that it is the only tense which unambiguously expresses the character of facticity. If we disregard the future tense, which of its nature always has the value of expressing the possible, the virtual, then we can distinguish the preterite from the present tense precisely through this character of unequivocal facticity. For the present tense, as we know, is ambiguous. In several languages it can replace the future, but above all it also denotes a-temporal, logical, and ideal relations. The sentence, "the nightingale sings" [*die Nachtigall singt*] can express both the idea of a nightingale's singing going on right now, as well as the a-temporal property of the nightingale's ability to sing.* On the other hand, "the nightingale sang" can designate only a past fact. Though one senses the preterite to be the temporal form adequate to narrative literature, nonetheless one interprets this feeling incorrectly if one ascribes to it the "illusion of the past" or that of a "virtual past," etc. It has its cause in the "connotative" *valeur* of facticity, so to speak, which discretely underscores—or better, does not disrupt—the experience of the semblance of life produced and evoked by fiction. For one must not exaggerate this phenomenon to the point of saying that the narrative preterite became the tense of fictional narration *on account of* its facticity value. It would be more accurate to say that its aesthetically "beneficient" character lies in that it retains its facticity value, while it loses its value of designating past-ness. To be sure, facticity is the most conspicuous expression of its semantic unequivocalness, but this unambiguity only emerges clearly in comparison with the ambiguous present tense. It is therefore the ambiguity of the present tense which is the actual objective reason why its use as a narrative tense, as a

* German has only one form to express both the simple present and the present progressive tense: *sie singt* means both the a-temporal "it sings" and the temporal "it is singing." However, many verbs in English parallel German usage in this respect. If I hear the nightingale singing and I say "I like that," it is not clear whether I mean I like it "now" or "in general." Thus in many cases the English present tense form has the same ambiguity as the German.— Tr.

historical present, is not without risk. In passages narrated in the historical present there are almost always places which for other reasons have to be in the present tense (which not only can be, but *must* be). This applies to Goethe's narrative technique as well as to a novel written in such a disorderly fashion as Werfel's *Bernadette*, which is narrated throughout in the present tense. Let us cite one small passage from this work, a passage which in itself is a prime example of the logical confusion which arises from the unrestricted use of the present tense:

> Daher *kommt* es, daß Zeiten, die den göttlichen Sinn des Universums *leugnen*, vom kollektiven Wahnsinn blutig geschlagen werden, mögen sie in ihrem Selbstbewußtsein sich auch noch so vernunftvoll und erleuchtet dünken. Das erste dieser äffischen Phänomene *begegnet* der Mitschülerin Bernadettes, Madeleine Hillot. Madeleine *ist* äußerst musikalisch. Das Göttliche *ergreift* das ganze Wesen dessen, den es begnadet. Das Dämonische *will* es sich leicht machen und *wählt* daher unsere Talente, um sich Eingang zu bahnen. . . . Auch bei Madeleine *wählt* es das begabteste Organ, ihr Gehör. Eines Nachmittags *kniet* das Mädchen in der Grotte und betet einen Rosenkranz. . . .*

The italicized verbs demonstrate the very different meanings which the present tense has, meanings which are so obvious that we need not subject them to exhaustive interpretation here. But there are passages in *Elective Affinities*, too, which, because of the ambiguity of the present tense, show its disruptive effect as a historical present:

* It *is* for this reason that times which *deny* the divine order of the universe are gruesomely conquered by collective madness, no matter how reasonable and enlightened they imagine themselves to be. The first of these idiotic phenomena is what *happens* to Bernadette's fellow student, Madeline Hillot. Madeline *is* extremely musical. The divine element *takes* possession of the entire being graced by it. But the demonic *wants* to make it easy for itself, and therefore *chooses* our talents as its way of gaining entrance. . . . In Madeline's case, too, it *chooses* the most gifted organ, her hearing. One afternoon the girl is kneeling in the grotto, saying the rosary. . . .

Ottilie steht ihm (dem Chirurgus) in allem bei: sie schafft, sie bringt, sie sorgt, zwar wie in einer anderen Welt wandelnd: denn das höchste Unglück wie das höchste Glück verändert die Ansicht aller Gegenstände: und nur, als nach allen durchgegangenen Versuchen der wackere Mann den Kopf schüttelt, dann mit einem leisen Nein antwortet, verläßt sie das Schlafzimmer Charlottens. . . .*

To recapitulate, the critique of the historical present as a tense of fictional narration has served to demonstrate that both tenses in fiction have the character of a substratum. It has also served to demonstrate the reasons why the preterite as substratum is preferable to the present tense. However, that the preterite does weaken into a substratum, thereby allowing the semblance of life evoked by fiction to emerge, this has its logical foundation—let us stress once more—in the loss of its grammatical temporal function, which in turn is due to the fact that the content of narrative literature is fictive, i.e., not the experience-field of the narrator, but that of the fictive persons, where fictive I-Origines replace a real I-Origo.

Before we turn to the further relations implied by these conditions in fiction and investigate the spatial components of the fictive spatio-temporal system, we must first look, in connection with the tenses, at some recent phenomena of narrative literature—new since the first appearance of this book—which might place the validity of our analysis of the fictional tenses in question. Here it is above all a matter of present-tense forms to which our critique of the historical present does not apply, because these forms are not a *historical* present. Our examples from older narrative liter-

---

* Ottilie assists him (the surgeon) in everything; as if in another world, she performs her tasks, assists, and looks after things: for great misfortune, just as great happiness, changes one's view of everything: and only after every attempt has been made and the good man shakes his head and replies with a soft "no," does she leave Charlotte's room. . . .

ature, for instance the passage from Stifter's *Hochwald,* have already shown that present-tense forms occurring in literature are by no means always a historical present. The landscape depiction from the Stifter piece turned out to be a tabular present which was still rooted in a retained statement structure, in the statement-subject still present here, namely that of the author. In fact, beginning with this text, one can establish a connection with a present-tense form as it appears in representatives of the *nouveau roman.* Some novels by A. Robbe-Grillet—*Les gommes, Dans le labyrinthe, La jalousie, La maison de rendez-vous*—are written in a present-tense form which is not a historical present, and which therefore cannot be replaced by the past tense. This present tense, too, is connected with a statement structure, one which, to be sure, is much more concealed than that found by the "naïve" narrator of the nineteenth century, and which as such therefore represents a totally new structural element. The statement-subject present in the novel *La jalousie* (1957) is not that of the author; and only after some time does the reader notice that a statement-subject is there, one which is not developed into a first- or third-person figure, but one contracted to nothing but an eye: the eye of the jealous husband who is watching the behavior of his wife and a family friend (in part by looking through the jalousie windows, and thus the double meaning of the title expresses the psychic state of the jealous man objectified to his observing the affairs and movements of the suspected lovers). The novel therefore has more the structure of a first-person than that of a third-person form, however without this I's announcing itself as such, and precisely this—as we shall elaborate in the chapter on the first-person narrative—is the structure of statement. As will become clearer in the following chapter, this entails that the depicted persons are not portrayed as fictive persons, i.e., formed in their I-Originity, but rather described as statement-objects. Since this description arises successively as the jealous man's observation progresses from moment to moment, the present tense in this novel is to be designated as a tabular present. —In other of Robbe-Grillet's novels the cause behind the present tense form is still more hidden. In *Dans le labyrinthe* (1959) it is the narrating author himself who restricts himself to his perceptual eye, and who in a foreword bids the reader to "see only those things, gestures and events which are reported to him . . . ," which give a disordered description of the soldier wandering about with his duffle bag in a small deserted city. In *La maison de rendez-vous* (1965) there is again a figure incorporated into the novel which is a somewhat more developed first-person figure than the one in *La jalousie,* but one which is developed only to the extent that it appears calling itself "I," but without attaining personal contours. This character is a foreigner staying in Hong Kong who registers the events and situations which "obviously" begin in a house of pleasure and culminate in a criminal case, a murder. He registers these events insofar as he perceives them, whereby it is exactly the pure perception which is the source of the disjointed repetitions of situations and configurations reminiscent of *déjà-vu* experiences. We might mention that this technique of Robbe-Grillet's is based on the rejection of the "omniscient narrator" and consequently employs the "restriction" to a narrative attitude which describes only what is perceived through the senses. The epistemological aspect of these novels, which this narrative technique allows us to see, is that through such a narrative attitude no clearly surveyable action is created, but rather one which is obscured, unclear, and imprecise. For everything which is merely perceived presents itself in a fragmentary way.

Robbe-Grillet's novels—just as, for example, Günter Grass' *Hundejahre*—are particularly striking examples of the fact that in modern narrative literature the traditional forms of first- and third-person narration are frequently disrupted, or otherwise so interwoven that the structure of the novel can no longer be unequivocally determined. In this context we have merely wanted to call attention to the fact that, on the basis of these present-tense structures, present-tense narration can occur which is not a historical present. And it may have already become discernable that this phenomenon has its cause in a deviation from the structure of "genuine" fiction, from the actual third-person narrative—or more precisely from the structure of fictional narration—which we shall describe in the following chapters. But first we must complement the analysis of the fictional tenses and the temporal deictic adverbs connected with them with a study of the spatial components of the fictive spatio-temporal system of epic literature.

Spatial Deictics

We have demonstrated the loss of the function of designating past-ness undergone by the epic preterite through the evident linguistic phenomenon that deictic temporal adverbs can be combined with it. But in a later context (p. 96f.), it was argued that it is not such temporal adverbs as for example "today," "tomorrow," or "yesterday" which effect the experience of the Here and Now of the action and persons of the novel, and that these can be lacking completely and the experience of the Here and Now nevertheless will be evoked. On the basis of the formative material of literary fiction the fictive Here and Now can respectively be brought to mental representation and expanded into the semblance of temporal sequence, a fact which by no means, however, implies (as Lessing thought) that the process of narrative presentation (or the unfolding presentation of the drama) is therefore an empirical process occurring in time. The formation of fictive time, be this static or sequential, is achieved through particular formative devices, just as is so with the formation of space. One of these devices is the conceptual dating through the adverbial temporal demonstratives "today," "yesterday," "tomorrow," "a week ago," and so on, deictics which extend the originary point of the Now into the temporal coordinate itself (and that into the infiniteness of past and future). In the mathematical or physical sense they correspond exactly to the conceptual spatial deictics "behind," "in front of," "above," "below," "right," "left," etc., which extend the originary Here into the spatial coordinate (reaching into the infinity of the universe). Precisely these deictic adverbs, the temporal as well as the spatial, are particularly suitable criteria for elucidating the nature of fictional structure and the logical character of its non-reality. And they are so suitable because of their demonstrative, i.e., deictic character; for it is in the nature of this attribute that it cannot really be implanted within fiction, that it cannot be transformed into genuine semblance, as can all other raw material given by reality. This can be shown better with the spatial than with the temporal adverbs, for a "demonstrative" in space is a genuine pointing, whereas a verbal pointing in time is only a figurative one.

Connected with this is the fact that the spatial adverbs have been used more commonly than have been temporal adverbs to exhibit the problem of plastic mental representation, which is doubtless a central problem of narrative literature. This is the procedure followed by B. K. Bühler in his *Sprachtheorie,* for example. But since he, like all other theorists of language, did not distinguish between the conditions of real and those of fictional presentation, his theory, with respect to the latter, turned out to be incorrect. This is not noticeable at first glance because, from a linguistic-grammatical point of view, the spatial deictics behave in a less complex manner than do the temporal adverbs. Their use is not governed by the tenses, as is that of the latter. And therefore that indication providing conclusive proof of fictional conditions is lacking: the combination of temporal demonstratives with the preterite, which is possible only in a context of fiction. From the perspective of grammar, words like "here," "there," "left," "right," "east," "west," etc., are so to speak free: there is no verbal or syntactical context in which they cannot occur. No combination of the kind "Tomorrow was Christmas" calls attention to any special behavior of spatial designations to furnish a point of departure for a proof. The sentence "To the right stood (stands) a cupboard" is gramatically correct in every context, in a travel guide as well as in a novel. It is just this circumstance which misled Bühler into establishing a "theory of displacement," which he proposed to be generally applicable, in order to demonstrate how the process of plastic mental representation or narration (which is the same thing), the "deixis in phantasma," takes place. These relations are demonstrated in connection with the attitude of the I-Origo of the person speaking (and respectively of the verbal recipient), this concept, as we have mentioned above, being taken from Bühler's theory. The adverbs "here" and "there" are characterized such that "here" (and now) expresses a "displacement of Mohammed to the mountain," i.e., a mental transferral of the I-Origo onto the scene portrayed; whereas "there," on the other hand, expresses Mohammed's remaining in his own place. Bühler demonstrates this displacement-theory with the example of a novel's hero who is in Rome: "The author is faced with the choice of whether his narration should proceed with 'here' or with 'there.' 'There' he trudged the whole day long around the Forum, there. . . . This could just as well read 'here.' What is the difference? 'Here' implies a transferral of Mohammed to the mountain, whereas 'there' in such a context signifies that Mohammed remains in his own place of perception and accomplishes a kind of telefocussing."[87]

This example is very much apt to blur the relations present here. This is so precisely because a condition of reality is combined with an element of fiction—something which in itself would not be forbidden, but which is not suitable for elucidating the problem here in question. It also indicates that, as we have mentioned earlier, the difference existing between a reality statement and fictional presentation is not noticed or considered. This leads us to that particular circumstance which is responsible for the fact that with spatial deictics this difference cannot be read directly from the sentence components themselves, as is possible with temporal deictics in combination with the preterite. When Bühler speaks of the "deixis in phantasma," he has in mind the broader Greek meaning of mental representation in general, irrespective of whether it is a matter of the representation of real data or that of imagined constructs. And it is no accident that he demonstrates his displacement-theory only with the spatial deictics. Notwithstanding the fact that epistemologically and physically time and space do belong together, nevertheless the category of space is distinguished from that of time in that it is the "form of external intuition" [*die Anschauungsform des äusseren Sinnes*] (Kant); that is, it can always be psychologically transformed into concrete perception or representation of space. Spatial aspects we can perceive, and in turn also mentally represent to ourselves, whereas time, the "form of internal intuition" [*die Anschauungsform des inneren Sinnes*], is something we cannot perceive and mentally represent, but only know. In other words, we can have only a conceptual awareness of it. We cannot "point" in time as we can in space, and when Bühler wished to illustrate the capacity of the demonstrative words for effecting visual representation, he very prudently restricted himself to the spatial deictics. But in so doing he did not note that even within the realm of our mental representation of space there exists a sphere in which we cannot point, but only know—even though the knowledge in question here has another sense than that of temporal knowledge. In fictive space we cannot point, and it is in the domain of fiction that the theory of displacement breaks down.

This becomes evident when, in Bühler's example, we substitute an imaginary place for the geographically familiar locality of Rome as the scene of the novel. When Bühler maintains that through the word "here" the reader mentally transposes himself to the place where the hero is, and that through the word "there" he is obliged to view the character "from afar," it immediately becomes evident that, with respect to an imaginary place, "here" and "there" are meaningless as spatial relations between my real existence and any fictive locality where the hero of the novel happens to be. That there is something not quite right here Bühler himself surmised when he added that "psychologically speaking, the land of the fairy tale lies in a Somewhere which is not fixedly bound up with the Here."[88] But he did not realize that this is not due to the more or less purely imaginary scene of the "fairy tale," i.e., to the fictive world of literature, but indeed rather to the fictive orientational system prevailing in this world. Even in the novel set in Rome, "here" does not mean that Mohammed, i.e., author and reader, mentally transposes himself to the location where the hero is, nor does "there" mean that he remains in his place and performs some kind of telefocussing; rather, "there" is nothing other than "here" referred to the fictive figure, the fictive I-Origo of the person in the novel. This immediately becomes apparent when one combines a deictic temporal adverb with "there": "Today he trudged around there the whole day" is just as acceptable as "Today he trudged around here. . . ."

However, just like the temporal adverb "now," the spatial "here" is least suited to provide an explication of how language functions in the spatial deictics when these appear in fiction. The original, deictic meaning of the Here has suffered considerable depletion through usage. Not only is it true that everywhere, even in a historical account, in the reality statement, "here" can be substituted for "there" without any mental displacement of one's perspective being thereby noticeable; but in addition, "here" can function in all possible contexts, by no means only in those designating spatial relations, for example: "here we must stop a moment," and the like. How matters stand with spatial deictics in the reality statement on the one hand, and in fiction on the other, is something we can establish far more convincingly with the aid of those spatial constructions which extend the "here": "to the left," "to the right," "in front of," "behind," "to the west," "to the east," etc. To be sure, we can ask, in momentary acknowledgment of Bühler's theory, whether in a novel we do not also feel ourselves "displaced" into a plastically depicted room, such that we can orient ourselves with the fictive persons: to their left and right, before and behind them. Bühler demonstrates the process of such orientation in our mental representation of concrete things, namely through the participation of what he calls the "present tactile image." "Cologne/Deutz: left of the Rhine/right of the Rhine—as I assimilate this fact and render it a clear and conscious one, I sense the readiness of my arms to function *hic et nunc* as directional pointers. It is from observations of this kind that we must scientifically determine and explicate the facts surrounding displacement in the act of mental representation."[89] If we are dealing with the mental representation of spatial relations which actually exist somewhere, then Bühler is correct. For however difficult it is to effect orientational relations within mental representation, for instance, as we listen to or read a spatial description which is rendered through deictic adverbs—in principle it is nevertheless always possible. And in any event the informant is, with respect to the verbal recipient, in the more favorable position of being able to direct or channel his mental representation on the basis of a preceding act of perception. In other words, in the mental representation of a real "here," "there," "right," "left," etc., the reference to a real I-Origo is always retained; speech is operating within the field of linguistic pointing, and a deixis in phantasma is possible. Bühler continues: "In the case where 'Mohammed transposes himself to the mountain,' his own tactile image is pieced onto a fantasized optical scene. Therefore he as speaker is able to employ position-words like 'here,' 'there,' and directives such as 'in front of,' 'behind,' 'to the right' and 'to the left' in exactly the same way in the phantasma as he does in primary perception. And the same is true for the hearer."[90] But the concept of the phantasma, the "fantasized optical scene" (an expression which, moreover, in our usage causes one to think of a fictional world rather than of a real locale, but which Bühler nevertheless intends in the general sense of all mental representation), in its undifferentiated meaning, by no means completely accounts for the phenomena of mental representation. And the notion that, in the realm of the mind's representation of fictive things and events, orientation occurs via adverbs of place, forsakes us when we consider an actual text. We can demonstrate this with a small experiment which we shall conduct with a passage from *Buddenbrooks,* the description of the landscape room in the house on Meng Street:

> Durch eine Glastür, den Fenstern gegenüber, blickte man in das Halbdunkel einer Säulenhalle hinaus, während sich linker Hand vom Eintretenden die hohe weiße Flügeltür zum Speisesaale befand. An der anderen Wand aber knisterte . . . der Ofen.*

This depiction—although it occurs in a novel, a fictional context identifiable as such because the characters have already made their appearance in it—is a reality-description; and it could be interpreted as such even if perchance one did not know that here Thomas Mann was describing his family home. It is a purely verbal, indeed a structural circumstance, which, independently of the figures in the novel, actually makes this description tantamount to a guide-book entry. With the words "to the left of a person entering the room" the narrator refers to an imagined, but not to a fictive person: be it to himself or to the reader, indeed, to anyone who can be thought of as entering the room, such that the real I-Origo of the reader is invoked, and he can then, with the aid of his own "tactile image," effect a mental picture of the spatial relationships of the room. However, when we make our experiment and replace

* Through a glass door opposite the windows one looked out into the dimness of a pillared hall, while to the left of a person entering the room were the high, white folding doors leading to the dining room. Against the other wall, though, crackled . . . the stove.

the expression "of a person entering the room" with "of Konsulin Buddenbrook," we are suddenly no longer able to effect this orientation at all. The designation "to the left of Konsulin Buddenbrook," who is depicted as sitting beside her mother-in-law on the straight-backed sofa, cannot be corroborated via the image of the reader's own physical presence in the room. For now the expression "to the left" is referred to the fictive figure, whose position in the room we cannot represent to ourselves in exact spatial detail. Thomas Mann intended to provide as exact a description as possible of this room, which was real for him; and, in unwitting accordance with the laws of epistemology, he has referred the spatial orientation, which as such is real, to a real I-Origo, thereby momentarily abandoning the realm of fiction, so to speak.

This experiment demonstrates that, when they appear in fiction, something takes place with spatial deictics corresponding to that which occurs with temporal deictics. It also holds true for these adverbs that they do not refer to a real I-Origo, i.e., that of the author and therewith that of the reader, but to the fictive I-Origines of the figures in the novel. In the course of such a change of reference, though, they do not initiate any alterations in grammar, as do the temporal adverbs. Because of this they demonstrate even more tangibly than the latter what the cause of this change of reference is which applies in equal manner to both types of deictics. The cause consists in that *demonstratives in fiction recede from the field of deixis in language and transfer into that of symbol* —notwithstanding the fact that there they retain the grammatical resemblance of demonstratives, just as the epic preterite retains the grammatical appearance of the past tense. In fiction deictic adverbs, both temporal and spatial, relinquish the deictic, existential function which they have in the reality statement and become symbols, wherein the temporal or spatial perception is reduced to a conceptual level. When in Goethe's *Elective Affinities* the gardener describes the area surrounding the moss-covered cottage with the following words:

Man hat einen vortrefflichen Anblick: unten das Dorf, ein
wenig rechter Hand die Kirche . . . gegenüber das Schloß und die
Gärten . . . dann öffnet sich rechts das Tal. . . .*

or when in Stifter's works the persons in the novel frequently travel
"westward" or "eastward," we assimilate these directional indicators as designating relations which we know as belonging to space,
but which we can represent to ourselves as such only on the basis
of our own real Here, not on that of the fictive Here of fictive figures. In this respect the adverbs of space can also illuminate those
of time. Precisely on account of their originally deictic character,
the designations "today," "tomorrow," etc., in fiction have only the
function of reduced conceptual symbols which we know as designating temporal relations, but which we cannot experience as existential time. They can be lacking in fiction, and yet the illusion
of the Now would not be disrupted by their absence; just as spatial
deictics may also be absent in fiction without the illusion of the
Here of the action and characters being therefore disrupted. The
experience of the Here and Now which fiction (epic and equally so
dramatic and cinematic, as we shall see) conveys to us, is the experience of the mimesis of men in action, i.e., of fictive, spontaneously alive figures, who, precisely because they are fictive, are not
in time and space—even when, as montage, a geographically or
temporally known reality is the scene of the novel. For the experience of reality is determined not by the object of experience, but
by the experiencing subject. But if this subject itself is fictive, then
every geographical and historical reality known as such becomes
absorbed into the field of fiction, becomes transformed into "semblance." And neither author nor reader need then concern himself
with whether and to what extent that reality familiar to him is furnished with additional elements by the imagination. This is the
ultimate consequence, familiar to every reader of novels, arising

* One has a splendid view: below the village, slightly to the right the
church . . . opposite the castle and gardens . . . then on the right the expanse
of the valley. . . .

from those logical functions of language when it intends to engender the experience of fiction and not that of reality.

FICTIONAL NARRATION—A (FLUCTUATING) NARRATIVE FUNCTION

The Disappearance of the Statement-Subject and the Problem of the "Narrator"

Thus far we have both specified and endeavored to account for those phenomena—or better those symptoms—which in themselves reveal that fictional narration is of a categorically different nature and structure from statement (which, on the basis of the real statement-subject, is always synonymous with reality statement in the above-defined sense): the use of verbs of inner action with reference to the third-person, and derivable from this the narrated monologue [*erlebte Rede*], the disappearance of the narrative preterite's significance of designating past-ness, and the possibility (not the necessity) created by this of its combination with deictic temporal, particularly future, adverbs. These are not symptoms which as such are isolated; they mutually condition one another. They alone are elements which make fictional narration recognizable as a special verbal-grammatical phenomenon. But they are not the only ones—once their ultimate and decisive cause is established, still further characteristic features shall emerge.

We have already observed that the symptoms pointed out thus far are linked with the transferral of the real spatio-temporal system onto the fictive persons or I-Origines, which at the same time implies the disappearance of a real I-Origo, i.e., of a statement-subject. With respect to the relationships which follow, let us refer back to our analysis of statement structure and demonstrate this with a sentence which, taken in isolation, yields no evidence as to what kind of context it is from. It runs: "Then during the meal Mr. Arnoldsen gave one of his witty and imaginative toasts in honor of the engaged couples." This is a type of sentence which can occur in a letter (or in an oral account) which I receive from a person who has participated in the festivities described. In this case the sentence then contains the following features which constitute it as statement: the statement-subject, the letter-writer, reports about a circumstance, Mr. Arnoldsen's toast, as an occurrence experienced by him; the verb is in the past tense, thereby indicating that this occurrence is past in relation to the temporal point of the report about it, that it stands in the past of the statement-subject. As such it is an event which has actually taken place, i.e., which has existence independently of whether this statement-subject does or does not report about it. This event only then is a statement-object through the statement itself, that is, once it has become one. Conversely, this implies that the statement-subject is aware of the statement-object's reality (in this instance, of its factual occurrence in the past) as being independent of him, irrespective of whether its reality can be verified or not.—But, the sentence about Mr. Arnoldsen's toast is not a real sentence occurring in a letter, but rather one occurring in a novel, in *Buddenbrooks*. Furthermore, it is not spoken by any of the characters in the novel, but is a sentence of straight narration, or narrative report. As a sentence in a novel it does still have the form of a declarative sentence, but nevertheless it does not represent a declaration, since it no longer has the structure of statement. For now, should we ask after the statement-subject, we receive no answer to our query. Does the past tense "gave" signify that the event described, namely Mr. Arnoldsen's toast in honor of the engaged couples, took place in the past of the person telling it, i.e., in the past of the author of the novel? Did it take place at all? Can one submit the content of the sentence to a process of verification, for example by objecting that the person doing the reporting erred and that it was not Mr. Arnoldsen, but rather, let us say, Mr. Bertoldsen who proposed the toast, or that the toast wasn't at all as witty as it was purported to be? All of this implies: is the author the statement-subject in this sentence; does

a statement structure exist here? All of these questions must be
answered in the negative. The sentence "Then during the meal Mr.
Arnoldsen gave a toast . . . ," as a sentence occurring in a novel, has
a different character from the very same sentence when it stands
in a letter. It is part of a scene, of an independently existing fictive
reality which *qua fictive reality is just as independent of a state
ment-subject as is a "real" reality.* In other words, whereas a real
reality is because it is, a fictive reality "is" only by virtue of its being narrated (and correspondingly a fictive reality is dramatic by
virtue of its being created with the media of dramatic formation).

We are now in a position to recognize the following fact: epic
fiction, the product of narration, is not an object with respect to
the narrative act. Its fictivity, that is, its non-reality, signifies that
it does not exist independently of the act of narration, but rather
that it only *is* by virtue of its being narrated, i.e., by virtue of its
being a product of the narrative act. One may also say that the act
of narration is a function, through which the narrated persons,
things, events, etc., are created: the *narrative function,* which the
narrative poet manipulates as, for example, the painter wields his
colors and brushes. That is, the narrative poet is not a statement-
subject. He does not narrate about persons and things, but rather
he narrates these persons and things; the persons in a novel are narrated persons, just as the figures of a painting are painted figures.
*Between the narrating and the narrated there exists not a subject-
object relation, i.e., a statement structure, but rather a functional
correspondence.* This is the logical structure of epic fiction, which
categorically distinguishes it from that of the reality statement.
Between the εἰπεῖν of narrative literature and that of statement runs
the boundary between "literature and reality," along which there is
no point of transition from the one category to the other and which,
as we shall see, signifies a decisive criterion for establishing the
locus of imaginative literature in the system of language.

In the sense of traditional grammar and theory of language the contention that there is this boundary running right through the system of language would be a startling and objectionable one, had we not been able to ground this fact through demonstrating those linguistic processes which take place on the plane of narrative fiction. These processes or phenomena, namely the change in meaning undergone by the preterite, the transition of demonstrative adverbs from the deictic onto the conceptual or symbolic plane of language, the possibility of employing verbs of inner action, are all symptoms and as such the results of that functional correspondence between the narrated and the act of narration which characterizes fictional narration. For these verbal phenomena are the symptoms of the fictive world, which is a created one and in which there is no real space and no real time.

Now, if we recognize the disappearance of a real I-Origo and therefore of a statement-subject as the decisive structural element of this fictive world, and in turn as the cause of the phenomena discussed above, it may appear as if these phenomena have been derived from two different causes, causes which, although they do not stand in contradiction to one another, are nevertheless unconnected. But conditions are precisely such that *the absence of the real I-Origo and the functional character of fictional narration are one and the same phenomenon.* Both are merely different aspects, even merely different modes of expressing the fact that this narrating is characterized by the experience of the non-real. This experience commences the moment the fictive figures or I-Origines appear, or (since context prepares us for it) the moment we anticipate their appearance. It is they that constitute narrative literature as fiction, as mimesis. And conversely, then, this implies nothing other than that it is the narrative act which engenders mimesis here. Only here does narration have the character of a productive function and not that of a statement; and with the beginning text of *Jürg Jenatsch,* and still more significantly with the passage from *Hochwald,* we were able to trace genetically that it is purely the process of fictionalization alone which categorically separates epic, functional narration from the reality statement. This process can be accomplished only with human figures (or respectively with personified, anthropomorphized animal figures, or even things, as for example in fables, fairy tales, and the like), because only man is a person, i.e., not merely an object, but also a subject. Fictionalization of portrayed persons means this: that they are portrayed not as objects, but rather as subjects, that is, as I-Origines.

The concepts "subject" and "object" appear here obviously in another meaning than that of the relational poles of the statement. The object of the statement signifies nothing but that which is stated, and the subject of the statement signifies the statement itself: they are concepts from the logic of statement. But if I speak of a person as an object, then I define this concept as the opposite to that of subject in the ontological sense of an I-saying being: man is an I, a subject, the being who says "I" both of and to himself. This is the exact opposite of the concept of object in the sense of an object or thing. The self as a specifically I-saying being stands opposite a world of objects, to which, as far as it is concerned, even all other human beings, i.e., all other I-saying beings belong. It knows of them only as objects, not as subjects, since each I-saying being knows only of itself as a subject; or if it knows of them as subjects, it does so only once they have articulated themselves. To be sure, I can indeed comprehend I-saying or person-objects in a way other than as thing-objects: on the basis of their own I-ness I can communicate with them as a You.[91] But—and this is what is of extreme importance in the context of our investigations—when a person-object is the object of a statement, then we can only state about him as an object—which fact we need elucidate with only one example: a sentence which runs "At this moment she remembered the words she had spoken to him" (Musil), immediately shows itself to be a sentence from a novel, a sentence occurring in fictional narration and not in statement. Only in such a sentence can verbs of inner action appear, which, as was shown, are that means, elementally concomitant to fictional narration, of portraying persons as thinking, feeling, remembering in the Here and Now of their living and experiencing, in their I-originarity, i.e., in their subjectivity—and moreover of portraying them as third-person subjects. Epic fiction is the sole instance where third-person figures can be spoken of not, or not only as objects, but also as subjects, where the subjectivity of a third-person figure *qua* that of a third-person can be portrayed. And conversely it is therefore precisely the fictive persons which withdraw the structure of statement from the narration of narrative literature, which establish not a relational, but instead a functional correspondence between the act of narration and that which is being narrated. And this implies, as has been demonstrated with the sentence from *Buddenbrooks,* that the author of a piece of narrative literature is not the statement-subject of that which is being narrated.

The problem of the narrator, or let us say less pretentiously, the term "narrator," must be briefly commented upon here. It is a term which doubtless has created some confusion because the structural difference between statement as a subject-object relation and fictional narration as a function has hitherto been disregarded. Certainly, in describing a piece of narrative literature it is terminologically convenient to avail oneself of this personifying expression. For of all art media narration evokes, or can most frequently evoke the impression of a "person" who posits himself in a relationship not only to the figures he creates, but to the reader as well. In positing a "fictive narrator" to circumvent a biographical identification with the author one merely appears to void the personification of the "narrator." There is no such thing as a fictive narrator which, as is obviously presumed, would be conceived of as a projection of the author, or indeed as a "figure created by the author" (Stanzel). There is also no such fictive narrator in cases where this impression might be awakened by interspersed first-person flourishes such as

"I," "we," "our hero," and the like, which we shall discuss in detail in what follows. *There is only the narrating poet and his narrative acts.* And only in cases where the narrative poet actually does "create" a narrator, namely the first-person narrator of the first-person narrative, can one speak of the latter as a (fictive) narrator. The epic poet and also theorist of the novel Michel Butor, a representative of the *nouveau roman,* also reserves the concept of narrator for the first-person narrator and, almost surprisingly, but yet in confirmation of our theory, calls the third-person narrative a "narrative without a narrator."[92] Yet traditionally when one speaks of the narrator, what is meant is nevertheless the third-person narrator. Now, as regards this term, it is suitable for the description of the system of literature and its strict linguistic classification if one does not burden the concept of the narrator with that confusing ambiguity which arises when the term is applied both to the epic poet and to the εἰπεῖν, but instead reserves it solely for the former. It is to be classified on the same plane with the concepts "dramatist," "lyric poet," indeed further with "painter," "sculptor," "composer"—that is, it is to be employed as the designation for that particular kind of art which an artist pursues, but not for the artistic medium he uses.

To talk of the "role of the narrator," then, has just as little significance as to talk of the role of the dramatist or the painter. Even today one rarely advances beyond those insights developed by Käte Friedemann in her book entitled *Die Rolle des Erzählers in der Epik* (1910), a book which, written in refutation of Spielhagen's "theory of objectivity," embodies what for her time were extremely significant and advanced ideas in the theory of literature. Certainly, Friedemann was correct in defining the "narrator" as a "medium organically inherent within the work of literature itself." But since she did not grasp the nature of this medium as a function, she merely appears to be correct when she states: "He is the one who evaluates, who is sensitively aware, who observes. He symbolizes that epistemological conception common since Kant, which states that we do not comprehend the world as it is in itself, but rather as having passed through the medium of an observing mind."[93] Again she is only seemingly justified in asking: "How does the poet arrive at a knowledge of the psychic life of the characters?"[94] Then thirty years later, when Julius Petersen expands upon this aspect by comparing the narrator with a "director who stands between the persons on the stage and assigns them their places, movements and intonations," and, what is more, places this narrator "in the role of the psychologist" and has him "assume the tasks of the latter, so that responsibility for describing and portraying psychic processes falls on him"[95]—it becomes all the more clear that we are dealing here with sometimes more, sometimes less adequate *metaphorical pseudo-definitions* which in literary jargon have become condensed and overused slogans, like the "authority" or the "omniscience of the narrator," or which have even become mythologized in their comparison with God's omniscience and precisely for this reason have provoked criticism.[96]

At the base of this widespread view—which indeed, as far as I can see, is almost the sole dominant one[97]—lies the mistaking of the character of fictional narration and its categorical difference from statement. It has gone unrecognized that, for example, the "evaluative" attitude of the narrator (as epic poet) is not the same as the evaluative attitude of a historian, of an interpreter of literature, or of a psychologist *vis-à-vis* his respective objects of investigation. The evaluative attitude of the epic poet is an aspect of his specific, mimetic medium of portrayal, his narrative acts, just as is the light and shadow that the painter puts into his painting. It is an aspect of that creative function which is present even in those instances where it is not at all conspicuous as such: not only in dramatic literature, but also—as we shall presently show in detail —in epic literature itself. The question of how the dramatist arrives at knowledge of the psychic life of his characters could with equal justification be posed of the "narrator." But just as one would not answer by saying that the dramatist arrives at this knowledge of the psychic life of his characters by way of "experimenting," so also the exponents of the "narrator"-interpretation would probably not come to such a conclusion. This shows nothing other than that the question is also inadequate in reference to the epic poet, that, in other words, it has not been recognized that like the dramatist, he, too, is a "mimetes." That is, he creates his characters, he produces them, but he does not evaluate, judge, or come to a knowledge of them.

The Problem of the Subjectivity and Objectivity of Narration

However, exact proof that in fictional narration there is no statement-subject identical with the "narrator" at work can be produced only through an examination of precisely those concepts which characterize the structure of statement. These are concepts which, however, hitherto have always been employed not only for the description of narrative literature, but also for the differentiation among literary genres. We are dealing with the concepts of subjective and objective, which are usually applied to literary genres such that epic and drama as objective are contrasted to the lyric as a subjective genre, but with the difference of degree that, due to the "epic I," the epic is more subjective than the drama, though not as subjective as the lyric. Thus the naturalistic theories of the novel proposed by such authors as Spielhagen and Holz maintain that through the furthest possible exclusion of the narrator, i.e., through the greatest possible degree of dialogue and therefore dramatization of the novel an "objectivity" in narrative literature would be attained which would approach that of the drama. And when such an injunction was rejected, as by Petersen, for example, this was done with the stipulation that the subjective factor in narration should not be excluded from narrative literature. We are citing his formulation because it very clearly expresses the traditional conception of this "subjective factor": "The mediating pose of the narrator entails a constant interplay between objectification of the subjective and subjectification of the objective. The subjective narrative form seeks to evoke the impression of the narrator's objective truth through reference to substantial material, such as things remembered or statements given by an eye-witness. . . . The objective narrative form becomes subjectified through the personal intrusion of the poet, through the narrator's addressing his audience as in interpolations of an explanatory, didactic or contemplative nature."[98] And Jean Paul spoke no differently when he compared epic and drama: "Far more objective than the epic is the drama, which—crowding the person of the poet completely behind the canvas of his painting—must therefore run its course in an epic sequence of lyrical moments without his intervention."[99]

It is predominantly the conception that, as Petersen says, "the objective narrative form is rendered subjective via the intrusion of the poet," which introduced the concept of the subjective, and as its opposite that of the objective, into the theory of the epic. However, inadequate use of these concepts obscures not only the structure of epic literature itself, but also that of the entire system of literature; for what we are dealing with here are concepts of logic itself. Their meaning must be clearly elaborated if it is to be recognized that fictional narration is never "subjective," not even when it appears to comport itself ever so subjectively.

We shall demonstrate this first of all with three examples of narrative modes, or narrative styles, which in the traditional terminology are customarily characterized according to the degree of their respective objectivity or subjectivity.

Example 1:
    Durch diese schöne Anstrengung mit sich selbst bekannt gemacht, hob sie sich plötzlich, wie an ihrer eigenen Hand, aus der ganzen Tiefe, in welche das Schicksal sie herabgestürzt hatte, empor. Der Aufruhr, der ihre Brust zerriß, legte sich, als sie im

Freien war, sie küßte häufig die Kinder, diese ihre liebe Beute, und mit großer Selbstzufriedenheit gedachte sie, welch einen Sieg sie, durch die Kraft ihres schuldfreien Bewußtseins, über ihren Bruder davon getragen hatte.   (Kleist, *Die Marquise von O . . .*)

Example 2:

Treibel war ein Frühaufsteher, wenigstens für einen Kommerzienrat, und trat nie später als acht Uhr in sein Arbeitszimmer, immer gestiefelt und gespornt, immer in sauberster Toilette. . . . In der Regel erschien die Rätin sehr bald nach ihm, heute aber verspätete sie sich, und weil der eingegangenen Briefe nur ein paar waren, die Zeitungen aber, in denen schon der Sommer vorspukte, nur wenig Inhalt hatten, so geriet Treibel in einen leisen Zustand von Ungeduld und durchmaß, nachdem er sich rasch von seinem kleinen Ledersofa erhoben hatte, die beiden großen nebenanliegenden Räume, in denen sich die Gesellschaft vom Tage vorher abgespielt hatte. . . . Die Szenerie war wie gestern, nur statt des Kakadu, der noch fehlte, sah man draußen die Honig, die, den Bologneser der Kommerzienrätin an einer Strippe führend, um das Bassin herumschritt.   (Fontane, *Frau Jenny Treibel*)

Example 3:

Dann ging er, ein Nachtlager suchen; im Wirtshaus war man noch wach, der Wirt hatte zwar kein Zimmer zu vermieten, aber er wollte, von dem späten Gast äußerst überrascht und verwirrt, K. in der Wirtsstube auf einem Strohsack schlafen lassen.

(Kafka, *Das Schloß*)

Example 4:

Jetzo setzten sich nun die sämtlichen Meister in Bewegung und auf die Stühle—ein Tizian, Fra Bartholomeo di Sa. Marco, ein Da-Vinci, ein Kaufmann (wahrscheinlich Angelika Kaufmann)— vorwärts, nebenwärts, seitwärts, hinterwärts, vor den Spiegeln. Herrlich und ungebunden und im großen freien Stile malten und zeichneten alle—der Nase wurde nur im Vorbeigehen auf dem Gesicht gedacht. . . .   (Jean, Paul, *Der Komet*)

Example 5:

Es wird doch, hoff' ich, kein Leser Worble's gelehrte Anspielungen . . . als zu unwahrscheinliche und mir bloß geraubte absprechen. Diesen Leser müßte man sonst daran erinnern, daß gegenwärtiger Verfasser selber tausend Mal mehr Gleichnisse für seine 'Grönländischen Prozesse' schon im ersten Jahr seiner akademischen Laufbahn in Leipzig, also in einem noch jüngeren Alter, herausgebracht und herausgegeben. Denn Worble war, als er von Henoch zum Prinzenerzieher installiert wurde, gerade anderthalb Jehre älter als ich, nämlich neunzehn und ein halbes Jahr. . . .

Ich frage überhaupt die ganze Welt, wie war es denn anders zu machen, um Nikolaus durch die Städte zu bringen? Und was mich dabei besonders freut, ist, daß sogar Libette, die Schwester, in alles einging, ja in manchem vorausging. . . .

(Jean Paul, *Der Komet*) *

* *Example 1*
Having come to know herself through this intense psychological exertion, she suddenly lifted herself up, as if aided by her own hand, out of the depths into which fate had plunged her. The tumult that ravaged within her breast abated once she was in the open country, and she poured kisses on the children, these her dear prize; and with great self-satisfaction she pondered what a victory she had achieved over her brother through the strength of her guiltless conscience.

(Kleist, *The Marquise of O . . .*)

Example 2
Treibel was an early riser, at least for a Kommerzienrat, and never appeared in his office later than eight o'clock, always with boots and spurs on, always in the most immaculate toilet. . . . As a rule his wife appeared very shortly after him. But today she was late, and since there were but few letters having come in, and since the papers, which already carried the signs of oncoming summer, had little content, Treibel lapsed into a mood of muted impatience, rose suddenly from his leather sofa and crossed through the two large adjoining rooms where the social activities of the previous day had taken place. . . . The scene was just as yesterday; only instead of the cockatoo, which was still missing, one saw Mrs. Honig outside, who was walking around the pond leading the Frau Kommerzienrat's Bolognese dog on a leash.

(Fontane, *Frau Jenny Treibel*)

Example 3
Then he went out looking for a place for the night. At the inn people were still awake; the inn-keeper didn't have a room to rent, but, taken unawares and confused by this late guest, he was willing to have K sleep on a stack of straw in the bar room.

(Kafka, *The Castle*)

According to traditional terminology, passages 1 to 3 would be classified as examples of objective narration. There is no narrator's voice interfering with the flow of narration. In all three cases a concrete situation is described: the marquise of O . . . as she gains control of herself, goes outside and kisses her children; Kommerzienrat Treibel and his wife as one follows the other into the office; K as he is seeking lodgings for the night at an inn. All three narrative types are oriented directly to the situation, without circumlocution or digression. But if for this reason we were to designate them as objective, such a term would nonetheless seem inadequate to us. That is, we would not be able to judge whether one of these narrative modes is more objective than the other, i.e., whether the situation is depicted more objectively in one instance and less so in the other.

Let us first compare the passage from Kleist with that from Kafka.

Example 4

And now these sundry masters set themselves into motion and onto their stools—a Titian, a Fra Bartholomeo di Sa. Marco, a Da Vinci, a Kaufmann (probably Angelika Kaufmann)—forwards, sideways, to and fro and backwards before the mirrors. Splendidly and unrestrainedly did all paint and sketch, and in a grand, free style—only in passing did they think of putting in a nose on a face. . . .

(Jean Paul, *Der Komet*)

Example 5

I hope no reader will take Worble's scholarly allusions . . . as being too improbable and condemn them as being pirated by me. He would then have to be reminded that the present author himself published and edited a thousand times as many such similies for his *Grönländische Prozesse,* and moreover that he did so being only in the first year of his academic studies at Leipzig, and therefore at a younger age than Worble. For when he was installed by Henoch as the prince's tutor Worble was exactly a year and a half older than I, namely nineteen and a half. . . .

Now I ask you, everyone, was there any other way to have brought Nikolaus through the cities? And what especially pleases me about it is that his sister, Libette, got into everything—and in many areas was indeed quite prominent. . . .

(Jean Paul, *Der Komet*)

The one from *The Marquise of O . . .* exhibits a vocabulary which is more emotionally accentuated than does the one from Kafka's *The Castle*. In the latter there are only two more emotionally tinged expressions that describe the inn-keeper's state: taken unawares and confused. But in the former we have a whole array of such expressions: intense psychological exertion, the tumult which ravaged within her breast, great self-satisfaction, the strength of her guiltless conscience, and finally also the metaphorical description of her collecting herself: "suddenly she lifted herself up, as if aided by her own hand, out of the depths into which fate had plunged her." But is the marquise portrayed less objectively than is the inn-keeper in the Kafka piece?

We will not answer this question immediately now, but rather we shall answer it by way of digressing to a little experiment which will first afford us the possibility of exactly determining those narrative conditions present here. Let us assume for a moment that the Kleist passage represents a reality-report which a person is giving about the marquise of O. . . . Not all, but nevertheless several of the expressions in this passage could also appear in a reality-report, for instance, "she raised herself up out of the depths. . . ." But when we make this change in context we notice immediately that there is now a totally different relation between this mode of expression and the object of the statement, the marquise. Indeed, we note that it is only under such conditions that we can meaningfully speak of a "relation," or even of an "expression" at all. What is established is a relation between the matter itself and a person stating about it, a person who is very involved with it, and who expresses his empathy for the marquise's fate with those words which he deems to be adequate for such expression. And even if someone else were to comment on the same subject-matter in a way such as the following: "Then the marquise composed herself and asserted control again," then we would quite justifiably find this to be legitimately more objective than the first formulation, less colored with the subjective sympathetic attitude of the speaker than the other. But when we take this passage and return it to its original context, i.e., to that of a novel, this relational system which was established in the context of the reality statement immediately collapses. The sentence "She raised herself up out of the depths into which fate had plunged her" no longer expresses any involvement of a speaker, nor any more or less subjective judgment on his part (or, as K. Friedemann says: evaluation). For now the state of affairs rendered by the sentence is not an object of judgment, but rather a fictive life and existence, running its course in its fictive Here and Now. But as a fictive life, as semblance, it runs its course just as independently of a statement-subject, of someone who makes judgments about it, as does the real life—*qua* act of living—of real persons.—And now let us proceed with the second part of our experiment and assume that the sentence we made up, namely, "Then the marquise composed herself and assumed control again," is not a reality-statement, but rather a sentence occurring in a novel. In this case, then, even this sentence would not represent a judgment made by a speaker or statement-subject, but rather, just as the passage from the actual text, it would represent a creative forming of the marquise's situation at a given moment. Narrative techniques of a similarly "objective" nature are found in many Kleist passages: "This news threw Squire Friedrich into a state of extreme alarm" (*Der Zweikampf*); "In his tormented soul Kohlhaas was toying with . . . a new plan to lay Leipzig in ashes" (*Michael Kohlhaas*).

Now, we do sense a difference between the last two Kleist passages and the one from *The Marquise of O. . . .* But how is this difference to be defined? We may be tempted to apply the term "objective narrative technique" to the *Zweikampf* and *Kohlhaas* passages, as well as to the passage from Kafka. But is the portrayal of the marquise's situation to be designated as more subjective? Even in posing this question one sees that the designation "objective narrative technique" is just as inadequate as the term "subjective"—for the one could be meaningful only if the other were also. The difference consists in that in this particular passage the marquise is portrayed in her inner state, in the I-originarity of her psychic experience, to which the modifying adjectives and predicates give expression. In the other examples expression of the inner life being lived "here and now" is not lacking but is restricted in deference to the presentation of external circumstances and events. In each of these instances it is limited to one phrase that characterizes the psychic state of the person involved in the action: "extreme alarm," "in his tormented soul," "taken unawares and confused." But again in *Zweikampf* as well as in *Kohlhaas* there are passages where the presentation of psychic conditions has precedence over that of external event, as for example: "As she saw Squire Friedrich's mother . . . enter, Lady Littegarde rose from her chair with that expression of dignity that was peculiar to her, and which became even more moving because of the anguish which had spread over her entire being" (*Der Zweikampf*). And conversely in *The Marquise of O . . .* there are passages consisting of pure reporting of external action: "In a short time the square was subdued, and the commandant . . . retreated with failing strength towards the portal just as the Russian officer, very flushed, stepped from it. . . ."

No further examples are needed to make it clear that in narrative fiction it is never a question of whether we are dealing with subjective or objective narration. For here there exists no subject-object correspondence between the narrated and the narrative act —no relation and in turn no correlation. The difference we sensed between the two types of passages is grounded in the fact that at one time the characters are depicted in acts which are directed outward, as being in the stream of external occurrences, whereas at another time they are portrayed more in their subjective experiencing, in the quiet (or disquiet) of their inner being. In a work of narrative literature both types of narration alternate with one another, just as straight reporting and dialogue alternate. Now, as one of the stages in the development of narrative literature, we do have the phenomenon that the descriptive presentation of psychic life was increasingly cultivated in the course of the nineteenth century. Both the technique of rendering the novel into extensive dialogue as well as the use of the narrated monologue to render not only streams of conscious, but also of subconscious experience (as in Joyce), are narrative forms whose function is just such presentation of the psychic life. But no one will argue that the mental associations of Leopold Bloom and Stephen Daedalus in *Ulysses* are more subjectively—or in the sense of the dramatization theory more objectively—narrated than the novels of Kleist and Kafka. In all these cases a fictional field is produced, a fictive world of persons and events. And only this one criterion is decisive in the choice and evaluation of these respective stylistic devices in narration: namely whether the persons are seen and portrayed more "from without" or more "from within," i.e., more as objects presented as acting, feeling, and thinking in such and such a way, or more as subjects who, so to speak, "present themselves." Between these two narrative techniques many modulations can be found, both within the individual work and with respect to the styles characteristic of various periods and authors. The mode of presentation can evoke the appearance of an "objective" reality-report, i.e., one directed toward the matter to be depicted; in this case the presentation of the persons involved in the action is less oriented toward bringing their subjective experiencing to view. External events have priority over the persons. And this capacity of narrative literature to portray events in chronicle form is one of the reasons, perhaps the primary reason, why the categorical difference between statement and fictional narration has remained unnoted, and that the fictional "narrator" was likened to the historical narrator or reporter and was thus personified, conceived of as a genuine statement-subject, hence leaving the logical and phenomenological conditions of literature undisclosed. For even between the "most objective" fictional narration, i.e., straight narration directed toward the presentation of a given state of affairs, and an ever so concrete and vivid historical narration there runs the intransgressible boundary which separates fiction from the reality statement. However tautological this may sound, this boundary-line is fixed and established solely in that a given material becomes "fictionalized": the persons in action are portrayed as being so "here and now," and therefore necessarily as experiencing "here and now," concomitant to which is the experience of fiction, of non-reality. As was already discussed in detail in the section on verb tenses, this takes place precisely through those narrational forms which cannot logically occur in the reality statement: the verbs of inner action, monologue, and *erlebte Rede,* and further through abundant use and elaboration of such forms as can appear in reality-reports (e.g., in eye-witness accounts), but which in that context are nevertheless restricted by the limitations which are always posed by the presence of a real I-Origo, by the presence of the genuine statement-subject: dialogue and situation verbs. However, even the most paltry fictionalization, which only minimally renders the fictive characters' I-originarity in any concrete fashion, even this is divorced from the realm of the reality statement. Even such minimal fictionalization "reduces the realness" of the narrator to a function, and in place of a polar-relational correspondence establishes the functional correspondence between the narrated and the narrative act, to which the concepts "subjective" and "objective" are no longer applicable.

From the point of view of the "theory of subjectivity" it may be objected that this exposition as such does not refer to narrative modes of the kind we have analyzed in examples 1 to 3, but only to the type represented either by the Jean Paul passages, where the narrator manifests his presence through the words "I" and "we" and through addressing his readers, or by narrative modes which are highly reflective. But here is one of those points where we have opportunity to refer to the method of the logical study of literature, and at the same time to the way in which such study can and must prove fruitful for the evaluation of the aesthetic problems of literature. As we have done above, in connection with the questions of temporal structures, so can we also refer here to the methodology of modern linguistics, and moreover in a more fundamental way than in the previous instance. The logical investigation of literature corresponds to "universal grammar" (as this has been construed by de Saussure, Marty, Hjelmslev, Jespersen, et al.) insofar as it seeks to disclose those universal structural laws and forms which make it possible to recognize apparently disparate phenomena as being only modifications of the same structure. But here, it seems to me, the logic of literature is in a more favorable position than is the logic of grammar. Works of literature exist as self-contained structures that are already manifest. And whereas there exists a rather vast number of languages, the multitude of individual works of literature, on the other hand, is divided into only three structural forms, to one of which not only every actual, but also every conceivable individual literary work must and does conform. And even if we ourselves trace these three structural forms, i.e., epic, drama, and lyric back to only two, namely mimesis and lyric, nevertheless in the course of such tracing the method of universal poetological investigation still prevails. This method must be preserved in the investigation of even the most specialized literary forms, if any system of literature may be propounded at all.

Applied to our present problem, this means that, from the perspective of the logic of fictional narration, even the apparent subjectivity of such narrative styles as that of Jean Paul, Sterne, Fielding, and also that of other, even non-humoristic authors, must dissolve as such and prove to be a different phenomenon. Should such disclosure prove unsuccessful, that would be an indication that our proof of the functional character of fictional narration is not valid and correct. However, should it succeed, as we hope to be able to show, then the functional character of epic narration and those characteristics peculiar to it will be all the more clearly, and all the more subtly, delineated.

Let us begin with our example 5, a passage from Jean Paul's fragment *Der Komet*. According to traditional terminology this text is a typical example of subjective narration, because the narrative I, and even the authorial I intrude into the narration, thereby "subjectifying the objective." Let us now compare example 5 with example 4, a passage from the same novel. We have intentionally used one and the same work from which to choose one passage where the narrator-I does not intrude (where the narrational form would therefore be "objective"), and another where such intrusion is largely the case. Now, let us once more conduct a little experiment. Let us introduce such first-person intrusion into example 4, as, for instance: "And now these sundry masters set themselves into motion and onto their stools; a Titian, Fra Bartholomeo di Sa. Marco, a Da Vinci—the reader may think of their great namesakes, as do I, or he may not—a Kaufmann (probably Angelika Kaufmann, for who of us, upon hearing this name, would not remember the lovely artist in Rome?). . . ." Does the scene depicted seem less objective because of these first-person intrusions and addresses to the reader than it would without them? If the passage from Fontane (example 2) were to read: "Treibel was an early riser, at least for a Kommerzienrat (for to the extent that I have the honor of knowing such people, they are generally speaking not early risers), and he never got into his office later than 8 A.M. . . . As a rule his wife appeared very shortly after him, but today she was late . . ."—would the scene be in any way altered? That such, as we immediately note, is not the case indicates already that no change in the sense of a more subjective narrative form is effected through first-person intrusions into a third-person fictional text. For such intrusions by no means cause a relation to be brought about between this I and the depicted persons and events, such that they would be brought into its field of experience. They are and they remain just as fictive as they would be without first-person intrusion; that is, they are just as little the object of a statement with it as without it. Rather, both with and without first-person intrusion the depicted persons and events are the product, the function of the narrative act. Therefore, when in example 5 Jean Paul takes delight in saying that Worble, when he was installed as the prince's tutor, was one and a half years older than he, Jean Paul himself, was when he published his *Grönländische Prozesse,* we just as little as the author establish any kind of relation between him and the figure Worble. Similarly, we also do not establish any relation between the sister Libette's behavior, either—her "getting into everything, and indeed in many areas being quite prominent"—and the joy which the narrator, in first-person form ("which particularly pleases me") expresses over this. In other words, these figures are not on this account more "subjectively" narrated than are Kafka's inn-keeper, the marquise of O . . . and the Kommerzien-rat Treibel. For only where we are dealing with an experienced, i.e., a real state of affairs does the concept "subjective" make any sense. But is Jean Paul's conception of his characters Worble and Libette more subjective than Fontane's, Kleist's, or Kafka's conception of theirs? Is this part of his novel more subjective than those others where his narration is without any first-person intrusions? If, for example, Libette, who got into everything, were a real person, and the account of her a reality account, then the remark "which especially pleases me" would have the status of a critical comment about a state of affairs which as such would exist objectively, i.e., independently of anyone stating about it, and which precisely for this reason could then be judged by him. Only now do we approach the significance and function of so allegedly subjective a narrative style as that of Jean Paul.

That this style is a play of "romantic irony" is no new conclusion.

The intrusion of the author into his narrative, or the entrance of the poet, the director, or a feigned public into the (romantic) drama was always designated as a disruption of the illusion. But it was not clearly enough perceived that thereby the illusion of fiction is far less disrupted than stressed, underscored. And the reason for this can be disclosed only once the difference between a fictive experience and the experience of reality, between fictional narration and reality statement has been logically elucidated. This can be demonstrated better with epic than with dramatic fiction, since we can present this difference more exactly in the problem of narration versus statement. The appearance of the first-person narrative form in pure fiction, in the third-person narrative, evokes for that moment the appearance of the fictive figures' being real persons. The creative narrative function is occasionally interrupted by a statement form, and the field of fiction becomes the experience-field of a statement-subject, of a real I-Origo, whose narrating—for this moment—is not fictional, but historical. But this signifies a play on the narrative function, and in turn therefore on fiction itself. Fiction is momentarily feigned as a reality report, but this without our being cast from its sphere. For in cases like these the reader nevertheless knows that he is reading a novel and, precisely because of this, even ever so impetuous first-person capriccios of the "narrator" will not only not disrupt the illusion of fiction for him, but will first make him smile to himself in awareness of this illusion—just as the narrator, in the moment he appears as the author, smiles to himself in awareness of this role. In this play on historical and fictional narration—for a play on one is at the same time a play on the other—humoristic style has, if not its ideological basis, at least one of its most subtle possibilities of expression. One denies oneself access to the poetic and aesthetic structure of a humoristic novel of this type if one takes the "subjectivity" of first-person intrusion seriously and understands it to be the commentary of a genuine statement-subject, as subjectification of the objective. In a fictional text such intrusion is flourish, arabesque, a play of the narrative function turned upon itself.[100] It has no "existential" significance, i.e., it is not referred to a real I, regardless of whether the "narrator" may comport himself as such. First-person intrusions in the third-person novel, i.e., in pure fiction, just as little render it a first-person novel as, for example, the inclusion of poems in a novel would render it a "lyrical" novel (as we shall demonstrate below). For whereas the first-person narrative as a literary form does not stand subject to the logical laws of fiction, nevertheless within fiction these laws are so powerful that they can never be suspended or rendered ineffective "in earnest," but only "in play," and this means not at all. Non-reality, once it is constituted through the fictive persons, cannot admit reality into any area within its realm. That is, non-reality cannot assimilate a real I-Origo and thereby become its genuine field of experience.

By way of objection, though one could refer to our own example from Stifter's *Hochwald*, it could be pointed out that nevertheless such mixtures of historical and fictional narration do occur. And just for this reason we must now return to this example, because in contrast it clearly illustrates the "pseudo" first-person form of a humoristic style such as Jean Paul's, and in turn the irrevocable structure of fiction.

We directly sense that the first-person intrusion in Jean Paul does not suspend the structure of fiction, and that, on the other hand, this is precisely the case with the two Stifter passages analyzed above. In both instances the authors introduce themselves into the narration and thereby set themselves in a relation to their own novel. But wherein lies the difference between the two? With Stifter the first-person intrusion occurs outside of the field of fiction established by the novel. When in the extensive introduction, and more briefly again at the beginning of chapter two, he describes the setting of the novel as a place known to him, he is not yet narrating the novel proper; and in the second chapter, once the action of the novel, i.e., once fictional narration has already begun, it is once more interrupted. This means that the real I-Origo which appears here does not posit itself in a relation to the figures in the novel; and it is just for this reason that it is a genuine, real I-Origo, namely that of the author. The aesthetic effect of such narration is that of what might be called an involuntary disruption of the illusion, one which has no special meaning or specific artistic intent, but arises from the author's so to speak naïve impulse toward historical and geographical exactness. Here the awareness of fiction is not strengthened, as it is in the humoristic disruption of illusion common to romantic irony, but rather the fiction, so to speak, remains indifferent toward this historical interruption. Indeed, in terms of both the fictional work and the reader it is a matter of indifference whether the setting of the novel was once known to the author or not. Similar naïve and involuntary disruptions of the fictional illusion are to be found in Balzac, who indeed considered the writing of novels to be "history," believing that through unrestrained montage-technique in his *Comédie humaine* he was presenting his own *histoire contemporaine*. And we might also refer to the strategic and historical-philosophical remarks which Tolstoy, without any concern as to the continuity of the novel, inserts into *War and Peace*. All of these three great prose writers are, then, representatives of their "historical" century, a century in which it is not merely coincidental that one finds such "naïve" combining of historical and fictional narration. But just such examples as these are instructive for the literary theorist, because they demonstrate that even within the same fictional work these two kinds of narration separate like oil and water, and that they in no way blend to an artistic unity. Particularly not when this occurs in naïve, uncritical ignorance of those laws which govern fictional and historical (i.e., statement) as being categorically separate types of narration. The example from Stifter demonstrates that the field of fiction cannot become related to the field of real experience through the naïve intrusion of the reality statement. It is only symptomatic that here the reality statement does not set itself into a relation to the fictive persons, and that therefore fiction remains undisrupted, or more precisely: it is disrupted only insofar as it is simply interrupted.

We have already seen that in the passage from Jean Paul it was a completely different case, one of fiction's remaining undisrupted by the first-person intrusions which occur there. In contradistinction to the Stifter text, here the real I-Origo does set itself into a relation to the fictive persons; but nevertheless they do not attain any relation to it. Rather, we become all the more clearly aware of their fictivity. The cause for this lies in the non-naïve, consciously humoristic way in which it is done.[101]

Even the subject-matter of *Der Komet* renders this a distinctly humoristic, indeed comical novel. And even if we have been able to show that here, with the aid of first-person intrusion, the narrative function engages in a play upon itself (and in turn a play on fiction), nevertheless it can be objected that such first-person intrusions by no means occur only in Jean Paul's comical novels, but also abound in his serious, sentimental novels. Such an objection would therefore imply that the conclusion we have drawn from the *Komet* passage, namely that of the narrative function's play on fiction, is obviously too narrow and does not suffice to refute the notion of the subjectivity of such a narrative style as being erroneous. But if we examine the function of first-person intrusion in a novel such as *Titan*, for example, we will see that the more narrowly comic-humoristic novel represents only a special case of a narrative technique which we can term humoristic in a broader sense because it incorporates the problem of fictional narration as a problem *per se*, and it does so regardless of the subject-matter of the novel. We must dwell a moment longer on this type of the humoristic novel—which began with Cervantes and became more refined in the eighteenth century, the century of critical philosophy—because this significant phenomenon in the history of literature concretely illustrates those systematic relations which concern us here. For the logical structure of literature is not an abstraction from phenomena; rather it can only directly be inferred from them. And conversely, the laws we find will serve to elucidate these phenomena. On the one hand, we derive the structure of the humoristic novel through the distinction between reality statement and fictional narration, and on the other it is just this type of novel which provides the clearest means of gaining a knowledge of this distinction. Consequently it also furnishes the material for the exact description of fictional narration, i.e., of epic fiction itself.

Jean Paul's *Titan* is just as little a humoristic novel in the narrow sense of "comic" as is Henry Fielding's *History of Tom Jones*. Though dissimilar in style and content, these works do share one common trait: both have interpolations which are concerned with the narrating of the novel *per se*. In Fielding this is carried out both more systematically and more simply than in Jean Paul, and for this reason we shall begin with the former. Fielding consciously strove to be "the founder of a new province of writing" (II,1), and this awareness is clearly reflected in that he realized the special nature of fictional narration, that it obeyed different laws than did all other narration, "so I am at liberty to make what laws I please therein" (II,1). He was concerned with solving the problem that on the one hand the novel should give a picture of reality, "a history," not a "romance" or "novel" in the narrow sense (and therefore he titles the novel *History of Tom Jones*), and on the other that it can only present a fictive reality, for which the author himself must make his own laws. He must do so precisely because narrated reality—just because it exists as narrated—is not real reality, nor can it, basically, "represent" such at all. In working on this problem, Fielding encountered a phenomenon which otherwise had not occupied theorists of the novel until the present time, namely that of the representation of time. The relation between fictive and real or historical time is one of his fundamental concerns. And he tries to express this by putting the narrated time as a heading above the title of each individual chapter: "Containing the time of a year," "containing about three weeks," "two days," "twelve hours," etc. He saw a problem here precisely because while telling his story he noticed that time could not be narrated, that in fiction the consciousness of time is lost, since fiction does not merely name and date events, as does historical narration, but rather evokes the semblance of life. And this semblance, just as does real life, runs its course without reflection on the temporal span in which it is taking place. He noticed this, but without arriving at a clear comprehension of the logical and structural constituents of this phenomenon which are inherent within fictional narration, when he says: "When any extraordinary scene presents itself, we shall spare no pains nor paper to open it at large to our readers, but if whole years pass without there proceeding anything worthy of his notice . . . we shall leave such periods of time totally unobserved" (II,1). He did not notice that with this sentence he suspended that narrated time which he wanted to designate with his chapter-headings, that neither the narrator nor the reader pays attention to the time in which the narrated events and experiences unfold, since "narrating-time" [*Erzählzeit*] is not "narrated time" [*erzählte Zeit*]. Indeed, he did not note that it is not at all time which is narrated, but action, life, and that therefore the chapter-headings designating temporal stretches are superfluous—in his novel as well as in any other. But Fielding's problem was not that of the representation of time as a category of experience (it has become such only in the modern stage in the development of the novel); rather, for him it was a criterion and a sort of crux for the fictional character of the reality portrayed in the novel. This is an uncommonly astute observation in this epoch (1745), which for all its technical pragmatism in literary endeavors nonetheless sought to achieve a knowledge of that locus within the system of thought and language which is peculiar to fiction. And it is from this perspective that we are to judge those theoretical and reflective interpolations with which he introduces each of the eighteen books of *Tom Jones*. They contain his theory of the novel, commentary on the differences and similarities between history and the novel and so on, and by consciously incorporating this critical theory into the novel itself he renders the latter humoristic, and this quite apart from the novel's subject-matter. That the basic attitude in *Tom Jones* is a humoristic one lies neither in the theoretical observations nor in the story as such. In itself, neither is humoristic in the proper sense of the term. But the fundamentally humoristic tone is achieved in that through these theoretical comments we are continually kept aware that a novel is not reality, but illusion, semblance, fiction: a life depicted not as life, but—as Novalis was to say later—as a book. However non-humorous in content that semblance of reality may be which the novel narrates, it nevertheless appears in a humoristic light precisely in that it is a "made" reality, and its creator can play with it, can suspend it and then re-establish it. That is, this semblance of reality is humoristic because it need not take itself seriously, so to speak. Thus, we ought to find things like references to chapter divisions, for example, only in humoristic novels: that is, reminders of the fact that what is narrated there is only the content of a book, and therefore is not laden with the gravity and dead seriousness, the cruel arbitrariness of real life. Again and again we read: "As we have seen in the chapter before," or "this being the most tragical event in our whole history we have to treat it in a special chapter," and the like. Here it is clear that these intrusions of the narrator into the narrative are falsely construed, in poetological terms, if one designates them as subjective style. It is not a matter of the narrator's subjective interest *per se,* in his capacity as narrator or author, but instead just the opposite: it is a particularly "objective" attitude the author has toward his work, the consciousness of the free play which can be engaged in with the substance-less, stylized, fictive reality of the novel with its division into chapters, its arbitrary abridgments, contradictions, and expansions.

From Fielding's theoretical and creative problems we can see that this sovereign aesthetic humor also stamps those of Jean Paul's novels which are not expressly humorous. In *Titan,* too—as in *Komet* or *Wuz*—there is a "play" upon the narrator and his product; the narrator makes it known that this world is there only because of him, i.e., by virtue of the fact that it is narrated. "I think the corner I've cut for man from Whiston's comet map is wide enough. Before going on I will stipulate that I occasionally will be permitted to call Don Gaspard simply 'the knight,' without tagging on the whole golden fleece" (*Titan,* First Jubilee). And so neither *Titan* nor *Hesperus* nor *Die unsichtbare Loge* lack those elements of humoristic style characteristic of the epoch: alleged discussions of the origin and publication-history of the respective novel, for example, the extensive "Inaugural lecture for *Titan* (9th Cycle at the close of the First Jubilee), or the many explanations of book and chapter titles.

We have not been concerned here with an intensive analysis of the humoristic style characteristic of Jean Paul and the English authors named. Rather, we have referred to the narrative technique so common to that epoch because it allows the essence of the epic narrative function to emerge quite clearly. And it is not merely coincidental that the representatives of this technique understood, interpreted, and artistically evaluated it as being that characteristic peculiar to fictional as distinguished from historical narration (as we have only briefly sketched here). The sport Jean Paul makes of his characters, in the humorous as well as in the serious works (the boundary between these two types being fluid in his works as a whole) has a cause which he was more or less consciously aware of: that he repeatedly delighted in calling to mind the unique "creative act" of the novel's narrator, not to narrate *about* people, but to narrate *them*, i.e., by means of narration to produce them in the "subjectivity" of their existence. Such a process has its sole logical locus in narrative literature, whose laws it then determines. And the source—or one of the sources—of epic humor are precisely those instances where the poet does not completely submit to the law of narration, i.e., where he does not totally disappear into the narrated, but rather becomes aware of this law. By its very nature the play on fiction can only occur in the humoristic novel, for non-humoristic narration would negate both its product, fiction, and itself, if it were not to take itself seriously, ie., if it were itself to become aware of its fictivity, or if it were to make others aware of it. And just for this reason epic humor is an especially good means of illustrating fictional narration, which emerges in its uniqueness precisely in those instances where it is manipulated not "naïvely," but "critically" (in the Kantian sense).

What a humoristic style of this kind illustrates, however, is the fact that it does not properly define this state of affairs to call it subjective, despite all the first-person intrusions. Doubtless we do sense the arabesque play of Jean Paul's narrative technique, the narrative function's play upon itself, to be a "digression from the point" (as he himself has expressed it), namely, as verbose. But there are other types of narration which do not form a play upon themselves, but which we could nevertheless experience as verbose, and which, according to our own particular tastes, we might in some circumstances find tedious.

Consider heavily *reflective narration,* which more or less directly interprets the action and characters: it explains, expounds upon, and reveals the broader connections behind them, thereby often seeming to "digress from the point." But if we examine this narrative mode more closely, the essence of fictional narration in its categorical distinction from statement will be all the more clearly discernible. In this context it is of particular importance that one not allow oneself to be deceived by initial impressions. This happens quite easily if one does not penetrate to the structural elements involved here. Let us once more cite several examples:

Example 1:
Wilhelms Gedanken wandten sich nun bald auf seine eigenen Verhältnisse, und er fühlte sich nicht wenig beunruhigt. Der Mensch kann in keine gefährlichere Lage versetzt werden, als wenn durch äußere Umstände eine große Veränderung seines Zustandes bewirkt wird, ohne daß seine Art zu denken und zu empfinden darauf vorbereitet ist. Es gibt alsdann eine Epoche ohne Epoche, und es entsteht nur ein desto größerer Widerspruch, je weniger der Mensch bemerkt, daß er zu dem neuen Zustande noch nicht ausgebildet sei.
Wilhelm sah sich in einem Augenblick frei, in welchem er mit sich selbst noch lange nicht einig werden konnte. Seine Gesinnungen waren edel, seine Absichten lauter. . . .
(Goethe, *Wilhelm Meisters Lehrjahre*, 5. Buch, Kap. 1)

Example 2:
"Die meisten Menschen, selbst die vorzüglichsten, sind nur beschränkt; jeder schätzt gewisse Eigenschaften an sich und andern; nur die begünstigt er, nur die will er ausgebildet wissen."

(Ebd., 8. Buch, Kap. 5)

Example 3:
Wenn Ulrich hätte sagen sollen, wie er eigentlich sei, er wäre in Verlegenheit geraten. . . . War er ein starker Mensch? Das wußte er nicht, darüber befand er sich vielleicht in einem verhängnisvollen Irrtum. Aber sicher war er immer ein Mensch gewesen, der seiner Kraft vertraute. Auch jetzt zweifelte er nicht daran, daß dieser Unterschied zwischen dem Haben der eigenen Erlebnisse und Eigenschaften und ihrem Fremdbleiben nur ein Haltungsunterschied sei. . . . Ganz einfach gesprochen, man kann sich zu den Dingen, die einem widerfahren oder die man tut, mehr allgemein oder mehr persönlich verhalten. Man kann einen Schlag außer als Schmerz auch als Kränkung empfinden, wodurch er unerträglich wächst; aber man kann ihn auch sportlich aufneh-

men, als ein Hindernis. . . . Und gerade diese Erscheinung, daß ein Erlebnis seine Bedeutung . . . erst durch seine Stellung in einer Kette folgerichtiger Handlungen erhält, zeigt jeder Mensch, der es nicht als ein nur persönliches Geschehnis, sondern als eine Herausforderung seiner geistigen Kraft ansieht. . . .

(Robert Musil, *Der Mann ohne Eigenschaften*, I, Kap. 39) *

These three passages, whose number could be multiplied at random, all have one common trait: they are "verbose" in that

* *Example 1*
Wilhelm's thoughts soon turned to his own situation, and he felt himself not a little ill at ease. A person cannot be put into a more dangerous situation than when through external circumstances a great change is effected in his condition without his way of thinking and feeling being prepared for it. Then there is a new era without a new era, and the contradiction that arises becomes the more great the less the person notices that he is not yet equal to his new condition.

Wilhelm saw himself free in a moment when he could not yet be one with himself. His thoughts were noble, his aspirations pure. . . .

(Goethe, *Wilhelm Meister's Apprenticeship*, Book 5, Ch. 1)

Example 2
"Most people, even the most accomplished ones, are limited. Each values certain qualities in himself and in others, and only these qualities does he encourage, only these will he see cultivated."

(*Wilhelm Meister's Apprenticeship*, Book 8. Ch. 5)

Example 3
If Ulrich would have had to say what kind of a person he really was, he would have been at a loss. . . . Was he a strong person? That he didn't know; in this respect he might have been fatefully mistaken. But certainly he had always been a man who had confidence in his own strength. Even now he did not doubt that this distinction between possessing one's own experiences and qualities and their remaining alienated from one was only a difference in attitude. . . . Quite simply put, a person can take those things that befall him, or that he does, in either a more general or a more personal fashion. One can feel a blow not only as pain, but also as a personal offense, whereby it increases insufferably; or one can be sporting about it and accept it as a hurdle. . . . And exactly this phenomenon, that an experience acquires its meaning . . . only through its position in a chain of consistent acts, is seen in every person who regards experience not only as something that happens to one personally, but as something which challenges his spiritual strength. . . .

(Robert Musil, *The Man Without Qualities*, I, Ch. 39)

they are reflective. Are they digressive, too? Do they digress "from the subject," and might one be tempted to exhort them to "get to the point?" In so formulating it, we note that this is an inapt question. Once more we can illuminate this state of affairs by applying the comparison to the reality statement. Only with respect to the latter does the injunction to get to the point make any sense. For there "the point," the matter at hand, always exists independently of its being reported, and as such it cannot be "influenced" either by the report itself or by the reporter. Let us assume that the first sentence from the *Wilhelm Meister* passage, "Wilhelm's thoughts soon turned to his own situation," is a reality report, such that one person is telling someone else about a given circumstance in the life of an acquaintance of his, Wilhelm. Wilhelm himself might have told this person that his thoughts had turned to his own situation. In this case the sentences which follow in the passage would represent the reflections of the person reporting. They would refer only to himself, and would be an expression of his subjective way of viewing people and things. They would have nothing to do with the person and the matter in question here, and the recipient of the report could then appeal to the speaker, saying "Come now, it doesn't interest me in the least what you think in general about sudden changes that can appear in a person's life. Get to the point. What was the matter with Wilhelm, and how did his situation straighten itself out?" For a real person who at one point or another in his life feels and acts in such and such a way is not described any more closely, or in any more depth, when another person reporting about his situation augments his report with ever so perceptive philosophical and psychological observations. (Even in cases where one seeks to understand and interpret the behavior of a real person through psychological interpretations of his character, his social circumstances, etc., which could have determined such behavior, these interpretations are always the subjective conception of the person reporting and have nothing to do with the person himself who is the object of these state-ments.) We sense immediately that these referential relationships present themselves quite differently when we are dealing with Wilhelm Meister *qua* figure in a novel. Confronted with such an observation as "A person cannot be put into a more dangerous situation . . . ," we are not tempted to cry "get to the point." For then we would have to be able to account for what "the point" is here. And, as we tried to show by comparing fictional and state-ment structure: these relations in fiction are not assignable. Just as temporal and spatial relations in fiction escape all assignability because here it is only a matter of a conceptual awareness of such relations and not of these themselves, so also does the question as to what the "point" at hand is in a novel elude clear-cut, fixed assign-ing. In the novel we cannot separate the person Wilhelm Meister from the narration of this person. For he is not a person *about* whom something is being narrated. In this context the observa-tions that accompany the sentence which says that he soon turned to his own situation and felt not a little ill at ease, are not any subjective reflections and digressions of a person reporting about Wilhelm, reflections which would have to do with this reporter, but not with Wilhelm himself. Rather, such observation serves to shape the figure Wilhelm in precisely the same manner as do sentences which render his actions, speech, and thought. Just as little as we can distinguish a "narrator" from that which or that about which he narrates in the sentence "Wilhelm's thoughts soon turned to his own situation," or for example in the concrete situation depicted by the sentence "The count gave his wife his hand and led her down-stairs" (Book 3, Ch. 2), so also can no such boundary be indicated for the reflective type of sentence. The logical relations present here will become clearer if we compare example 1 with example 3, the passage from a comptemporary novel, Musil's *Man Without Qualities*.

This passage is similar to the one from *Wilhelm Meister*. Here, too, the narrative lapses from direct concern with the character Ulrich into a discussion of general problems and conditions, beginning with the sentence: "Quite simply put, a person can take those things that befall him, or that he does, in either a more general or a more personal fashion." But we note a certain difference between the older and the more modern text. It consists in that in the latter passage the generalizing reflections seem to be somewhat more intimately connected with the character Ulrich than are those in the *Wilhelm Meister* passage with the character Wilhelm. Just as little reference is made in the later sentences from the Musil passage themselves to the thoughts of the characters portrayed as is made in the case of the Goethe passage. Nevertheless, these sentences do appear to be more Ulrich's thoughts than those in the Goethe passage appear to be those of Wilhelm. But this is not a principal difference; it is merely one of style. It immediately betrays to us that the Musil novel is the more modern of the two works. We have already pointed out on several occasions that in the course of the nineteenth century the techniques of fictionalization had become more and more refined, the presentation of the psychic life came increasingly more to employ the devices of directly subjectifying the characters. That is, the fictive I-originarity of the figures became more and more explicitly developed, culminating in the bold methods of Joyce. But even if the sentence "Wilhelm's thoughts soon turned to his own situation, and he felt himself not a little ill at ease" does have more the style of a statement in the proper sense than does the sentence "If Ulrich would have had to say what kind of a person he really was, he would have been at a loss. . . . Was he a strong person?"—still the difference is merely one of degree. That we cannot as readily transpose the second sentence into a reality statement as we did the first is due only to its particular narrative style. That is, here the style of fictional narration emerges clearly right away. But nevertheless the *Wilhelm Meister* sentence has the same structural features.

Upon close examination we see that it, too, exhibits those characteristics of fictional narration which are not possible in the reality
statement, such as "he felt not a little ill at ease" (which as reality
statement would change "felt" to "was"). The verb of inner action
shows Wilhelm in the fictive Here and Now of his thinking and
feeling existence; it merely accomplishes this with less finely drawn
contours than does the form of the modern novel. In other words,
the figure Wilhelm appears less subjectified than the figure Ulrich.
And since the figure is portrayed in a more "objective" style of
presentation, so also do the further reflective observations in the
Goethe passage seem more detached from this figure than in
Musil, more "objective," if you will. But we cannot confuse this
designation of a stylistic difference with the proper meaning of the
concepts "subjective" and "objective." Subjectivity or respectively
objectivity does not refer to the author, who in the case of the reality report is indeed identical with the narrator, but who is not
identical with him in fictional narration (as little as is the painter
with his brush). As was demonstrated above, these concepts in
fiction merely refer to the aspect under which the fictive persons
are made to appear, and the noticeable difference is only one of
narrative style. Therefore we can as little in the Goethe as in the
Musil text entreat the narrator to "get to the point." Both forms
of reflective observation are interpretative, fictively integrated configurations and not statements, differing only in degree, but not in
category.[102] Thus the question what the "point" in a novel is cannot be answered because it cannot be posed. The example from
Musil shows clearly (elucidating the Goethe passage in this respect) that in no way is any "objective fact" like that of the reality
report, i.e., a given action, event, situation, etc., the "point," the
"content" of a novel, such a content as would in any way be sep-
arable from its artistic presentation. For which reason we ultimately cannot reproduce the "content" of a novel. When we do
this, or presume to do it, we merely seek to indicate some points

of reference, with the aid of which we can recall the novel's "content;" and there are cases where a single sentence can reproduce the "content," thus understood, of even the longest novel.

As to the behavior of "digressive" observations in fictional narration—and ultimately to the behavior of fiction itself—we may shed light upon this from another side by comparing example 1 with example 2 above. This, too, is from *Wilhelm Meister*, but here the quotation marks indicate that it is a piece of dialogue: one of Jarno's reflections made in a conversation with Wilhelm. It is the same general type as that of example 1, but since it is "put into the mouth" of one of the fictive persons we automatically would not categorize it as diffuse or even digressive. For we find ourselves in the dialogue system of the novel, which is one of the central components of the fictional system, or the fictional field. The reflections immediately appear as being the concerns of the fictive person, not those of the narrator (in the sense of the author). But just this phenomenon is proof—albeit indirect, but precisely on that account convincing—that even the narration done by the narrator as straight narration is an appurtenance of the fictive persons and not his own, so to speak. Goethe's narrative style is particularly well suited to demonstrate just this point. The characters' speech shows a style which is essentially no different from that of the straight narration. We can quite easily exchange the reflective observations in our two examples, i.e., make example 2 into straight narration and arrange example 1 as a piece of dialogue, beginning with the sentence: "A person cannot be put in a more dangerous position. . . ." This goes particularly well here because the style of the dialogues in *Wilhelm Meister* is less individualized for any given character. But even here it is not a matter of a difference in kind, but only in degree. Here the boundary between the material of straight narration and that of dialogue in the novel is only slightly defined. But exactly this reveals that the function of narration is ultimately none other than the formation of dialogue, and therefore also of soliloquy and narrated monologue. If it could at all be required that the narrator's presence "disappear" as much as possible, that the novel be reduced to a system of dialogue,[103] it was theoretically possible only because the narrative function in straight narration is only one in a composite of formational structures in fiction, and therefore can be integrated with other compositional structures. Such an integration is clearest in the case of the narrated monologue.

Above (pp. 84ff.), in connection with the questions of verb tense, the narrated monologue was decisive in instructing us about the relations of fictive I-originarity. It also provided the most conclusive proof that fictional narration establishes itself via the verbs of inner action. Naturally, it is in close connection with these relations and not merely coincidental that it serves us now in attaining a more complete knowledge of the fictional narrative function itself. It has already been noted several times that the form of the narrated monologue cannot always be clearly distinguished from the "voice of the narrator." In other words, the boundary where the narrator ceases to speak, as it were, and delegates speech to the figures, cannot always be pinpointed.[104] The studies which have been made about the occurrence of this form in medieval literature[105] must move precisely on this boundary-line, since in medieval literature the narrated monologue doubtless was not refined to a consciously employed technique, but rather to a certain degree was suffused in the narrator. But it could only be suffused in him because this narrator in the medieval epics, too, is a fictional narrative function. Thus E. Lerch has also pointed out that almost imperceptibly the interpreting voice of the narrator is heard along with the reproduction of the conscious or unconscious thoughts of the persons in the novel, in that he thinks their thoughts, but with his words.[106] Indeed, it is by no means sufficient to characterize the narrated monologue by saying that it is a means of presenting the mute thoughts of the characters' stream of consciousness from their own perspective.[107] Certainly there are forms where this is the predominant impression evoked:

> The way she said "Here is my Elizabeth!"—that annoys him. Why not "here's Elizabeth" simply? It was insincere. And Elizabeth didn't like it either. For he understood young people; he liked them. There was always something cold in Clarissa, he thought. . . .   (Virginia Woolf, *Mrs. Dalloway*)

But the narrational stratum which the narrated monologue can occupy is often very much broader. It can be so encompassing as to constitute the narrative function entirely, and it cannot be decided where the boundary is to be drawn which separates the "interior," i.e., the psychic processes which are developed in this presentational form, from an exterior, i.e., from objectifying interpretative acts. Our Musil example displays this phenomenon very clearly. The general observations, which are not, as in the above passage, concerned with a person in the novel who stands in close relation to the main character, are at once both Ulrich's and the narrator-*qua*-author's observations. But they are the narrator's only because they are Ulrich's, i.e., because they serve to mould his inner and outer situation. Which is a further criterion for the fact that what we have to deal with is the narrative act itself, and not a narrator.

What is important here is to make it clear that the narrated monologue can illuminate the essence of fictional narration as a function and not as a statement because it is the ultimate result which fictional narration is capable of producing, so to speak, from itself, a result to which the reality statement by its nature cannot attain. A form such as that of the Musil passage, which is comparable to the *Wilhelm Meister* piece in structure and content, shows that the reflections in this latter piece are not the concerns of an observer or narrator who is independent of the fictive action; rather, they serve only in the creation of the character, even if they do bear less of a formal connection with the figure than in the Musil passage. The character Wilhelm is as little "the point" as are Ulrich and Peter Walsh (*Mrs. Dalloway*) "the point" from which the narrative act can digress, as such a narration would if he were a real entity, namely a real person, and the narrative acts, therefore, not fictional but historical. That the latter assumption cannot at all be made in the case of Ulrich or Peter Walsh is due to a narrative style which is from the start more fictionalizing in its form. But there is no principal or structural difference here.

This becomes all the more clear when we return to the Kleist text and compare it with the other two. We can see that the broad, reflective narrative form signifies nothing other than an elaborated extension of the narrative function itself, differing only stylistically, but not categorically, from that of the other passages. When we read in the Kleist passage: "and with great self-satisfaction she pondered what a victory she, through the power of her guiltless conscience, had achieved over her brother," we must admittedly listen more closely in order to note that here, too, narration and narrated coalesce, and we cannot ascertain where the boundary runs which separates the more or less spontaneously accomplished psychic processes from the interpreting voice of the narrator. And this boundary cannot be specified, for it does not exist. In a fictional context the interpretation of psychic processes and these processes themselves are one and the same thing, and—as we have already demonstrated above by taking the opposite approach—another interpretative word would produce other psychic processes. For they exist only by virtue of their being narrated. The narration is the action, the action is the narration. And this holds just as much for the narration of external as for that of inner action.

Let us consult the Fontane text (p. 144ff.) in order to illustrate this once more. As a depiction of an external situation, it differs from the Kafka passage in its greater detail, and by exhibiting stronger fictionalizing aspects than the latter. Aside from the situation verbs (which are abundantly utilized in every work of epic literature), such fictionalizing aspects in the presentation of external situations are to be seen—above all in modern texts—in the use of deictic adverbs, such as: "The setting was like yesterday," and also in the detailed description of the actions and goings-on, in short, the description of the animated "setting." In such depictions the coalescence, the identity between narration and narrated cannot be demonstrated as well, because from the very outset we experience nothing but this identity here. That is, we cannot distinguish exactly between compositional elements which are interpretative and those which are more descriptive or chronicle-like in nature. And of course just this is the consequence of the fact that that which is narrated is fictive. Adjectival expressions such as "the most immaculate toilet," "the trivial newspapers," etc., designate qualities that are so bound to the portrayed entities themselves that they are not especially conspicuous as interpretative features which would be contrasted to the pure naming of the entity (as would to a greater or lesser degree be the case in the reality statement, where for example these concepts could be contrasted to an opposite judgment, where the newspaper might be judged by one person to be trivial, but by another to be rich in content). But this small passage nevertheless does contain one feature in which we can see the process of this coalescence itself taking place, a feature which therefore not merely coincidentally betrays much about Fontane's particular style. When we read the sentence "only instead of the cockatoo, which was still missing, one saw Miss Honig outside, who was walking around the pond leading the Frau Kommerzeinrat's Bolognese dog on a leash," we are compelled to smile in amusement. We find this humorous. But it is a different kind of humorous style from that of Jean Paul. It does not come about through a play of the narrative function on itself, on fiction. Fontane's sentence is completely "matter-of-fact": the cockatoo was not there yet; outside Miss Honig was walking the dog. One tiny word, one small coupling sequence in the sentence is what makes us smile: the word "instead," and the way it connects the cockatoo and the lady in waiting. Whereas for example, the sentence "instead of the cockatoo one saw the Bolognese dog" would not occasion any amused smiles, it does have a comic-humorous effect to see a person put on a par with an animal in this way. But the humor here is very subtle and submerged. Ultimately it is directed at the Frau Kommerzienrat, in whose bourgeois eyes society animals and ladies in waiting stand on the same level of servitude, as in the same sentence Miss Honig stands in the service of the Frau Kommerzienrat's society animal, the little Bolognese dog. Thus the interpretative humor here is reduced to a single word, an adverb, and coalesces indistinguishably with the report-like form of depiction.

The Dialogue-System

In our attempt to demonstrate the distinction between fictional narration as a functional structure and reality statement as a relational or subject-object structure, we were already led to those elements of which narration is composed as soon as we introduced the discussion of narrated monologue. That dialogue belongs among these elements, indeed that as long as there is narrative literature it will form a central component of narrative substance, is self-evident. On the other hand, it is equally clear that it has not been given its full due. Precisely because dialogue appears to lend itself as a particularly simple narrative device does it require closer analysis.

At first glance dialogue appears to contrast so greatly to straight narration, i.e., to the descriptive or reflective reportorial form, that our demonstration of its coalescence with other compositional forms, above all with narrated monologue, appears to have no general validity. Nevertheless, it can be shown that such a somewhat traditional description of our reading experience, and in turn of the structure of a novel, does not correspond to the actual phenomenon. If we consult our reading experience, it informs us that we do not become conscious of any greatly noticeable difference between the substance of straight narration and that of dialogue. This does not mean that as we read we do not notice, and would not be able to establish in each instance what was straight narration and what was dialogue. The phenomenon is rather of a different nature, namely, grounded in the fact that *the narrative function appears as fluctuating in a particular way.* We have already observed this in the way in which the narrative function presents itself in the narrated monologue, where it at once disappears and becomes suffused into the figure, such that it can no longer be distinguished whether the figure is "spontaneously" presenting itself or whether it is being presented. But that is only a criterion which is quite considerably pronounced. This phenomenon of narrative fluctuation stamps fictional narration in every moment of its progression, since in every moment fictional narration produces life—at one instance more, at another less imbued with meaning. Always producing, engendering, it is always immanently in play within this life, these figures, and their world: now nearer, now farther off, now fusing entirely with them, now withdrawing from them again—but without "losing sight" of them, thus being able, so to speak, to "disappear" within these figures themselves, or to be absorbed by them. This occurs to an even more absolute degree in dialogue and monologue than in *erlebte Rede.* And it need scarcely be mentioned that these three forms are interrelated, and that they, in varied distribution and modulation, express the unique nature of fictional narration. Indeed, they are also the most valid proof that this narration is not a narrating of things as past, but rather one which always produces the semblance of present-time. Like the narrated monologue, dialogue, too, has as its indigenous locus only third-person narration, i.e., pure fiction. For only here can narration so fluctuate that "reporting" and dialogue blend within the unity of the narrative function. And this is possible only because the narrative act, too, is fictional, and is at every moment ready to "become" the fictive figures.

But when we examine the function of dialogue more closely, we see that it in itself is a confirmation of the "impersonal" functional character of epic narration, namely only one of the forms which the latter can assume. This can be seen in that conversation by no means only presents the characters themselves in their own being and existence; to a substantial degree it also assumes the purely depictional function of narration. In a novel it is not only straight reporting, but also dialogue which informs us as to various relations, external situations and events, and other persons. This applies in such a large measure already to Homer, the father of the Western epic, that just for this reason Aristotle particularly lauded him. Had Goethe, who saw in Richardson's epistolary novels a sign of the dramatization of the novel, not completely overlooked this phenomenon in Homer, he might possibly have modified his definition of the rhapsode. For when the narrator, as Aristotle advocates, speaks as little as possible "in his own person" (αὐτόν . . . δεῖ . . . λέγειν), but upon a short introduction immediately has a man or woman enter (*Poetics,* Ch. 24)—does this narrator really then appear as "one who is reciting what is completely past, a wise man who in tranquil circumspection is surveying past events" (Goethe, December, 1797)? As we have said, Homer himself rejects this definition of narration *qua* narrator, a definition which in more or less modified forms has been retained up to present-day literary theory. In the Homeric epics the compositional elements of narration are divided almost totally into address and reply, first-person narration, and soliloquy. That these speeches are not the psychological-existential presentation of psychic processes, as they are in modern epic literature, lies in the essence of the epic of antiquity, where events are not shaped and created (symptomatically or even symbolically) for the sake of the persons, but where the latter have the function of being the carriers of the events, functional parts of an event-filled world-scene. But, in the context of our investigations, this is not the essential element. The decisive factor is the recognition which the originator of the Western epic imparts, that the apportioning of even plot material to the speaking persons and the "narrator" divests the latter of precisely that character which has erroneously been associated with this concept, and through which association the concept of the narrator has itself given rise to false interpretation. When even Goethe, to some extent rescinding his earlier definition, says a few sentences later that "the rhapsodist should be a higher being who does not himself appear within his poem; best of all let him read behind a curtain, so that one would abstract from all personality elements and imagine himself as listening only to the voice of the muse in general," we sense precisely the fact that, to put it in our terminology, the "rhapsodist" is not a statement-subject, and that that which is wrought and created through narration has nothing to do with the narrator, the rhapsodist, such that "we perceive only the voice of the muse in general," the "spirit of narration," as one modern epic writer, Thomas Mann, has said. Indeed, we can see quite clearly from Homer's narrative form that fictional narration is a function which can assume now this, now that form, independently of that logic and grammar of language which governs the statement of a subject about an object. For this logic makes it impossible for reported action to be built up in the conversational exchanges of third persons, or even to be made known in monologue. He who in the Homeric epics speaks "to his sublime soul" is as little the object of a statement about the fact that he is speaking, as is the speaker in a drama, even though in the former case the character's speech is introduced by some kind of indication that he is speaking. The fact that such indicators can be lacking, as is surely not so with Homer, but is often enough the case with the modern novel, is in itself an indication that, to overstate it some-what, in fictional narration, narration itself is not what is of principal importance. This means: the narrative act is a formative, shaping function, of which one can just as well say that it is set beside other shaping functions such as dialogue, monologue, and *erlebte Rede*, as one can also say—indeed, more precisely—that, *fluctuating*, it assumes now this, now that form.

How within the nexus of a work of narrative fiction these forms interlace, so that in reading we are not at all attuned to the difference between straight narration and dialogue, can be demonstrated with a few examples:

Example 1:

"Schön, recht poetisch", nahm endlich Sorti das Wort, "aber aufführen"—"keine Drukker" platzte Ruprecht heraus.—"Zu viel Verwandlungen" meinte ein anderer. "Kein einziger brillanter Abgang. Aber was hat denn all das Teufelszeug mit meinem Gedichte zu schaffen?" fragte der erstaunte Otto in seiner poetischen Unschuld. "Wird sich schon geben, mein Liebster", entgegnete Sorti gelassen, "wird sich nach und nach schon geben mit der zunehmenden Bühnenkenntnis." Nun steckten alle die Nasen in das Heft, und ein jeder fing an, nach seiner Art daran zu mäkeln. Der Dialog war zu phantastisch, er sollte noch einmal überarbeitet, herabgestimmt und natürlich gemacht werden. Der Held dagegen erschien zu einfach, die Dame gar zu verliebt. Da hielt sich Otto nicht länger, diese Mädchengestalt war ihm gerade die schönste, er hatte sich, wie es jungen Dichtern wohl begegnet, nach und nach im Schreiben selber in sie verliebt. "Das Lieblichste", rief er aus, "das Heimlichste, Wahrste und Beste, was ich wußte, hab ich gegeben und nicht einen Buchstaben ändere ich an dem ganzen Stück." Hiermit schleuderte er das Manuskript zornig auf den Tisch und ging rasch in den Garten fort, und es war ihm in einiger Entfernung, als hörte er die Schauspieler hinter sich lachen. (Eichendorff, *Dichter und ihre Gesellen*)

Example 2:

Das Wirtshaus war äußerlich sehr ähnlich dem Wirtshaus, in dem K. wohnte. Es gab im Dorf wohl überhaupt keine größeren äußeren Unterschiede, aber kleinere Unterschiede waren doch gleich zu merken, die Vortreppe hatte ein Geländer, eine schöne Laterne war über der Tür befestigt. Als sie eintraten, flatterte ein Tuch über ihren Köpfen, es war eine Fahne mit den gräflichen Farben. Im Flur begegnete ihnen gleich, offenbar auf einem beaufsichtigenden Rundgang befindlich, der Wirt; mit kleinen Augen, prüfend oder schläfrig, sah er K. im Vorübergehen an und sagte: "Der Herr Landvermesser darf nur bis in den Ausschank gehen." "Gewiß", sagte Olga, die sich K's gleich annahm, "er begleitet mich nur." K. aber, undankbar, machte sich von Olga los und nahm den Wirt beiseite. Olga wartete unterdessen geduldig am Ende des Flurs. "Ich möchte hier gerne übernachten" sagte K. "Das ist leider unmöglich" sagte der Wirt. "Sie scheinen es noch nicht zu wissen. Das Haus ist ausschließlich für die Herren vom Schloß bestimmt. . . ." (Kafka, *Das Schloß*)

Example 3:

Als Duschka in den Mittagsstunden des folgenden Tages bei Jekaterina Iwanowna anklopfte und nach dem Diakon fragte, war sie so ernst und sah so verwacht aus, daß es der sogleich auffiel; und noch ernster wurde sie, als sie hörte, der Vater Diakon sei schon am frühen Morgen weggegangen—über Land—und komme erst am späten Nachmittag wieder. Am Abend gehe er abermals aus. "Wann wird dieser spätere Nachmittag sein?" fragte Duschka halb sich selbst und halb Jekaterina Iwanowna, und dann entschied sie, sie werde es gegen sieben Uhr noch einmal versuchen.

Als sie vor Beginn des Nachmittagsunterrichts noch einmal nach Hause ging, gewahrte sie schon von der Straße her, daß Ilja am Fenster seines Zimmers stand. Und kaum hatte sie die Tür hinter sich geschlossen, als er bei ihr anklopfte und eintrat. Sie meinte, er sehe blasser aus als sonst, und sein Gruß war eilig. "Hast du ihn gesehen", fragte er. "Nein", er war ausgegangen—über Land . . . Sie hatte gehört, daß er sie duzte . . . "Ich fahre heute weg" sagte er. Sie blickte ihn erschrocken an.

(Edzard Schaper, *Der letzte Advent*)*

---

* *Example 1*

"Nice, really poetic," Sorti said finally, "but to perform it"—"no color," blurted Ruprecht.—"Too much scene shifting," said another. "Not a single

The Fictional or Mimetic Genre

These passages, which could not be too brief if they are to make the phenomenon in question both visible and experienceable, are samples chosen at random. Everyone knows that they are paradigmatic for all narrative literature, however different style, content, or even literary *niveau* may be. Each of these three texts manifests a different style of combining straight narration and dialogue. But

---

brilliant exit. But what does all that damned nonsense have to do with my piece?" asked Otto, astonished in his poetic innocence. "It'll get better, my friend," said Sorti calmly, "it'll gradually get better as your stage knowledge increases." Now everyone buried his nose in the text, and each began in his own way to pick it apart. The dialogue was too fantastic, it should be reworked, toned down, and made natural. The hero, on the other hand, was too simple, the young lady too infatuated. At that point Otto could not contain himself any longer. This character, the girl, he considered the best part; he had, as often befalls young poets, while writing himself gradually fallen in love with her. "I have given the sweetest, the most furtive, the truest, and the best I know how," he cried, "and I'll not change a single letter in the whole piece." With that he angrily hurled the manuscript onto the table and went quickly away into the garden, and he was some distance off from them as he heard them laughing behind him.

(Eichendorff, *Dichter und ihre Gesellen*)

Example 2

On the outside the inn was very similar to the one K lived in. In the whole village there were probably no great external differences at all, but smaller differences could be seen right away: the front steps had a railing, an attractive lantern was fastened over the door. A piece of cloth fluttered above their heads as they entered, it was a flag with the colors of the castle nobility. Once in the hall they immediately encountered the inn-keeper, obviously on one of his rounds of inspection; he looked at K with his small eyes, scrutinizing or drowsy, as he passed, and said: "The Land Surveyor is permitted to go only as far as the bar." "Certainly," said Olga, who immediately took K's part, "he's only accompanying me." But K, unthankful, freed himself from Olga and took the inn-keeper aside. "I would like to stay here overnight," K said. "Unfortunately that is impossible," said the inn-keeper. "You don't seem to know yet. The inn is meant exclusively for the gentlemen from the castle. . . ."

(Kafka, *The Castle*)

Example 3

When Duschka knocked on Jekaterina Iwanowna's door in the afternoon hours of the following day and asked for the Deacon she was so somber and looked so worn from waiting that it struck the other woman right away. And

they are all similar in that the descriptive material (of the given excerpt) is conveyed partly by straight narration, and partly by dialogue. We could, of course, take the trouble to demonstrate this "statistically," by division under two headings, for example. But that is not necessary. Directly we see that in each of these three texts, and yet in the most different ways, there exists between those parts consisting of straight narration and those of dialogue such a close continuity in terms of style and content that they have interfused and coalesced into *one* aesthetic configuration—in the exact sense of Gestalt psychology, we may say. Nevertheless we do notice differences in both the kind and the degree of this coalescence among our three text types. We get the impression that in the Kafka text dialogue and straight narration do not merge as fluidly into one another as they do in the Eichendorff and Schaper passages. And this has its cause—which, however, does not detract from the phenomenon itself.

The passage from Kafka's *The Castle* is concerned with the presentation of objects, things: the inn, characterized by its balustrade, lantern, and the flag of the castle nobility. What the persons K, Olga, and the inn-keeper say does not have direct reference to the visual features of the house, but rather to its special nature: K may not spend the night there, because it is reserved for the

---

she became more and more somber when she heard that the Deacon had left early that morning—across country—and would only be coming back in late afternoon. In the evening he was going out again. "When in the late afternoon will it be?" Duschka asked, half to herself and half to Jekaterina Iwanowna, and then she decided she would try again toward seven o'clock.

When she went home again before the start of the afternoon instruction, she noticed from the street that Ilja was standing at the window in his room. And she had scarcely closed the door behind her when he knocked and came in. She said he looked paler than usual. His greeting was hurried. "Have you seen him?" he asked. "No," he had gone out—across country. . . . She had heard that he was addressing her with the familiar "you" . . . [cf. Tr. footnote, p. 94]. "I'm going away today," he said. She looked at him, shocked.

(Edzard Schaper, *Der letzte Advent*)

gentlemen from the castle. But despite this content-boundary be-tween straight narration and dialogue, the overall content of the passage appears to us as a single interwoven complex. In the con-versations the uncanny inn is further delineated, in its "internal features" to some degree, these having been anticipated in the por-tions of straight narration by the opaquely revealing words "no great differences, but smaller ones could be seen right away."

Whereas here report and dialogue rather artistically interlace in the formation of an uncannily opaque outer sphere, examples 1 and 3 present more traditional and therefore far simpler examples for the continuity of Gestalt between dialogue and straight nar-ration. They occur a century apart from one another, and precisely on that account are conclusive evidence of this necessary and essential property of fictional narration. In the passage from Eich-endorff's *Dichter und ihre Gesellen,* too, the material is divided be-tween dialogue and straight narration. But here this division pro-ceeds more fluidly. The state of affairs here is more of an emotional character. The speakers, Otto and the actors, are each in his own way inwardly involved with the matter at hand: Otto's first literary production, which is submitted to the actors for their evaluation. The choice of words in the straight narration is oriented toward the respective way in which the thing is experienced, and not, as in the example from Kafka, to the thing itself: "Otto, astonished in his poetic innocence," "calmly," "pick apart," "blurt out," etc. Above all, the attitude taken toward the matter at hand is ex-pressed already by way of the straight narration, be it as the con-tent of indirectly repeated conversation ("the dialogue was too fantastic, the young lady too infatuated"), or as the content of the young playwright's temperament ("this character, the girl, he con-sidered the best part . . ."). What is said, thought, or felt—dialogue and straight narration, in other words—merges indistinguishably together and forms a scene *unit*, whose action proceeds from the psychic stratum.

The piece from Schaper's *Der letze Advent* is constructed in a way similar to, and yet different from the Eichendorff passage. It is such a simple and natural presentation of a given piece of action that we can scarcely separate the reportorial and conversational components of this action itself and Duschka's conception of it. This is further complicated by the fact that part of the action is narrated in indirect discourse, that is, *reported in straight narration* as conversation, so that this in itself renders direct speech and straight narration not strongly distinct from one another. Furthermore, it has the effect that straight narration still retains the tone of conversation, and, without at any point becoming absorbed into *erlebte Rede,* leaves us much more with the impression of the disconcertedness and anxiety in Duschka's soul than with that of the external action itself.

The *indirect discourse form,* which in the Schaper example is so conducive to the conflux of dialogue and straight narration, ought at this point to be investigated with regard to its function in fictional narration. It is distinguished from the narrated monologue or *erlebte Rede* in that it can render not only the content of what is thought, but also that of what is actually said. But above all it is distinguished from *erlebte Rede* by its very form, by the use of a *verbum dicendi.* Whereas narrated monologue is exclusively a presentational form belonging to fictional narration, it is a well-known fact that indirect discourse occurs frequently in the reality statement. Indeed, in that context it is the only legitimate form for rendering the statements of third-persons. Although in this form the two categorically different modes of reporting do seem to approximate one another closely, nevertheless the boundary between them is by no means rescinded by it, but remains clearly intact. To be sure, one must pay close attention and distinguish very precisely in order to notice it. What aids us in so doing is none other than direct discourse itself, which once again has its only natural and legitimate place in fictional narration. When in the reality statement we render the words of another person in the indirect form, for example: "he said that all tickets were sold out;" or in double indirect form: "he said he heard that all tickets were sold out;" or even the repeating of a discussion among several persons: "he said things stood so and so; she, on the other hand, said they were different"—we will not be tempted to have this reproduction alternate with direct discourse. For we always project ourselves into the reported speech in the capacity of the person reporting. We do this through the use of the *verba dicendi*, and, in proper usage, through the utilization of the subjunctive. Both devices signify: I am only repeating what the other person has said, I myself take no responsibility for it, so to speak. The reporter's attitude toward what he is reporting is always suggested along with the actual indirect discourse, and can be accentuated to a greater or lesser extent according to the state of affairs in question. This attitude can be directed either more toward the originator of the statements reported or more toward their content. Whatever the case, indirect discourse in the reality statement has (at the least) a threefold stratification, consisting of the primary statement-subject, the secondary statement-subject, and his statement-object. This stratification, i.e., the presence of the primary statement-subject, the real I-Origo, emerges more clearly (often emotionally) in oral than in written indirect discourse, especially in very objective presentations. But even in written indirect discourse it is still there. We shall include two further examples, which are designed to demonstrate the difference between indirect discourse in the reality statement and in fiction. For the purposes of such a comparison we may only use a written document which is at the same time the document of a reality statement. In this context the historian and novelist Ricarda Huch presents us with useful material for comparison, which will also serve to elucidate further example 3 above, and beyond that, on the basis of this particular problem further to elucidate the fluctuating narrative function in fiction.

In Ricarda Huch's purely historical study *Wallenstein* we read:

> Wallenstein tue das närrischste Stück von der Welt, daß er auch die Katholiken angreife, sagte der sächsische Geheime Rat Schönberg: würde er nur die Evangelischen bedrücken, so hätte er damit ein leichtes Spiel; und er bewies damit, wie wenig Verständnis er für Wallenstein hatte.*

Let us juxtapose to this a portion of the beginning of her work *Der grosse Krieg in Deutschland,* one of the nicest examples of literary, i.e., mimetic historical writing, which neither can nor intends to be used as a historical document because its literary features consist precisely in the fictionalization of historical events. It is a special kind of fictionalization, which is not "novelistic" in the usual sense, but which, in that it is fictionalization, nonetheless lies beyond the boundary separating fiction from the reality statement. We perceive this in the indirect discourse form, which in this work is the essential linguistic means of producing this highly ingenious fictionalization. It can be seen in the very beginning of the work, and is typical for the narrative technique of the entire book:

> Im Jahre 1585 wurde im Schlosse zu Düsseldorf die Hochzeit des jungen Herzogs Jan Wilhelm mit Jakobe von Baden so pomphaft und majestätisch gefeiert, wie es dem Ansehen des reichen Jülicher Fürstenhauses entsprach. Nachdem die Festlichkeiten abgelaufen waren, verabschiedete sich der Kurfürst von Köln, Ernst von Wittelsbach . . . von der Braut, die seine Nichte war, und sagte zu ihr, er scheide leichteren Mutes, als er gekommen sei; denn es habe oftmals an seinem Gewissen genagt, ob die Heirat, zu der er sie in wohlwollender Meinung und Absicht auf ihr Glück überredet habe, sie auch wirklich zufriedenstellen werde. . . .

---

* Wallenstein was doing the most foolish thing in the world in attacking the Catholics too, said the Saxon privy councilor Schönberg: if he would suppress only the Protestants, he would have an easy time of it; and with these remarks he proved how little understanding he had of Wallenstein.

Jakobe lächelte mit Augen und Mund halb gutmütig, halb spöttisch und erwiderte: "Mich dünkt die Umgebung nicht so prächtig und die Familie nicht so höflich wie Euch . . . Mein Schwiegervater . . . ist ein alberner Greis. . . ." Ja, sagte der Kurfürst ein wenig verlegen, er habe nicht gewußt, daß es so häßlich um den alten Herzog stehe . . . doch . . . sie solle nur bekennen, daß sie mit Jan Wilhelm wohl versehen sei. Dabei streichelte der Kurfürst ihre vollen dunkelerrötenden Wangen. . . . Mit ihrem Gemahl sei sie zufrieden, sagte sie.*

Wherein lies the clearly perceptible difference between this indirect discourse and that in the *Wallenstein* study? It is not three-layered; indeed, it is not stratified at all. There is no primary statement-subject speaking here, repeating the statements of third-persons. These are speaking directly. This is due to the fact that the verb "to say," which in the indirect discourse of the reality statement constitutes this tripartite stratification, alters its meaning in the fictional sense. In *Der grosse Krieg* we are not being told, as we are in the *Wallenstein* text, that someone is saying something (and this utterance then becomes subject to judgment). Rather, the persons speaking are speaking "here and now," that is, they are fictive persons (even though they are historical figures). Here in-

---

* In the year 1585, in the castle at Düsseldorf, the marriage of the young duke Jan Wilhelm to Jakobe von Baden was celebrated with such pomp and majesty as befitted the image of the wealthy Julian sovereignty. After the festivities had come to an end, the Elector of Cologne, Ernst von Wittelsbach . . . bade farewell to the bride, who was his niece, and told her he was leaving in brighter spirits than he had come; for it had often preyed on his conscience whether the marriage, to which he, in well-meaning conviction and intent, had persuaded her, would really make her contented. . . .

Jakobe's eyes and mouth fell into a smile half benevolent, half mocking, and she said: "I do not find the surroundings so splendid, nor the family so polite, as you do. . . . My father-in-law . . . is a foolish old man. . . ." Yes, said the Elector, a bit embarrassed, he hadn't known that things stood so miserably with the old Duke . . . but . . . she should only admit that she was well provided for with Jan Wilhelm. As he said this he stroked her full, deeply blushing cheeks. . . . With her husband she was satisfied, she said.

direct discourse is no longer genuine indirect discourse, just as the "narrator" here is not a statement-subject; it is no more dependent upon an introductory *verbum dicendi* than is direct discourse, because the verb "to say" here is not an introductory, but a situation-verb, just like the verbs "smiled," "stroked." And for this reason, here as well as in the Schaper text, the (pseudo) indirect discourse form can easily alternate with direct discourse. The marked preference for the indirect over the direct form in *Der grosse Krieg* is a stylistic device for retaining traces of the historical events behind the fictionally vivified figures—events in which they themselves are depicted as acting and experiencing—and for retaining these traces as something in fact "historical," investigated and recorded as such by the science of history; and yet, at the same time, as a device for reconverting those events into something which is taking place "here and now." But this ever so sparing and cautious transmutation of reality into fiction is so effectual that at once the meaning-contents of the verbal forms change and obey that law which is imposed upon them solely by virtue of the fact that persons are portrayed not as objects, but in the Here and Now of their fictive subjectivity or I-originarity. Therewith the boundary between historical account and fictional narration emerges as one categorically separating the two kinds of narration. In fiction any and every system of reference between the narrative act and the narrated disappears. Dialogue and soliloquy, indirect discourse, and *erlebte Rede* coalesce with straight narration, and vice versa, into one configuration, into the Gestalt of a fluctuating function, which produces fiction by assuming now this one, now that one of its several forms. All the forms which this function, fictional narration, exhibits, and through which, as we have seen in each case, it is categorically distinguished from the reality statement, are marked by the fact that the narrative function does not describe an object, as does the reality statement, and therefore it cannot understand, interpret, judge, and evaluate it in any of several different ways. Instead, interpreting it engenders a world, such that engendering and interpreting are one single creative act, the narrated is the narration and the narration the narrated.

This formula, which summarizes the results of our preceding investigations (including the criticism against the notion of the "role of the narrator"), might encounter contradictions even if one accepts the proof of the functional continuity between narration and the narrated: contradictions arising from the reading experience. For even if there is a functional continuity, are we not able to distinguish very well between a narrator and that which he narrates? Isn't it exactly this which distinguishes our experience of a novel from our experience of a drama, irrespective of whether we read the latter or see it performed on stage? In which connection the additional fact of the difference in length between these two fictional forms enters into this experience as a more or less conscious element.—So let us consider this question of our reading experience and see if it can be correctly interpreted and answered. We will not content ourselves with vague impressions, but we will enquire after the way in which one describes and interprets a novel on the one hand and a play on the other. This question can be answered most illuminatingly from the perspective of the conditions present in the drama. We interpret plot, characters, and thematic content, and in so doing we are referred to the words which the playwright "has the dramatic figures say." But do we not proceed in exactly the same fashion when we interpret a work of narrative literature? Do we distinguish what the author has the persons say and what he has the narrator say? Do we say, for example: now the narrator says that Duschka knocked on Jekaterina Iwanowna's door in the afternoon, and then Duschka herself says "When in the late afternoon will it be?" (for this is the first direct discourse which appears in the portions of the text we have cited). No, at the most we report: Duschka knocks at Jekaterina's door, she looks somber, etc. In the world formed in the literary work concerned, straight narration and dialogue interlace for us, in quite the same way in which the various forms which the narrative function can assume fuse together into the total Gestalt of the literary work, no differently from the way the colors in a painting merge together into the painted objectivity presented therein. For even the conversations which the poet has his characters have in the novel are the narration of the novel, just as is that indirect discourse in which these conversations can be rendered.

But, one might further object, can we not extract the reflective parts of the novel, the author's reflections, as not belonging to the fictional nexus, and in this way clearly distinguish the narration from the narrated? We showed in the example from *Wilhelm Meister* that reflective passages, too, can without particular accentuation be divided between the speaking or thinking persons in the novel and the straight narration. And even when certain passages are suited to such extraction, they do not differ in this respect from those many "sententious maxims" which we find in classical drama. Even if these sayings have become so "common" that one often has to look up what their original context was, this is nevertheless not the fault of these maxims themselves, nor of the poet who once set them into the mouth of his Wallenstein or Tell. And the poet who with reference to his character Wilhelm says, "A person cannot be put into a more dangerous position than when, through external circumstances, a great change in his situation is effected," is in his capacity as narrator no more an "observing, evaluating, emotively responding" person than is the playwright Schiller, who has his Wallenstein say: "Youth is fast finished with the word/ Which is as hard to handle as the sword's edge."

On the basis of the reading experience there is still another, counter-objection which can be raised. It is true that we cannot always separate the reflective portions into those belonging to the straight narration and those belonging to the dialogue sections.— But are there not cases, particularly in the modern novel, where the figures are so strongly characterized by the way they think and speak that these features are directly associated with them in our interpretation? We need hear only a few quotes from the discussions between Settembrini and Naphta in Thomas Mann's *The Magic Mountain* in order to know immediately which speeches or thoughts belong unmistakably to the one and which to the other, and moreover to know that they are said by one of these characters and not by the narrating poet. And what is true in this particular instance is also more or less true of all narration which strongly individualizes the figures in the novel. Even this phenomenon, however, is only a confirmation of the functional character of the narrative act. In face of just such "embodiments" of the intellectual content the fact that these figures and what they say are narrated, produced by a narrative function, escapes our awareness in our interpretative image of the work. And this apperceptional experience of the reader is all the more symptomatic when, for example, in the chapter entitled "Operationes Spirituales," the preponderance of the discussion among Settembrini, Naphta, and Hans Castorp is formed in indirect discourse, which, as has been shown, in fiction does not have the structure of the reproduction of third-persons' speech, but rather forms them as stating subjects in precisely the same way as dialogue does, and which therefore can easily alternate with the latter. A small passage from this chapter of *The Magic Mountain* will shed light on this aspect of the reading experience:

> . . . Die Philanthropie seines Herrn Widersachers, sagte er, arbeite darauf hin, dem Leben alle schweren und todernsten Akzente zu nehmen; auf die Kastration des Lebens gehe sie aus, auch mit dem Determinismus ihrer sogenannten Wissenschaft. Aber die Wahrheit sei, daß der Begriff der Schuld durch den Determinismus nicht nur nicht abgeschafft werde, sondern sogar durch ihn noch an Schwere und Schaudern gewönne.
>
> Das war nicht schlecht. Ob er etwa verlange, daß das unselige Opfer der Gesellschaft sich ernstlich schuldig fühle. . . .

Allerdings. Der Verbrecher sei von seiner Schuld durchdrun-
gen wie von sich selbst . . . Der Mensch sei, wie er habe sein
wollen. . . . Ed möge sterben, da er die tiefste Lust gebüßt habe.
Die tiefste Lust?
Die tiefste.
Man kniff die Lippen zusammen. Hans Castorp hüstelte. Herr
Ferge seufzte. Settembrini bemerkte fein:
"Man sieht, es gibt eine Art zu verallgemeinern, die den Gegen-
stand persönlich färbt. Sie hätten Lust, zu töten?"*

Even more clearly here than in the example from Ricarda
Huch's *Der grosse Krieg*—and so precisely because of the not
merely reportorial, but reflective character of this discourse—the
indirect discourse form is proof of the impersonal, functional character of the narrative act, irrespective of which of its forms it
assumes. Indistinguishably straight narration, direct discourse, indirect discourse, *erlebte Rede*, etc., flow together in their fluctuation—and not only in our subsequent image of the work, but even
during the reading process itself. They merge as equally into the
totality of the narration as they do into the totality of the narrated,
because the narration is the narrated, and vice versa. And whether
one or another of the narrative forms predominates is a question of

---

* . . . The philanthropy of his honored opponent would take from life all its
stern and grimly serious aspects; even with the determinism of its so-called
science, it was aimed at the castration of life. But the truth was the concept
of guilt would not only not be eliminated by determinism, but because of it it
would actually take on an added severity and horror.
That wasn't bad. So, he was demanding that the wretched victim of society
be convinced of his guilt. . . .
Quite. The offender was as entrenched in his guilt as he was in his own
self. . . . Man was as he had wanted to be; let him die, for he had gratified his
deepest desire.
His deepest desire?
His deepest.
They pursed their lips. Hans Castrop coughed. Herr Ferge sighed. Settembrini shrewdly remarked: "One sees, there is a way of generalizing that gives
the object a personal tinge. You would like to kill?"

style and not of structure, and depends upon the author's individual style, or even upon the literary period. In the third-person novel of the eighteenth and nineteenth centuries, generally the basic narrational substance is composed of straight narration, which stands in clear contrast to dialogue and monologue. Hemingway's or Salinger's narratives show dialogue as the basic narrational substance (but not like Diderot's novels in dialogue, *Jacques le Fataliste* and *Le neveau de Rameau*, which do not belong to the category of the novel, to epic fiction, because, structurally similar to philosophical dialogues from Plato to Hemsterhuys, the dialogues expounding various themes or telling various anecdotes here do not have the function of forming and creating fictive persons). There are narratives, like H. E. Nossack's *Unmögliche Beweisaufnahme,* for example, which are constructed predominantly in indirect discourse, whereas *erlebte Rede* and interior monologue still prevail in the novel of Natalie Sarraute. But in any given instance it is a matter of the quantitative extent of the elements of the fluctuating narrative act, whose number can be counted on the fingers of one hand. And one hardly need mention that the predominance of one or another of these elements has its significance for the tenor and type of the respective narrative.[108]

Summing up our investigations of fictional narration, we may now say that the narrative act (of the narrative poet or narrator) does not represent an additional *person* present in narrative, but not in dramatic literature, but that instead it is one more *form* of the mimetic function which the narrative poet has at his disposal, but the dramatist does not.[109] This form of the mimetic function can disappear altogether, and nevertheless fiction will arise, namely dramatic, or even cinematic fiction. This means that the epic narrative function is replaced by other functions, as we shall see more closely below.

These remarks have once more caused that boundary to emerge clearly which runs between the logical and the aesthetic investigation of literature, and to which we must pay particular attention in fixing the relation in which epic and dramatic fiction stand to one another.

Dramatic Fiction

THE RELATION OF DRAMATIC TO EPIC FICTION

Heated controversies can arise at that frontier separating the logic from the aesthetic of literature, especially when the former claims to categorize dramatic literature within the same genre as narrative literature. The structural diversity of the two fictional forms seems to aesthetics to be too great for it to be able to accept the sober and outwardly very technical-looking arguments which the logic of literature will first offer. The latter, for instance, will refer to the fact that again and again epic material, i.e., material that has already been fictionalized, has invited re-contouring into dramatic form, and will cite as examples the history of the Faust chapbook, the Nibelung material, and the creation of serious and light dramatic-operatic art based on narrated material, as in the case of Wagner's *Tristan*, Tschaikowsky's *Eugen Onegin* (based on Pushkin's epic), Offenbach's *Tales of Hoffman*, and others. (Also, the less common, but symptomatic case occurs where a poet has recast his own epic work into a drama, as Pär Lagerkvist did with his novel *The Hangman*.) Aesthetics will disregard such allusions because it would guard itself against their implied devaluation of the narrative structure of epic literature, against any subordination of the structural and stylistic peculiarity of narration to its fictionalizing function. As regards the drama, aesthetics will fear that its delicate architechtonics will not have been done sufficient justice if those differences between epic and dramatic literature, which had been stated as generic ones, were to be dissolved by no matter how logically founded a common classification.

But an examination of the many comparisons of form and content which poetics has made between epic and drama shows that, without being aware of the fact, it is operating within *one* genre. As that criterion which betrays this we can cite the fact that comparisons of drama to the epos have led to opposite results from a comparison of drama with the novel, and again that a comparison made of the epos and the novel was essentially no different from one made between epos and drama. If, for example, Goethe and Hegel assigned to the epos the priority of occurrence, of event over "persons portrayed in their inner character,"[110] and to the drama the reverse, nevertheless a modern literary theorist, Wolfgang Kayser, arrived at the opposite conclusions in his comparison between the novel and the drama. He assigns drama the priority of event, and "to the private world of the novel the priority of figure," i.e., of the individual's existence.[111] But similar results were also reached in comparing the novel with the older epos,[112] while under still different perspectives and with opposite conclusions novel and epos have been compared only with respect to the way they present their worlds.[113] The possibility of as well as the discrepancy between these comparisons can be explained by the poetological correlation of epic and dramatic literature as the mimesis of men in action, whose relation to their "world" is not conditioned by the structure of the mimetic forms but by the historical development of world conditions and the conception of man and world connected thereto. And even Goethe, who had ascribed the "presentation of man from within" only to the drama, had to concede that his own "Epopöe" *Hermann und Dorothea* "departs from the Epopöe in this respect and approaches the drama" (Dec. 23, 1797). Such a judgment, which completely disregards aesthetic structure, the presentational form, is symptomatic enough, and unintentionally points to that ordering principle which underlies the system of literature.

The differentiation between dramatic and narrative literature on the basis of presentational form could lead to more exact results. But such can only be achieved when this difference in presentational form, i.e., narration and the formation of characters through dialogue, is not made to signify a difference in genre. That this is so becomes especially clear in those attempts of literary theory to bring what it juxtaposes and distinguishes as the three genres of epic, dramatic, and lyric literature into a structural connection with one another. From within the most varying points of view epic and lyric have been contrasted to drama, drama and lyric to the epic, and of course also epic and drama to lyric. J. Petersen attempts the first classification when he defines the epos as the reporting of an action in monologue, the lyric as the presentation of a state in monologue, and the drama as the presentation of an action in dialogue.[114] The concept of monologue is more decisive here than that of report or presentation, because at its base lies the notion that the "epic I" is of the same nature as the lyric I (a false conception which overlooks the fact that epic report, too, presents, but that the lyric statement does not, as we shall demonstrate in detail below). Classifications of drama and lyric taken together and contrasted to epic have been undertaken from the perspective of "presence": "The content of a lyric poem or a drama is absolutely present; it is not merely observed, but directly experienced by the poet or myself." E. Winkler, who quotes this statement from Lipps, does, to be sure, go on to say that a significant difference exists between lyric and drama. However, in that he establishes this difference as one within the "genre of emotive experience"—lyrical emotive experience is static, dramatic lively, dynamic[115]—he creates a correlation between lyric and drama which the phenomena themselves in no way appear to confirm.

That on the basis of their mimetic-fictional character epic and drama belong together is, as we have mentioned before, something which literary theory has not readily stressed because it could obscure the specific aesthetic-technical qualities of these two forms.

However, that in the creation of epic literature, too, the primary thing is the mimetic impulse and not narrating *per se* as a particular attitude of consciousness, is the structural insight which Aristotle achieved, and to which too little attention has been paid over the years. The epic poet does not set out to narrate for the sake of narrating, but in order to narrate *something*, i.e., for the sake of the narrated. Let us cite M. Kommerell's conception of this, in confirmation of our point: "A novel's inner existence is pre-verbal. Before it is written in words the persons are there, their voluntary congregation and the coincidences which bring them together, the novel's scope with its major scenes and images, with its unforgettable stages of the flow of action. . . ."[116] So described the process of the conception of a narrative work also holds true for that of a dramatic work, and no matter how high a value we can or ought to place on the strictly stylistic aspects of the narrative function, still we ought not to mistake the fact that the narrative poet is primarily a "mimetes," and that the What of his narrative first determines the How. Statements from writers themselves confirm this insight, which ultimately goes back to Aristotle. Thus, for example, Alfred Döblin did "not recognize any difference whatsoever between the drama and the novel. . . . For him the goal of both is immediate, pressing presentification."[117] And even when an epic poet like Thomas Mann expressly establishes differences between dramatic and epic character formation, in favor of the latter (*Versuch über das Theater*), nevertheless the awareness is expressed that as a narrator he is following mimetic procedures, even if he is doing so with other means and under other presuppositions than the dramatist.

From the perspective of the classification of literary genres the decisive element is neither the particular style used nor the special ability of the narrative function to present the outer and inner existence of the figures in a different and more inclusive manner than the drama, but rather the specifically fictionalizing function of the narrative function as such. For the locus of drama within the logical system of literature is determined solely by the absence of the narrative function, by the structural given that the figures are formed through dialogue.[118] The aesthetic, specifically dramatic properties of the drama are derived from this fact in just the same way as those of epic literature are derived from the narrative function. From it is derived the drama's constitutive characteristic of being performable on stage. For whether it was the purely mimic or the literary, mimetic impulse which founded the origins of dramatic form, the restriction to the forming of characters through dialogue alone includes its mimic potential: the characters formed as speaking and only as speaking can, in speaking, present themselves. It seems to me that this is not only the poetological, but also the phenomenal perspective from which dramatic literature, read as well as performed on stage, is experienced, and not that of "action," which has frequently been cited and which has been claimed more for the drama than for the novel. For action is a very relative concept, which precisely in its relativity is applicable to both mimetic forms without the form of the drama's guaranteeing in any given instance that its action is "dramatic," and without epic form's guaranteeing that the narrated action is "epic." The dramatic character of Kleist's *Novellen* has often been cited; the epic possibilities in Goethe's *Tasso* are not difficult to recognize; and confronted with a character such as the Princess in that play, Hugo von Hofmannsthal regretted that she was a dramatic and not an epic figure.[119] In these conditions lies no doubt one of the reasons why recent literary theory has been reluctant still to classify the categories of the dramatic and the epic (and in connection with them those of the tragic, comic, and the humorous) among the "genres" (Emil Staiger). But on the other hand, even if we find the action in a drama not very dramatic in the literary, aesthetic sense, nevertheless this action is contingent upon the poetological form of the drama, the system of dialogue and consequently the self-presenting persons, insofar as these possess the potential for mimic-scenic embodiment.[120] That is, the potential for transmuting from the modus of mental representation to that of perception. But this in turn means that these persons can step out of the infinite realm of mental representation and into the limited sphere of reality, which demands *that* concentration of events which is the structural core of dramatic fiction. How this concentration of the action has in the changing styles of various epochs adapted itself to—or broken away from—the laws of the stage, i.e., the laws of perception, are matters of investigation for the aesthetics of literature, which for its part need take no further consideration of the basic situation (from the standpoint of linguistic theory) from which dramatic action ensues: namely dialogue, the self-presenting persons.

THE LOCUS OF THE DRAMA

We are now at the point where we can more precisely describe the locus of drama within the system of literature. Looking back at the beginning of our investigations, we note first that the drama is far less conducive to study from the perspective of the logic of language than is either epic or lyric literature. It offers no opportunity to grasp the laws of creative language as we have defined it in comparison to non-creative language. For just that linguistic form which of all mimetic presentational forms the drama has preserved, namely direct discourse, as such offers us no poetological criteria. It can do this only as a form of the fluctuating narrative function, which is identified as fictional narration in part through dialogue. Drama has its locus in the system of literature within that enclave in the general system of language which is formed by epic literature, far from the frontier which the fictional narrative function draws against this general system. In the case of the drama Hegel would have been least able to conclude that art was dissolving and transmuting into the prose of scientific thought. For the drama is that particular literary work of art where the word is no longer free, but bound. It has become the figure, like the stone from which a statue is formed. To put it differently, the figure no longer is in the medium of the word, as is so in epic fiction, but rather the word is in the medium of the figure—which in turn is merely another formulation of the fact that the narrative function has become nil. "In regard to form," Hegel says with reference to tragedy (which here stands for drama in general), "in that language enters into the content, it ceases to be narrative, just as the content ceases to be one which is mentally represented."[121] In the formula for the drama, namely that the word is in the medium of the figure, we have the foundation of the fact that the logical locus of dramatic fiction cannot be oriented in the functions of language themselves, as can be done in determining the locus of epic fiction. The reality statement becomes ineffective and irrelevant as an instrument of comparison precisely because the fictional narrative function has disappeared. But in place of the reality statement *reality itself* enters as the orienting factor in the logic and phenomenology of dramatic fiction. This takes place in an extremely covert and complex manner, which has long brought a great deal of confusion to dramatic theory, but which on the other hand throws the unique fictional character of dramatic fiction— more compact and more intensive in comparison to epic fiction— into bold relief.

The dramatic formula that the word is in the medium of the figure implies that the locus of the drama is to be determined not primarily with respect to the word, but with respect to the problem of the dramatic figure. And this in turn establishes that the logic of the drama is inadequate without epistemological perspectives— which, therefore, implies that the problem of reality itself has a certain relevance for the elucidation of dramatic structure.

As was already stated, the dramatic figure is so constructed that, unlike the epic figure, it exists not only in the modus of mental representation, but is determined and designed for transferring over into the modus of perception (the stage), that is, into the same physically defined reality as that of the audience. This means that this dramatic figure is conceived under the dual perspective of literature and (physical) reality, and that it is characterized by those forms of appearance that are concomitant to this circumstance, to the physical realization or embodiment of fiction.[122] However, this aspect by no means first appears when we see the play on stage. On the contrary, the decisive criterion for the logic of the drama is precisely that already as a written work it falls under both of these modi.

The word's being in the medium of the figure comprises two aspects which are interdependent, but are nevertheless inversely opposed to one another. *It means that the word becomes figure and the figure word.* From these two formulae is to be inferred that peculiar encounter of fictional and real planes which is the contingency for both the creation and the poetic existence of the dramatic figural world.

The formula that the word becomes figure and nothing other than it, is the expression of the objectivity, indeed the materiality of the dramatis personae, which is constituted by the disappearance of the narrative function and the distribution of the material to be presented among autonomously articulating, self-presenting persons. Therewith they obtain just that aspect which real persons in the framework of physical reality also have, the "Others," those people outside of and before me, whom I see and hear, and with whom I speak. They are objects, things, for me, even if objects informed with an ego. They are objects to which I stand opposite and which stand opposite to me, such that I can never attain a whole, complete picture of them. I know only that of them which they themselves portray to me, be it through their words or through their deeds (whereby under certain circumstances the latter can alter the picture I have of a person from what he says). However, my image of the objectively experienced world standing opposite me is always fragmentary—which is one of the most essential features of the experience of reality. The dramatic figure, too, shares this fragmentary character of reality as a form of experience, even if in a special, modified way. To a certain extent he represents the pure Platonic idea of fragmentarily experienced reality—and the situation where the audience is before the actor facing them on the stage is, strictly speaking, symptomatic of this fact. For vis-à-vis living reality the experience of the fragmentary is in a perpetual state of potential completion, which can be integrated to a high, if never to an absolute degree. Other people, my fellow-man, I can "become acquainted with," just as I can broaden my knowledge of my fragmentarily presented surroundings in that I circulate about in them. And this process of acquaintance is not only associated with what this Other objectively existing opposite me has in one form or another given me to know; my own comprehending intuitive penetration and psychological interpretation are also at work along with this—a kind of work to which, in principle, no limitations are set because the object of my knowledge is itself an infinite, inexhaustible, developing living whole.—Now, to be sure, the poetic figure is also always offering new possibilities for interpretation, and literary history and criticism have given us a concrete and changing picture of this over the years. It is substantiated by the fact that the practical interpreters of a work of dramatic literature, the directors and the actors, can and customarily do give a literary character highly differing performances—actor A will play a different Hamlet from actor B's. Nevertheless we sense directly that matters stand quite otherwise with the interpretation of life, of living people, than with the interpretation of literature and the literary character. Here it is not the object of interpretation itself which changes but the interpreter. The literary character does not change. The possibility for its interpretation approaches that frontier which is characterized by the fact that the persons do not form the words, but the words the persons, that these "are constituted by the sentences" and not vice versa.[123] This applies not only to the dramatic, but also to the epic figure—and considered from within the realm of fictional literature, it is precisely the epic figure which does not "deny" this state of affairs. The dramatic figure, however, does—having absorbed its constituting sentences into itself. And just for this reason it can become "embodied" through the means of physical reality and can represent the semblance of life, or life-likeness."[124]

These circumstances also illuminate the problem of the dramatic figure as seen from the theory of language. As figures formed purely through dialogue, they are formed exclusively as statement-subjects. That they, i.e., that dramatic fiction is nevertheless detached from the statement system of language—and moreover absolutely so in comparison to epic fiction—is something which might appear to be contradictory. But the contradiction is resolved when we recall the demonstration that all statement is reality statement only by virtue of a "genuine," namely a real statement-subject. The statement of a fictive statement-subject is a fictive reality statement. This would be a tautological observation if it were not founded in the absence of precisely that criterion which first constitutes the reality statement at all: subject-object polarity. We cannot say of a fictive person, who is "constituted by the sentences," that he is making a subjective or objective statement, just as we cannot verify his statements, either. Here again the categorical difference between a functional and a relational continuity asserts itself. The speeches of fictive persons are nothing but elements of their formation, elements of their thus-and-so characterized creational being. It is true of both dramatic and epic fiction that in their realm there is as little subject-object polarity present as there is time and space. That is, there are no reality constituents, although, as we have said, the dramatic figure can represent the semblance of reality to a higher degree than can the epic figure.

The structure of the dramatic figure will be further disclosed if we analyze the second part of the dramatic formula: *that the figure becomes word* and nothing but word. Only once we consider this aspect does the peculiar duality of the dramatic figure's form of existence emerge completely; only then is it shown in its essential fragmentariness, which on the one hand distinguishes it as fiction from reality, and on the other distinguishes it as specifically dramatic fiction, as opposed to the epic figure. At this point in the phenomenology of the drama it is disclosed in an almost paradoxical way that it, the drama, which can take on the semblance of reality, displays the purely fictional character of fictional literature in a higher degree of intensity, to a certain extent in a more elemental way, than does epic literature—and moreover that it does so on the basis of its "likeness to life."

To begin with, the formula that the figure becomes word brings this dramatic figure close to reality, namely in precisely that sense in which in reality, too, one person makes himself known to another. This is the phenomenon which we, as reader or spectator, on the one hand get from the effect of the dramatis personae on our selves, on our conception of them, and which on the other hand we get from viewing them as they act and interact, i.e. which we get from the drama's intrinsic action *per se*. It is at this point in the, as it were, all too "reality-like" structure of the drama that various augmentational techniques set in. Ranging from old to new, these include the use of a chorus, of monologue, or even that device whereby mute thoughts become audible, a technique through which, for instance, Eugene O'Neill, in his play *Strange Intermezzo,* daringly exceeded those limitations which are imposed upon the dramatist.[125] Both these augmentational techniques as well as the internal construction of the various dramas are instructive in the context of our investigations because they provide an indication of the drama's dual form as literature. Indeed, to express it somewhat bluntly, they point out the drama's conflict between its having, as literature, to present a more extensive reality, and its being referred and directed to only perceptible reality. Statements made by two great modern authors bring us directly into this problematic arising from dramatic structure.

Hugo von Hofmannsthal grounds his criticism of the demeanor of the Princess in Goethe's *Tasso* in the fact that, as a dramatic figure, she cannot employ silence, too, as a means of self-portrayal. "I think she should have become a tranquil, serene woman . . . a figure like the canoness, whom the 'Confessions of a Beautiful Soul' are about, or like Ottilie in *Elective Affinities.* But in the drama there is probably no place for such lucidity, and since the figures can only portray themselves by speaking, and not by silent existence and non-verbal contemplation of that world in their transluscent inner life, I think that in this case the genre has forced him [Goethe] to ruin the nicest figure by having her speak and declaim about herself where it would be precisely her role, as a great lady as well as a beautiful soul, not to speak."[126] And in a still earlier essay, "Über Charaktere im Roman und Drama" (1902), written in the form of a conversation between Balzac and the Orientalist Hammer-Purgstall, he has Balzac designate the dramatic character as a "contraction of the real person. What captivates me about the real person is exactly his breadth."[127] From diverse points of view these two statements illuminate the fragmentary nature of dramatic character-formation. Hofmannsthal has Balzac—who believed he was able to reproduce the breadth of his nation's reality with the breadth and multiplicity of his novels—deny "reality" to the dramatic figure and his world. The criticism of the character Princess Lenore, too, is based on the fact that the true reality of such a woman cannot appear in dramatic form, because she cannot be portrayed in the tranquil depths of her being, in "her translucent inner life," alone with herself, silent. She can be portrayed only in speech, which really does not befit her. She can be portrayed only as "an allotropy of the corresponding real person," as is stated at another point in the Balzac essay.[128] Thomas Mann expressed this matter in similar terms in his *Versuch über das Theater* (1908). He considers the situation of the audience before the "abbreviated" stage world symptomatic of the "silhouette-art" of the drama. "Where is the dramatic scene," he asks, "which would excel the scene in a modern novel in the precision of its visual features, in intensive presence, in reality! . . . The novel is more precise, more complete, more knowing, more painstaking and deeper than the drama in everything that concerns knowledge of man in body and character, and in contrast to the view that the drama is the true plastic literary work, I profess that I find it far more an art of the silhouette. I find the narrated person alone to be rounded, whole, real and plastic. One is an on-looker in a play; one is more than that in a narrated world."[129]

However, the reality problematic discussed in these statements by Hofmannsthal and Thomas Mann is far more complex than it appeared to be to these two literary theorists, whose own creative endeavors made them so initiate and knowledgeable in such matters. They compare that "reality" which can be formed in the drama with the reality which narrative literature can create—to the benefit of the latter—and they equate this narrated reality with an actual, total reality. But upon closer examination one sees that ultimately the situation of the audience before the stage—where, as Schiller remarked, it "is stringently confined to the sensuous present" (to Goethe, December 26, 1797)—corresponds far more to the fragmentary character of empirical reality in the sense developed above, and that the dramatic figure and his world more closely approximate this empirical reality than does the epic figure. The way in which the epic figure and his world present themselves to us far exceeds what can be presented in physical and historical reality. There is only one "epistemological" locus where we can experience man in his "transluscent inner life," and that is in narrative literature. There we experience him as the "product" of the engendering narrative function, whose essential characteristic of being "producing" and not "reproducing," finds its strongest substantiation in just this phenomenon. Where this narrative function is lacking, i.e., in dramatic literature, it is replaced by a creative function of character-formation which is comparatively restricted: namely that function characterized by the inverse formulae that the word becomes figure, and the figure word. Let us stress once more that these formulae describe only literary dramatic fiction as such. They describe it in precisely that fragmentary aspect which more closely approximates it to the experience of physical and historical reality than epic fiction, and just for this reason they render it more visibly a "mimesis" of this reality than does the latter. It is dramatic mimesis which, on the basis of its logically and epistemologically dual structure, more tangibly discloses *that* problem of mimesis in literary theory which the notion of imitation had totally obscured: that mimesis of reality is not reality itself, but that reality is merely the raw material of poetic productivity, and it can undergo what we can loosely term symbolic subjugation and transformation in all degrees, even up to the point where any kind of experienceable reality whatever disappears. The problems which here enter into the theory of dramatic literature no longer belong properly to its logic. But they originate precisely at that place within the system of literature where the relation between the mimesis of reality and reality itself emerges more clearly and requires elucidation more than anywhere else: the locus of dramatic fiction, which can wholly achieve its form of existence not merely in mental representation, as does epic fiction, but also in physical perception. This means that the drama, understood not only as literature, but as a piece for theatrical performance, fixes itself under that perspective of mimesis thus understood, so that the widely discussed problematic of the stage can be traced back to its fundamental and constitutive elements.

The Reality of the Stage and the Problem of Stage-Present

The problem of dramatic fiction cannot be illuminated without our considering the phenomenology of the stage. That perspective of mimesis under which the latter falls may even be considered as the solution to the age-old problematic of that "reality" which the stage presents, and in turn to the problematic of time as that form in which, since the flourishing of the theory of the unities in the Renaissance, the problem of stage reality has been given its essential expression.

This is an instance where first of all we must again cast a comparative glance at narrative literature. Moreover, we must do so with a view to the discussion of time in modern literary theory. This problem is indeed more topical to narrative than to dramatic literature, for which it may with a certain justification be considered as being already exhaustively treated. Even if such be the case, we must stress that only the problem of time in the drama and not in the epic is legitimate in the proper sense. And although it may at first seem paradoxical, this is so even though time as a problem of creation and of subject matter can only become thematic in narrative literature. This pseudo-paradox is connected with, and also resolved by, the fact that time as a form of physical reality, i.e., as reality itself, does not enter into the structure of epic fiction. That fiction created by epic literature persists in the modus of mental representation, and does not require completion in the modus of perception. But, as we have endeavored to demonstrate, *qua* fiction it also is autonomous over against that other temporal form which likewise exists in the modus of mental representation, but which is valid only for historical thought: the past. When in recent times, based on Günther Müller's theory,[130] time as a factor of physical reality, namely as "narrating time" [*Erzählzeit*], has been employed as a measurement of length and temporal duration applicable to the production and physical existence of a narrative work as a book, as well as a standard of measurement for the fictive world and the action depicted within it, and when from the relation between "narrating time and narrated time" there have been conclusions drawn as to the structure and interpretative meaning of certain narrative works—these procedures are based on an incorrect understanding of both the form of existence of epic literature and the problem of time within it. Narrating time is consumed not only for narrating the temporal progression of epic action, but also for the presentation of objects, things, and of reflective passages (presentation which can be more or less "diffuse"). To demonstrate this point with the simplest example, the description "blonde hair" requires less narrating time than the expression "lustrous blonde hair." But time appears in epic literature only as a fictive element of the fictive epic world, as a compositional element no different from the spatial elements portrayed therein. In most cases the temporal element is given along with the progression of the action, more or less unemphasized, and, as we may only briefly indicate here, it only becomes a problem of structure or even of meaning when it as such becomes thematic, as is the case in modern epic literature, for example in Joyce's *Ulysses*, Thomas Mann's *The Magic Mountain* and the Joseph novels, and Virginia Woolf's *Mrs. Dalloway*. And, with respect to a narrating time, the same would apply to the drama if it only existed in physical reality as a book. The play *Wallenstein*, too, which occupies an entire volume in the Säkular edition of Schiller's works, has a longer "narrating time" than *The Robbers*, whose plot obviously extends over a longer period of fictive time than does the Wallenstein trilogy.

But the "narrating time" of the drama should be transposed into "playing time." The dramatic work converts from the modus of mental representation to that of sensuous perception, thereby consigning itself to the conditions of spatio-temporal reality. This is the source of the discussion of time in the drama, and the reason why time as a factor of dramatic art was one of the first elements recognized as a problem whose solution is more a matter of stage technique than of literature itself, as more a problem of dramaturgy than of drama.[131] It is no coincidence that it first became topical in that epoch in which, as D. Frey has shown, the drama was received by the audience as an objectively, and above all as a plastically experienced stage work. as an other, aesthetic (or fictive) reality which was detached from their own.[132] This was in the Renaissance and, in its full development, in the Baroque period. The problem of the classical unities—regardless of whether they have always reverted to the problematical passage from Aristotle on the sun's revolution—is grounded in the fact of the box-stage, as a problem of the relation of the spatio-temporal reality of the "audience in the pit" to the obviously fictive, but yet at the same time "genuine" spatio-temporal reality of the stage, which is experienced as both detached from, and yet in the physical sense as belonging to, the auditorium—and which has been so treated in the course of the historical development of the theater.[133]

Let us briefly recall the classical discussion of the dramatic unities, for in exposing those fallacies which this discussion harbors, we shall be able to discern not only the literary form of the drama, but that of stage reality as well, as being a mimetic form. What we are concerned with is the familiar question of the approximation of the fictive action's temporal duration to the real temporal duration of the play's performance, which for the five-act dramas of French Classicism amounted to two hours. Corneille, for example, in his "Discours sur les trois unités," posits the coincidence of these two times as the ideal. And the presupposition for this—which was by no means clearly expressed—was that the spectator projected the reality, and therefore the temporal immediacy of his physical presence in the theater, onto that of the action unfolding before him and the actors enacting it, and that above all these stood in the same reality as the spectator. But the epistemological error emerges precisely in the difference between these times which in his argument Corneille admitted as possible, as one not deviating from "verisimilitude." "Si nous ne pouvons pas la renfermer dans ces deux heures, prenons en quatre, six, dix; mais ne passons pas de beaucoup les vingt-quatre heures de peur de tomber dans le dé-règlement, et de reduire tellement le portrait en petit qu'il n'ait ses dimensiones proportionées et ne soit qu'imperfection."[134]

No cognizance was taken of the fact that even a relatively small difference between the duration of the action and that of the performance involves the categorical distinction between fictive and real time, and that with respect to this it is irrelevant whether the difference between these two times is one of hours, days, weeks, or even years.[135] Indeed, neither was it noted that this difference is also present when both times do coincide, or more precisely, when they are thought of as coinciding, and that it is valid to say only for the performance, but not for the depicted action, that it lasts so and so long. It is a duration which for its part can only be ascertained with a clock, and is irrelevant precisely because the audience is as little attentive to it as the reader of a novel is to the time it takes him to read.[136] For the phenomenon which applies to the drama, performed as well as just read, is the same one which is valid for narrative fiction: that the person who apperceives it, in this case the spectator in the audience, is *not* present with his I-Origo in the fictive, imaginary world unfolding before him, irrespective of whether it unfolds before his inner eye, i.e., only in mental representation, or before his physically perceiving eye. The stage as a physical, perceptible form can easily obstruct the realization that it is just as much an imagined, fictive space as is the scene of a narrated action, that in its realm, too, time and space have only conceptual, and not deictic form. And if above we at first said, in our introductory remarks to the problem, that by virtue of its scenic embodiment the dramatic figure enters into the same physical reality as that of the audience, then we must now modify this formulation to read that the intrinsic physical reality of the stage is nonetheless not the same as that of either the audience or the actor himself.

The classical theory of the unities did not dispose of these problems inherent within it, and it could not do so for reasons of stage technique. Although advances in stage technique have made it possible to illustrate the course of the imaginary time of the action, for example through spatial and lighting effects, the revolving stage, etc., and have thus come closer and closer to eliminating the problem of dramatic time, nevertheless, even today this classical theory is further from being superseded than one might think. In modern dramatic theory it has been retained in the form that time in the dramatic work is a present time.[137] The theory of stage-present corresponds to the theory of past-ness for the epic, and indeed with more justification, even if for reasons other than those perhaps implicit within this theory. In fact, the theatrical stage corresponds to nothing other than the preterite form in narration. Not the dramatic form, the dialogue as such, but the phenomenon of the play's performance is the basis for the notion that "the action is portrayed as present,"[138] that "the drama portrays a self-contained action . . . in immediate present time,"[139] and that it "takes place in a perpetual present time. On stage it is always now,"[140] (to choose just a few random definitions from the abundance of like-sounding ones). These definitions adhere to the illusion of the spectator's experience so faithfully that they would scarcely have required express formulation. But they prove to be problematic, and even erroneous, when one examines whether such a determination of the dramatic present really designates a different kind of temporal experience from that of a narrated action. When in act two of Ibsen's *Rosmersholm* Rebecca West says to Rosmer: "Yesterday evening when Ulrik Brendel left I gave him two or three lines to take to Mortensgård," the spectator has experienced this "yesterday" a few minutes previously in his own time, i.e., in the first act of the play, when Brendel leaves the stage with Rebecca. That she "then" gave him a letter for Mortensgård, i.e., "then" in the (concealed) dramatic action (but not, as it were, behind stage), is something we learn only through what she says. Nevertheless we experience this, to be sure perceived, but yet fictional "yesterday" in no different fashion from the "yesterday" of our Fontane text, "the setting was like yesterday," which we similarly have experienced a few minutes previously in our own time—even though here it is our reading and not our viewing time. Conversely, we experience the "present" setting of Treibel's room, i.e., the scene itself, how the Kommerzienrat enters the room, sits down on the sofa, and unfolds the newspaper, as just as "immediate" as the scene with Rebecca West and Rosmer. Not, as Thornton Wilder says, only on the stage, but also in the novel, in the epic, is it always "now"—the difference being only that in the former we experience this Now in acts of perception, whereas in the latter we experience it in acts of mental representation, in intuitive cognition instead of in direct concreteness. And only by way of such comparative observations can one discover how matters stand with the Here and Now of the scenically embodied dramatic world. The relations of the Here and Now in drama are no different from those of epic fiction; in drama there is just as little a temporal present as there is in the novel. Dramatic action occurs in a Here and Now, even if in the entire play there are no indicators which set a fictive past or future in relation to a fictive present. It is the Here and Now of the fictive I-Origines to which the action of dramatic, as well as of epic fiction is referred. And even if the tangible, sensuously perceptible reality of the stage and the actors at first appears to obscure the fact, and although it appears to run counter to our "sensuous" experience, nevertheless this sensuously perceptible reality is just as much without function *qua* reality as is the grammatical value of the epic preterite *qua* past-ness. That is, the pseudo present time of stage-present is just as invalid as a temporal modus as is the epic preterite. Just as the latter fades out as a morpheme, leaving only the verb's semantic content relevant for the engendering of the fictive world, so also is the stage, as one wise saying has long since established, merely boards that signify the world; and these boards can be treated—even if in a different medium—in exactly the same manner as the fictional narrator, contrary to all grammatical rules, deals with the epic preterite. In confusing the real present-time and reality of the stage with the fictive present enacted upon it, theories of stage-present were committing the same error as one would if one were to confuse the actor with the fictive character he is portraying. Surely, stage and actors belong to reality just as the audience does; they change, and they perish. Wednesday, the 6th of May, 1767, was the present for Madame Hensel, who at that time played Miss Sara Sampson on the stage of the Hamburg National Theatre, as it was also the present for the theater critic Lessing, who was sitting in the audience (*Hamburgische Dramaturgie, 13. Stück*). But Mellefont's room at the inn which Sara enters, she herself, Mellefont, and the other characters exist in no more real a present than they would if they were characters in a novel. If we analyze our experience in the theater more closely, we note that here just as well as in a reading situation we are conscious of the fact that the real Here and Now of the stage, and in turn our Here and Now in the audience, is not identical with the fictive Here and Now of the action of the play. Immersed in the action unfolding before us, we forget the stage as stage, just as we forget the past tense form of verbs in fictional narration—indeed, radically phrased, as we forget the narrative act itself. When Goethe characterized the difference between dramatic and epic presentational forms through the mime and the rhapsodist respectively, what he had in mind was the Homeric epos, where he conceived of the epic poet as being at once the same one who recited the work (and thinking thus, he personified the narrative act into a narrator).[141] However, the principal thing is not the reciting of the epos, i.e., the rhapsodist himself (he disappeared with the art of printing, but the epos form persists), but the εἰπεῖν, as that function which he employs. To the epic mimetes only the dramatic mimetes is comparable, to the narrative only the dramatic poet. But comparable to the act of narration, to the mimetic function of the epic mimetes, is the mime, i.e., none other than the stage itself, the mimetic function, or more precisely a portion of the mimetic function of the dramatist.

The stage, together with the actors, is only a part of the mimetic function of the dramatist, whose art work is a verbal work, just as is epic literature. But the stage is the non-literary partial function which the verbal art work constructed through dialogue can (not must) make use of. In the totality of the scenically embodied dramatic work it stands for that part of the narrative function which is omitted in the structure of the drama (which latter forms only characters): namely the function of producing a physical environment for the action. But it does not stand for this part of the mimetic function in the genuine, literary sense. Instead it is a surrogate-function, which, like every substitute, consists of a different material from that which it is to replace. Stage and actors are a different material or medium from that of the epic narrative function: unlike the latter, they do not belong to literature itself as its substance, and they are not shaped and developed by the poet; indeed, they are beyond his creative capacity. And precisely for this reason could this surrogate-function arise as an independent and unique art, that of stage and acting technique; just for this reason could purely literary fiction be interfused with the physical reality of the stage, and that play of the various times and modes of present emerge which has confounded past dramatic theory.

However, it is here that we also find the purely poetological reasons for the various methods and endeavors of stage technique to cause the reality of the stage boards to be forgotten in favor of the fictive world which they "signify." For of course it lies in the particular manner in which scenic embodiment must replace the epic narrative function, i.e., in the physical restrictions of this embodiment, that dramatic fiction has the capacity and the tendency to assume the appearance of a reality which is analogous to that of the audience.

These possiblities were assessed and utilized in the theaters of the various periods according to differing conceptions, technical facilities, and changing trends in fashion and taste. The specifically decorative stage technique, the illusory stage, which began with the backdrops, thunder machines, etc., of the court theater of the Baroque, and which strove for an ever more exact imitation of reality, can be understood as an intention to give fiction the greatest possible resemblance to, or illusion of, perceptible reality. The underlying conception of art which must be considered the leading one here, and which generally speaking is often the chief one in the contemporary theater, endeavors to cause the merely fictive presence to be forgotten in favor of real present-time, and the merely "signifying" stage boards to be forgotten in favor of the real ones— to which end they, like the actors themselves, must be costumed. Seen in terms of epistemology, the reverse procedure underlies the efforts of modern directors to reduce the imitated, pseudo objective reality of the stage as much as possible and, by making the stage "non-illusory," to cause the latter to be forgotten in favor of the purely fictive world of the play, and not confuse its "present" with that occupied by the stage as a physical object. The thought behind this stage technique is that of freeing dramatic literature as much as possible from those sensuous phenomena concurrent to its scenic embodiment, that is, as little as possible to disrupt or restrict through sensuous impression that symbolization which is the essence of all art.[142]

Peculiarly enough, the ultimate consequence of eliminating

stage reality from the structure of dramatic literature was possible only with the help of technical advances. The radio drama [*Hörspiel*] may well be the only form which realizes, or appears to realize the second aspect of the formula: that the figure becomes word and nothing but word. However, the problematic of the radio drama consists in that scenic embodiment, and therefore the total perceptibility of the piece, is reduced to audio perception. And this causes the mode of being of these figures in the literary work to assume a reduced grade. Hearing a drama occupies an intermediate position between seeing and reading it. Mental representation, which is totally suspended in complete sensuous perception, and which on the other hand is fully engaged in the act of reading, is incorporated into auditory sensuous perception at more or less half-strength. Hearing a drama is distinguished from reading it in that the actors in a radio drama give a so to speak inner shaping to the characters, but the audience (listeners) can distinguish these characters only through the different voices of the actors. This is a somewhat irritating process, to which many prefer the reading of a drama, simply because pure mental representation expands the literary figures, which were projected only as speaking ones, into their psychic-corporeal totality. In such a process the imagination operates in a manner which is principally no different from the reading of a novel. Except that in the latter case the possibilities are given for channeling this mental representation with greater precision; and it depends on the style of narration to what degree these possibilities are utilized. But the half-reduced representation which the radio drama presents totally inhibits spontaneous mental representation. For here even in our mental representation the word no longer becomes the figure, but remains word and voice. Indeed, precisely as word becomes voice it divests the purely literary word of its function of shaping and moulding the figure.

But the intent here is not that of an aesthetic evaluation of the radio drama, the illusory and the abstract stage—in short, of the various kinds of and experiments in scenic embodiment. We have attempted to characterize them briefly in order to show the varied behavior of that surrogate-function which the stage represents in the total structure of drama, and in turn the function of perceptibility, which here is the sole factor of importance. For the much-discussed problematic of time does, to be sure, have its cause in the embodiment of dramatic literature on the stage; still, epistemologically speaking, it was erroneous to treat it as a problem both of literature itself and of the stage. Despite its physical reality and sensuous perceptibility the stage, too, is mimesis, just as the epic world existing purely in mental representation—a surrogate mimesis, to be sure, one which does not have its mode of existence as part of literature itself, but which merely serves the latter. But the paradoxical problem of the stage and its relation to dramatic literature consists precisely in that on the other hand it also does affect the poetic structure of the drama, because as perceptible mimesis it requires figures capable of presenting themselves, figures which can pass from the mentally represented world of literature into the —however mimetic—perceptual world of the stage.

The problems arising from the epistemological investigation of these two types within the fictional genre enable, or indeed compel us also to subject to analysis yet a third, even if not totally legitimate type of fiction, namely the film.

Cinematic Fiction

At first glance it does not seem quite in keeping that within the framework of a logic of literature we should also give some consideration to the film. Photography, i.e., technology, to which the film owes its existence, does not seem to have any legitimate place in the realm of the verbal art work. Indeed, the specific problem of the logic of literature, which is grounded in literature's linguistic structure, does not appear to have any validity for the film. But just as the logic of the drama is only completely realized and elucidated once its structure as a stage piece, and hence once the phenomenology of the stage, has been included, so we can also say that the technical aspect of the film does not prejudice its existence as a fictional, and in turn as a literary form. For we shall see that the film does exhibit a definite logical structure, and that it does so not only despite, but also because of its technical, photographic dimension. On the other hand the photographic factor is, to be sure, also the reason why the logic of the film is more complex than either that of the drama or that of narration, since because of this factor it is not quite autochthonous, but must be established only with reference to these other two forms, which are "genuine" fiction in the literary sense.

The intricate problems in the phenomenology of the film can be unraveled most easily from the perspective of the movie-goer. The latter's situation is distinguished on the one hand from that of the theater-goer and on the other from that of the reader of a novel in a peculiar way, which may be initially expressed by the fact that the movie-goer, unlike the theater-goer or the reader of a novel, does not completely understand what he does and experiences when he sees a film. Is he viewing a novel or a theatrical piece? Is the action narrated, or is it a dramatic presentation? This question is by no means easily and readily answered; and only once a careful comparison of the situation of the movie-goer with that of the novel reader and the theater-goer has been made will the structure of cinematic fiction be thrown into relief.

Above all, the situation of the person viewing a film is reminiscent of that of the spectator in the theater: it being namely that of a spectator and not that of a reader. We see and hear; we apprehend the film via sensuous perception, not via mental representation, as we do a novel. Nevertheless, in a movie-house we are not a spectator in the same way as we are in the theater. We see something different from what we do in the theater—and it is primarily this matter of seeing which is important here. What we see in the theater unfolds on the stage. This is a natural, i.e., a three-dimensional space, the extension of the space occupied by the audience, and it is not the physical conditions but only convention which prohibits us from going up onto the stage and mingling with the actors. The movie screen, on the other hand, is a two-dimensional surface, and what we see on it has nothing to do with the spatio-temporal conditions of our own physical existence—just as little as a painting does. But the curious and paradoxical thing we experience is that precisely the two-dimensional film conveys a more natural spatial experience than the three-dimensional stage. Indeed, to express this phenomenon quite pithily, the two-dimensional, i.e., the film, produces a three-dimensional spatial experience, whereas the three-dimensional stage produces a two-dimensional one, or in any event one which is extremely fragmentary.

At this point in the analysis it becomes necessary to investigate more closely those structural conditions of cinematic art which are purely technical: namely photography. Its relation to the film is obviously the same as that of narration to the novel, and that of dialogue to the drama. In all three cases the epic, dramatic, or cinematic work is the product of its respective creative technical medium. But in establishing this comparison we immediately sense that it is not completely valid. To begin with, photography does distinguish itself as such from the other two, which are literary techniques. But even this statement is not totally correct. It is not completely correct to separate photographic technique used for purposes of the film from the other two, purely literary techniques. These, namely the epic and the dramatic technical tools, are the word, language, whereas photographic techniques as such are not linguistic, but rather ones of pictorial reproduction. Nonetheless the film, unlike photography *per se,* belongs not to the realm of the plastic arts, but to that of literary art. Photography as an art can be compared with painting, which has already been done (and for our context it is irrelevant whether such comparisons have been positive or negative). The film, however, cannot be compared with painting, but rather only with the two literary arts, epic and drama. Should we ask why, we will encounter a paradoxical phenomenon whose basis is again of a technical nature. It is not through the photographic image as such that the film is comparable to the literary arts; rather, it is the *animated* photographic image, the *motion* picture, which enables such comparison. But what does even the animated photographic image have to do with literature? In posing this question, we are admittedly no longer considering merely the presentational medium of epic and drama, i.e., language itself; but rather that which it respectively creates and presents: human life, men in action. Notice, then, that the technically reproductive art, i.e., photography, which could compare and even compete with painting so long as it was capable of photographing only unanimated people and things, entered as even more of a rival into the realm of literary art as soon as it was able to photograph animated persons and objects. For therewith it appropriated to itself, if only imitatively, one of the secrets of all life, namely motion, and could then, like the literary arts, produce the illusion, the fiction of human life.

But this does not answer the question as to what we, as the viewer of a film, experience. We cannot answer this question simply by saying that we see a movie. Such a reply does not have the same unambiguous meaning that it has when we say we are reading a novel, or that we are reading or seeing a play. Considered as a literary form, neither the novel nor the drama requires elucidation through still another literary form. A novel is a novel, a play a play, and we know directly for what reasons it is so. But when we see a movie we can ask whether we are seeing a novel or a drama; that is, in order to elucidate its literary structure we need other literary forms, namely those of the novel and drama. This fact already emerges clearly in the analysis of the situation of the movie-goer, this being, as was already mentioned, that of a spectator: we see and hear. But now the peculiar circumstance arises where at once we also find ourselves in the situation of a reader of a novel—insofar as we place the emphasis here on the concept of the novel and not on that of the reader. For not everything which we see in a film can also be seen on a theatrical stage. We can, however, read it in a novel. When, for example, the sun on the distant horizon slowly sinks into the sea, when a plane lifts off from the ground and disappears into the sky, when couples dance through spacious ballrooms, snowflakes whirl and settle on trees and fences —in such instances we do see something, but we see something which is narrated. The animated image, or motion picture, has a narrative function; it replaces the word at work in the epic narrative function. This is the reason that in the film we can view pure milieu depictions without persons, while the stage, on the other hand, cannot be shown without characters. For the stage has no autonomous function within the piece which is being enacted upon it. It does not belong to the piece itself; it is not a part of the dramatic work. But what we see in the film belongs as completely without exception to it as does everything which we read in a novel belong to the latter. The animated picture, which exercises a narrative function, brings the film closer to epic than to dramatic fiction. When we see a film we are viewing narrated material, a novel.

But is this definition completely correct? Do we not also, and indeed primarily, see a drama, a theater piece, when we see a film? Something like an expanded drama, expanded upon through the pictorial narrative factor of the motion picture? For we see just that which we cannot experience or see in reading a novel, but can on the stage: speaking and moving actors, dramatic characters. Since the advent of the talking film it is precisely this, i.e., the film's dramatic aspect, which seems to have particularly entered the foreground. And cinematic art has since abundantly availed itself of existing dramatic literature: Shakespeare's *Hamlet, Julius Caesar, A Midsummer Night's Dream,* Strindberg's *Miss Julie,* and other plays of world literature have been filmed. In the talking film the narrative picture actually does seem to function only as an expanded stage, and in the best, most efficacious illusion to improve upon the latter's fragmenting restrictions and scenic effects, replacing its unnatural effects with natural ones which the motion picture is able to produce. But it is precisely here that the actual theoretical problem of the film is hidden. A unique phenomenon emerges here; and that relation of epic and dramatic elements which mesh to form the structure of the film may well prove to be the most complex relation possible of all literary forms.

First, let us again consider the film's dramatic structural component. In order to avoid any possibility of misunderstanding, let us emphasize once more that under dramatic structure we understand nothing other than the pure dialogue form of the drama, which form is the ultimate reason that a play can be performed. We shall begin by comparing the dramatic form of the film with that of the theatrical stage piece. In doing so, we encounter a phenomenon which can be demonstrated especially well in the filming of already existing dramatic works like the ones menioned above: *Hamlet, Julius Caesar, Miss Julie,* etc. The relation of these works to their filmed versions differs considerably from the relation in which they stand to a staged version—even in cases where the movie retains the text of the play unchanged. A symptom of this phenomenon is the fact that the theatrical stage in no way exercises any effect upon the literary existence (and worth) of these works. They exist independently of whether or not they are performed, be it on the Shakespearean stage or that of Reinhardt or Piscator. And they also exist independently of whether they are good or bad. The form of these plays, which has been created by the poet, remains unviolated and unaffected, and can be revived again in any period —for everyone who has a reading or viewing experience of them. These works *are*, they are eternal, preserved in the works of the respective author. But the films *Hamlet, Julius Caesar,* and *Miss Julie,* on the other hand, do not exist outside of the movie screen. The situation is not such that they are, but that they were: namely when they were being shown, and they will only be again when they are shown again. Despite their unaltered dramatic texts they do not exist as autonomous literary works removed from the temporal moment, but only as scripts, as scenarios which have no significance of their own within the totality of the film, but constitute only one function among others in cinematic art. *Qua* films they are no longer Shakespeare's or Strindberg's works. They have been altered in that their original dramatic form has been combined with an epic element which does not belong to this form. The milieu of the movie *Hamlet,* for example, no longer functions merely as a stage upon which the dramatic work is being played, but rather is a part of the cinematic work *Hamlet,* exactly as it would be if it were to be narrated in a work of epic literature. And this process not only concerns the milieu presented but also affects the cinematic figures, the actors. Unlike the dramatic figure, they not only present themselves through speech, but they are in addition extensively described. For example, in the Shakespearean play Ophelia is not shown on stage as being in the brook, dead; rather, the queen merely reports this to Laertes. But in the movie *Hamlet* she is seen drifting on the water, entwined in garlands and branches—and she is no longer a dramatic, Shakespearean figure, but a narrated, an epic figure. For as an epic figure, being portrayed as dead, a corpse floating on the water, she can have a legitimate literary existence, whereas as a dramatic figure she cannot. Which, by the way, is a particularly clear illustration of how the motion picture shifts photography, which as such belongs to the graphic arts (epistemologically considered), into the literary realm. A painted—or even a photographed—portrait of Ophelia in the brook has no reference to the literary domain (except as a picture in a book, which obviously has nothing to do with the problem with which we are concerned).

This brings us to the point where we must now investigate the epic aspects of the film and determine whether it is really completely correct to say that the cinematic figure has an epic but not a dramatic form. In broader terms the question can be phrased thus: if it is correct that being filmed renders a drama epic, so that despite the speaking actors what we see is a novel, is it then also correct that the filmed novel has the same structure as the narrated one? In other words, if a drama is rendered epic through being filmed, does a filmed novel remain a genuine novel?

It is doubtless no coincidence that the motion picture industry has preferred to film novels. The novel provides a better basis for a film than does a play, because the film can more completely correspond to the depictions in a novel. The cinematic image works like the narrative function: like the latter it can build up a total picture of the respective narrated world, can integrate particulars into a whole: the corner of a room becomes, we know not how, the room itself, the room a house, the house a street, the street a city, and so on. The cinematic image, like the narrative function, can show not only inanimate things, but also taciturn persons— persons wandering, sitting, ruminating, silently occupied. In a quite different manner from on the stage, the facial expression has an autonomous function; it need not be only the mien accompanying speech. The gesture, the facial expression, the tear, and the smile speak for themselves, and often speak more clearly than the articulated word. Indeed, the smile we see surely has more communicative and concrete visual appeal than does the narrated and therefore only mentally represented smile. And we no longer differentiate between that which is spoken and that which is pictorially narrated. The cinematic pictorial function fluctuates; it narrates space, corporeity, and speech just as the epic narrative function does. Like the latter, it also narrates recollections, dreams, and fantasy, in that through the "flash-back" it reverts "back" from the Here and Now of the action and shows past events. This is a favorite film technique, which makes the assimilation of the cinematic pictorial function to a narrative function quite clear.[143] All in all, the film's narrational power is so great that the epic factor of cinematic art seems to be more decisive for its literary classification than does the dramatic factor.

But let us pause for a moment and ask again whether this is entirely correct. The relation of the epic and the dramatic in the film only renews its complexity, still leaving the question unsatisfactorily answered as to whether we see a drama or a novel when we sit in a movie. The complication arising here is of an extremely particular nature. In order to resolve it we must revert to the phenomenon of the animated image. The animated picture, as we have endeavored to show, is the reason why the film, which itself is a product of photography, has its phenomenological locus not in the realm of the plastic, but in that of the literary arts. And precisely as a motion-picture the cinematic image fulfills to a great extent the function of the narrative act in narrative literature. The animated image is narrative, and appears to constitute the film as an epic, not as a dramatic form. A drama, when it is filmed, is given epic qualities. At this point, however, we will come up against a boundary if we pursue the comparison between cinematic and genuine epic narration any further. This frontier is established by the fact that even the motion-picture is a *picture*. Because it is a picture the cinematic image must halt at this frontier, on whose other side the realm of mental representation, of combinative thought commences. Thus the very picture-quality of the filmed image is the reason why in some respects a filmed novel is reduced to the structure of a drama, to that of a theatrical piece, and therefore why we experience a filmed novel as dramatized. For what does the picture-quality of the filmed image mean? On what basis does it constitute the film's dramatic structural element? It means that we apprehend the film, just as the theatrical work, in perception: through seeing and hearing.[144]

The ramifications of this fact are manifold. First, let us remain with the cinematic figures. In their capacity as epic figures they are restricted in the following way: although we can view and interpret them in the film as portraying or expressing themselves silently, i.e., in gesture and mien—and this for the duration of unlimited periods of time—nevertheless we can as little discover from the cinematic as we can from the dramatic figure exactly what he is tacitly thinking and feeling. But we can experience this in a novel, which is the only place in the system of language where human beings can be presented in their inner life, in their non-verbalized thinking and feeling, as we have extensively demonstrated. In literature it is the dramatic and the cinematic forms which fashion human beings in that form of reality in which we and our fellow-man live: the communication-form of the articulated, i.e., either the spoken or the written word. Only the novel, only narrative literature can create persons in a form which is not bound to and circumscribed by articulated communication, auditory perception.

There is another way in which the motion-picture's narrative function proves to be curtailed by its physical restrictions, that is, by the modus of perception. And this one concerns not only the creation of persons, but also that of the world of objects. Here is an example:

Amenhotep—Nebmarê's Witwe thronte ihm gerade gegenüber auf hohem Stuhl mit hohem Schemel, gegen das Licht, vor dem mittleren der tiefreichenden Bogenfenster, so daß ihr ohnedies bronzefarben gegen das Gewand abstechender Teint durch die Verschattung noch dunkler schien. *

This highly pictorial scene from Thomas Mann's *Joseph and His Brothers*, can without any qualification be thought of as an impressive technicolor shot. Nevertheless, the setting as an epic construction in a novel produces a different experience from that gotten from a picture. The additional element in the scene as part of a novel is the factor of interpretation, of inference. In this instance the narrative act's faculty of interpretation restricts itself completely to straight physical description, without metaphorical or other periphrastic devices. Through the subtle, comparative description "bronze-colored to begin with, but darker still because of the shading," the Egyptian queen Teje's external appearance is made to transcend the given situation, forming a more comprehensive picture of her. Indeed, the situation itself does not appear in plastic consolidation, but in its causal structure, as it were, such that even the purely material relationships among the objects— "against the light," "long, arched window"—guide our mental representation of what is so visualized. For this visualization is interpretatively produced. The filmed image would forego this kind of visualization, indeed all visualization whatever. For one mentally visualizes only what one is not seeing in direct visual perception. And in our present example this means that on film the wealth of references in the novel depiction would not appear: that, for example, the darkened face is to be ascribed to the window behind, or even the mere fact that this window is full-length. The specta-

---

* Amenhotep—Nebmarê's widow, sat opposite him enthroned on a dais with a tall footstool, against the light, in front of the center long, arched window, so that the shading made her complexion, which was bronze-colored to begin with, contrasting nicely with her dress, appear to be even darker yet.

tor's visual contemplation is not channeled; it is left to him whether or not he establishes a relation between the darkened face and the window behind it.

With this phenomenon the point is reached where, even within the sphere of the mere depiction of physical objects, the epic and cinematic narrative functions part ways, and each strives to attain those ends set by the limits of its own creative potential. As we have tried to show, the epic narrative function engenders the fictive world interpretatively; the latter lives and "is" through the signifying word which constructs it, from the simplest and most materialistic portrayal of objects and things and extending into all manner and degree of intellectual interpretation of the novel's action and world. As so and only so interpretatively produced is this fictive world experienced through the reader's acts of understanding as he reads the novel. Cinematic narration, on the other hand, can give only indications—no matter how much the director may succeed in embedding interpretative functions within the filmed image. For since such interpretation is not conceptually anchored, but—like the things of objective reality—is relinquished to the sphere of perception, the experience of what is captured on film, just as that of objective reality, is left to each individual spectator as his individual experience.

We are now at the stage where we can precisely determine the relation of the film to epic and dramatic literature. The motion-picture as such is the reason why the film is both drama rendered epic and epic rendered dramatic. The factor of motion in cinematic photography turns the latter into a narrative function, which in turn makes the movie actor largely an epic figure. But the picture-factor of photography restricts the film's capacity for forming characters to dramatic formation, i.e., to dialogue; and in addition, it divests the portrayal of the objective world of its causal structure. In the film dramatic and epic techniques mesh, resulting in a special form of dramatized epic and epically rendered drama, both in one—a blend wherein in a peculiar but nevertheless structurally and epistemologically well-founded manner each of these two factors is at once both enlarged upon and restricted.

Surveying our expositions in this chapter, let us recapitulate and conclude by turning our attention once again to the logical structure of literary fiction, the fictional genre. That we had to begin our analysis with epic fiction, and that the latter occupied the major portion of this chapter, is due to the system of language. Epic fiction is not only the purest fictional structure in terms of logic and language; it is also the only form which presents us with the possibility of precisely developing the concept of literary fiction. Only through comparison of the functions and properties of fictional narration with those of the reality statement could the essence of the non-real, i.e., the field of fiction, which is not the range of experience of a narrator but the product of the narrative function, be shown. All fictional structures are thus defined by the intransgressible boundary which separates fictional narration from statement. For even though this boundary is no longer visible in dramatic and cinematic fiction, since the narrative function has been replaced by different functions that belong to the realm of perception, nevertheless as a criterion in the logic of language it is still definitive and conclusive even for these fictional structures. As became clear in each of our investigations, statement served as a catalyst for the purpose of separating and distinguishing those partly linguistic, partly presentational functions which produce fictional structures.

We believe that in this way we have been able to demonstrate that narrative fiction grows out of the same creative and formative impulse as dramatic fiction (as Aristotle already saw), that the epic poet does not narrate primarily for the sake of narrating, but in order to create a world of fictive characters—and this without detriment to the fact that the formative narrative function can seem to become independent and so to speak forget its task of producing fiction. That nonetheless the structural law of fiction is preserved unblemished, revealing just such instances of narrative independence as humoristic illusion in most cases, is something we have also attempted to demonstrate.

From this perspective cinematic fiction, too, belongs in the logically defined realm of literary fiction, although not on an unequal basis with epic and dramatic fiction. Even it, in its capacity as fiction, is not totally conditioned by the technical medium of motion-photography that partially replaces the narrative function; for it is also conditioned by the creative, mimetic impulse. In connection with this, let us conclude this chapter on fiction by referring once again to our introductory investigations into the definition of the concepts "literature" and "reality." The logical approach to literature, which is the topic of this book, could lead one to forget that mimetic works are more than just constructs thus and so structured by the laws of thought and language. They are *literature*, art. The aesthetic law which governs them, and which provides the impetus for them, is mimesis. Mimesis is "imitation" of reality; it is antiquity's word for fiction when applied to literary structures. And we have shown that already in Aristotle the word carries this meaning. The concept of imitation has been given an all too naturalistic tinge in literary theory. But when we combine with it the meaning of non-reality and semblance, it becomes expanded, and reveals that that pseudo-reality which is semblance —and which in the various types within the fictional genre can be constructed with several different formative devices—precisely because it is semblance, i.e., non-reality, has the mode of being of a symbol. Reality itself merely is. It does not *mean*. Only the non-real has the power to convert the real into sense, into meaning.

4

THE LYRICAL GENRE

The System of the Reality Statement and the Locus of the Lyric

To an even greater extent than our previous remarks, the following commentary and attempted definitions run the risk of being misunderstood. Today more than ever, spurred on by the situation in the modern lyric, the theory and interpretation of lyric poetry is oriented toward the purely linguistic artistic phenomenon which comprises the lyric poem; and it is of the conviction that only from this standpoint can one at all approach lyric art. And properly so, since a poem presents no such formal and structural problems as fictional literature does—narration, the creation of time, the mode of being of fiction itself, etc.—and is absolutely identical with its linguistic form. When in what follows this aspect of lyric literature, in itself a primary one, is developed as a phenomenon of only secondary importance, we must bear in mind that this is being done within the framework of that theme with which this book is exclusively concerned: the classification of the system of literature as founded in the theory of language, i.e., the relation of literary genres to the statement system of language.

If we recall Hegel's statement that literature is that particular art in which art itself begins to break down and assume its point of transition to the prose of scientific thought, then we can now use the results of our investigations into the theory of language and determine in what cases and to what extent his pronouncement is or is not valid. And if we may consider it sufficient to see the insights of great and original thinkers substantiated in the phenomena themselves (as little as it is fruitful to use such insights dogmatically as a point of departure), then we can regard as satisfactory confirmation the fact that Hegel's statement has its validity just at that point where Aristotle drew the dividing line between mimetic and elegiac art, where he separated ποιεῖν from λέγειν. Hegel's statement does not, or not yet, hold true for that sphere of literature which is the realm of ποιεῖν, of mimesis. Here the intransgressible boundary which separates fictional narration from reality statement, and therefore from the statement-system of language, makes it impossible for literature to revert to the "prose of scientific thought," that is, to the statement-system. For here the process of "making" is at work, in the sense of forming, shaping, fashioning; here is the workshop where the *poietes* or *mimetes* creates his figures, using language as his instrument and construction material just as the painter uses color and the sculptor stone. Here literature is completely within the domain of the plastic arts, which create the semblance of reality. That this semblance, the law of fiction, first becomes effective in literature when fictive persons are created, whereas a landscape painting is mimesis even without depicting human figures, has its reason in the special nature of the construction material of literature, namely language, which outside the realm of mimesis is the medium of speech (in all its modifications). We may also formulate it conversely and say that language is statement in every instance where is does *not* create fictive I-Origines. And the only reason this formulation is not as epigrammatic as it may to all intents and purposes seem to be, is that it does indeed express those two opposing logical possibilities over which thought expressed in language presides: the potential to be either the statement of a subject about an object, or the function (in the hands of the narrator or the dramatist) which creates fictive subjects.—However, by no means does the boundary separating these two aspects of language coincide with that boundary which divides creative and non-creative language (as we have defined above). *That* creative language which produces the lyric poem belongs to the statement system of language. And this is the basic, structural foundation for the fact that the manner in which we experience a lyric poem as literature is quite different from the way we experience a fictional, i.e., a narrative or a dramatic work of literature. We experience it as the statement of a *statement-subject. The much-disputed lyric I is a statement-subject.*

In making such an assertion we seem to be only confirming the traditional definition of the lyric as the subjective literary genre, thereby taking a step backward and away from the modern description of a poem as a verbal structure. A step back to Hegel, for example, the actual founder of German phenomenological theories of literature. "In the lyric," he says, "it is the . . . need (of the subject) which finds its satisfaction in self-expression and the coming to a knowledge of the soul in this expression of itself."[145] With this statement, what German poetic theory has designated as *Erlebnis-lyrik* is expressed as having the specific subjectivity of empirical experience: the "subject" is meant as a person, the personal I of the poet, his interiority [*Innerlichkeit*], and thus the subjectivity of the lyric is contrasted to the objectivity of the epic. The concepts "subjectivity" and "objectivity" are workable, but nonetheless vague and imprecise orientations in the realm of literature (as we have seen in the analysis of the narrative function). They are inexact because it has been overlooked that they are correlative concepts, and are therefore meaningful only when this correlation itself is valid: in the logic of judgment and statement. If conditions are such that the structural principle of lyric poetry is a statement-subject, namely the lyric I, then this genre cannot be compared with and thus related to those literary genres which are not constituted through a statement-subject. Its locus as literature can be determined only within that sphere into which it as a verbal structure categorically belongs: in the statement-system of language.

But if the lyric I is fixed not as merely a "subject" in the personalized sense of this concept, but instead as a statement-subject, then, as we shall attempt to show, the concept of subjectivity will be eliminated from the theory of the lyric, and it will be possible to categorize even the most modern forms and theories of lyric poetry, such as text and text theory, within this generic concept. This may appear to be contradictory at first because the concept of the statement-subject, and therefore that of statement itself, entails subject-object correlation. In the first chapter, using a series of statements from all sentence modalities within all three types of statement—the historical, pragmatic, and theoretical—we demonstrated the various degrees and relationships within this correlation: ranging from the absolute objectivity of a mathematical proposition, whose statement-subject has only the character of inter-individual universality, to the tangible subjectivity of an emotionally tinged command. It was also seen that neither the type of statement nor the sentence modality is the definitive factor for the degree of subjectivity or objectivity, but rather the attitude of the statement-subject—such that a theoretical statement such as those sample sentences from Kant and Heidegger can be more subjective than that of either a historical or a pragmatic statement-subject.

In the description of the general statement-system we could content ourselves with presenting just the subject-object correlation. But now, with respect to the lyrical statement-subject, we must investigate several additional aspects. It is necessary to ask whether the lyrical statement-subject participates in the other three statement types, or whether it is distinguished in any way from these; and if so, what does this reveal about the character of lyric poetry—which means the genesis and mode of being of the lyric work of art.

To this end we must give preliminary consideration to a further essential feature of statement: its character as *communication, information,* understood in the broadest sense. This implies that statement, be it ever so subjectively tinged, is always directed to its object-pole. That is, whether as asserting, enquiring, wishing, or commanding, it carries the intent and purpose of being effectual in the particular context indicated by its content, i.e., its statement-object: asserting in order to inform, enquiring in order to obtain information, and commanding or wishing in order to effect something. Husserl gave pregnant expression to these relations when speaking about philosophy as being a very subjective discipline: "Philosophy is the philosophizer's quite personal affair. It must arise as *his sapientia universalis,* i.e., *his* knowledge tending toward universality—but as a genuinely disciplined and systematic knowledge. . . ."[146] In the context of this passage Husserl was not concerned with the character of the theoretical statement as such, but with the philosopher's existential decision "to live with this as his aim." But nevertheless implied in Husserl's formulation is the directedness of the philosopher's statemental attitude. The intention of someone engaged in even ever so "personal" philosophizing is not that of "expressing *himself*" (Hegel), but that of "bringing to giveness" (to express it in Husserl's terms) the matter with which he is concerned. All three statement categories, which comprise those aspects of our verbal life concerned with communication, are directed away from the subject-pole to the object-pole. Another way of expressing this is that their intention is that of performing a function in an objective context, which in turn is always a context of reality, regardless of what specific kind of reality the respective topic might represent. And let us emphasize again that here it is irrelevant to what degree the statement-subject might make his presence felt. And, as far as the structure and function of a statement is concerned, even if its verbal quality is not altogether irrelevant, still it is only of secondary importance. The lyrical, or to phrase it in more old-fashioned but less mistakable terms, the poetic surge which Kant breaks into in our example cited from the *Critique of Practical Reason* does not make this statement-subject a lyrical one. And when Rilke, whose letters always bear the distinctive imprint of his particular creative style, describes the sleigh-ride in Skåne and the steps ascending into the "void," the lyrical valeurs of this depiction nonetheless still do not render the historical statement-subject represented by the letter-writer Rilke —i.e., someone intending to give information—a lyrical one. Here, too, language is in the service of communication designed for transmitting information.

These conclusions are, of course, self-evident. They alone contribute nothing to an understanding of either the lyric I or the lyrical genre. But there is one phenomenon where the function of the statement-subject is not so self-evident or obvious. We find this exhibited in hymnals and prayer books. As concrete illustration, let us consider the following examples:

> Nach dir, Herr verlanget mich.
> Mein Gott, ich hoffe auf dich. Laß mich nicht zu Schanden werden, daß sich meine Feinde nicht freuen über mich.
> Wende dich zu mir und sei mir gnädig; denn ich bin einsam und elend.
> Die Angst meines Herzens ist groß; führe mich aus meinen Nöten.   (25. Psalm, 1, 2, 16, 17)

> Wie der Hirsch schreiet nach frischem Wasser, so schreiet meine Seele, Gott, zu dir.
> Meine Seele dürstet nach Gott, nach dem lebendigen Gott. Wann werde ich dahin kommen, daß ich Gottes Angesicht schaue?   (42. Psalm, 2, 3)*

---

* Unto Thee, O Lord, do I lift up my soul.
  O my God, I trust in Thee. Let me not be ashamed, let not mine enemies triumph over me.
  Turn Thee unto me, and have mercy upon me, for I am desolate and afflicted.
  The troubles of my heart are great: O bring Thou me out of my distresses.
                                          (Psalm 25:1, 2, 16, 17)

  As the hart panteth after the water brooks, so panteth my soul after Thee, O God.
  My soul thirsteth for God, for the living God. When shall I succeed in seeing his countenance?
                                          (Psalm 42:1, 2)

In allen meinen Taten
Laß ich den Höchsten raten,
Der alles kann und hat;
Er muß zu allen Dingen,
Soll's andern wohl gelingen
Selbst geben guten Rat.

So sei nun, Seele, seine
Und traue dem alleine
Der dich geschaffen hat.
Es gehe wie es gehe,
Dein Vater in der Höhe
Weiß allen Sachen Rat.

> (Paul Fleming, Gesangbuch für die evangelische Kirche in
> Württemberg, Nr. 324)†

Wenn ich ihn nur habe
Wenn er mein nur ist,
Wenn mein Herz bis hin zum Grabe
Seine Treue nie vergißt;
Weiß ich nichts von Leide,
Fühle nichts als Andacht, Lieb' und Freude.

Wenn ich ihn nur habe,
Laß ich alles gern,
Folg' an meinem Wanderstabe
Treugesinnt nur meinem Herrn;
Lasse still die andern
Breite, lichte, volle Straßen wandern.

> (Fr. v. Hardenberg)‡

† In all my deeds/I let the Highest (one) counsel me/
Who holds all things in His power and possession/He must in all things,/
Where others are to succeed,/Himself give good advice.

So now, soul, be His/And trust in Him alone/
Who has created you./However things may go,/
Your Father on high/In all matters can give counsel.

‡ If only I have Him,/If only He is mine,/If my heart unto the grave/
Ne'er forgets His fidelity,/Then I shall know no sorrow,/
And shall feel only devotion, love and joy.

If only I have Him,/Gladly shall I leave all else/
And follow with my traveling-staff/Faithfully in the way of my Lord;/
And in peace let others/Traverse broad, glittering, crowded highways.

The Psalms of David, the hymns of Fleming, Gerhardt, Harden-berg, et al. all exhibit features of the lyric poem: poetic diction, verse, rhyme. And they bear that form in which the major portion of lyric poetry appears: namely the first-person form, as the state-ment of an I which is in this case glorifying, beseeching, praying, confessing faith. But the prayer, the psalm, and the hymn, which in the church service do have the first-person form of a poem,[147] nevertheless do not belong to (and have customarily not been counted as part of) the realm of the lyric as a literary genre. This is due not to the content of the psalms and hymns, but to the statement-subject appearing in them. It is a *pragmatic* statement-subject, and as such objectively oriented, like the historical and theoretical statement-subjects. Prayer is part of the church service, just as are the sermon and all the rituals performed by clergy and congregation. It falls within the context of church ritual, within that objective or real context which is the specifically religious sphere, and it brings the individuals in the congregation into a relation with this sphere. The I of prayer is the congregational I, and to what extent the individual worshipper experiences this con-gregational I as a personal I cannot be indicated—nor does it have anything to do with the inherent structure of the prayer offered as a congregational one. And even when the individual worshipper, at church or in his room, says the prayer as the personal expression of his piety, or of his misery in times of need, the I of the prayer remains nonetheless just as much a pragmatic I as is that of the actual individual who in the moment of praying identifies himself with it for his own personal ends. Even if the prayer has lyric form, he does not experience it as a lyric poem—precisely because, according to the degree of his pragmatic religious engagement, he refers the I of the prayer to himself.

But psalms and hymns represent particular forms which, in a special way, are revealing for an investigation of the structure, the logic of literature. For they *are* poets' creations, regardless here of what rank and reputation the respective poet may have. And they do indeed change character when we no longer encounter them in church ritual or in the hymnal, but in the poet's works. For the person who has never experienced the hymn "If only I have Him,/ If only He is mine" in church, but only as a poem in the collected works of Novalis, as the fifth of his "Sacred Songs," it is completely divorced from the context of reality set by the Protestant divine worship. He experiences the poem's religious content, the intimacy of the sentiment, the melodic quality of the verse, and he experiences them as the religious sentiment of the I who is expressing it, as this I's experience. And what kind of an I is it which he experiences? It is the lyric I of this lyric religious poem, the I which has given its piety this and only this expression, this and only this form. How does this phenomenon come about? Through nothing other than the context in which the reader encounters the poem. For this is no chance context, but the one into which the poet has set his work. By including this one in his collected poetry and not merely having it serve the ends of church worship, he is indicating that the poem has no practical purpose, that the statement-subject does not intend to be a practical, but a lyric I. The pious poem has no function in a context of reality, but is only the artistic expression of a pious soul.

Novalis' "bi-faceted" sacred song is not unsuited to take us further into the phenomenology of the lyric I, and in turn into both the structure of the lyric poem as well as that of the lyrical genre in general. In the preceding context it served as an index of that locus within the statement-system of language where the lyric as a literary genre is to be found. As the work of a poet which also serves a practical purpose, that of worship, it represents a borderline-case, wherein we are able to discern when we are dealing with a lyric I and when not. The identifying feature here is nothing other than the altered conception of the I of the poem (irrespective of whether or to what degree we are consciously aware of this change), and not the poem *form per se*. For in principle every statement can be put into the form of a poem, without, however, turning it into a lyric poem. And even if the prayer, on the basis of its content, i.e., its religious concern, does lend itself to a poetically beautiful rendering, nevertheless it lies on the same level—even though aesthetically at the opposite pole—as the occasional poem (here meant not in the Goethean, but in the profane sense) and the advertising jingle. For the foundation and classification of the literary genres as grounded in theory of language, it is of utmost importance that we stringently separate the *lyrical statement-subject*—which constitutes the lyric—from the *form* of lyric poetry. Because the lyric is located within the statement-system of language, its own characteristic form can be transferred onto any statement; and conversely, where a lyrical statement-subject is present, the form in which it "is speaking" by no means must meet the aesthetic claims of a lyric form as a work of art. Such is the case with bad poetry, for example. But there is a very great danger of being misunderstood when we say that every statement-subject which posits itself as a lyrical (and not as a historical, theoretical, or pragmatic) one, constitutes a lyric structure. It is the same process which also classifies every light novel as part of the epic fictional genre. Only that there this process is more tangible and can be immediately recognized, since fictional narration exhibits those established characteristics which separate it from the reality statement. But the logical genesis of the lyric poem does not evince such characteristics, since the poem resides within the statement-system and since its form is transferrable onto each statement type. The lyrical genre becomes constituted through the so to speak "announced" intention of the statement-subject to posit itself as a lyric I, and this means by the context in which we encounter the poem. However, neither for fiction nor for the lyric is the aesthetic form the decisive criterion for an individual work's belonging to either of these two literary genres.[148] Thus an ever so poorly composed novel will nevertheless belong

within the system of literature (whereby "literature" is not understood in the aesthetic sense), but a however brilliantly written
essay will not. The (unintentionally) funniest Friederike-Kemp-
ner poem will also belong to it, but the 42nd Psalm of David will
not. And the fifth of Navolis' "Sacred Songs" belongs to it when
we encounter this work in a collection of poems, but not when we
encounter it in a Protestant hymnal.

By now it may have become clear that the intent of these definitions is simply that of fixing the logical locus of the lyric within the
system of literature. To summarize once again, this locus lies in the
statement-system of language, in contradistinction to the fictional
genre, which is detached from this system. But it is situated in a
part of the statement-system which is distinct from all three categories of the communicative statement, beyond the frontiers of
this sphere, so to speak. We have defined the communicative statement in that, regardless of the degree of its subjectivity, it is oriented away from the subject-pole to the object-pole, thus having
a function in an objective context, or a context of reality. Furthermore, we have indicated, with the example of the prayer-poem,
that the lyrical statement does not "intend" (as we must say) to
have such a function, and that its subject-object polarity is different from that of the communicative statement. Only a closer investigation of these various relations, i.e., an investigation into the
nature and behavior of the lyrical statement-subject, will further
elucidate the (logical) genesis of the lyric poem as a verbal art
form.

Lyric Subject-Object Correlation

Let us resume our discussion by again referring to the borderline-case represented by the Novalis prayer-poem, for which pur-

pose we shall now cite it, the fifth of the "Sacred Songs," in its
entirety:

Wenn ich ihn nur habe,
Wenn er mein nur ist,
Wenn mein Herz bis hin zum Grabe
Seine Treue nie vergißt;
Weiß ich nichts von Leide,
Fühle nichts als Andacht, Lieb' und Freude.

Wenn ich ihn nur habe,
Lass' ich alles gern,
Folg' an meinem Wanderstabe
Treugesinnt nur meinem Herrn;
Lasse still die andern
Breite, lichte, volle Straßen wandern.

Wenn ich ihn nur habe,
Schlaf' ich fröhlich ein,
Ewig wird zu süßer Labe
Seines Herzens Flut mir sein,
Die mit sanftem Zwingen
Alles wird erweichen und durchdringen.

Wenn ich ihn nur habe,
Hab' ich auch die Welt;
Selig wie ein Himmelsknabe,
Der der Jungfrau Schleier hält.
Hingesenkt im Schauen
Kann mir vor dem Irdischen nicht grauen.

Wo ich ihn nur habe,
Ist mein Vaterland;
Und es fällt mir jede Gabe
Wie ein Erbteil in die Hand;
Längst vermißte Brüder
Find' ich nun in seinen Jüngern wieder.*

---

* If only I have Him,/If only He is mine,/If my heart unto the grave/
Ne'er forgets His fidelity;/Then I shall know no sorrow,/
And shall feel only devotion, love and joy.

We shall no longer consider this spiritual song as a prayer, but as a lyric poem in the defined sense of the statement of a lyrical statement-subject positing itself as such. In this capacity it is a suitable point of departure for observing that process which engenders the lyric poem. This process is not to be understood as an individual one peculiar to this particular poet, or indeed as one which might be biographically explained, but instead solely as logico-linguistic, as that process which takes place within the subject-object correlation of the lyric statement. As such it does, to be sure, have infinitely differentiated manifestations, whose very differentiations constitute the infinite possibilities of lyric statement and those art forms produced by it. And only in this sense is this process individual, both with respect to individual lyric poems and poets, and also to period styles. The structure of the older lyric presents itself differently in this respect from that of modern poetry.

The fifth of Novalis' "Sacred Songs" is a suitable point of departure for investigating this process precisely because it can also function in the capacity of a song in divine worship. As such it is functioning in a context of reality, namely that of religious worship, as the confession of the heart's love for its Lord, for Christ. As we have seen, the impersonal congregational-I changes to the

---

If only I have Him,/Gladly shall I leave all else,/
And follow with my traveling-staff/Faithfully in the way of my Lord,/
And in peace let others/Traverse broad, glittering, crowded highways.

If only I have Him,/Happily will I go to sleep,/A sweet balm, eternally,/
His heart's stream will be to me,/And will with gentle subduing/
All things soften and possess.

If only I have Him,/Then I also have the world;/Blessed as an angel/
Who holds the Virgin's veil./Kneeled in vision,/
I cannot shudder in the face of worldly things.

Where I only have Him,/[There] is my fatherland;/And every gift falls/
Into my hand like an inheritance;/Long-missing brothers/
Among His servants I now find again.

I of the poet when we read or hear the poem outside of the context of religious worship. The character of the statement-subject changes, but that of the statement-object does not—quite in keeping, since the *poem* does not change. The object-nexus within the poem remains, even if it does not function as worship: "He," the Lord, the possession of whom fills the heart with a joy to which in the five stanzas the five different conditions, some directly and some metaphorically named, attest. The objective continuity of these statements is so clear that all the interpreter has to do is to establish them as the expression of the pious joy of the lyric I "speaking" here. Not too much has yet taken place between the subject- and object-poles of this religious statement created into a poem. Not much, but yet something has indeed already happened. It appears in the fourth stanza—and it is hardly a matter of chance that in those hymnals where this song was included, this stanza was either altered or eliminated.[149] Certainly it is possible that the reason for this lies in the erotic overtones of the third and fourth lines, but possibly also in a certain difficulty in establishing their meaning. And with this we have named an element which is essential for lyric subject-object correlation. Not only the third and fourth lines in themselves, but also the continuity between the two preceding and the two following lines presents certain difficulties in interpretation. In the context of our study we are not concerned with the interpretation of the stanza —for example with the question whether the comparison of blessedness with an angel who holds the Virgin's veil could be inspired by a painting depicting such a scene; whether the "world" in line 2 is meant as the opposite of the "worldly things" in line 6, i.e., as the higher, divine world of Christ, before the vision of which all earthly things fade and hold no more terror.—We are not concerned with these individual questions, but only with the process taking place in the statement, a process which becomes noticeable precisely through those questions of interpretation which are to be posed with respect to this portion of the text. For in this fourth stanza the connections have become *more indistinct* (for which reason it calls for exegesis). The three statements in this stanza, each covering two consecutive lines, are more disparate than the statements of the other four stanzas. In cases where this fourth stanza was omitted from hymnals, we can interpret this omission as an indication that the I of this stanza was not so readily transposable to a congregational-I as was that of the others. In this one we can see that process which constitutes the lyric statement, and which so to speak no longer fulfills the "unequivocal" pragmatic purpose of a prayer.

Nonetheless, despite its fourth stanza, this prayer-poem cannot be used to give sufficient demonstration of this process. It was useful to us only as a phenomenon on the border between a pragmatic and a lyrical statement-subject, and thus in such a capacity it served as a preliminary indication of that process which is constitutive of the lyric in contradistinction to the non-lyric statement. This process, which takes place between the statement-subject and statement-object, shall now be demonstrated with the aid of several examples. The poems are chosen in chronological order, which is intended to make this process evident through the increasing difficulty involved in interpreting them. At the same time, this process can be seen as an explanation—as one among other possible explanations—for the fact that older lyric poetry presents fewer difficulties in understanding than does that of the modern era.

As our first example we have chosen Mörike's famous spring poem "Er ist's" ["It is he"]:

> Frühling läßt sein blaues Band
> Wieder flattern durch die Lüfte;
> Süße, wohlbekannte Düfte
> Streifen ahnungsvoll das Land.
> Veilchen träumen schon,
> Wollen balde kommen.

—Horch, von fern ein leiser Harfenton!
    Frühling, ja, du bist's!
Dich hab' ich vernommen!*

The poem does not present any difficulties of interpretation. It is immediately discernible what it is about. The object-pole in the statements of each line is clear: spring, explicitly named in the first word—or more precisely the coming spring, but first evoked as such only in the fourth, fifth, and sixth lines, through the words "full of promise," "already," "soon." But the first two lines already contain another image: a blue ribbon, fluttering in the breeze. It does not wave by itself, and if we were to answer the question who is making it wave, *we* would have to say "the" spring [*der Frühling*]. But in so answering we are doing something different from what the poem does. The poem says "spring," and only through omitting the article before the name of the season does it make of it a proper name, an (in the German) masculine personification, which it can then have as waving its azure band. But the interpreter cannot repeat this metaphor as a statement. Should he say something like: "this is a metaphor which is possibly meant to express the blue spring sky," then he is again doing something different from what the poem does. The poem does not speak of the sky directly, but merely presents the image of a fluttering blue ribbon, which as such is far removed from the easily identifiable object-pole, namely spring. The next four statements are closer to the object-pole: they name concrete, "familiar" signs of spring: sweet fragrances, violets. And in the words "full of promise," the adverbial modifier of the streaking, sweet scents, there is the direct intimation of the promise of spring. But close

---

* Spring lets his azure band/Flutter in the breeze again;/
Sweet, familiar fragrances/Streak, full of promise, over the land./
Violets are already dreaming,/Soon about to appear./
—Listen, from afar, a low harp note!/Spring, yes, it is you!/
It is you whose faint refrain I've caught!

scrutiny also reveals that the statement about the violets is more indefinite. They are already dreaming, soon about to come. As simple and unobscure as these statements are, we cannot tell whether they are speaking of violets which are already there, as buds perhaps, or whether these, too, are only "in the air" as the presentiment, the promise of spring—or whether, still more indefinite, they are there, but only in the imagination of the poet. In a manner we scarcely notice, the explicit objective reference evades our questioning, our interpretation. It becomes completely remote in the last statement. Like the ribbon metaphor, this is a transformative interpretation of the poet's—but transformed no longer into an image of something visible, but of something only audible. And even so this spring-sign is not concrete, like for instance the song of a lark—a favorite requisite of spring poems in Romanticism—but rather is transformed into something which has no overt reference to the real object-nexus: namely the low, distant harp note. And ultimately the presentiment of spring becomes epitomized in this wholly imaginary note. It, this note, is spring; it is this which the lyric I, now making an overt appearance in the poem, has become aware of.

Let us reflect on what the analysis of this simple little poem shows as its structural principle of organization. A child can understand the poem, for it is perfectly clear what it is about. The object-pole of the statements made by the lyrical statement-subject is the coming of spring. But now we are confronted with the phenomenon that, once we have read the poem in its entirety and when we then consider it as a whole, what remains for us as our primary impression and experience of the poem is not the coming spring as such, the implicit meaning-content, but spring's fluttering blue ribbon, dreaming violets, a low harp note. Something has taken place in the subject-object structure of these statements which never occurs with the informative statement. They have, so to speak, withdrawn from the object-pole and gone into a mutually interlocking order or contiguity, and have thereby taken on meaning-contents which in no way refer—at least not directly—to the object-pole. These new contents are not oriented toward an object-nexus, nor are they controlled and directed by it. They do not form any objective context, any context for communication; rather, they form something different, something which we shall call a *sense-nexus* [*Sinnzusammenhang*]. This means that the statements have withdrawn from the object-pole and have entered the subject-pole. And this is the process which engenders the lyric poem. The poem arises in that statements form a cohesive bond, guided by the sense, or poetic meaning, which the lyric I wishes to express with them. How the lyric I achieves this, what linguistic, rhythmic, metric, and acoustic devices it employs, to what degree it does or does not make an inner continuity visible—this comprises the aesthetic aspect of its creative acts. And from the resultant poem it cannot be distinguished whether the statement's form and contiguous order yield the sense-nexus or vice versa. In the lyric poem form and meaning are identical.

We find the Mörike poem simple and easy to understand because, what with all sense-related, metaphorical glossing of its statements, the implicit meaning-content nevertheless remains clearly intact. The meaning which the poem is created to express, namely joy in the advent of spring, can be directly construed; and only a closer scrutiny of the words, images, and internal relations of the poem made the process of the statements' withdrawal from the object-pole noticeable. *We can establish the formula that the more lucid or abstruse the object-nexus, the more easy or difficult it is to construe the sense-nexus.*

As a second example we have a poem that exhibits an increased, though still only a medium degree of interpretative difficulty, a poem which belongs to the more modern period: Georg Trakl's "Music in Mirabell." But let us emphasize right away that the degree of interpretative difficulty in a poem is absolutely not conditioned by the poem's temporal origins, even if it is generally valid to say that modern poetry manifests a higher degree of interpretative difficulty than does that predating the modern period. But even something as early as Goethe's "Selige Sehnsucht," for example, has obscurities in meaning, not to mention the poetry of Mallarmé, with which Hugo Friedrich sets the beginning of the modern period. And indeed, contrary to the Goethe poem, it is for "modern" reasons that Mallarmé's poetry is difficult: exactly for those reasons which make the Trakl poem a different and more difficult problem for interpretation than the Mörike poem. We have chosen it for our purposes because the lyric subject-object-correlation is more clearly discernible here, since the lyric statement-subject does not announce itself in the first-person form. (The diverse nature and mode of appearance of the lyrical statement-subject will be investigated more closely in the next section.)

Musik im Mirabell

Ein Brunnen singt. Die Wolken stehn
Im klaren Blau, die weißen, zarten.
Bedächtig stille Menschen gehn
Am Abend durch den alten Garten.

Der Ahnen Marmor ist ergraut.
Ein Vogelzug streift in die Weiten.
Ein Faun mit toten Augen schaut
Nach Schatten, die ins Dunkel gleiten.

Das Laub fällt rot vom alten Baum
Und kreist herein durchs offne Fenster.
Ein Feuerschein glüht auf im Raum
Und malet trübe Angstgespenster.

Ein weißer Fremdling tritt ins Haus.
Ein Hund stürzt durch verfallne Gänge.
Die Magd löscht eine Lampe aus,
Das Ohr hört nachts Sonatenklänge.*

* ### Music in Mirabell

A fountain sings. The clouds stand/In clear blue, the white, fragile ones./ Pensive, quiet people walk/In the evening through the old garden.

Upon preliminary reading this poem, too, does not appear to present any particular difficulties. From the three assertive sentences of various lengths comprising the four lines of the first stanza we thoroughly believe to experience a continuity of explicit meaning-contents. An old garden: in which a fountain is singing; above which are soft white clouds in the clear blue; and through which quiet, pensive people are walking. But although we have used all the material presented in the stanza for the establishment of this object-continuity, still the stanza itself does not completely correspond to it. We have incorporated prepositions—a fountain in the garden, clouds above—which do not appear in the poem; and we notice that their absence disbands that continuity which we have established with the aid of them. The sentences: A fountain sings. The clouds stand in the clear blue, etc., are in paratactic, disjunct juxtaposition. They are not integrated with one another, and precisely the easy establishment of the integration marks the subtle boundary that exists even here between the informative and the lyric statement. This phenomenon reasserts itself in diverse manner in the lines which follow, carrying over into the stanzas. The statements in the second stanza appear only as disparate symbols for the garden growing dim in the evening, but symbols which evoke a subtle disintegration of the still relatively closed continuity of the first strophe, a commencing disorientation, and in turn a growing sense of the uncanny, which becomes verbalized in

---

The marble of ancestry has turned grey./A swarm of birds streaks into the distance./A faun with dead eyes looks/After shadows that glide into the dark.

The foliage falls red from the old tree/And whirls in through the open window./A fiery glimmer flickers up in the room/And paints faint [sad] spirits of fear.

A white stranger steps into the house./A dog races through decayed walkways./The maid extinguishes a lamp,/The ear at night hears sounds of sonatas.

[Translated by Liselotte Gumpel.]

the final words of the third stanza, "spirits of fear." But just this strophe seems to posit an unexpected point of orientation, a perspectival focal point in which the statement-subject seems to be concealed: a tree before an open window, a room, from which someone is looking into the garden, intimated by the directional adverb *herein* ("whirls in toward"). But since a direct indication to this effect is nevertheless still lacking, the establishment of such an object-relation is not permissible. Indeed, it becomes evident that exactly through the omission of such a perspective, despite the spatial designators, the disorientation increases, reaching the point where the lines "A white stranger steps into the house" and "The ear at night hears sounds of sonatas" admit of no answer to the question as to an objective causal relation, for example, whose ear hears the sounds of sonatas, and where these are being played. And now the poem's title also becomes peculiar, with its concrete, topographical place-name, and, despite that the word "music" seems to define the last line more exactly, seems to be dissolved into something indeterminate, something non-localizable.

Going through the lines and stanzas of the Mirabell poem in this way reveals a strange, almost paradoxical phenomenon. Compared to the statements comprising the lines of the Mörike poem, the single statements here, which all have the form of objective assertions, are by far more concrete, more realistic. No metaphors occur. Even the surface subject-matter is more definite and concrete: a place, house and garden, by oncoming darkness. Nevertheless it could be established that the statements withdraw far more radically from this explicit meaning-content, thereby dispersing, dissolving into a mood of anxious lost-ness and uncanniness into which the poem crystallizes. And exactly to the extent to which the objective causal continuity is disintegrated and made indiscernible does the semantic cohesion, or sense-nexus, also become obscure and can no longer be unequivocally stated as a fixed and readily discernible one, as it can in the case of the Mörike poem.

As an example of an almost entirely abstruse object-relation we shall use a work belonging to the modern period, a short Paul Celan poem consisting of six sparse lines:

Ins Nebelhorn

Mund im verborgenen Spiegel,
Knie vor der Säule des Hochmuts,
Hand mit dem Gitterstab:

reicht euch das Dunkel,
nennt meinen Namen,
führt mich vor ihn.   (*Mohn und Gedächtnis*, p. 45) *

The three lines of the first stanza name three parts of the body, posited as isolated beings, each of them in a material semantic content which is just as exactly specified as it is difficult to penetrate. The colon at the end of the stanza indicates that the second person plural imperatives comprising the three lines of the second stanza refer to the parts of the body previously named. These are enjoined to undertake something with the lyric I which is doing the stating here (and which now announces itself overtly in the first-person pronoun form), with regard to which enjoinder the second and third imperatives, "call my name,/lead me before him," are clearer than the first, "pass on the darkness to one another." As is often the case, it is possible that an implicit object-relation could at least be sparked by the last word in a poem. In this poem it is "him," the accusative of the masculine personal pronoun. If we

---

*   *Into the foghorn*

mouth in the concealed mirror,
knee before the pillar of disdain,
hand with the grid-iron stave:

pass on the darkness to one another,
call my name,
lead me before him.

                [Translated by Liselotte Gumpel.]

assume that it refers to a male person, we find no explicit reference; one does not occur. The only remaining grammatical possibility in German is to refer this accusative to one of the masculine nouns which appear in the poem: mouth, mirror, disdain, name. The most obvious thing is to refer it to the substantive immediately preceding, "name." Then, construing a possible, very uncertain and very abstruse object-relation, one could interpret that the lyric I does not experience itself as a personal whole, but as mouth, knee, and hand, which have no mutual connection, each standing in a different relation, alienated from one another and above all alienated and obscure to the I to which they belong. Possibly the statement "pass on the darkness to one another" adverts to such an interpretative meaning. The I's self-identity is not established by the parts of the body named, which are so totally distinct from one another—or can at least be felt to be so, such that one might ask what mouth, knee, and hand have to do with each other—but far more readily by the name. Name is person to a far greater degree than are mouth, knee, or hand. These are called upon, first to acknowledge the name (of the I), and then to lead "me," the lyric I, before this, that is, at least to confront the lyric I with its name.

This attempt to interpret the six lines of the Celan poem necessitated a completely different procedure from that followed for the simple Mörike poem, or even that followed for the Trakl poem. It was no longer possible to indicate a more or less recognizable objective causal relation and then observe how the lyric I withdraws its statements from such a relation, subtly and yet distinctly with Mörike, and in more radical, obscure fashion with Trakl. Instead we had to follow the reverse procedure with the Celan poem, namely to begin with the individual words and statements and bring them into an integral relation—into a merely possible, not a certain and unequivocal relation. In this way we had to attempt to construe a sense-nexus, and by this means to penetrate to a possible object-nexus. But, in contradistinction to the Mörike poem, and even to the Trakl poem, here the sense-nexus and the object-nexus coincide. They cannot be separated from one another, as can spring and the presentiment of spring in the Mörike poem, or oncoming night and a sense of anxiety in the Trakl work. In the Celan poem there is no extra-subjective objectivity, no object-nexus. For it cannot be discerned whether or what kind of a possible objective experience lies behind the poem. If our interpretation is fairly adequate, what the poem seems to state are metaphors of a possible experience of identity or non-identity of the I with itself. And even this experience we can only interpret as a possible meaning for the poem. The more abstruse the object-nexus, the more difficult it will be to interpret the sense-nexus.

The process which, with the aid of the above examples, we believe to be able to exhibit as that of lyric subject-object correlation, seems to correspond most of all to the Symbolist theory of poetry. Let us cite Mallarmé's famous remarks in this regard, of which W. Vortriede maintains that they "contain the Symbolist aesthetic *in nuce*."[150] "Nommer un objet c'est supprimer les trois quarts de la jouissance du poème, qui est faite de deviner peu à peu: le suggérer, voilà le reve. C'est le parfait usage de ce mystère qui constitue le symbole: évoquer petit à petit un objet, pour montrer l'état d'âme, ou inversement, choisir un objet et en dégager un état d'âme par une série de déchiffrements."[151] What Mallarmé calls symbol, and what more or less nebulously expresses the idea of the lyric poem for the Symbolist movement, expresses particularly in its second formulation (inversely opposed to the first) that process which we have endeavored to describe as the withdrawal of the statement from the object-pole—except that Mallarmé goes back to the relation between the object and the expression of it, the *état d'âme*. But in the two formulations *évoquer un objet* and *choisir un objet* we can clearly discern that lyric subject-object relation in which the process of the transformation of the object takes place. Symbol here means nothing other than the apprehension of the object by the lyric I, its transformation into an *état d'âme*, whereby in turn it becomes symbolic of this state. But it depends upon the kind of "de-ciphering," i.e., upon the verbal structure of the poem resulting from this process, to what extent the object is discernible. For *poésie pure*, pure verbal configuration, is the declared aim of the Symbolist movement. In Hugo Friedrich's analysis of Mallarmé's poems "Sainte" and "Éventail (de Mme Mallarmé)," an analysis which traces the withdrawal from objects, he says: "What takes place is not the presentification of a thing, but the withdrawal from it; the thing does not become distinct, but the process of de-substantization does."[152]

This brief reference to the central theory of Symbolism is meant to serve here only as particularly lucid supporting evidence for our statemental formula for the structure of the lyric. But *poésie pure*'s emphasis on the liberation of the poetic word (without this process' ever having been adequately described, however) directs our attention to several extreme forms of the modern lyric in contemporary times, as well as to their companion poetics, which developed with the aid of linguistics and text theory. The phenomenon and problem common to both developments is the predominance of language, the emphasis—and also the over-emphasis—on the fact that poems are made out of words. We must examine whether in the face of this phenomenon lyric subject-object structure, or respectively the theory thereof, is to be retained intact. Or, to anticipate the answer to this question, we believe this structure can be employed as a definitional tool for classifying such phenomena within the system of the lyric.

Basing his argument on such innovators of poetic language as Mallarmé, Arno Holz, and in the twentieth century Gertrude Stein, Max Bense says, in one of his many writings devoted to this question, that "for this poesie words are not pretexts for objects, but rather objects pretexts for words. One speaks, as it were, about-faced, that is with one's back to things: about words, metaphors, contexts, lines, sounds, morphemes and phonemes. It is a matter of poesie on the meta-linguistic level, of hermetic poesie."[153] As a rather instructive, and to be sure relatively primitive example, we shall use an Arno Holz text, one which Bense has reprinted as illustration:

Die alten
eisenholzlaffetigen
buckelbildrigen, buckelringigen, buckelschildrigen
Bronzekanonen,
Bronzehaubitzen, Bronzemörser, Bronzehaufnitzen
Bronzebasilisken,
Bronzekartaunen und Bronzefalkaunen
unten im Hafen werden
abgeprotzt:
. . .

(Phantasus) *

One might pose the question whether this doubtless new and radical language and manner of describing things doesn't ultimately represent only an extreme outcome of lyric subject-object structure. Indeed, Bense's definition, that for this poesie objects are pretexts for words, seems to me to be precisely another expression for the lyric statement process in general—and moreover only an extreme development of the formulation that words are pretexts for objects. It is to be stressed that both these formulations hold true only for purely descriptive poems, i.e., poems describing

*
The old
ironwoodcarriaged
castimaged, castringed, castinsigniaed
bronzecannons,
bronzehowitzers, bronzemortars, bronzehownitzers
bronzebasilisks,
bronzemuzzleloaders and bronzefalconets
below in the harbor are being
dismounted:

. . .

material objects. The two inversely opposed formulas express extreme positions within the lyric statement-process, in which the object-pole can be either more or less discernible or more or less indiscernible. If words appear as pretexts for objects, then we have the first case, whereas the reverse indicates the second. But in both formulations it is the words which are the decisive factor. They are the tools for the lyrical statement-subject who describes things, objects; whereby in the case under consideration here we are to think of such *Dinggedichte* which do not make the object symbolic, or symbolically transparent, but which lyrically describe or "fashion" the "thing itself." *Dinggedichte* of this kind are especially instructive, and also subtle paradigms, because here even the lyrical statement-subject presents itself as being object-oriented, intent upon an adequate description of the thing. And it is therefore no coincidence that such poems lend themselves quite easily to being designated as "texts," and that they group themselves, as it were, around that boundary which runs between lyric and informative statement. A *Dinggedicht* such as Rilke's "Roman Fountains," which nowhere points to any other meaning beyond a purely descriptive one of the phenomenon at hand, namely a fountain consisting of three basins in perpendicular succession, is still far removed from this boundary and well within the realm of the lyric because it presents itself, in sonnet form, *as* a poem—moreover in a poetic language which through a metaphoric quality that is by no means imposed, but subtle, contained in the carefully chosen words themselves—"gently inclining," "in silent reception of that softly speaking," "moving onward without nostalgia"—announces that the statement-subject's intent here is that of lyric statement. This poem would at least in principle conform to Bense's formula that objects are pretexts for words, since the object here has become the impetus for a poem, or more precisely for a lyric statement which then draws back onto the words. And in such a poem, which has the traditional lyric form, we cannot discern whether the object is "only" the occasion, or even the pretext for the verbal "event," or whether this latter, i.e., the words, are oriented toward the object. Expressed in terms of our structural formula, the process entailed in this *Dinggedicht* through the statement-subject's positing itself as a specifically lyrical one, namely the process whereby the statements withdraw from the object-pole, can be discerned not only through the external sonnet form, but is even more recognizable through the poetic, metaphorical language—such that, as in the Mörike spring poem, with all the lucidity of the object-relation, the images evoked by the metaphorical qualities of the words remain as the final impression of the poem.

But it is a different matter with the Arno Holz text. The idea that objects, here the cannons, are the pretext for the words, is in agreement with Holz' own theoretical endeavors as well as with his actual creative practice. Both aim at the mastering of reality through language, with the result that language, namely the "process of differentiation" necessary to this mastery, is rendered an autonomous construct of word-series and word-associations. "Holz . . . seeks to bring language to a total verbalization [*Verwörtlichung*] of the thing meant; that is—to a process wherein language must not seek its possibilities in secret meaning-spheres, but in the exposing enrichment of the word's productivity."[154] In point of fact, the "verbalization of the thing meant" conforms to both Bense's requisites and our own structural formula. The objects, namely the cannons, disappear beneath the words, which become independent and remain existant as linguistic sounds, having their own world and their own intrinsic worth. The statements in this piece, reduced to substantives and attributive adjectives in word-series, have receded from the object-pole and formed their own contiguity. But, unlike the Trakl and Celan examples, this process does not obscure the object-pole. Precisely because the process is a purely linguistic one, not motivated by interpretative meaning-contents, and the theme of the text is merely the relation between the object of description and the descriptive language, the object-pole remains clear. This does not contradict the formulation that the object disappears in the words, that it becomes, or is to become total verbalization. It is the intent of this lyric statement to have the object emerge again in the "impressions" which the words evoke, impressions which are to be understood as having been inspired by the object (there is a relationship here with impressionism in painting). And so considered, this object-poetry borders closely on communicative statement.

Notwithstanding all stylistic differences (temporally conditioned as they are), there is a line from Arno Holz to a modern lyric poet like Francis Ponge, whose best-known work is entitled "Le parti pris des choses" (1942), "partisanship for things." This work, which consists of 32 prose pieces, scarcely awakens the appearance of lyric poetry, and this is not because of the prose form *per se* (which can present itself as being a specifically lyric prose form, as for example Trakl's "Offenbarung und Untergang"). Here the prose form reinforces the material description of the objects and phenomena which the respective titles indicate as the particular subject-matter at hand: *Pluie, L'orange, Le bougie, La cigarette, L'huitre, Le feu,* to name only some of these texts, all of varying lengths. In his most important theoretical writing, "My creative method" (written in French, despite the English title), Ponge gave a very precise definition of his method of creative description, and summarized the result in the following sentence, which is printed in capital letters:

> Parti pris des choses
> égale
> Compte tenu des mots.

The partisanship for things amounts to giving an account of words. That he is dealing with a verbalization, or more precisely in Ponge's case, with the object of description's becoming word, he has himself expressed with regard to his text "Le galet" (*The Pebble*), by saying that this pebble he wants to "remplacer par une formule logique (verbale) adéquate." If the right words were not in the dictionary (*le Littré*), then he would have to create them (*créer*). The essential feature of this creative method, however, is the insight into the word's function not actually to denote the object, but the idea (or even the concept) of the object. And this object-idea is so to speak not the object's affair, but the subject's, whom it would befit Ponge's intentions to designate as the language-subject. For it is not a matter of a lyric, or indeed of any statement-subject at all, but of a given word in a given language. "Il s'agit de l'objet comme notion. Il s'agit de l'objet dans la langue française, dans l'esprit français (vraiment article de dictionnaire française)."[155] The object in the French language is the French word for object.

Although the relationship between language and object, or reality, that Ponge has in mind is the problem of the intentionality of language in general, it remains for him a specifically literary problem and not a philosophical one, as it is for Wittgenstein; and thus for him the poet is superior to the philosopher: "Supériorite des poètes sur les philosophes,"[156] although he hesitatingly asks whether the word *poète* should be used here. Indeed, it can be applied to Ponge's text only to the extent that what we are talking about is the purely linguistic effort involved in obtaining the word which will express the object-idea—but not any endeavors with regard to lyric form, such as meter, rhythm, or tonal qualities. From the standpoint of traditional lyric poetry, or even of lyric that approaches prose form, one would read a text such as the following as *material* for a poem—material which, to be sure, does already contain poetic devices such as comparisons and metaphors, but which has not yet undergone the process of creation into a poem:

Le feu fait un classement: d'abord toutes les flammes si dirigent
en quelque sens. . . .

(L'on ne peut comparer la marche du feu qu'à celle des ani-
maux: il faut qu'il quitte un endroit pour en occuper un autre; il
marche à la fois comme une amibe et comme un girafe, bondit du
col, rampe du pied). . . .

Puis, tandis que les masses contaminées avec méthode s'ècrou-
lent, les gaz qui s'èchappent sont transformés à mesure en une
seule rampe de papillons.   (Lyren, Frankfurt a. M. 1965, p. 48)

Thus, according to our own criteria, Ponge's texts lie outside the
borders of the lyric and within the sphere of the communicative
statement—as he himself does call them *définitions-descriptions*.
The predominance of language, its being made absolute or "concrete," seems to me to be the reason for the abolishment of the lyric
form *qua* form—a process extending into the most recent developments in "concrete poetry," which works on the graphic plane with
words, syllables and letters, and produces "visual texts." With such
manipulation of linguistic elements as graphic material, the frontier is reached where lyric subject-object correlation is no longer
valid or applicable, and precisely for this reason, it appears to us,
this concrete-visual form of poetry no longer falls within the category of the lyric.[157]

With the aid of these few examples we have followed lyric
subject-object correlation as it approached, and then extended its
bounds and became informative statement. In this connection
there is one more phenomenon within the domain of the lyric
which needs to be mentioned, one which—in a different manner
from the *Dinggedicht*—can also be considered as being specifically
object-oriented: i.e., political poetry. The concept of political lyric
is to be understood only in the sense that a political situation as
such is the subject-matter of the poem, and is not merely the occasion for emotional reaction and creativity. Examples of the latter
would include Andreas Gryphius' "Über den Untergang der Stadt

Freystadt" [On the Downfall of the City of Freystadt], or the poems of sorrow and lament occasioned by the crimes of the Nazis, such as Nelly Sachs' collection "In den Wohnungen des Todes" [In the Habitations of Death], or Paul Celan's "Todesfuge" [Death Fugue]. Although there is certainly a broad gamut of transition between emotional and critical-objective poems occasioned by political situations and events, it is nevertheless legitimate to call only the latter genuine political lyric. And whereas the category of emotional poems displays all the criteria of lyric subject-object correlation and is thus well beyond the periphery of the informative statement, political lyric proper by its very nature, occupies a position close to these bounds. The lyric I of a Heine or Brecht poem that deals with historical events—to orient ourselves on pinnacles of political lyric a century apart from one another—is in many instances very close to a historical, theoretical or pragmatic statement-subject. When Heine, in his poem "Michel nach dem März" [Fritz after March] (1851), breaks into a very personal and satirically bitter lament over the shattered hopes for freedom, in lines like the following:

Solang ich den deutschen Michel gekannt,
War er ein Bärenhäuter;
Ich dachte im März, er hat sich ermannt
Und handelt fürder gescheuter.

Wie stolz erhob er das blonde Haupt
Vor seinen Landesvätern!
Wie sprach er—was doch unerlaubt—
Von hohen Landesverrätern.

Das klang so süß zu meinem Ohr
Wie märchenhafte Sagen,
Ich fühlte wie ein junger Tor
Das Herz mir wieder schlagen.

Doch als die schwarz-rot-goldne Fahn,
Der altgermanische Plunder,
Aufs Neu erschien, da schwand mein Wahn
Und die süßen Märchenwunder.

Ich kannte die Farben in diesem Panier
Und ihre Vorbedeutung:
Von deutscher Freiheit brachten sie mir
Die schlimmste Hiobszeitung.

Schon sah ich den Arndt, den Vater Jahn—
Die Helden aus andern Zeiten
Aus ihren Gräbern wieder nahn
Und für den Kaiser streiten.

. . .

Derweil der Michel geduldig und gut
Begann zu schlafen und schnarchen,
Und wieder erwachte unter der Hut
Von vierunddreißig Monarchen.*

or when Brecht, in his Svendborg poems, expresses himself la-
conically and dialectically about the Hitler war which he forsees:

Wenn der Anstreicher durch die Lautsprecher
                    über den Frieden redet
Schauen die Straßenarbeiter auf die Autostraßen
Und sehen
Knietiefen Beton, bestimmt für
Schwere Tanks.

---

* As long as I've known the German Fritz/He's been an apathetic lot;/
I thought in March, he's taken courage/And will act more sensibly
from now on.

How proudly he lifted his blond head/Before his country's patriarchs!/
How he spoke—which was forbidden—/Of lofty traitors.

It sounded so sweet to my ear,/Like legendary sagas./
Like a youthful simpleton I felt/My heart begin to beat again.

But as the black, red and gold flag,/The old-German trumpery,/
Appeared anew, my lunacy went,/Along with sweet fairy-tale miracles.

I knew the colors on this banner,/And their ominous foretoken./
Of German freedom they brought to me/The very worst Job's tidings.

I saw Arndt, Father Jahn,/The heroes of yore/
Near from their graves again/And fight for the Kaiser.

. . .

Meanwhile the good and patient Fritz/Began to sleep and snore,/
And awoke again in the keeping/Of four and thirty monarchs.

Der Anstreicher redet vom Frieden.
Aufrichtend die schmerzenden Rücken
Die großen Hände auf Kanonenrohren
Hören die Gießer zu.

Die Bombenflieger drosseln die Motore
Und hören
Den Anstreicher vom Frieden reden.
. . .*

the lyric process as such is to a certain extent only weakly marked.
The statements that have assumed poem form remain to a great
degree object-oriented, and are consequently direct, underscored
further by the naming of the respective political or historical figures. But even though in both cases this process, i.e., that of the
genesis of the lyric poem, seems weak, the statements appearing
scarcely withdrawn from the object-pole, there is nevertheless a
formative element at work here which does order the statements
into a poem. In both poems this element is of a similar nature, even
though varied accordingly to individual and period styles. It is
namely a *discrepancy,* which with Heine is expressed in the first-
person as the experience of hope and disillusionment, and with

---

* When through the loud-speaker the house-painter
    speaks of peace
The street workers look at the highways
And see
Knee-deep concrete, designed for
Heavy tanks.

The house-painter speaks of peace.
Straightening their aching backs,
Their husky hands on cannon-barrels,
The cement pourers listen.

The bomber pilots throttle their engines
And hear
The house-painter speak of peace.
. . .

[Brecht speaks of Hitler as "der Anstreicher," the housepainter, because in
his youth he made his living by this occupation, having been refused by the
Academy of Arts in Vienna.—K.H.]

Brecht by the simple statements about the war preparations which the street workers, cement pourers, bomber pilots etc., are engaged in, and the voice of the "house-painter" speaking of peace through the loudspeaker. In that the phenomenon of discrepancy is the formative element and theme, it also proves to be the moment of lyric poetic meaning which guides the statements and—in a different manner in each case—organizes them into a poem. It is easy to see that Heine's rhyming lines and regular stanzas can throughout be resolved into a typically Heine prose, whereas, almost paradoxically, Brecht's unrhymed, non-metrical and irregular lines and stanzas nonetheless resist such dissolution—the reason being that here the element of discrepancy is structurally treated in a more antithetical manner than in Heine's post-March poem, thereby revealing itself as a more inherent, and also a more decisive moment of lyric meaning. But it is true of both poems (which here stand as paradigms of political lyric) that, with all their proximity to communicative statement, a specifically lyric subject-object relation, i.e., the positing of a lyrical statement-subject, nevertheless renders them poems. And Brecht's Svendborg poem shows that the external form is not the decisive criterion for this phenomenon.

With these few examples we have attempted to describe lyric subject-object correlation as a structure which is distinguished from the object-oriented communicative statement in the very fact that the object is not its goal, but its impetus. Otherwise expressed, *the lyric statement does not aim at having any function in an object- or reality-nexus*. But this circumstance, i.e., that the object is not the goal but only the occasion for the lyric statement, is the reason for the infinite variability of the lyric subject-object relation, which for its part determines the amount of difficulty involved in understanding a poem. In this respect, as we have already remarked, it can serve as a general criterion in the history of lyric poetry that in the modern poem the object-relation is more abstruse than in the poetry of earlier periods. And our three poems by Mörike, Trakl, and Celan were chosen from the standpoint of this structural phenomenon in the history of the lyric. But, as we have also mentioned (p. 249ff.), this general characteristic is not true of each single poem. The object-referent of Goethe's "Selige Sehnsucht" [Ultimate Aspiration] is more difficult to construe than is that of Nelly Sach's poem "Schmetterling" [Butterfly]—a comparison that can be considered paradigmatic for many instances, and which we have chosen for discussion of a further, although only secondary phenomenon of lyric statement-structure, namely that of *the poem's title*.

The Nelly Sachs poem reads:

Welch schönes Jenseits
ist in deinen Staub gemalt.
Durch den Flammenkern der Erde,
durch ihre steinerne Schale
wurdest du gereicht,
Abschiedsgewebe in der Vergänglichkeiten Maß.

Schmetterling,
aller Wesen gute Nacht!
Die Gewichte von Leben und Tod
senken sich mit deinen Flügeln
auf die Rose nieder,
die mit dem heimwärts reifenden Licht welkt.

Welch schönes Jenseits
ist in deinen Staub gemalt.
Welch Königszeichen
im Geheimnis der Luft.*

---

* What a lovely Beyond/is painted in your dust./Through the flaming core of earth,/through its stony crust/were you passed,/wefts of good-bye measured in mortality.

Butterfly,/good night of all beings!/The weights of life and death/settle with your wings/upon the rose,/which withers with the homeward ripening light.

What a lovely Beyond/is painted in your dust./What regal signs/in the secret of the air.

The object-relation here is indicated not only by the direct naming of the butterfly, but even in the very title, which then serves as a guideline to understanding the first stanza. In lyric poetry the title has a far more essential function than in the fictional genre. It derives this function in and through the statement-structure of the poem, namely in the relation of the subject-pole to the object-pole. As in the above case, it can illuminate the sense-nexus of the lyric statements by its very naming of the object. But it can also, as with the poem "Selige Sehnsucht," point directly into the nexus of sense, the subject-relation, without at the same time elucidating it. In this poem, too, there is a butterfly:

> Keine Ferne macht dich schwierig,
> Kommst geflogen und gebannt,
> Und zuletzt des Lichts begierig,
> Bist du, Schmetterling, verbrannt.†

But in this case the insect is not the object-referent, but a symbol of the heart which is consumed in the flame of love, and which addresses itself in the image of the butterfly. How sensitive and, so to speak, easily displaceable the subject-object relation of the lyric statement is, can be seen if we make the conceivable assumption that Goethe had also entitled his poem "Butterfly." Immediately this would then present itself as the original object-referent which had been withdrawn into the symbolically transforming subject-sphere of the lyric I, a process which, on the other hand, the Nelly Sachs poem does clearly exhibit. The title, therefore, can indicate both the subject- and the object-referent. In both these types of

---

† Distances to thee are shrunken,
  And thy agile flight is doomed,
  And at last, with radiance drunken,
  Art thou, butterfly, consumed.

[Translated by Ludwig Lewisohn, in: *Goethe's Poems and Aphorisms,* ed. Friedrich Bruns, Oxford University Press, 1932.]

title bestowal, which occur in innumerable variation, there are cases where the object-referent or respectively the sense-referent is illuminated, and others where it tends more to be obscured. In our context this is meant to make two things clear: first, that even a title indicating the object-referent does not signify that the statements comprising the poem are object-oriented, i.e., that they have a function in a reality-nexus; and second, the fact which at first appears the contrary, namely that in every lyric statement an object-relation is nevertheless preserved, regardless of how much this might be resolved into and saturated with poetic meaning from the sense-nexus—and therefore difficult to interpret. For, as we have already emphasized, it is inherent in the lyric statement that it is the statement of a subject about an object. Even when this object no longer comprises the statement's theoretical or practical goal, even when it is no longer recognizable in its reality-based substance, still it has not disappeared from the statement. It remains the reference point of the lyric statement, but now it is not there for the sake of its own intrinsic value, but as the nucleus which produces the sense-nexus. But this is only another description of the lyric phenomenon, merely one more way of saying that the statement is loosed from a real context and recoiled into itself, i.e., onto the subject-pole.

At this point, in conclusion of the analysis of lyric subject-object structure, we must clarify the question we have already brought up as to why the lyric poem is a reality statement even though this statement has no function in a context of reality. For when we examine our experience of a poem, it seems to be primarily defined in that we experience it as a reality statement, just as the account of a specific experience communicated by word of mouth or in a letter. And then only secondarily, as we analyze the meaning of a lyric statement (such as we have attempted in the above examples), do we augment this initial experience with the modification that we neither derive, nor do we expect to derive, any objective reality or truth from the poem. What we expect to derive and re-experience is nothing factual, but something meaning-ful. And this attitude we have is not a totally new inner experience vis-à-vis the lyric poem. We are acquainted with it in modified form from other, non-lyric communication. If someone gives us a concrete and vivid account of the enjoyment derived from some experience of a work of art, of nature, or of any other pleasure in life, it can happen that we for our part are more intrigued by the person's subjective impressions and the way he expresses them than by the actual thing that inspired him; and we would probably say something like "he gave such a delightful description of the party that it was truly a pleasure to listen to him." This banal example from everyday experience indicates the direction we take in experiencing the lyric poem, even before we proceed to an interpretation of its meaning-nexes. But in such cases of extra-poetic depiction where it is possible that we might be more interested in the How than in the What, this What is nevertheless still there along with the How as the reality intended (that is, it is more or less still there, according to the extent of our interest in it or its own intrinsic value). On the other hand, as we have already demonstrated, in the case of the lyric poem its very context, the fact that it is a poem, frees us of all "interest"—in the Kantian sense of the aesthetic experience—in the intrinsic value of the What, that is, in the value it would have in a real context. The fact entering into our experience of a lyric poem, namely that we incorporate a possible, more or less discernible object-relation into our interpretation only because of its function for the sense-nexus, implies that we are principally freed of all interest in the intrinsic value of the object. In this manner the person experiencing the poem, the interpreter, complies with the will of the lyric I: just as the latter, through the context of the poem, proclaims its intent to be understood as a lyric I, so does this context in turn channel our experience in the enjoyment and interpretation of the work. We experience the lyric statement-subject, and nothing but this. We do not go beyond the experience-field in which it confines us.[157a] But this means that we experience the lyric statement as a reality statement, the statement of a genuine statement-subject, which can be referred to nothing but this subject itself. And precisely what distinguishes the experience of lyric poetry from that of a novel or a drama is that we do *not* experience a poem's statements as semblance, as fiction or illusion. Our grasping the poem through acts of understanding and interpretation is to a large extent a process of "re-experiencing." We must consult ourselves, if we will understand the poem. For we always stand in direct confrontation with it, just as we do vis-à-vis the utterance of a real "Other," of a Thou who speaks to my I. There is no mediation of any kind. For there is only the word and nothing more (and here we are no longer considering the absolutizing of "words" commented on above).

If this is to be claimed, then we must pause again for a moment for a comparative consideration of the other genre in verbal art: fiction. Is it a special criterion of the lyric poem, and of our experience of it, that we orient ourselves to the word? The word, language, is, after all, the "material" of all literature, and it is, or seems to be, just this which links the genres together into the unity of literature. Precisely at this point it becomes clearer than elsewhere that we are to regard this material not merely as such, i.e., as something homogeneously operative in the genres, but must pay close heed to the different function it has in the fictional genre on the one hand, and in the lyrical on the other. But even if we totally disregard its purely logical functions, i.e., what distinguishes its operations in the fictional genre from those in the statement system, even then the function of the word as such is different for the fictional from what it is for the lyrical genre. Whereas in the lyric it has an immediate function, the same as in every statement outside of literature, its function in fiction, on the other hand, is one of mediation. There it has no inherent aesthetic value, but instead serves the other tendency of art, namely to be formational: the word serves in the formation of a fictive world, a world of semblance, mimesis. Thus only in the fictional, but not in the lyrical genre is the word material in the proper sense. It is material just as is color in painting, and stone in sculpture. But language in the lyric poem is just as little material as it is in non-lyric statement. It serves no purpose other than the statement itself; it is identical with it, immediate, direct. What we encounter in the lyric poem is the immediate lyric I.

The Constitution of the Lyric I

The preceding explication of lyric subject-object structure makes further discussion of the lyric I appear superfluous. But considering the infinite variety of forms the lyric can manifest itself in, it is not enough to demonstrate that the lyric I is a genuine, a real statement-subject. For precisely because the lyric reality statement intends no function in any real context, so does the lyrical statement-subject become problematic, and the topic of much debate in literary theory. What is disputed, and also has not yet been answered by our structural analysis of the lyric statement, is the question of the identity or non-identity of the lyric I with the empirical I of the poet. There have been many opposing conceptions in the past regarding this topic. Whereas the "more naïve" literary historians of the past had no compunction about identifying the lyric I with the poet, and were well pleased every time they discovered the woman for whom a love poem was meant, one is nowadays often cautiously intent on ruling out any connection between the I of the poem and that of the poet. The fine Goethe interpreter, Paul Stöcklein, cries with indignation and amusement, "The readers believe 'I' is Goethe and 'you' is Friederike—biographism!" and confidently states that just as "every word changes its meaning in a poem, likewise does every "I" and every 'you.'"[158] Wellek and Warren formulate the lyric I as a "fictive I,"[159] whereas Wolfgang Kayser at least looks upon the modern attacks on the subjective character of lyric poetry with some questioning, even though he does concur with them, since the concept of the subjective "still directs attention to the real subject, the speaker."[160] But, to return to Stöcklein's pregnant statement, there was one reader of Goethe, a woman, who would never have allowed herself to be dissuaded from the belief that this I was Goethe, and this you Friederike. This was the great Goethe admirer Rahel Varnhagen, who on October 11, 1815, had re-read the poem "Mit einem gemalten Band" [With A Painted Ribbon], and written to her husband about it. We shall cite her comments as testimony of a psyche which grasped the phenomena with particular immediacy and instinctive certainty:

"Und so endet's:

> Fühle, was dies Herz empfindet,
> Reiche frei mir deine Hand,
> Und das Band, das uns verbindet,
> Sei kein schwaches Rosenband!

Wie mit verstarrendem Eis auf dem Herzen blieb ich sitzen! Einen kalten Todesschreck in den Gliedern. Die Gedanken gehemmt. Und als sie wiederkamen, konnt' ich ganz des Mädchens Herz empfinden. Es, es mußte sie vergiften. Dem hätte sie nicht glauben sollen? . . . Ich fühlte dieser Worte ewiges Umklammern um ihr Herz: ich fühlte, daß die sich lebendig nicht wieder losreißen. . . . Und zum ersten Male war Goethe feindlich für mich da. Solche Worte muß man nicht schreiben; er kannte ihre Süße, ihre Bedeutung; hatte selbst schon geblutet. . . ."[161]*

---

* And it ends:

> Feel thou what this heart is feeling,
> Frankly give to me thy hand,
> Let the tie around us stealing
> Be no fragile rosy band!

We must not think it altogether out of the question that even those who adhere to the "most objective" theory of lyric poetry, that even today ingenuous readers still experience this poem as one stemming from the young Goethe's most intimate amorous experience, even if they do not, like Rahel, extend the biographical references beyond the poem. But these references are summed up by the poem itself, in the protestation about the "fragile rosy band." For we cannot detach our knowledge of the biographical references which Goethe included in his poetry of this period from these and other Friederike, Lili, and Charlotte poems. Emil Staiger, the founder of structural stylistics, says just as candidly as Rahel once did that in " 'With a Painted Ribbon,' in 'May Song,' Friederike is present. Goethe's being is permeated with her, just as he for his part rejoices in the feeling that her being is permeated by him."[162]

What is to be said in the face of such diametrically opposed interpretations of the lyric I? As Rahel Varnhagen's and Staiger's concurring statements show, these various conceptions cannot be explained according to the different eras, for example, by the advanced methods of literary study and research. To begin with, from our poetological perspective we have to answer that it is just as inadmissible a biographism to say that this I is not Goethe, and this Thou not Friederike, as it is to maintain that they are. This means there is no exact criterion, neither logical nor aesthetic, neither intrinsic nor extrinsic, that would tell us whether we could identify

---

[Translated by William Gibson, in: *Goethe's Poems and Aphorisms,* ed. Friedrich Bruns, Oxford University Press, 1932.]

I sat there as if ice were hardening over my heart. Seized with a cold, deadly fright. My thoughts choked. When they returned, I could empathize completely with the girl's feelings. It, it *had* to poison her. She should not have believed that? . . . I felt the *everlasting* grip of these words around her heart: I felt that *alive* they would never be loosed from it. . . . And there, for the first time, Goethe was hostile for me. One must *not* write such words; he knew their sweetness, their meaning; had himself bled before. . . .

the statement-subject of a lyric poem with the poet or not. We possess neither the possibility, nor therefore the right to maintain that the poet meant the statements in the poem—regardless of whether or not they have the first-person form—as those of his own experience; nor can we maintain that he does not mean "himself."[163] This is something we can as little decide for the lyric as we can for any other, non-poetic statement. The form of the poem is that of statement, and that means that we experience it as the experience-field of the statement-subject—which is precisely what makes it possible for us to experience it as reality statement.

How do these various relations come about, and how are they to be explained? Do we not find a contradition here of our demonstration, or better of our interpretation, of lyric subject-object relation which says that the lyric statement has no function in a context of reality? Does this not also indicate that the statement-subject, too, intends just as little to be considered a "real" one as it does not to have its statements interpreted as referring to reality, as being object-oriented? But here there emerges that logical phenomenon which, so to speak, forbids the lyric I this freedom. It does indeed have the power to form its statement as one which is not objectively oriented, in other words not oriented to reality, but it does not have the power to eliminate itself as the genuine, real statement-subject. When it posits itself as a lyric I, this influences only the object-pole, but not the subject-pole of the statement. The object, the possible reality-referent or context, can be transformed through its apprehension by the subject. But the statement-subject *cannot* be transformed. For—to express it metaphorically—when it says: I will not be understood as a historical, theoretical, or pragmatic statement-subject, it is only saying: my statement is not to be understood as historical, theoretical, or pragmatic.

What are we, the interpreter, to do with this lyric statement-I? Should we, out of dread of unmodern biographism, say that the I which exclaims "Wie herrlich leuchtet mir die Natur!" [How majestic nature seems to me!] is not the I of Goethe, but, say, a fictive I, a non-real, contrived I—then we would be proceeding no differently than if we were to say that the statements of the *Critique of Pure Reason* were not those of Kant, or that those in *Being and Time* were not Heidegger's, but some fictive statement-subject's. It follows from the structure of statement, such as we have explicated it in depth, that the statement-subject is always identical with the person stating, the speaker, or the author of a reality-document. Therefore the lyrical statement-subject is identical with the poet, just as well as the statement-subject of a work in history, philosophy, or the natural sciences is identical with the author of the respective work. That is, identical in the logical sense. But, whereas in the case of such reality-documents this identity-factor presents no problems, because the statement-subject plays no role in their content—their being completely object-oriented—in the case of the lyric I it must be modified to a certain degree. Logical identity does not imply that every statement in a poem, or even the entire poem, has to correspond to a real experience of the creating subject. For example, research has established that the apostrophized mistress in the *Minnelieder* was in most cases not a person who actually existed, or who actually existed as the poet's beloved, and that the love expressed in the poem was not a real love, i.e., not one the poet actually experienced. But this is totally irrelevant for the structure of the *Minnelied* as a poem. The love which is expressed, be it stated in ever so strict accordance with the norms of this particular poetic form, is the experience-field of the lyric I, irrespective of whether the I has experienced it as an actual or only an imaginary love. And, outside of literature, the lie and the dream are also the experience of the lying or dreaming I. Except that in the case of the non-literary statement, which is efficacious, i.e. functioning for a context of reality, we are justified in subjecting its content to verification. But we are no longer justified in so doing when the lying or dreaming I posits itself as a lyric I, withdrawing into the "non-binding" context of the poem and thus free-ing itself from the purposes and constraints of objective reality. Then we no longer can, no longer may, ascertain whether the state-ment's content is true or false, objectively real or unreal—we are dealing only with subjective truth and reality, with the experience-field of the stating I itself.

In the context of this discussion on the nature of the lyric I, and also with respect to the concept of *Erlebnislyrik* as developed in German literary studies, let us now devote some brief explicatory remarks to the concept of *experience* [*Erlebnis*], or respectively *experience-field*. *Erlebnislyrik* is a historically conditioned concept which stems from Dilthey's psychological theory of literature, and which is a popular designation for the lyric poetry of personal feel-ing and expression arising at the close of the eighteenth century and contrasting with an essentially conventional, socially im-printed, formal lyric poetry of preceding periods. With reference to this term, then, the concept "experience" is understood psy-chologically and biographically. But *Erlebnis* is also a legitimate concept in German epistemology, employed above all by Husserl as a comprehensive concept for all acts of consciousness (those of perception, mental representation, cognition, fantasy, etc.). He speaks of conscious experiences, and also equates consciousness with experience, expressly using the latter as a term which ex-presses the intentionality of consciousness, as consciousness of something—for which reason he also calls these conscious experi-ences "intentional experiences."[164] Understood in this compre-hensive, epistemological, or phenomenological sense respectively, it is legitimate to apply the concept of experience to the lyric state-ment without limiting it to that idea of experience meant by *Erlebnislyrik*. It can be referred to the statement-subject in gen-eral, insofar as this is the subject of experience manifesting itself through the statement act (as an extension of the cognitive subject, whose relation to the statement-subject was discussed above, page 32ff.). If, however, the experiencing subject manifesting itself in the communicative statement, i.e., in Husserl's sense if here the experience itself, is intentionally directed toward an object, then we can say that the experiencing subject manifesting itself in the lyric statement, the lyric I, substitutes for intentionality the incorporating of the object into itself, irrespective of the varying degree to which it does so. We may formulate it thus: the lyrical statement-subject does not render the object of experience, but the experience of the object, as the content of its statement—and, analogous to our description of statement structure, this implies that the subject-object correlation is not cancelled out. And it may also have become clear that in this process it makes no difference as to the kind of "experience": it is as valid for the *Dinggedicht,* political poetry, the poetry of ideas, as it is for that of personal emotions—indeed, for all lyric poetry whatsoever. *The experience can be "fictive," in the sense of its being invented, but the experiencing subject, and in turn the statement-subject, the lyric I, can be encountered only as a real and never as a fictive subject.* For it is the constitutive structural element of the lyric statement, and as such it behaves no differently from that of the non-lyric statement: likewise structuring both first-person and non-first-person sentences.

Nevertheless the lyrical statement-subject does distinguish itself from the non-lyrical one, and it does so not only through its relation to the statement-object, but also in that it is *more differentiated and sensitive* than the communicative statement-subject—to the same degree to which the lyric statement itself is. The lyric I can present itself as a personal and individual I, so that, as we have pointed out, we do not possess the possibility for deciding its identity, or more precisely, the identity of its experience as this is stated in the poem, with that of the poet. Theodor Storm, in titling his moving dirge:

Das aber kann ich nicht ertragen,
Daß so wie sonst die Sonne lacht;
Daß wie in deinen Lebenstagen
Die Uhren gehn, die Glocken schlagen,
Einförmig wechseln Tag und Nacht.*

with "Einer Toten" [To My Dead Wife], is indicating the empirical reference, the personal, existential situation out of which the poem grew. If in a poem from our times, Hilde Domin's "Mit leichtem Gepäck" [Travelling Light], the lyric I forbids itself habitation to a home:

Gewöhn dich nicht.
Du darfst dich nicht gewöhnen.
Eine Rose ist eine Rose.
Aber ein Heim
ist kein Heim.
. . .
Ein Löffel ist besser als zwei.
Häng ihn dir um den Hals,
du darfst einen haben,
denn mit der Hand
schöpft sich das Heiße zu schwer.
. . .
Du darfst einen Löffel haben,
eine Rose,
vielleicht ein Herz
und, vielleicht,
ein Grab.   (*Rückkehr der Schiffe*, S. 49)†

---

* But I cannot bear/That the sun laughs as before,/
  That, as in the days of your life,/The clocks run, the bells chime,/
  And day and night still uniformly alternate.
† Do not accustom yourself.
  You may not accustom yourself.
  A rose is a rose.
  But a home
  is no home.
  . . .
  One spoon is better than two.
  Hang it around your neck,

then here harsh experience has become harsh expression, behind which there faintly sounds lament, but lament which, because it is not loud, is not uttered directly. Despite all differences in poetic form, the empirical reference here is no different from what occurs in a poem from the very early period, Walther's jubilant

> Ich han mîn lêhen, al die werlt! ich hân mîn lêhen!
> nû enfürhte ich niht den hornunc an die zêhen,
> und wil alle boese hêrren deste minre flêhen. *

If in such poems—which here are representative of an endless number of similarly structured ones—the lyric I appears in a personal, even more or less autobiographical form, still this does not stand in contradiction to the phenomenon we have described, namely that the lyric statement does not function in a context of reality, that it does not inform. What Goethe formulated for his own creative experience, namely, that the poem "contains nothing which has not been experienced, but at the same time nothing as it was experienced,"[165] is, with graded variability, true of all lyric poetry, even for poems based on ever so personal life-experiences. And Goethe's dictum prohibits both denying the lyric I's identity with the I of the poet, as well as establishing the identity of what is stated in lyric form with "real" experience.

> you may have one,
> for with the hand
> Hot things are hard to get.
> • • •
> You may have a spoon,
> a rose,
> perhaps a heart,
> and,
> perhaps,
> a grave.
>
> (*Return of the Ships,* p. 49)

* I have my fief, everyone! I have my fief!
Now I'll not fear February on my feet,
And of all mean gentlemen will beg all the less.

Such comments are obviously occasioned by the wealth of those poems where the lyric I presents itself as a more or less personal I, appearing in the first-person form or concealing itself behind a second-person address, which could either mean it is addressing itself or referring to a genuine Thou. But the whole question as to the constitution of the lyric I generally becomes the more irrelevant to the degree to which this I becomes more impersonal, more indeterminate, such that neither a specific situation nor even a direct relating of the poem's subject-matter to the statemental I appearing in first-person form enters as an integral factor in the poem's content and experience-effect. To this category belongs much of the older didactic poetry. The I which in Schiller's "Worte des Glaubens [Words of Belief] says "Drei Worte nenn' ich euch, inhaltsschwer" [Three words I name you, laden with meaning], is so close to the theoretical statement-subject of a philosophical doctrine that it becomes paled, abstract, irrelevant as an I. However, it does not on that account coincide with a theoretical I, but rather, through poetic context and form, shows itself to be nevertheless a lyric I.—These examples represent what are logically speaking extremes of first-person reference. Between them, in infinite nuance, are all the others. Quite different from the effect of the lyric-philosophic I in "Worte des Glaubens" is that of the "we" in these tercets from the young Hofmannsthal, in which the statemental I is embedded:

> Wir sind aus solchem Zeug wie das zu Träumen
> · · ·
> · · · nicht anders tauchen unsere Träume auf*

or that of the I which in the subsequent tercet, in the poem "Manche Freilich" ["Many, doubtless . . ."], suddenly breaks into subjective statement:

* We are of such stuff as dreams are made on
· · ·
· · · not otherwise do our dreams arise

Ganz vergessener Völker Müdigkeiten
Kann ich nicht abtun von meinen Lidern,
Noch weghalten von der erschrockenen Seele
Stummes Niederfallen ferner Sterne.†

How can we grasp it? In those existential depths from which come these lines of empathy with the slave-like sufferings of humanity, it cannot be ascertained if or whether there is a boundary between an I as a formal element, which could be replaced with "we" or the impersonal "one," and the experiencing I of the poet.— The I can be directly named within the fantastic-surrealistic, grotesque fairy-tale-like reference of its statement, as in the following poem by Christoph Meckel, where there is also the possibility that this I is that of a role poem (which will be discussed later):

Was mach ich mit allem Getier
das über Nacht kam zu mir?
Zuschanden reit ich den Hund
und richte das Käuzchen zugrund
die Schlange erhalte ich mir
der Has, den ich aß, schreit in mir,
der Bär wird zerstückt und geschlacht
der Rabe zum Sprechen gebracht   (*Wildnisse*, S. 27) *

Does the "I" at the beginning of Karl Krolow's poem "Schlaf" [Sleep]:

Während ich schlafe,
Altert das Spielzeug,
Das ein Kind in Händen hält,

---

† The weariness of totally forgotten peoples
  I cannot loose from my eye-lids,
  Nor ward off from my dismayed soul
  The silent falling of distant stars.

* What do I do with all the animals /That came to me overnight? /
  I ride the dog to ruin /And drive the screech-owl to rack /
  The snake I'll keep for myself, /The hare I ate is screaming in me, /
  The bear is being cut up and slaughtered, /The raven brought to speak.
                                        [*Wilderness*, p. 27]

Wechselt die Liebe ihre Farbe
Zwischen zwei Atemzügen.
Das Messer im Türpfosten
Wartet vergeblich darauf,
Mir in die Brust gestoßen zu werden.
Auch die Mörder träumen jetzt
Unter ihren Hüten.
Eine stille Zeit. Schlafenszeit.
Man hört den Puls derer,
Die unsichtbar bleiben wollen.
Die Weisheit der unausgesprochenen Worte
Nimmt zu.
Behutsamer blühen nun
Die Pflanzen.
Es sind keine Augen da,
Die sie bestaunen können.   (*Ges. Gedichte*, S. 193) †

make this reflection on the phenomon of time for sleep into a poem
of personal experience? Or does the "you" which addresses itself in
Rilke's "Rosenschale" [Bowl of Roses]:

Zornige sahst du flackern, sahst zwei Knaben
zu einem Etwas sich zusammenballen,
• • •
Nun aber weißt du, wie sich das vergißt:
denn vor dir steht die volle Rosenschale
• • • ‡

have a personalizing function in this classic *Dinggedicht?*

† While I sleep,/The plaything ages,/That a child holds in its hands,/
Love changes its color/Between two breaths./The knife in the doorpost/
Waits in vain/To be thrust into my breast./Even the murderers are
  dreaming now/
Under their hats./A quiet time. Time for sleeping./One hears the pulse
of those/Who wish to remain invisible./The wisdom of unspoken
words/ Increases./The plants/Are blooming more warily now./There
are no eyes there/To admire them.   (*Collected Poems*, p. 193)

‡ You saw them, angry, flare up, saw two boys
  Interlock into a ball of something
  • • •

When H. Henel justifiably defines the concept *Erlebnisgedicht* as a purely formal one, saying it is "a type of poem where events are presented in the form of an experience,"[166] and designating the first-person form as its decisive criterion, still, considering the infinitely many meaning nuances exhibited by the lyric I, it seems also justified to classify this specific idea of an *Erlebnisgedicht* within the more comprehensive, structural concept of *Erlebnis* which we have set forth above. This makes it possible to describe the countless transitions from one type of poem to another, with the result that—to formulate it somewhat provocatively—on the one hand sometimes even a *Dinggedicht* where no I appears in any form can still be an *Erlebnis*-poem in the sense of personal experience, whereas on the other hand it is difficult to make such demarcations precisely because a poem presents the experience-field of the lyric I in the very *variability and indeterminability of its significance*. And just this variability is a further structural criterion distinguishing lyric from non-lyric statement. We have demonstrated it with several examples which could be multiplied almost *ad infinitum*. To conclude this discussion of the nature of the lyric I, which was occasioned by the remarks as to its fictive or real status, let us say once more that the respective difference or identity between the lyric I and the empirical I of the poet also belongs to this character of indeterminability. In and of itself it is the least relevant question as far as the structure and interpretation of a poem is concerned; and only the fact of its indeterminacy itself served as evidence of the character of the lyric poem as reality statement, i.e., as the statement of a real statement-subject, which *qua* lyric merely behaves differently from the non-lyric one in that it constitutes a different subject-object relation.

But it was the task of the logic of the lyric to disclose the cause

---

But now you know how that is forgotten,
for before you stands the bowl filled with roses
• • •

wherein the experience of the lyric poem is contained: the experience of our being confronted with a reality statement, no matter how unreal the content or how imperceptible the statement-subject may be. And precisely here runs the boundary which in the phenomenological sense already separates the lyrical and the fictional genres. In the case of the latter, logical enquiry could engage its more coarse grammatical and linguistic artillery to ground the phenomenon of non-reality, of fiction. For it could be demonstrated both that and why fictional narration (which the phenomenology and logic of fiction enables us to recognize) can avail itself of linguistic and grammatical forms which the reality statement must exclude. And only once these structural relations have been described can any clarification be made of the problem of the relation between literature and reality, a problem which, as we said at the beginning, had been left unclarified in many respects and was often treated in all too popular a fashion. From the logico-phenomenological perspective it has become evident that this problem can only be meaningfully posed with respect to the fictional genre. The lyrical reality statement cannot be compared with any kind of reality, any more than can the non-lyric statement. In both instances this could occur only in the sense of a verification, which, however, is not what is meant when we pose the problem of literature and reality. As we saw, verification is prohibited simply in that the statemental I posits itself as a lyric I. We are dealing only with *that* reality which the lyric I signifies as being *its,* that subjective, existential reality which cannot be compared with any objective reality which might form the semantic nucleus of its statements. For only two phenomena which are isolated and distinct from one another can be compared.

Fictive reality, the non-reality of a novel or a drama, on the other hand, can be compared to objective reality in any number of ways. This is evident in the reverse, almost banal phenomenon that we can live in the world of a novel as if it were reality. As we read we can take an interest in the fate of the fictive persons just as if real people were involved. We can examine the events in a historical novel as to their empirical accuracy; or we might even criticize a novel or a drama because "in reality such people and events can't exist." No further reference is needed to such more or less banal problems—which do, nevertheless, have their logically legitimate place. Fictional literature is mimesis of reality because it is not statement, but rather formation, "facsimile," whose material is language in the same sense as marble and color are that of the plastic arts. Fictional literature is mimesis because its stuff is the reality of human life. The recasting it undertakes with this stuff, even when it is so absolute as to be surreal, is nonetheless of a categorically different nature from the transformation which the lyric statement-subject brings about with the object of its statement. The lyric I transforms objective reality into a reality of subjective experience, for which reason this still persists as reality. But fictional literature recasts reality into non-reality; that is, it "contrives" reality—where we must set this concept in quotation marks because contrived reality is identical with non-reality, with fiction. As we have demonstrated, its epistemological difference from the lyric is grounded in this fictive world's not being the experience-field of the author, or respectively of the narrator or dramatist. It can only be structured as a fictive world in that it is created as being the world of fictive persons.

In these distinctions we have the foundations for the fact that a lyric poem is an open structure, whereas a work of fiction is a closed one. And once again, this is not a matter of aesthetic concerns: that for example a poem can be artistically more self-enclosed than a novel. Rather, it is the constitutive relations of language which are responsible for these diverse aspects. The lyric poem is an open logical structure because it is constituted by a statement-subject; and this is as such the reason "for the ultimate inexplicability from which and in which it (the poem) lives," as one modern poetess,

Hilde Domin, formulates it, tracing the interpretative variability of the poem back to just this.[167] A poem is open as to interpretation; and this is true in principle even for the simplest, most directly approachable poem. Conversely, even the most opaque, surrealistic novel is in principle interpretable. For it is a closed structure: it is segregated from the open realm of statement by its mimetic functions. It scarcely needs to be pointed out, then, that the difficulties involved in the analysis of an intricate and exacting novel or drama (such as a Kafka novel or a play by Pirandello) are on a different plane from the interpretation of a lyric poem.

In the context of these reflections on the difference between fiction and the lyric, it remains for us to consider the case of the *interpolation of poems into a novel,* a phenomenon occurring principally in the epic of German Romanticism. It seems to me that an understanding of their aesthetic function and effect can be reached if we base our observations within the framework provided by the logic of literature. This is not the place for an in-depth analysis of those individual novels containing lyric inserts.[168] We shall characterize only two such types of inserts that are very different from one another. One type is represented by the songs of Mignon and the Harper in *Wilhelm Meister's Apprenticeship,* and the other by the novels of Eichendorff. In both these cases, too, the phenomenon immediately presenting itself to us can be grounded in a logical structure.

Before we undertake this, we must raise the fundamental question which, from the standpoint of the logic of literature, cannot be evaded, namely whether the very factor of lyric inserts in an epic fictional work does not completely upset the logical theory which we have developed. If it is correct that the lyric poem is experienced as a reality statement, whereby we are not able to say anything definite about the relation of the lyric I to the empirical I of the poet, then how does a poem behave in a fictional context, where the I of the novelist, the authorial I, doesn't even exist? But even as we ask this, the difference we directly sense between poem inserts in *Wilhelm Meister* and in such Eichendorff novels as *Ahnung und Gegenwart, Dichter und ihre Gesellen,* and *Taugenichts,* is disclosed. When we call to mind any of the *Wilhelm Meister* songs: "Who never ate his bread with tears," "Only he who knows yearning knows what I suffer," "Do you know the land," etc., we immediately associate them with the fictive character who sings or recites them. However much the poetic beauty of this lyric makes it stand out against the narrative prose, thus making it seem that the poems have an autonomous lyric existence, nevertheless they still completely retain their reference to the context of the novel. This means that the respective lyric I in these poems is at once known to us as the fictive I of the Harper, Mignon, etc. These poems receive their meaning from the figures, and contribute for their part to the characterization of these figures. This applies even to a poem whose content is as general as "Who never ate his bread with tears." It does, certainly, attain its own unique meaning when it is taken out of the novel and thereby completely assumes the statemental mode of the lyric. But once back in the novel, it again loses this autonomous meaning, and what now attains form and expression through it is the tragic existence of the Harper—a more mysterious form, a deeper, "more mute" expression welling up out of ineffable depths, than (for Goethe's artistic intentions) it would have been possible to achieve in a narrative prose form. Goethe's lyrical genius here is in the service of his epic-fictional art: in these mysterious songs of Mignon and the Harper the mysterious figures themselves reach their culmination.

A wholly different impression is left by the innumerable songs sung by the characters in Eichendorff's novels. If we read these in a book of Eichendorff's collected poetry footnoted with references such as "from *Ahnung und Gegenwart,*" "from *Dichter und ihre Gesellen,*" it would be difficult even for someone well ac-

quainted with this poet's works to say from memory what character
sings them, or even which novel they belong to.

Laß, mein Herz, das bange Trauern
Um vergangenes Erdenglück,
Ach, von dieser Felsen Mauern,   (*Ahnung und*
Schweifet nun umsonst dein Blick.   *Gegenwart*)

Hörst du nicht die Bäume rauschen
Draußen durch die stille Rund,
Lockts dich nicht hinabzulauschen   (*Dichter und ihre*
Von dem Söller in den Grund?   *Gesellen*)

Und wo noch kein Wandrer gegangen
Hoch über Jäger und Roß,
Die Felsen im Abendrot hangen   (*Dichter und ihre*
Als wie ein Wolkenschloß.   *Gesellen*)

Schweigt der Menschen laute Lust:
Rauscht die Erde wie in Träumen
Wunderbar mit allen Bäumen.   (*Taugenichts*)*

* Cease, my heart, your anxious sorrow
Over past earthly joys,
Alas, from these stone walls
In vain your glance now steals.

(*Ahnung und Gegenwart*)

Don't you hear the trees rustling
Outside through the stillness about,
Are you not enticed to listen
From the balcony down into the
    depths?

(*Dichter und ihre Gesellen*)

And where no wayfarer has ever gone,
High above huntsman and steed,
The cliffs hang in the twilight
Like a fortress of clouds.

(*Dichter und ihre Gesellen*)

When the clamorous mirth of men
    is hushed:
The earth sighs as in dreams
Wondrously with all its trees.

(*Taugenichts*)

—No examples, no special sequence is necessary. Everywhere in these poems it rings and sings, sighs and nighs, dimmers and shimmers, roars and soars, all to the same tune. Everywhere nature and soul express one another in similar mood-images, metaphors, and symbols; and pervading this realm of romantic *Stimmung* are the same figures from German history and folklore, the same players, huntsmen, vagabonds, noble and rustic maidens. But here our concern is not that of treating the stylistic aspects of lyric inserts in the novel. There is only one point that is essential for our problematic: the fact that, contrary to the *Wilhelm Meister* songs, these poems represent fractures in the continuity of the respectively epic or lyric formative telos. No matter how these songs are introduced, whether a Count Friedrich, a Leontin, a Lothario, the I of the Ne'er-Do-Well sings them, or whether someone hears them being sung either from near or from afar, still, as soon as the poem commences it breaks away from the medium of the singing epic figure and out of the novel's context altogether. And it is highly significant that in many instances the singing figure becomes vaporized into what is expressly referred to as a mere "voice in the distance." But whether or not it is expressly stated as such, the singing figure always becomes one voice amidst the chorus of the others in the mood-symphony of the whole novel. But in terms of the phenomenology of such a "lyric-musical" novel, this means that the unity of the work's structure becomes broken. Since we cannot bring these songs that are sung, or that are narrated as sung, into any meaningful connection with the fictive figure concerned, and since, unlike the *Wilhelm Meister* songs, they do not contribute to the characterization of the figure, we experience the lyric I present in them as dissociated. The lyrical and the fictional experience of these novels break apart from one another. For since they are after all novels which build up a world of fictive persons and events, we cannot simply project both elements together onto a common level of mood. Rather, we are so to speak repeatedly surprised to discover how independent of each other these elements are, which for the structure of fiction means: that the figures in the novel are untouched by their own songs, by their own "musical" existence. Set into the fictive sphere the *Wilhelm Meister* songs, nevertheless, wholly realize the existential essence of the lyric poem; but the Eichendorff songs remain in their own non-fictive, lyric domain within the larger fictive sphere of the novel without blending with the latter. From a logical point of view, therefore, they reveal more of the essence of the lyric poem than do the *Wilhelm Meister* songs: namely, as belonging to a realm of language and experience which is categorically separated from fiction.[168a] And it is only a symptom of their behavior that they have at least an equally legitimate, if not a more legitimate place in Eichendorff's collected poetry than in the novels. This does not mean to say that in the novels one would get by without them. On the contrary, it is this very circumstance which—as has often been done—one can most fruitfully exploit for the aesthetic analysis of these novels.

The fundamental features of the logic and phenomenology of the two basic genres into which the realm of literature falls have now been elaborated. Whereas—thanks to the variety of its presentational means and types of mimetic functions—the fictional genre consists of several different forms in which it can manifest itself, the lyrical genre, on the other hand, is not differentiated. For we only experience a genuine lyric phenomenon where we experience a genuine lyric I: a real statement-subject, which guarantees the character of lyric statement as reality statement regardless of whether or not this I names itself in the first-person form. We have attempted to demonstrate that this circumstance both defines the autochthonous essence of lyric poetry, and is as well the determining factor for its unique, delicate position within the general statement realm of language. And this sensitive, subtly marked difference must be incorporated into the structural definition of the lyric. And although it is a subtle difference, it is one which, nevertheless, in principle can be assigned in each individual case. The boundary separating the lyric from the non-lyric statement is not fixed by the external form of the poem, but, as was shown, by the relation of the statement to its object-pole. That we experience the lyric poem as the experience-field of the lyric I, and only as that of the lyric I, comes about in that its statements are not directed toward the object-pole, but instead draw the object into the sphere of subjective experience, thereby transforming it.

These various relations have been briefly recapitulated here because they provide us with the criterion for analyzing a number of special literary forms and determining their locus within the system of literature more precisely than it has been possible to do from the standpoint of a merely intrinsic interpretation. These are on the one hand the major form represented by the first-person narrative, and on the other minor forms whose most prominent example may be considered the ballad. Both these literary types lie outside the two main genres, and therefore they can be termed special forms. They are special with reference to their logical structure, which in the case of the ballad and its related forms is the fictional, and in that of the first-person narrative the statement structure. More precisely, they are special forms because they have "disavowed" their innate structure and gained the right of residing in the respective otherwise-structured genre: the ballad in the lyrical, the first-person narrative in the fictional genre. That these conditions are such because of reasons of form does not (to prevent any misunderstanding) imply that their respective form is of secondary importance for the phenomenology of the ballad on the one hand, and that of the first-person narrative on the other. On the contrary, their form is the condition for the special place which these phenomena assume within the system of literature.

5

SPECIAL FORMS

The Ballad and Its Relation to the Picture Poem and the Role Poem

The ballad's special form as an epic-fictional work within the lyrical genre is one which is not immediately evident. Only once we have more closely examined that area within the lyrical realm where it has found its unique place can we establish the foundations and trace the systematic genesis of that special phenomenon which it represents. To that end the concept of the lyric is to be employed in the stringent definition which we have developed as its categorical difference from fiction: namely as a type of literature within the scope of the experience-field of a genuine statement-subject. If we adhere to this as our point of departure, we shall see that the lyric experience-field can contain elements that have the inherent tendency toward fictional formation, and hence the tendency toward structural estrangement from the lyric realm. What is the nature of these elements, or more to the point, of these objects of lyric statement?

They must be such objects as by nature lie farther off from the existential nucleus of the subject-pole than others, and, in addition, such as are not of an ideal, but of a plastic nature. For ideal objects, too, can be relatively remote from the subject-pole, as for instance those of didactic, epigrammatic and certain types of philosophical poetry. But that area of the lyric statemental realm where the ballad is to be located is occupied not by intellectual, but by *figurate* statement-objects. And those types of lyric poetry which on these grounds have their systematic, and also their historico-genetic locus in the vicinity of the ballad are the picture poem [*Bildgedicht*] and, though more ambivalently so, the role poem [*Rollengedicht*].*

With respect to the structure of the lyric statement, the concept of figure [*Gestalt*] has a twofold implication. First, it is an object to which the I responds more in terms of visual contemplation than in terms of emotion. And secondly, a figure is an object of a particularly versatile or multi-faceted nature. The concept of figure belongs in the realm of art, not in that of nature or of human life. And specifically it means the human figure, as defined in art on the one hand by the plastic representational arts, and on the other by fictional literature. When, so defined, the figure as the product of art appears within the realm of the lyric, we have a phenomenon that is unique in the total system of literature, the picture poem. We shall first consider this form and examine it in its relation to the ballad.

A *picture poem,* having developed from the epigram of antiquity, describes a painting or a piece of sculpture. And from Helmut Rosenfeld's valuable study *Das deutsche Bildgedicht* we learn that those cases are few where a picture poem has something other than figural paintings as its subject-matter.[169] (With poems based on sculptures the alternative is altogether lacking.) It is in any event these figural poems which are essential for that special area within the lyric realm with which we are at present concerned. As we have said, these poems as such represent a unique

---

* [The term "role poem" has another standard equivalent in English studies, namely the term "dramatic monologue poem," as employed by Browning and T.S. Eliot.—Tr.]

juncture in the system of literature, a juncture at which lines from
the lyric and the two forms of the fictional genre converge, such
that the locus of the picture poem in the lyric realm is an extremely
delicate one, where the structure of the poem can be altered by
slight shifts in the attitude of the lyric I. For the human figure
created by the plastic arts can be a mere lifeless (however aesthetically experienced), as well as an animate object of contemplation.
And now, as we trace in several examples the attitude that the lyric
I of the picture poem can assume, it will be seen that the latter's
logical structure is determined by nothing but the human figure,
i.e., by the artistic formation of *that* object which can also be
created as a subject.

From the wealth of representational poetry which German literature exhibits we shall choose a sculpture-poem by Herder, and
a portrait-poem by Rilke to begin our discussion. One of the so-
called picture-epigrams[170] which Herder composed in his espousal
of ancient tradition describes a Hellenistic group sculpture:

Amor und Psyche

Die Hand, die dieses holde Haupt berührt
Und still hinab es zum Geliebten führt,
Der leise Hauch, der um die Lippen schwebt
Und sanft den Arm und sanft den Busen hebt—
Der Blick, der nicht zur Sprache werden kann
(Denn Seelen schaun sich ineinander an)
Indes sich Herz zum Herzen schüchtern drängt
Und Geist an Geist, an Lippe Lippe hängt—
Der nur verlangend süßester Genuß
Des Wiederfindens—seht, ist dieser Kuß.
Es schwebt in ihm des Himmels reinstes Glück.
Anschauend tretet, tretet still zurück. *

---

*   ### Amor and Psyche

The hand that touches this sweet head
And gently brings it down toward the beloved,
The soft breath that hovers about the lips

Even if one did not know that this poem describes a piece of sculpture, it still conveys to us the lyric I's attitude of descriptive contemplation, expressed verbally in the imperatives "behold" and "step silently back." What is conveyed through the words that animate the figures and instill emotions within them nowhere exceeds the contours of the sculpture, and says nothing about it which cannot be gathered from its own features—and here it is immaterial whether another viewer would have seen other emotions depicted in it. The essential thing here is that the lyric I retains the figures in the tension of the subject-object relation, never releasing them from its experience-field. Indeed, this relation expressly enters into the poem even despite the subjective, animating interpretation, as is similarly the case with Rilke's famous sculpture-poem "Archaic Torso of Apollo." Let us compare the Herder poem with another of Rilke's poems, a portrait-poem which is not as well-known, but is nevertheless very instructive for our problematic:

Damenbildnis aus den achtziger Jahren

Wartend stand sie an den schwergerafften
dunklen Atlasdraperien,
die ein Aufwand falscher Leidenschaften
über ihr zu ballen schien;

seit den noch so nahen Mädchenjahren
wie mit einer anderen vertauscht:
müde unter den getürmten Haaren,

And gently raises the arm, the bosom—
The glance that cannot be put into words
(For two souls gaze at one another)
While diffidently heart presses to heart,
And spirit to spirit, lips to lips do cling—
Only the sweetest desirous pleasure
Of reunion—behold, is this kiss.
There wafts in it the purest joy of heaven.
Step, step silently back in contemplation.

in den Rüschenroben unerfahren
und von allen Falten wie belauscht

bei dem Heimweh und dem schwachen Planen,
wie das Leben weiter werden soll:
anders, wirklicher, wie in Romanen,
hingerissen und verhängnisvoll,—

daß man einmal etwas erst in die Schatullen
legen dürfte, um sich im Geruch
von Erinnerungen einzulullen;
daß man endlich in dem Tagebuch

einen Anfang fände, der nicht schon
unterm Schreiben sinnlos wird und Lüge,
und ein Blatt von einer Rose trüge
in dem schweren leeren Medaillon,

welches liegt auf jedem Atemzug.
Daß man endlich einmal durch das Fenster winkte;
diese schlanke Hand, die neuberingte,
hätte dran für Monate genug.*

*   *Portrait of a Lady of the Eighties*

Waiting, she stood at the thickly folded
dark satin draperies,
which seemed to canopy over her
a sumptuousness of false passions;

since the still so near maiden years
as though exchanged with someone else:
weary under her high-piled tresses,
in frilly gowns inexperienced,
and as though overheard by all the folds

in her nostalgia and dim planning
of how life should now proceed:
differently, more real, like in novels,
enraptured and portentous,—

that for once one might have something among one's
                              privy possessions,
so one might soothe oneself
in the fragrance of memories;
that finally in one's diary

In this work, which according to the author's intentions we are to
interpret as a portrait-poem,[171] (and which we could scarcely
interpret otherwise), something different occurs from what takes
place in Herder's Amor poem. The very conspicuous past tense
alone takes the figure out of the merely pictorial[172] and imperceptibly transforms it into a mimetic situation, which then becomes
further intensified through a type of narrative monologue technique: "That for once one might have something among one's privy
possessions," "that one might once beckon from the window. . . ."
The figure begins to live spontaneously of itself, its fictive I supplanting the lyric I of the poem as the latter begins to cease its
statement and instead turn into a fictive narrative function that
here fluctuates from straight narration over into the *erlebte Rede*
form. But the artistry of the poet sustains our awareness that it is
nevertheless a picture which was the occasion for such novel-like
interpretation, and the tension created by the shifting between the
statement of a lyric-descriptive I and an engendering narrative
function not only gives this portrait-poem its charm, but also makes
it instructive as to the unique role which the human figure plays
in the structure of the total system of literature.

We shall consider a further picture poem by Rilke, one which in
itself, and surely not lastly also because of its historical subject-
matter, stands in close proximity to the ballad: "The Last Count
of Brederode Escapes from Turkish Captivity." The pictorial situation (taken from an obscure historical painting[173]) is likewise
changed into an epic scene with the aid of the past tense:

---

one would find a beginning which does not already
in the writing become meaningless and lies,
that one might carry a rose petal
in one's heavy, empty locket,

that leans on every breath.
That one might once beckon from the window;
for this slim, newly-ringed hand
that would be sufficient for months.

Sie folgten furchtbar, ihren bunten Tod
von ferne nach ihm werfend, während er
verloren floh, nichts als: bedroht.
Die Ferne seiner Väter schien nicht mehr
für ihn zu gelten; denn um so zu fliehn
genügt ein Tier vor Jägern.*

The flight is seen as motion, as action:

>   bis der Fluß
> aufrauschte nah und blitzend. Ein Entschluß
> hob ihn samt seiner Not und machte ihn
>
> wieder zum Knaben fürstlichen Geblütes.
> Ein Lächeln adliger Frauen goß
> noch einmal Süßigkeit in sein verfrühtes
>
> vollendetes Geisicht. Er zwang sein Roß
> groß wie sein Herz gehn, sein blutdurchglühtes:
> †es trug ihn in den Strom wie in sein Schloß.

This picture-sonnet is informative for the problem of the ballad because it does not contain visible evidence of its origins in a motif taken from a painting. And here, too, the lyric I approaches being

---

* They followed in fearsome pursuit, casting their motley death
  at him from afar, while he
  fled, lost, nothing but: menaced.
  The remoteness of his ancestry seemed no longer
  worthy to him; for to flee so
  befits a beast in the face of huntsmen.
†   Until the river
  surged up near and gleaming. A resolve
  lifted him and his peril and made him

  again a youth of royal blood.
  A smile of noble ladies poured
  sweetness again into his too early

  matured face. He forced his steed
  to pace as gallantly as his sanguine-glowing heart:
  It bore him into the river as into his royal castle.

replaced by a fictionalizing narrative function. But we chose one of Rilke's representational poems which is close to the ballad form precisely because, even though it appears in this modern form and is furthermore conditioned by this poet's extremely complex artistic awareness, the frontier can still be sensed which nevertheless holds the poem firmly within the autochthonous lyric sphere, so that the narrative fictive situation, the action and figure, is kept intact as a lyric phenomenon. The secret is that the figure is conjured up as a sort of poetic vision and at once elevated to a higher level of pictorial quality, where the presentational and fictionalizing resources of the narrative function are not utilized beyond those aspects of their creative potential which to a certain extent are still lyric. (An artistic procedure characterizing others of Rilke's figural poems which did not originate from pictorial motifs, such as "Orpheus. Eurydice. Hermes" and "Alkestes.") A far more naïve ballad atmosphere—as is not surprising—is at work in C. F. Meyer's picture poem "Die Fei" [The Nymph]. Here the pictorial motif, from a painting by Schwind, is completely resolved into narration, with all the narrative function's devices of straight narration and direct speech, whereby in the artistic, symbolic interpretation of the water nymph as a betrayed lover, a lyric I is no longer present.

The instances are not too frequent where a picture poem is at the same time a ballad, but such cases are nevertheless significant for the systematic investigation of the connection between the ballad and the sphere of the lyric. This connection (and in turn the complex phenomenology of the lyric's frontiers, within which the ballad, too, is to be found) is developed still further in the phenomenon of the *role poem* [*Rollengedicht*], whose locus in the system of literature is of even more interest than that of the picture poem. It lies at a juncture in the generic realms where at once lines of descent from the picture poem extend over into the ballad and intersect with other lines originating in the lyric realm which

branch out to the first-person narrative. The reason for its ambivalent position is its *first-person form*. Historically considered,
this form is the reason why it is the role poem which constitutes
the seminal origins in the development of the ballad form by way
of the intermediate picture poem. Rosenfeld establishes the representational epigram of antiquity as one root in the genesis of the
role poem: namely "the fiction that the sculpture or painting is
speaking and introducing itself."[174] As he demonstrates, this is a
phenomenon which recurs in the epigrammata of the medieval
period, in the scroll titles and later in the so-called picture-sheets
of the Renaissance. Now, when such a picture-sheet contained several figures, the rudiments were there for the balladesque form of
the role poem: for the most part a dialogue form, but in cases where
the poet appears as the interpreter of the sculpture or painting
there commences a genuine fictional narration.[175]—But as the
picture poem is only one of the sources in the genesis of the
ballad—and one which first becomes relevant only for the art
ballad—so also is the role poem *qua* picture poem only one of the
ballad's genetic points of origin. Among the clearest examples of
the role poem are the "Two Portrait Descriptions" in Wackenroder's *Confessions from the Heart of an Art-Loving Friar:*

> »Warum bin ich doch so überselig
> Und zum allerhöchsten Glück erlesen
> Das die Erde jemals tragen mag?«°

says Mary;

> »Hübsch und bunt ist die Welt um mich her
> Doch ist mir nicht wie den anderen Kindern«†

° Why should I then be so overblessed,
  And selected for the highest bliss
  That the earth ever can sustain?
† Pretty and colorful is the world around me!
  Yet I am not like the other children.°

° [Translated by Mary Hurst Schubert, in: *Wilhelm Heinrich Wackenroder's
Confessions and Fantasies*, Pennsylvania State University Press, 1971.]

says the child Jesus of the so "described" painting entitled "Die heilige Jungfrau mit dem Christuskind und der kleine Johannes." It becomes obvious that the picture poem *qua* role poem immediately and of necessity relinquishes its character as a picture poem, because the figures now present themselves. And it is precisely this first-person form which renders the role poem an "ambiguous" structure, enabling it to be either a genuine lyric form or a fictional one, a type of ballad. Thus role poems can also be found, though infrequently, among folk ballads. As illustrations we shall cite the ballad "Der Spielmannssohn" (dating back to the early nineteenth century), about the musician's son who courted a king's daughter:

> Als ich ein kleiner Knabe war,
> Da lag ich in der Wiegen,
> Als ich ein wenig größer war,
> Ging ich auf freier Straßen.
> Da begegnet mir des Königs Töchterlein,
> Ging auch auf freier Straßen:*

and the role monologue in Arnim and Bretano's *The Boy's Magic Horn* about the girl compelled against her will to become a nun:

> Gott geb ihm ein verdorben Jahr,
> der mich macht zu einer Nonnen†
>
> . . .

*
> When I was a very young lad,
> I lay in the cradle,
> When I was a little older
> I strolled the open streets.
> There met me there the king's young daughter,
> Strolling the open streets.
> . . .

† May God give him a wretched year,
> Who makes a nun of me.
> . . .

302

It can also occur that ballads are divided into long role monologues followed by straight narration, as for example in the humorous English folk ballad "The Brown Girl":

> I am as brown as brown can be
> My eyes as black as a shoe
> . . .
> My love has sent me a love-letter
> Not far from yonder town
> . . .
> Now shall you hear what love she had
> Then for this love-sick man;
>
> When she came to her lover's bed-side
> Where he lay dangerous sick,
> She could not for laughing stand
> Upright upon her feet.

On the basis of such phenomena the role poem has been designated as a sub-category of the ballad.[176] And doubtless we do experience first-person figures like the musician's son, fair Barbara, or even Fontane's Cromwell ("Cromwells letzte Nacht") [Cromwell's Last Night] as being just as fictive as the third-person figures of most ballads. And likewise we experience these role poems as one of those several forms that fictionalize the figures, as a monologue (and often monodramatic) variant juxtaposed to the dialogue form (as for example in the "Edward" ballad and in Brentano's "Großmutter Schlangenköchin"), and as one variant of the composite, fluctuating narrative function in epic literature.

In that we do not simply characterize the ballad as a minor epic form and thereby relegate it to the fictional genre, but instead designate it as a special form conditioned by its relation to both the fictional and the lyrical genres, we are alluding to Goethe's famous definition which he gave in the commentary to his own poem "Ballade" in "Kunst und Altertum." Disregarding circumstances of historical development, differences in form and content, and distinctions between art and folk ballads, he saw in the ballad a "mysterious" form, from which "an entire poetics [could be] expounded, since here the various elements are not yet separate, but collective, as in a living proto egg. . . ."[177] And in the notes and commentary to the *West-East Divan* he further refers to the ballad as illustration that one can "often find the three genuine forms of natural poesie . . . epos, lyric and drama . . . occurring simultaneously within the shortest single poem."[178] In the ballad commentary he cites the refrain, the recurrence of the same end sound, as that feature which "gives this form of literature its decisive lyric character." But in the notes to the *Divan* the concept of the lyric is more general, posited as "a natural form of poesie." And as is the case here, as far as I can discern, so is it also with subsequent descriptions of the ballad that the lyrical element is a concept based on far more vague notions than that of either the epic or the dramatic. For the epic moment, and epic in the older sense derived from the verse epic, namely the narrating of an event and therefore of figures involved therein, is a fundamental element of the ballad, and is as unequivocal as it is inevitable. The dramatically tense manner of narration comprises the dramatic element; and the lyric moment could be variously construed: on the one hand formally, from the division into stanzas (with its greater or lesser, but always limited number of stanzas), and from the "singability" of the folk ballad, frequently underscored by the refrains. On the other hand, the ballad's lyric character was allied with elements such as mood and lyrical-poetic diction, and was essentially associated with the art ballad of the late eighteenth and nineteenth centuries. The imprecise notion of the lyrical moment as a mood factor is evident, for example, in Wolfgang Kayser's comments on Heine's and Eichendorff's Loreley poems, as well as in his remarks on another Loreley poem written by the Portuguese A. Garrett. What is expressed in the latter is interpreted as "the anxiety in anticipation of the encounter with the siren," and in Heine's poem "the melancholy note arising from the encounter in retrospect." Eichendorff's "Waldgespräch" [Sylvan Conversation] and "Der stille Grund" [The Silent Dell], Kayser adds, "stand exactly on the periphery between ballad and lyric."[179] Leaving the Portuguese poem aside, and presupposing that Heine's "Loreley" is familiar, we shall cite the two Eichendorff poems which Kayser has categorized together under this rubric. For precisely in their striking diversity they serve to determine the exact locus of the ballad in the system of literature.

Der stille Grund

Der Mondenschein verwirret
Die Täler weit und breit,
Die Bächlein, wie verirret
Gehn durch die Einsamkeit.

Da drüben sah ich stehen
Den Wald auf steiler Höh',
Die finstern Tannen sehen
In einen tiefen See.

Ein Kahn wohl sah ich ragen,
Doch niemand, der ihn lenkt,
Das Ruder war zerschlagen,
Das Schifflein halb versenkt.

Eine Nixe auf dem Steine
Flocht dort ihr goldnes Haar,
Sie meint, sie wär alleine,
Und sang so wunderbar.

Sie sang und sang, in den Bäumen
Und Quellen rauscht' es sacht,
Und flüsterte wie in Träumen
Die mondbeglänzte Nacht.

Ich aber stand erschrocken,
Denn über Wald und Kluft
Klangen die Morgenglocken
Schon ferne durch die Luft.

Und hätt' ich nicht vernommen
Den Klang zu guter Stund',
Wär' nimmermehr gekommen
Aus diesem stillen Grund.*

Waldgespräch

Es ist schon spät, es wird schon kalt,
Was reit'st du einsam durch den Wald?
Der Wald ist lang, du bist allein,
Du schöne Braut! Ich führ' dich heim!

»Groß ist der Männer Trug und List,
Vor Schmerz mein Herz gebrochen ist,
Wohl irrt das Waldhorn her und hin,
O flieh! Du weißt nicht, wer ich bin.«

So reich geschmückt ist Roß und Weib,
So wunderschön der junge Leib,
Jetzt kenn' ich dich — Gott steh' mir bei!
Du bist die Hexe Loreley.

*

The Silent Dell

The moonlight dazzles/ The valleys far and wide,/ The brooklets, as if astray,/ Run in the secludedness.

Yonder I saw/ The forest standing on a steep slope,/ The dark fir trees reflecting/ In a deep lake.

I think I saw a skiff jutting up,/ But no one to steer its course,/ The rudder was in splinters,/ The little boat half sunk.

A nymph on the rock/Braided her golden locks./She thought she was alone/ And sang so wondrously.

She sang and sang, the trees/ And springs murmured softly,/ And the moonlit night/ Sighed as in dreaming.

I, however, stood there terrified,/For o'er the forest and chasm/ The morning bells were already ringing/ Distantly through the air.

And had I not heard/ The peals at that right hour,/ I would never have gotten/ Away from those still depths.

Special Forms

»Du kennst mich wohl — von hohem Stein
Schaut still mein Schloß tief in den Rhein.
Es ist schon spät, es wird schon kalt,
Kommst nimmermehr aus diesem Wald!«†

Structurally speaking, both Heine's "Loreley" (1824) and Eichendorff's "Silent Dell" (1837)—the latter having undoubtedly been influenced by the first—belong to the autochthonous realm of the lyric. Indeed, according to H. Henels definition they would qualify as *Erlebnislyrik*. For as statement-object the nymph, just as the moonlit landscape of which she is a part, stands in the experience-field of the lyric I, here stating in the first-person form. She does not attain to her own I-originarity. However, the I which speaks in "Sylvan Conversation" is not a lyric I, but the I of a fictive figure, which then enacts a scene in dialogue with the I of the sorceress Loreley. Here we have a ballad structure. (Whereby a potential first-person role form, which could possibly suggest bewitchment, would not impair the poem's structure as a ballad.) The two poems do not stand together on the periphery between ballad and lyric poem. This border runs between them.

But the essential factor is that Kayser actually does distinguish the ballad from the lyric poem, and establishes transitional forms between them; he correctly emphasizes that "rigorous theoretical

Sylvan Conversation

† It's late at night, it's turning cold./ What makes you ride alone
through the forest?/ The woods are deep, you are alone,/
You lovely bride, I'll take you home!

"Great is man's deceit and cunning,/ From sorrow my heart is broken,/
The hunting horn's cries scatter 'round,/ O flee, you know not who I am."

So richly adorned both steed and lady,/ So wondrously lovely her
young form,/ Now I know you—God be with me!/ You are the sorceress
Loreley.

"You know me well—from yonder climb/ My castle looks, silently,
deep into the Rhine./ It's late at night, it's turning cold,/
You'll never escape these woods again."

demarcations would be as impertinent as their premature con-
demnation as 'impure' forms."[180] Nevertheless, the very distinction,
without which there could be no transitions established, is itself,
though not a theoretical, still a structural demarcation between
the two phenomena. And precisely for this reason it does not suffice
to define the ballad as a form "in which an action is construed and
narrated as a portentous encounter." For it is only the circumstance
that fictional narration is taking place which first makes a more
exact demarcation possible. It means that we no longer construe
the content of the ballad as the statement of a lyric I, but as the
fictive existence of fictive subjects. Where a narrative function is
at work we do not have any lyric phenomenon. On the other
hand, the poem form in turn neutralizes the epic-fictional phenomenon.

There may not be much gain in thus analyzing the lyric-epic
structure which the ballad represents, instead of stating it simply
as the phenomenon it represents in the history of literature. But
more than any other form of poetry the ballad draws our attention to its historicity and development, and in the face of such a
phenomenon it must be particularly stressed that within the limits
of our topic our primary concern is not that of tracing the ballad
through the various period styles in terms of its characteristic content, style, and symbolic features, but solely that of attempting to
establish its structural locus in the system of literature. And from
this perspective it seems legitimate, and also to lead to exact lines
of demarcation, when one fixes the ballad as a fictional figural
poem. In this broad sense, then, the concept of the ballad can serve
as a general heading under which can be subsumed such variants as
have been categorized according to different kinds and styles ranging from the popular ballad to poetic romance forms—which is
the practice with collections appearing under the title "a collection
of ballads." On the other hand, the structural designation as a
ballad would have to be denied those poems so titled if they do
not exhibit such qualities, as for example Hofmannsthal's "Ballade

des äußeren Lebens" [Ballad of the Outer Life], or in more recent times Christoph Meckel's vision of the fall of Venice, which bears the title "Ballade." As illustration we shall quote only the first of five similarly structured stanzas:

> Aufflog Venedig
> als es mit Fischen und Gondeln oft gespielt
> und Finsterwasser gewälzt zur Genüge
> mit allen Molen und Palästen
> von den murmelnden Kieselbänken.
>
> . . .

(Wildnisse, S. 12) *

Needless to say, we are not criticizing that sense in which these poets have nevertheless chosen to call their works ballads.

In conclusion, and at the same time in anticipation of the chapter which follows, let us turn our attention once more to the *role poem*. Its place within the lyric realm is far more indeterminate and ambivalent. Until now we have considered it only in terms of its relation to the ballad and the picture poem. But it manifests an additional dimension, namely its direct relation to the lyric statement, to the lyric I itself. The crucial element here is the simple fact that the role poem is a first-person poem. And by no means is the picture poem always the kernel for the role poem: the latter is not always specifically monodramatic in nature, i.e., put into the mouth of a fictive figure who speaks in the first-person. This seems to be the case, and indeed is mostly so where the "part" is indicated not only by the title itself, but can also be directly inferred from the content of the poem. Within the lyric sphere a poem bearing

---

*   *Ballad*
Upward flew Venice
as with fish and gondolas it often played
and murky water swished to satisfaction
with all its jetties and palaces
from the murmuring pebble shoals.
• • •

(Wilderness, p. 12)

the title "Erstes Liebeslied eines Mädchens" [A Girl's First Love-Song] presents itself to us as a role poem because we know its author as the man Mörike, whereas with the same poet's "Lied eines Verliebten" [Song of a Man in Love], the possible role-character is far less obvious. This role poem can be identical with a poem whose first-person form is genuine; the title's vague reference to "a man in love" can be a more or less transparent camouflage for the empirical I of the poet. In short, despite the role-form the genuine lyric instance may occur in which we can say nothing definite about the relation of the lyric I to the I of the poet. But it would be incorrect to conclude that every first-person poem is to be designated as a role poem. What is involved here is the positing of an I which is more or less clearly feigned. And we are only justified in speaking of a feigned lyric I when it is made known as such to us by the poet. In the role poem expressly and unambiguously recognizable as such the lyric I enjoys its clearest degree of feint, and this feignedness decreases in direct proportion to the clarity of the poem's role-character, disappearing entirely in those poems which in no way present themselves as role poems. Thus the title of the role poem is of some significance.

In the context of our investigations, the in itself structurally insignificant instance of the role poem in the lyrical realm has only a systematic importance. For it presents itself as the lyric counterpart to the major epic form of the first-person narrative, since it confronts us with the problem of the feigned statement-subject. And it is precisely this problem which becomes relevant for the phenomenology of the first-person narrative—in a curious inversion which, nevertheless, corresponds exactly to those logical conditions present here. For it is the feigned statement-subject which renders the first-person narrative a poetological counterpart not only to the role poem, but also to the ballad. Moreover, it is an inversely opposed counterpart to the latter: if the ballad is a structural alien in the lyric realm, the first-person narrative is the same in the fictional province—a classification which may sound especially provocative as far as the first-person narrative is concerned. For which reason let us emphasize once more that first-person narration is not to be denied the character of narrative literature. In the context of our linguistic-statemental concerns, the sole problem of interest is that the first-person narrative is a form of literature whose structure is distinguished from that of the third-person narrative in that it is non-fictional, and is thereby subject to other laws than the latter.

The First-Person Narrative

First-Person Narration as Feigned Reality Statement

The first-person narrative shall first be considered in its proper sense as an autobiographical form which reports events and experiences referred to by the first-person narrator. The frame or inset-story [*Rahmenerzählung*], where a first-person narrator reports on third-person characters, shall for the time being be disregarded. Only the genuine first-person narrative is decisive for that locus in the system of literature occupied by first-person narration: novels of the same type as *Simplizissimus, Werther, Nachsommer, Green Henry,* and picaresque novels ranging from *Gil Blas* to *Felix Krull,* and also Proust's *A la recherche du temps perdu.* For only that I which presents itself here is a structural alien in the fictional realm. Just as the ballad has brought its fictional structure over into the lyric sphere, so has the first-person narrative brought its own, the statement structure, into the epic domain. For the origins of first-person narration lie in the structure of autobiographical statement.

But of what significance is this fact—which in itself is neither new nor astonishing—for the classification of the first-person narrative within the system of literature? It becomes evident that it is only this classification which first illuminates the autobiographical origins of the first-person narrative and discloses those grounds on which it differs from autobiography proper, via its character as narrative literature. That here we shall encounter conditions structurally similar to those of the lyric is founded in that logical structure which is common to both the lyric and first-person narration, and which is conditioned by the locus of both in the statement system. And it is here that that problem at once emerges which comprises the structural, and in part also the aesthetic problematic of the first-person narrative. If we go back to the two primal phenomena displayed in the two major genres: the non-reality of the fictional genre and the reality-statement of the lyric, we would not be willing to concede that the first-person narrative conveys the experience of a reality-statement in the same sense that the lyric poem does. On the other hand, neither can we say without qualification that it conveys the experience of non-reality, of fiction. Or more precisely: the experience of non-reality which nonetheless forcibly asserts itself no matter how "self-expressive" many cases of first-person narration may be, such as Stifter's *Nachsommer* and Thomas Mann's *Confessions of Felix Krull, Confidence Man,* cannot be logically grounded as it can in genuine fiction, in the third-person narrative. For it is an innate characteristic of every first-person narrative that it posits itself as non-fiction, i.e., as a historical document. And it does this on the basis of its first-person properties.

In order to clarify these relations, we must again focus upon the concept of that particular I through which the first-person narrative constitutes itself. Its form is no different from that of any other statement in the first-person, be this a lyric poem in the grammatical first-person (irrespective of whether or not it is a role poem), or any non-literary first-person statement, the most immediately comparable example of which is the extended autobiographical presentation. That is, the I of the first-person narrative is a genuine statement-subject. We can fix this I more exactly by distinguishing it with equal precision from both the lyric I on the one hand, and the historical, theoretical or practical statement-subject on the other. The I of first-person narration does not intend to be a lyric I, but a historical one, and therefore it also does not assume the forms of lyric statement. It does narrate personal experience, but not with the tendency to present it as being only subjectively true, as being *its* experience-field in the more concentrated sense, but instead, like every historical I, is oriented toward the objective truth of the narrated. And should we question this, say in the light of such first-person novels as *Werther*, i.e., of such novels as have strong emotional overtones and express subjective moods, we can counter such a potential objection by noting that this same range of more to less subjective or respectively objective autobiographical account also characterizes the "genuine" autobiographical statement (which represents a special instance of all statement in general, where the same conditions prevail).

Indeed, it is this concept of the "genuine" reality statement cropping up rather naturally here which leads to that specific literary type represented by the first-person narrative. Its opposite is the non-genuine reality statement, which is equivalent to the *feigned reality statement.* The concept of the feigned, which is also essential in defining the role poem, designates that place in the system of literature where the first-person narrative is to be found. In order to determine the special features of this locus, we must again turn our attention to the categorical distinction between the concepts "feigned" and "fictive" (see p. 55f. above). The concept of the feigned designates something pretended, imitated, something inauthentic and non-genuine, whereas that of fiction designates the mode of being of that which is not real: of illusion, semblance, dream, play. To be sure, the child at play can feign an adult, but in that it is only playing and not deceitfully pretending to *be* a grown-up, it is playing the fictive role of an adult, just as the actor does not feign the character whom he personifies but portrays him as a fictive figure. The positing of fiction is a totally different attitude of consciousness from that of the literary feint. And language, too, conforms to this distinction when it produces the various forms of literature. It operates differently in the creation of epic fiction than in the creation of a first-person narrative.

Applied to first-person narration, the concept of the feigned discloses that extremely variable phenomenon of experience which the several types of this narrative convey. This is the first difference we notice upon comparing the first-person novel with the third-person or fictional form. Whether in the form of the old epic or that of the modern novel, a third-person narrative always evokes the same experience of non-reality, accompanied by all the phenomena which we have described in detail above. There is no scale of gradations between a more or a less intense fictivity. And it was shown that the feigned intrusion of the narrator as the person of the author, a device employed predominantly with humoristic intent, does not impair the fictive phenomenon. Jean Paul's *Komet* is not experienced as being less fictional than Fontane's *Frau Jenny Treibel,* for example, nor as less fictional than any given fictional narrative whatever, for that matter. On the other hand, on the basis of our general intuitive impression, it does seem that *Simplizissimus* adheres more closely to experience, or is more real in terms of experience, than is Thomas Mann's *Felix Krull,* and that *Green Henry* is a "more authentic" autobiography than *Nachsommer.* And for similar reasons it seems we need just as little discuss the degree of feint in Werfel's utopian first-person novel *Star of the Unborn* as we do that of that I which, as Tristram Shandy, engages in a play upon its own pre-nativity. The principal thing here is the graded scale of feint according to which, if one were to take the trouble, one could classify all first-person narratives in world literature. Such a scale implies that the degree of feignedness can be so slight that it cannot be determined with certainty whether we are dealing with a genuine autobiography or with a novel. And this is the case with the well known first-person narrative stemming from the period c. 2000 B.C., *The Life of Sinuhe*—Sinuhe probably being an actual historical figure, a high-ranking dignitary. But, according to G. Misch, the view which several modern historians hold, namely that this work is an authentic memoir, is not justified.[181] Just such a borderline case as this is instructive for an understanding of the logic and phenomenology of the first-person narrative because so ancient a document yields no tangible evidence upon which its autobiographical authenticity can be established. Thus, the logical locus of the first-person narrative is determined by the concept of the feigned reality statement, which distinguishes it from fiction on the one hand, and from the lyric on the other. But these remarks serve only as a description of the phenomenon displayed by the first-person narrative. We have now to demonstrate it as the necessary symptom of the latter.

A constitutive feature inherent in the concept of the feigned reality statement is the fact that here the *form* of reality statement occurs. That is, we have a subject-object correlation, whose decisive characteristic is that the statement-subject, the first-person narrator, can speak about other persons only as objects. He can never free them from his own experience-field. His I-Origo is always present and never disappears, which, as we have demonstrated in depth, would result in the emergence of fictive I-Origines in its place. And this law, which others have already recognized and designated as the unity of perspective or of point of view, carries the effect that the characters appearing in a first-person narrative are seen only in relation to the first-person narrator. This does not mean that they must stand in some sort of personal relation to him, but only that they are seen, observed, and depicted from his and only from his point of view. G. Misch, who does not view autobiography, i.e., the genuine autobiographical statement, as the sole origin of the first-person narrative, sees as an equally important contributing factor in its genesis "the vividness of creative representation," which "flows more freely and pleasurably as first-person presentation than as the objectifying displacement into a third-person."[182] He concludes this on the basis of the frequent occurrence of the first-person form in the fairy-tales and legends of primitive peoples, and associates with it the traditional explanation that this form had always been and would continue to be a favorite choice for the purposes of rendering the miraculous credible. How matters stand with this contention we shall see at a later point. At the present juncture we must examine Misch's statement that productive representation lends itself more easily to a first-person presentational form than to third-person narration. When we compare these two forms from the perspective of the logical structure which takes effect as their aesthetic experience, we see immediately that this is not so. It is the logical form which makes it clear that productive representation, pleasurable fantasizing, the comporting of oneself as a "second creator," proceeds with far more ease and less risk in the realm of fiction, in the third-person narrative, than in the—however strongly—feigned reality statement, which is the form of the first-person narrative. For it is precisely this latter form and the law operative within it which set the limits for the free creative play of the imagination, ποιεῖν, limits which fiction need not concern itself about. And hence it is not a coincidental, but a structurally determined factor that those conclusively fictional presentational forms, the verbs of inner action applied to third-persons, and in turn the narrated monologue and even straight monologue—in short, the formation of third-person subjectivity—cannot occur in the first-person novel. It can occur neither with reference to the third-person characters nor to the first-person narrator himself, who in such a case would suspend himself as a person narrating and become the narrative function. These forms, then, designate the absolute boundary which the first-person narrative, as reality statement, cannot transgress. No feint of the first-person narrator, no matter how obvious, can cause this to change, can transform the first-person narrative into fiction.

Here, then, even within the realm of narrative literature itself, is an instance of that boundary which categorically separates epic fiction from the epic, novelistic reality statement. And this means that, at least at first glance, it is not the aesthetic approach, i.e., the investigation of content, which will necessarily characterize or even lead us to sense the first-person novel to be an alien within the epic sphere. Rather, it is the logical approach. And upon closer observation we see that in many critical aspects it is precisely the logical structure which gives a distinctive feature to the aesthetic aspects of the first-person novel, orienting interpretation in a direction other than that of a third-person novel. For the interpreter, too, "knows" of this world and of these persons only through the first-person narrator, whereas it would be wrong to say that we knew of the world and the characters in a work of fiction through the "narrator." It is precisely from the perspective of the first-person narrative that it again becomes clear that fiction is not constituted through a "narrator," but through a narrative function, and that the concept "narrator" is in fact terminologically correct only for the first-person narrative. For the first-person narrator does not "engender" that which he narrates, but narrates about it in the same manner as in every reality statement: as about something which is the object of his statement, and which he can only present as an object (or, in the case of persons, which he cannot also portray as subjects). Therefore the relationship between the remaining portrayed world of characters and the narrator can never be entirely omitted in the interpretation of a first-person novel. Precisely because it is the narrator's statement-object, this world of characters is never portrayed completely objectively: the narrator's subjective conception enters into his statements in the same logical and epistemological manner as in all reality statement. Pär Lagerkvist's novel *Der Zwerg* is a particularly clear, almost paradigmatic instance of first-person narrative structure. It is part of the content of this Renaissance tale that the reader knows of the persons described by the court dwarf only through the latter, only from his "dwarf perspective": namely in the distortion achieved by the view "from below," so that normal human proportions appear as deformed, warped, demeaned, and the question is left open as to whether or to what extent this view from below is perhaps the correct one. Here the first-person perspective is consciously incorporated into the novel as a factor of content, and a closer analysis of the work shows how carefully the forms of first-person narration are made to suit this perspective, which is namely the statement form. And within this perspective it is impossible for fictional narrative forms to occur—impossible not only for the narrated monologue, but for dialogue as well.

THE EPISTOLARY NOVEL

This brings us to the point where we are able to grasp the problematic proper of the first-person novel *qua* novel, i.e., to investigate how its poetologically paradoxical situation of being a statement structure in the epic-fictional sphere comes about. Its inversely opposed position with regard to the ballad will then become evident. We shall begin our investigations with a special form of the first-person novel, namely the epistolary novel, where the process in question here is most clearly observed. The epistolary novel represents that variety of first-person novel which least of all appears to be an epic form. And under this heading we may also classify the novel in diary form, which exhibits scarcely any formal differences from the epistolary novel. An essentially inherent feature of both these forms is that they depict a given restricted piece of outer and inner reality, such that there is not that temptation to which the continuous, extended first-person narrative is always subject, namely that of exceeding the bounds set by the statement form and going over into the epic-fictional province. Each individual letter looks back over a recent past time, a restricted piece of world and events, and the reproduction of conversations which were held "yesterday" or "recently" does not over-extend the possibilities of this reality statement. As a general feature, but one which emerges especially clearly in the diary and epistolary novel, we may note that the preterite in the first-person novel is not an epic preterite. It is a genuine, existential, grammatical past tense which indicates the letter writer's—however feigned —place in time. By its very nature the degree of feint in first-person narration carries over onto temporality, and the datings in Goethe's *Werther* are an almost touching indication of how relatively slight the degree of feignedness in a first-person novel can be: notations such as "May 4, 1771," etc., were easily established as identical with the real dates of Goethe's Wetzlar period. But such "autobiographical" datings are of no import for the logical structure of the first-person novel; indeed, it need scarcely be mentioned that they can be incorporated throughout into a work of fiction. What is of structural consequence is that "I was" and "it was" in the first-person novel signify the past of the narrator, whereas "he was" in fiction signifies the fictive present of the character. (And likewise for the present and future tenses.) In itself this semantic-phenomenological distinction grounds the difference between the experience conveyed by a first-person narrative on the one hand, and by a work of fiction on the other: the experience of—however feigned—reality in the one, and that of non-reality in the other.

For the reasons outlined above the preterite in the epistolary novel appears as particularly natural and close to reality, and it is due to this factor that this novel gives us the impression of being a less "epic" form than a first-person narrative like *Simplizissimus* or *Green Henry*, for example.—But the epistolary novel, too, is not a genuine, but a feigned reality statement, and as such a work of literature: a work which, in its structure, tends toward the epic-fictional form. How does this come about, and how does it make itself noticeable? Let us examine a passage from *Werther:*

Am 12. August. Gewiß, Albert ist der beste Mensch unter dem Himmel. Ich habe gestern eine wunderbare Szene mit ihm gehabt. Ich kam zu ihm, um Abschied von ihm zu nehmen. . . . 'Borge mir die Pistolen', sagte ich, 'zu meiner Reise'! 'Meinetwegen', sagte er, 'wenn du dir die Mühe nehmen willst sie zu laden; bei mir hängen sie nur pro forma'. Ich nahm eine herunter, und er fuhr fort: 'Seit mir meine Vorsicht einen so unartigen Streich gespielt hat, mag ich mit dem Zeuge nichts mehr zu tun haben'. Ich war neugierig, die Geschichte zu wissen. — 'Ich hielt mich', erzählte er, 'wohl ein Vierteljahr auf dem Lande bei einem Freunde auf, hatte ein paar Terzerolen, ungeladen, und schlief ruhig. Einmal an einem regnichten Nachmittage, da ich müßig sitze, weiß ich nicht, wie mir einfällt; wir könnten überfallen werden, wir könnten die Terzerolen nötig haben und könnten . . . du weißt ja, wie das ist. Ich gab sie dem Bedienten, sie zu putzen und zu laden; und der dahlt mit den Mädchen, will sie erschrecken, und Gott weiß wie, das Gewehr geht los, da der Ladstock noch drin steckt und schießt den Ladstock einem Mädchen zur Maus herein an der rechten Hand und zerschlägt ihr den Daumen. Da hatte ich das Lamentieren und die Kur zu bezahlen obendrein und seit der Zeit laß ich alles Gewehr ungeladen. Lieber Schatz, was ist Vorsicht? Die Gefahr läßt sich nicht auslernen. Zwar' — Nun weißt du, daß ich den liebhabe bis auf seine *Zwar;* denn versteht's sich nicht von selbst, daß jeder allgemeine Satz Ausnahmen leidet? . . .*

---

* August 12th. Surely Albert is the best person under the sky. I had an extraordinary scene with him yesterday. I came to him to bid farewell. . . . "Lend me the pistols," I said, "for my journey." "Fine," he said, "if you will take the trouble to load them; I have them up only pro forma." I took one down, and he continued: "Since the time my caution played such a hapless trick on me I have preferred to have nothing more to do with them." I was curious to know the story.—"I was staying in the country for some three months at a friend's home. I had a pair of pocket pistols, unloaded, and I slept without worry. Then one day, on a rainy afternoon, I'm sitting there idly, I don't know how it occurred to me: we could be attacked, we could have need of the pistols, and could . . . well, you know how it is. I gave them to the man-servant

This passage shows *in nuce* the temptation to which the first-person novel can become subject, and to which in most cases it succumbs: the temptation to make use of those fictional resources which, so to speak, are still permitted, still possible to use without altogether suspending the first-person or statement structure. Insofar as the first-person novel is distinguished from the lyric by its portraying not only the experience-field of the I as such, but also the objects of this experience in their unique objectivity and peculiarity, there is at work within it the tendency toward the epic. But this tendency is restricted by the law of statement, which admits of epic qualities only in their so to speak pre-fictional form. One such form of reporting which does not exceed logical possibilities, but only customary statement usage, is the verbatim, direct repetition of third-person speech by the first-person narrator, as in the example above, in Albert's story as it appears in Werther's letter, which is a first-person narrative of second degree, as it were. The natural form for reporting what another person has said is indirect discourse, which is put into the subjunctive, but which in more lengthy passages can often revert to the indicative. And even a passage from a letter having a direct form of report of this kind, or a quoted dialogue, manifests epic-fictional tendencies. For, as we have shown above, both individual speech and dialogue are among the most important resources of fictionalization, forming, as they do, a connective link between epic and dramatic form. In direct speech the figure is portrayed in his own reality independent of any statement context, in his own being-for-himself. As such,

---

to clean and load; and he was dallying with the maids, trying to frighten them and, God knows how—since the ramrod was still in—the weapon goes off and shoots through the ball of one girl's thumb, shattering it. I had to pay the price of her lament, and of her cure as well, and since that time I have left all my weapons unloaded. My dear fellow, what good is caution? Danger cannot be anticipated. Now of course—" You see, I am most fond of him until he gets to this "now, of course" of his; for isn't it self-evident that every general statement has exceptions?

this form of speech is a manifestation of human reality *per se*. And its only proper place in the total system of language is where a mimesis of reality is being created: in epic and dramatic fiction. For—as is self-evident in the drama—even in epic fiction it does not signify the reproduction of speech *by* another, the incorrectly termed "narrator," but is instead narrated reality, the fictive reality produced via the narrative act, just like the fictive character himself. It was demonstrated above how the fluctuating narrative function shifts into dialogue, narrated monologue, and so on. However, the first-person narrative has the form of statement, and regardless of how feigned, the letter, diary or memoir writer is a historical statement-subject and not a narrative function. For statement is not mimesis. In his reporting, direct speech is not a means of fictionalization; he is merely, as it were, "delegating speech" to the person about whom he is reporting. And direct speech occurring in the epistolary novel still shows this aspect. In such a novel it is indeed a marked germ of fictionalization, but, because of the properties of the letter as such, still a possible element of natural statement form. It is so exactly because the letter always speaks of a situation in the recent past, so that even a conversation having taken place then can be remembered, even verbatim, and the confines of the reality statement are thus not exceeded, or extended to the point of the improbable. Furthermore, linguistic form also confirms the observation that the epistolary novel is that first-person novel form which manifests the fewest epic tendencies. It divides the bulk of remembered reality into the various situations and temporal intervals proceding from the narrative process itself, and with each successive letter re-establishes the clear first-person reference, the I-Origo of the letter writer.

THE MEMOIR NOVEL

Dialogue assumes an entirely different aspect when it occurs in the properly autobiographical memoir novel. This new aspect is a

symptom of the (systematic) course which the first-person narrative can follow from a form close to the reality statement (such as is
possible for the epistolary novel) to an epic-fictional structure.
Closer analysis of the first-person narrator as the I of reminiscence
shall make this clear.

To begin with, there is the fundamental difference between the
narrative or respectively the writing situation in the epistolary
novel on the one hand, and in the memoir novel on the other. In the
former each recent situation and its temporal point progress from
one temporal present marked by the letter date to another, and in
this way they integrate into the—either more or less fragmentary—
totality of a life or of a life-segment. The writer of a memoir, on
the other hand, looks back from *one* fixed temporal present over the
whole of his past life. This basic situation entails a number of
elements which work together to give the memoir novel its essentially distinct aspect over against the epistolary form.

One of the principal implications of this situation is that the
originary point of the Here and Now of the person writing is not
continually renewed as it is with each new letter in the epistolary
novel, and that—which is essential—therefore we are not repeatedly made aware of it. It remains fixed, static, and never changes.
And from this fact ensue two further structural features that are
ultimately related. In that the fixed I of the autobiographical novel
(just as in genuine, non-literary autobiography) surveys its past
life and reproduces it, this I is also looking back upon past stages
of its own self. But this means that it differentiates the experiences
of these stages of its earlier self from those of its present stage,
whereas the writer of a letter or a diary knows and experiences
only the one Here and Now of his self in point. The autobiographer,
genuine as well as feigned, objectifies his earlier phases. He sees
the self of his youth as a different one from the present self which
is narrating, and in turn as one different from the self of a later
phase in his life. "At that time," writes Simplizissimus, about his
yet child-like ideas at the time he was a page in Hanau, "my most

precious possession was a clear conscience and an upright, pious spirit, accompanied by a noble innocence and simplicity" (I, 24), but later he says "the gracious reader will have seen in the previous book how ambitious I had become in Soest, how I sought and found honor, fame and favor in deeds which, had others done them, would have merited punishment" (III,1). This by no means rare example is of interest here only because of its structural significance for the possible variations of the first-person narrative. As paradoxical as it may seem at first, the character of the first-person novel as such can be lost to a certain degree through the narrator's objectifying the earlier stages of his self (which everyone does who speaks about himself from some temporal distance). The objectified self of these earlier phases is not always experienced with the same intensity as being identical with the first-person narrator, but rather more as a somewhat independent person who is only one among all the other persons in the narrative. The effect is that the subject-object relation of statement, though not suspended, recedes behind the first-person character in action in the narrative, who, as one might say, appears as one object among other objects, as one person among others. For, we recall, the other persons portrayed in the first-person narrative are always comprehended as objects and never as subjects (as they are in fiction).

This phenomenon becomes all the more strongly manifest the more the first-person narrative becomes not just a presentation of self, but one of world. And such an interrelation is not coincidental, insofar as the presentation of world (or the possibility thereof) is grounded in the retrospective situation wherein the first-person narrator looks back from a fixed temporal point. In surveying the totality of his life the narrator looks back on a given nexus of historical, geographical, epochal world, in which his life has run its course and where in the various earlier phases of his selfhood he encountered other persons, from which encounters there grew the ties, the destinies, the "stories" of his life. From the fixed point of his retrospection these present themselves as being more or less dissociated from him, "dead" like all things past, no longer belonging to the existential flux of present life.

These two interrelated factors, i.e., the objectification of one's own life-stages and the totality of the world-nexus established in retrospection, underlie the possibility, the "susceptibility" of the feigned (and often also the non-feigned) first-person narrative to tend away from the statement form and develop along the lines of fiction. One of the clearest symptoms of this is *dialogue,* which in the memoir novel has both a different aspect and a different function from in the epistolary novel. In the latter it does not yet have the character of fiction, but that of the delegation of speech, and it can be reproduced directly from memory. But in the memoir novel dialogue, which along with other devices for plastic representation vividly re-creates situations and episodes long past, no longer has the character of delegating speech, but that of literary creation. It fictionalizes the persons, just as in genuine epic fiction. And it fictionalizes not only the other persons conversing with these earlier I's of the narrator, but to the same degree also these very I's themselves. The fixed first-person narrator very closely approaches the narrative function as soon as he has the persons in his past exchange conversation with "himself" in his earlier phases. And, just as in the underlying, concealed stratum of logical structures all elements and symptoms condition one another, this phenomenon, too, is connected with the basic situation where we have the fixed narrative I. In that this I is not like that of the letter-writer whose self-awareness is renewed with each successive letter, and who must set the life and experience portrayed into relation to himself, it is possible for it largely to lose awareness of itself as the reference-point, as the statement-subject. The past life, that former world of people, things and events overshadows the statement-subject, even if he does portray himself as being present in every moment of this past life in the form of his earlier self—as indeed he must if the first-person narrative form is to be maintained. It is here that the structural nucleus of the memoir novel's epic potential lies; but at the same time we also find here the reason for the pronounced *variability of the first-person novel*. This is conditioned by a certain susceptibility which for its part is determined by the form of the reality statement, which is to be retained at all costs. As is also true of other realms of literature, this sensibility is doubtless more strongly embedded in the more critical, more style-conscious modern era than in earlier periods, where indeed there are instances, such as the Sesenheim scenes from Goethe's by no means feigned autobiography, where autobiographical statement goes over into animated epic depiction with dialogue. In Gottfried Keller's *Green Henry* the tendency toward fictionalization is so strong that even narrative forms which logically transgress the bounds of first-person statement crop up— which is not uninfluenced by the work's transition from a partial third-person to a first-person novel. About Agnes in her Diana costume at the Munich carnival we read: "Her eyes flashed darkly and sought her beloved, while in her silver-gleaming bosom the bold scheme she'd conceived made her heart pound"—whereas the most a first-person narrator can observe is the bosom's outer heaving, but not what is going on within it.[183] But such a passage is symptomatic of the first-person narrator's objectifying division into his previous I-phases, which mesh with those of the other, third-persons in the novel, to form a continuity. And this can occur in several ways: so that the I of the narrator, although portrayed as present, remains unnoticed, and the world picture arising from the fabric of his narrative, the other persons, the events and experiences taking place which have nothing to do with him, assume prominence and attain a life of their own, a life independent of this first-person narrator. They advance far beyond his field of experience. But at that point where they do exceed the latter's bounds, the form of first-person statement is breached, suspended. And this is the case—certainly out of conscious creative intent—in Herman Melville's powerful novel *Moby Dick*, where the first-person narrator, the sailor Ishmael, sometimes completely disappears and the sombre main character, Captain Ahab, is portrayed alone with himself, i.e., in his I-originarity, as a fictive figure. Such a striking form of "transgression" into the fictional in itself shows that the principal matter at hand here is not the first-person narrator *per se,* not his own existence and self-portrayal, but rather the existence, the independent being of other persons, and in the case of *Moby Dick* ultimately the existence of enticing evil itself, personified in the white whale.—If, on the other hand, those few but central situations in Thomas Mann's *Doctor Faustus* where Adrian Leverkühn, released from the experience-field of his biographer Zeitblom, are nonetheless conveyed to us by the latter, this is an indication that Zeitblom's relation to the object of his biography is more deeply rooted, that he himself as the chronicler is involved in the world- and life-sphere centering around the main character.

The Problematic of the Feint

These few examples taken from the wealth of first-person novels suffice to demonstrate that the reality statement form cannot be disregarded in the interpretation of the first-person narrative. This form is the structural law which is operative far into the aesthetic and "ideological" spheres—and which, indeed, proves instructive even when it is breached. Even in such instances the statement form still posits the boundary between fiction and the first-person narrative. And if preliminarily we could derive this from the forms of narration (being the symptoms of these laws), still this does not sufficiently elucidate the first-person narrative. The question posed by the latter's logical place in the system of literature, that of its being a feigned reality statement, has not yet been answered. That is, the concept of the literary feint itself must be more closely analyzed. Such analysis will show that this concept contains the decisive criterion which elucidates the relation of the first-person narrative to epic fiction on the one hand, and to the lyric poem on the other.

The fact that the lyric poem is a *genuine* reality statement implies that it completely realizes the concept of reality. For this concept is realized even when the reality concerned is not of an objective, but of a subjective nature, when—since reality is always experienced reality—the *experience* of the reality more than its objective constitution is what characterizes the statement. This means that it is also realized when the stated reality is ever so "unreal." For even the most extreme, dream-like, or visionary unreality is a reality experience—the experience of the lyric I (just as such unreality can also be the experience of the non-lyric, the dreaming or the visionary I). There can be no doubt as to the authenticity of this I, and therefore also none as to the authenticity of the lyric statement—and it is precisely this which marks the lyric experience. And this means that in the lyric it is not the form, but the full realization of the concept of reality which evokes the phenomenon of the genuine reality statement.

The exact opposite set of relations prevails in the case of the first-person narrative. Here it is through the form and not through the content of the reality statement, i.e., through the statement form and not the reality content, that the first-person narrative presents itself as a reality statement, and thus as a variable literary form, as a feigned reality statement whose degree of feint is subject to variation. Whereas an ever so unreal content in the lyric poem does not disparage its character as reality statement, the first-person narrative, on the other hand, appears the less real, i.e., the more feigned, the greater its unreal content is. Ernst Jünger's *Mar-*

morklippen adheres strictly to the first-person narrative form. Nowhere does it employ fictionalizing techniques to achieve its plastic
presentation of the milieu, the circumstances, the events, and persons portrayed. Everything remains the pure object of account;
none of the persons is portrayed in direct speech; nowhere is there
a dialogue situation created. Without exception, the form of the
historical chronicle is retained throughout. Nevertheless, the degree of feint in this first-person narrative is so great, its unreal
content so obvious, that it presents itself much less as reality statement than, for example, *Green Henry*, where the first-person form
is treated far more negligently. The form, then, does not guarantee
a real content. But on the other hand, it does guarantee that even
such a highly feigned account will not attain the character of fiction. At this point we see once more—and only from a different
vantage—that the concept of the unreal is not to be confused with
that of the non-real, with that of fiction. A third-person novel can
have an ever so naturalistic content, and can correspond ever so
closely with reality, and still it will be experienced as non-real, as
the fictive reality of fictive persons. The content of a first-person
narrative can be ever so unreal and fairy-tale-like, and can correspond ever so slightly with knowable reality, and still it as little
attains to fiction as does any other fantasizing statement. It is the
first-person statement form which maintains the character of reality statement in those statements of even the most extreme unreality.

But this still does not sufficiently clarify why nevertheless the
concept of reality might not also be realized by an unreal content,
as it can in the lyric. At this point we must bear in mind that the
first-person narrative assumes such an instructive logical position
in the system of literature precisely because it is to be distinguished
(in different ways) from both the lyric and the genuine reality
statement proper. With respect to the lyric it assumes the same
attitude as does the genuine reality statement: the I in first-person

narration does not intend to be a lyric, but a historical I. And as a result of this attitude the first-person narrative, be it an epistolary or a memoir novel, does not resemble the lyric poem in its outer form, but the extended and "prosaic" reality statement. It is a *mimesis of reality statement*—which is obviously something different from a mimesis of reality itself, which constitutes the fictional genre. *Qua* first-person reality statement it does entail self-expression, and it therefore cannot but come to contain some subjective truth. But at the same time, like all genuine first-person account, it also aims at setting forth objective truth and reality. It intends to narrate world not only as a subjective experience, but also world for itself, as a reality which stands opposite the I and is independent of it. Therefore the reality content of the first-person narrative is just as relevant for its structure as is that of the genuine, non-lyric reality statement. This is the reason why as a non-genuine, feigned reality statement, it does not realize the concept of reality, why in it a specific content of unreality is not to be credited to the subjective truth of the lyric I, but to the objective untruth of feigned reality, and in turn of a feigned statement-subject.

Only on the basis of such a structural analysis which elucidates the phenomena in question does it become evident how inadequate, indeed how erroneous the usual justification for the first-person form is: namely that it is a guarantee for the credibility of the narrated, and especially for unreal, fabulous events. This may actually be applicable for some first-person narratives. But we do not get the impression that through the use of the first-person form Ernst Jünger, for example, wished to make the world of his *Marmorklippen* credible as a real world. But what does not prove true for even one example of a type cannot suffice as the basis upon which the type as a whole is to be explained. That the concept of credibility is not covered by that of the feint is shown by a work such as *Die Marmorklippen;* but it is also made clear by so early a first-person portrayal of unreality as that of the Mummelsee in

Grimmelshausen's *Simplizissimus*. It is not with the intent of making the unusual society of the marble reefs—which does not conform to familiar conditions of reality in our world—and its environs more credible, of trying to create the illusion that they are empirically real, that these are presented as the experience of a first-person narrator. On the contrary, these human and social relations, which have been reduced to primal, archetypal situations, are presented as a construing, as a symbol of another reality. And that a similar symbolic intent motivates Simplex's story about the benevolent spirits of the Mummelsee is quite obvious. But even the first-person form of naïve, non-symbolic legends cannot be elucidated with the theory of credibility. For the phenomenon here in question implies the exact opposite. It is the feignedness of the first-person narrator which appears to a greater degree the more unreal the content of the statement is. It is not, therefore, the first-person form which causes the unreal to appear "more real," but rather vice versa: the unreality of the account causes the I giving it also to appear as unreal, as feigned. And on the other hand, in first-person narratives whose content is to a large extent real, there is in turn no need for recourse to the theory of credibility as a basis for explanation. For such narratives in themselves so closely approach genuine autobiography that in many instances only documentary investigation on the relation between art and empirical truth can decide. If we consider the totality of all possible and actual instances of first-person narration and do not draw conclusions on the basis of individual manifestations, then the contour, or better, the poetological law of its structure, will emerge clearly. It is conditioned and determined by the variability of the degree of feint, which in mathematical terms moves on a scale whose cardinal points are o and ∞. Whereby the example of *Die Marmorklippen* on the one hand, and the Sesenheim scenes in Goethe's autobiography *Poetry and Truth* on the other, both demonstrate that those various narrative forms within the general statement form are not the decisive criteria for the degree of feint. Goethe's genuine autobiography in these scenes makes use of fictionalizing narrative forms; the highly feigned first-person narrative of Jünger retains the form of historical statement. Both cases are extremes, exceptions. And if the majority of first-person narratives do not afford us a reading experience which is especially distinguished from that of a third-person narrative, the reason is that in most cases they are amply furnished with fictionalizing devices such as situation portrayals, conversations, and so on, which occur all the more spontaneously the more rich in world and characters the story is.

At this juncture we must once again point out the distinction between the first-person narrative and fiction, and counter an objection which is likely to arise. If we go back to our definition of fiction which states that it exists only by virtue of its being narrated, then how, one might ask, is the first-person narrator different from the narrative function? For in our immediate, "naïve" reading experience of most first-person novels we sense that here, too, that which is narrated exists only by virtue of its being narrated, and that the first-person narrator is himself a fictive person who is talking about other fictive persons. Indeed, even the authors of first-person novels themselves will scarcely feel or construe these first-person heroes as being persons less fictive than the third-person hero, and this despite the fact that they abide by the laws of first-person narration just as unconsciously as the person who speaks and thinks adheres to the laws of speech and thought. Despite ever so fictional elaboration, they will nevertheless not exceed that limit set by the first-person perspective, i.e., by the law of statement. But just this circumstance demands that we stress the importance of those concepts and terms which are to be employed in describing the phenomena which we find here. If we apply the concept of fictivity to the first-person narrator, he loses his poetological-phenomenological significance and is reduced to the factor of mere invention, of contrivance, which contributes nothing to the phenomenology of literature. To designate the first-person narrator as a fictive figure totally obscures his structural function as a statement-subject; and the only fictive statement-subjects are those persons speaking as characters in a work of epic or dramatic fiction. (But let us note parenthetically that this stringent differentiation is made precisely for reasons of the structure of language and their consequences for the phenomenology of the first-person narrative. In a more general and abbreviated discussion it is of course "permissible" to speak of the first-person narrator as being fictive, and in everyday usage to disregard the difference existing between the terms "feigned" and "fictive," and thus casually to include also the first-person narrative within the fictional genre.) The concept of the feigned statement-subject, which describes the first-person epic narrator (of a first-person narrative presenting itself as such), distinguishes him on the one hand from the genuine statement-subject of an autobiography, and on the other from the narrator-I of the author—and finally also from the lyric I. On account of the lyric I's being a genuine statement-subject we cannot and do not need to decide on its identity with the empirical I of the poet. But the feint of the first-person narrator directly implies that structurally he has nothing to do with the empirical narrative I of the author who invented him along with all the other persons in the novel (and that, therefore, it is equally irrelevant for both the first- and the third-person narrative whether and to what extent the author might be portraying himself in any of the characters).

If we maintain that the first-person narrative does not obey the laws of fiction, but those of the feint, then we must verify this with that criterion which was decisive for the structure of fictional narration, namely *tense*. If we compare the reading experience of a first-person novel with that of a third-person novel, we note that in the former the preterite retains its function of designating the past:

Mein armer Vater war Inhaber der Firma Engelbert Krull. . . .
Unten am Rhein, nicht weit von der Landungsbrücke, lagen ihre
Kellereien, und nicht selten trieb ich mich als Knabe in den kühlen
Gewölben umher. . . .*

Un jour, à l' heure du courrier, ma mère posa sur mon lit une
lettre. Je l'ouvris distraitement . . . .

These passages from Thomas Mann's *Felix Krull* and Proust's
A la recherche du temps perdu I bring us once more to the phenomenon of tense. Since the past time in which the reported events
took place is referred to the first-person narrator, the feigned
statement-subject, we shall designate it as a feigned, or to use a
more emphatic term, a *quasi-past*.

The quasi-past or respectively quasi-present of the narrator—
and in turn the poetological explication of the nature of the narrator—affords us another means of surveying the various structures within the realm of the epic. We see that it is also possible
for the first-person narrative to appear as an independent genre
in reduced and so to speak dependent form within fiction. The
analysis of these relations will shed more light on the concept of
quasi- or as-if reality as opposed to the semblance of reality.
Odysseus' tale in the Phaacean Court has long been considered a
classic example of the extended first-person narrative occurring
within a third-person narration, and has customarily been cited
as a prime case of first-person narrative in Western literature. And
erroneously so!—since no cognizance was taken of the distinction
between a fictive and a feigned first-person narrator. For a first-
person narration occurring within a third-person narrative, that is
a first-person narration given by a third-person hero, constitutes
a dual-stratified structure: a quasi-reality is based within a semblance of reality, the mimesis of reality statement within the

* My poor father was the proprietor of the Engelbert Krull Company . . .
Down on the Rhine, not far from the pier, were the company cellars, and as
a boy I often wandered about in the cool vaults. . . .

mimesis of reality. The first-person narrator Odysseus is not only an invented, but also a fictionalized figure, his own fictive I-Origo, and the past tense in which his deeds and the events concerning him are narrated signifies his fictive present, his fictive Here and Now. The past tense of his own first-person narration, on the other hand, signifies his past. How is this past to be logically defined? In order to grasp this we must begin with our reading experience. When the preterite tells of Odysseus as a third-person the reader experiences present-time, and he experiences past-time when Odysseus himself narrates. The preterite now appears in its proper function of designating something as past. But what kind of a past-time does the reader experience? Doubtless not his own (nor one known to him), but Odysseus' past. He experiences a quasi-past whose I-Origo is that of Odysseus, but with reference to whom this past is a "genuine" one. This genuine past of Odysseus is experienced by us as a fictive one only because we have encountered Odysseus from the start as a fictive figure. We know his "genuine" past only on the basis of his fictive present. The awareness of this fictivity supplants the character of the quasi-past and simply replaces it with that of the fictive past. In this process the character of the past itself, however, is always retained intact, since it is presented to us as a past experienced by the fictive person. A first-person narrative occurring within a work of epic fictional literature demonstrates with full phenomenological clarity the difference between the fictional and the genuine preterite, between "he was" and "I was." The genuine preterite can designate various modes of past experiences: experiences of real, quasi-, and fictive pasts. It is clear that these differences in our experience are determined by the type of statement-subject: by whether it is a real, a quasi- (i.e., feigned), or a fictive statement-subject. The first is what we have in the case of an indubitable reality statement which is documented or otherwise obviously recognizable as such, and the last is the instance of a first-person statement occurring in a work of fiction, be this an epic, dramatic, or cinematic work. And the quasi-past is what we have in the case of the independent first-person narrative.

But the relationship of these three possibilities to one another is not one of uniformity. Between a quasi- and a fictive past there is a categorical difference, and between a quasi- and a real past there is on the other hand a difference in degree, or a transitional relation. From the point of view of both theory of language and theory of literature the independent first-person narrative is not fiction, but a quasi- or feigned reality statement. And if often in our reading experience we do not differentiate the narrator in any random first-person novel from a fictive figure, this is due solely to the high degree of his feint. But that we are not to confuse this with fictivity is both founded in and proven by the fact that there are first-person narratives—such as the case of the Egyptian Sinuhe—which are to be interpreted as those of a real statement-subject. The quasi-reality, or the quality of being feigned, which is the definitive term for the first-person narrative, is distinguished from the fictive in that it is capable of *gradation*. There is a more or a less quasi-, but there is no such thing as a more or a less fictive. A high degree of feint in most cases also signifies an invented content. But an invented content is not the same as a fictive one. Historical figures in a novel, such as Napoleon in *War and Peace,* Heinrich von Kleist in Albrecht Schaeffer's *Rudolph Erzerum,* are as such not invented, but nevertheless *qua* figures in a novel they are fictive. That is, just like purely invented characters, they "are" only by virtue of their being narrated. If historical figures become first-person narrators, then it depends on the nature of the narrative to what degree the author renders them feigned. Where possibilities for checking are absent, as in *The Life of Sinuhe,* the periphery of genuine autobiography cannot always be ascertained. The autobiographical authenticity of a historical first-person novel such as M. Yourcenar's *Les Mémoires d'Hadrien* (1953), which is formally presented as a genuine autobiography (and is also supported by extensive documentation), can of course be verified. And if one objects that this is valid not only for the autobiographical, but also for every other historical third-person novel, this is quite correct, from the perspective of literary history. But nevertheless the decisive factor remains the presentational form. The form of fiction in and of itself posits a demarcation from reality of any kind. But the form of the feigned historical reality statement does not contain such a demarcation; indeed all the less so the slighter the degree of feint is—as we have demonstrated with the examples cited from both antiquity and modern times. The author of *Les Mémoires d'Hadrien*, by avoiding all fictionalizing techniques, such as dialogue, for example, has taken care to insure that the degree of feint will appear as very slight.

The phenomenology of the first-person narrative, therefore, reveals that this narrative is a non-fictional literary type occurring within the epic-fictional sphere, just as the ballad is a fictional type within the lyric realm. In both cases the respectively epic and lyric domains are "alien territory" with regard to the "innate" structural constitution of these two literary forms. And therefore the effect of the alien spheres remains a purely formal one. The structure of, and hence the experience produced by these two types of literature is not altered by their alien, host spheres: neither the non-reality of the ballad's content nor the—gradated—reality of the first-person narrative. The latter, in other words, belongs to the realm of the reality statement, along with all those shadings which statement itself can have. And, as we shall emphasize once more, within this concept is included the element of the unreal as well as that of the quasi-real, or feigned.

From this vantage point we can again shed light on those cases of the narrator's *first-person intrusion* in fiction. It is now more clear than in the previous context dealing with the narrative function that what we have here is a relation between feint and fiction which is of an entirely different structural nature from that of a first-person narrative occurring within a work of fiction. When the narrative function in a novel becomes independent and turns into a narrative or authorial I, the latter feigns a genuine statement-subject. But such feigning in no way affects the structure of the piece of narrative fiction. The narrator as it were presents a minia-ture first-person narrative which remains outside of the novel and whose hero is he himself. It separates itself from the novel proper like oil from water; and that which creates the novel is not this first-person narrator, but the narrative function. The authorial I, which is here engaged in a play upon itself, is never one of the fictive per-sons in the work. The first-person narrative of a character in the novel, on the other hand, is part of the novel's general system of dialogue and monologue, and the force of fictivity renders an ever so extended and apparently independent first-person narrative fictive.[184]

A third case is represented by the framework or inset story [*Rahmenerzählung*], which we shall only briefly touch upon here, since after the preceding remarks its structure no longer presents any particular logical problems. When we are dealing with a dual first-person narrative, where the narrator in the frame story repro-duces another first-person narrative in the framed story—a struc-turally more risky situation which is represented by Storm's *Der Schimmelreiter*, for example—the character of feint is all the more conspicuous precisely because it is the intent of this form to ob-struct it. For the framework narrator appears as the guarantee for the "historical" truth of the first-person account which he has heard. Precisely Storm's *Schimmelreiter* shows how this dual form, far more than a uni-stratified first-person narrative, defies the law of fiction, such that those epic and fictionalizing forms of dialogue, etc., which are also permissible in the first-person narrative, now prove themselves to be formally inadequate. There are elements of structural risk even in first-person narratives which have only one stratum: where a first-person narrator reports a third-person narrative. It is only through the most intense effort that Emily Brontë's *Wuthering Heights* preserves the first-person perspective of the woman house-keeper telling the story. And basically even this form is tolerable only when it is treated in so sovereignly humoristic a manner as in Thomas Mann's *The Holy Sinner*. The (too little noted) subterranean humor of the story of Pope Gregory on the rock is not lastly rooted in the play which the author engages in with the first-person narrator, the Irish monk, whom he makes into the "spirit of narration," which is nothing other than the narrative function itself.

Wer läutet die Glocken? Der Glöckner nicht. Die sind auf die Straße gelaufen wie alles Volk, da es so ungeheuerlich läutet. Überzeugt euch: die Glockenstuben sind leer. Schlaff hängen die Seile, und dennoch wogen die Glocken, dröhnen die Klöppel. Wird man sagen, daß niemand sie läutet? — Nein, nur ein ungrammatischer Kopf ohne Logik wäre der Aussage fähig. 'Es läuten die Glocken', das meint: sie werden geläutet, und seien die Stuben auch noch so leer. — Wer also läutet die Glocken Roms? Der Geist der Erzählung. . . . Er ist es, der spricht: Alle Glocken läuten, und folglich ist er's, der sie läutet. . . . Und doch kann er sich auch zusammenziehen zur Person, nämlich zur ersten, und sich verkörpern in jemanden, der in dieser spricht und spricht: ich bin es, ich bin der Geist der Erzählung, der . . . diese Geschichte erzählt, indem ich mit ihrem gnadenvollen Ende beginne und die Glocken Roms läute, id est berichte, daß sie an jenem Tage des Einzugs sämtlich von selber zu läuten begannen. . . .*

* Who is ringing the bells? Not the bell-ringers. They've run out into the streets, just like everybody else, because the bells are chiming so fiendishly. Rest assured, the bell-towers are empty. The ropes are hanging slack, and still the bells heave, the clappers boom. Are we to say that no one is ringing

Here the narrative function is engaged in a play similar to that in the novels of Jean Paul, only that here it does not become "embodied" as the authorial I, but as a framework first-person narrator, and causes not a genuine, but a feigned historical statement-subject to enter jocularly into fiction. But precisely because of this subject's humoristic and hence invalid feint, fiction need not concern itself here over the feigned first-person perspective. Obeying its own laws, it develops into a genuine mimesis of the legendary reality of the Gregorius story, a mimesis which will now in turn engage in its own play with the legend, which does indeed say that "the bells began to ring of themselves."

The first-person narrative forms a keystone in the system of logical structures comprising the network of creative literature. Its importance lies not only in those ample nuances of its unique structure which we have sought to elucidate; beyond this, it is of methodological value to our investigations. For in its peculiar capacity as a feigned reality statement, as an intermediate form of an extensive nature, it allows those contours once again to emerge clearly which within the general system of language categorically separate the two major literary genres, the fictional and the lyrical. In poetic form they mirror those relations which we discussed at the outset in order to gain access to the logical system of literature. For in its capacity as narrative literature the first-person narrative

---

them?—No, only an ungrammatical mind without any logic would be capable of that statement. "The bells are ringing," that means: they are being rung, be the bell-towers ever so empty.—So who is ringing the bells of Rome? The spirit of narration. . . . It is what says: All the bells are ringing, and therefore it is also what is making them ring. . . . And it can also contract itself to a person, namely the first-person, and become embodied in someone who speaks and says: it is I, I am the spirit of narration, who . . . am telling this story in that I begin at the propitious end and ring the bells of Rome, id est report that on that day of entry they all began of themselves to ring. . . .

demonstrates that even an ever so high degree of feint in a reality statement does not turn this into fictional narration. The reality statement proved to be such an effective heuristic tool because through its contrastive comparison with fictional narration—as the only literary structure capable of undergoing comparison—it allowed us to take cognizance of the latter's special laws. Between reality statement and fictional narration there runs the boundary, even the sometimes small, yet unbridgeable cleft which separates the fictional genre as a special realm from the general statement system, which includes both the lyrical genre and, in another part of its domain, the first-person narrative.

6

CONCLUDING REMARKS

If, at the conclusion of these observations, we return to those guidelines which Hegel's statement established for our investigation, we realize that this statement was valid only to the extent that it directed us to that specific spectrum of problems concerning the logic of literature, a problematic which Hegel himself did not elucidate. The proposition that "poesie" is that particular art wherein art itself begins to break down and "go over into the prose of scientific thought" is one which Hegel had, to be sure, deduced from the unique quality of the linguistic material of literature, which in itself is identical with language outside the realm of creative literature. But what he did not realize is that this general linguistic equipment is such a versatile instrument of thought and mental representation that it also possesses or is capable of developing those properties which nevertheless enable literature to establish itself as an art form and reduce neither itself nor art as such to "the prose of scientific thought." He had seen where the "dangerous" points of transition lie, but he did not see how language, when it produces literature, avoids these dangers: in that in the case of fiction it relinquishes the laws of statement structure, and in the case of lyric statement orients and conducts itself in accordance with the will of the lyric I not to function in a context of reality.

This brings us once again, in recapitulation of the results of our investigations, to the general question as to the function of the logic of literature for the aesthetic comprehension and interpretation of both literature in general and the individual literary work. This question has in part already been answered in our expositions of the logical problems themselves. Many of the analyses of logical structures directly touched upon the substance of literature as such, whereas on the other hand in many instances we encountered that boundary where the logician's authority had to retire before that of aesthetic judgment. Grounding the general nature of the narrative function or of the lyric I belongs to the task of the logic of literature; whereas describing the How, the style, the particular narrative technique, the artistic form, the content of the lyric statement, all belong to the task of aesthetic interpretation. In general, we can define the relation, or the collaboration, between the logic and the aesthetic of literature in that they approach one another all the more, the more deeply aesthetic investigation enters into questions of technique and structure, and they touch upon one another less when, for example, poetic or also philosophic content is being considered. The logic of literature is not concerned with merely "poetic" language, but with creative language, with that language which produces the forms of literature.

NOTES

1. Cf. F. Schneider, "Das Problem einer Sprachlogik," *Zeitschrift für philosophische Forschung*, VII (1953), Heft 1.
2. John Stuart Mill, *A System of Logic*, 8th ed. (New York, 1893), Bk. 1, Ch. 1, § 1.
3. Edmund Husserl, *Logical Investigations*, trans. J. N. Findlay, 2 vols. (London, New York, 1970), I, 248. [*Logische Untersuchungen*, II, 1 (Halle, 1928), 1.]
4. Ludwig Wittgenstein, *Tractatus Logico-Philosophicus*, trans. D. F. Pears and B. F. McGuinness (London, New York, 1963), 35f.: "It is not humanly possible to gather immediately from it [everyday language] what the logic of language is. Language disguises thought" (4.002). "All philosophy is a 'critique of language.'" (4.0031) [*Tractatus Logico-Philosophicus*, 9. Aufl. (London, 1962), p. 62.]
5. August Wilhelm Schlegel, *Über Schöne Literatur und Kunst*, in *Deutsche Literaturdenkmale des 18 u. 19. Jahrhunderts*, XVII, 1884, 261.
6. Irene Behrens, *Die Lehre von der Einteilung der Dichtkunst* (Halle, 1940), p. 4.
7. This interpretation of the concept of mimesis is corroborated by H. Koller in his book *Die Mimesis in der Antike* (Bern, 1954). Koller shows that even Plato, in the third book of the *Politics*, intended mimesis to mean representation in that, for example, he connects the word "dissimilar" (ἄνομοιως) with μιμεῖσθαι: Homer should be bidden not to presume to represent the greatest of the gods in such dissimilar fashion (οὕτως ἀνομοίως μιμήσασθαι); to copy with dissimilarity is senseless (p. 15). Plato terms as narration, διήγησις, everything told by mythologists and poets, and distinguishes simple narration, (ἄπλη διηγησις),

from μίμησις. Here, also, mimesis does not mean imitation; it means that the persons appear as speaking themselves. Plato expresses this in the following way: the poet assumes the voice and figure of another (... ἢ κατα φώνην ἢ κατα σχῆμα μιμεῖσθαι). Indeed, Plato does not wish to say that the persons of a literary work are copied from reality, but that the poet narrates them mimetically if he lets them speak themselves. Koller also accepts the meaning of representation for the concept of mimesis in Aristotle's *Poetics* (cf. n. 10). Cf. further W. Weidlé, "Vom Sinn der Mimesis," *Eranos-Jahrbuch*, XXXI (1962), 249-273. In partial criticism of Koller, Weidlé points out that the sense of expressiveness, which also enters into the concept of mimesis, is an additional element in the notion of representation (p. 259).

8. ἐποποιία δὴ καὶ ἡ τῆς τραγῳδίας ποίησις ἔτι δὲ κωμῳδια καὶ ἡ διθυραμβοποιητικὴ καὶ τῆς αὐλητικῆς ἡ πλείστη καὶ κιθαριστικῆς πᾶσαι τυγχάνουσιν οὖσαι μιμήσεις τὸ σύνολον (1447ᵃ).

9. ... μιμοῦνται καὶ ἤθη καὶ πάθη καὶ πράξεις (ibid.).

10. It is striking, and yet also characteristic, to note that Aristotle also reckons the Dithyramb under μιμήσες. This was a choral song accompanied by flute-playing, and it represented "action," namely the fates of Dionysus and other mythical figures. It was from the Dithyramb that the satyr play and tragedy developed, a well-known fact which we find already in Aristotle. From this we also appear to get clarification as to why "most flute and lyre playing" is named in the same context as the Dithyramb: obviously it is such instrumental music which accompanied dithyrambic and other "representational" literature.—And let us point out that, furthermore, mimesis originally referred to the dance and to that music accompanying it (Koller, p. 104).

11. Ἐπεὶ δὲ μιμοῦνται οἱ μιμούμενοι πράττοντας, ἀνάγκη δε τούτους ἢ σπουδαίους ἢ φαύλους εἶναι ... ἤτοι βελτίονας ἢ καθ᾽ ἡμᾶς ἢ χείρονας ἢ καὶ τοιούτους; ὥσπερ οἱ γραφεῖς (1448ᵃ).

12. οἱ ἄνθρωποί γε συνάπτοντες τῷ μέτρῳ τὸ ποιεῖν ἐλεγειοποιοὺς τοὺς δὲ ἐποποιοὺς ὀνομάζουσιν, οὐχ ὡς κατὰ τὴν μίμησιν ποιητὰς ἀλλὰ κοινῇ κατὰ τὸ μέτρον προσαγορεύοντες ... οὐδὲν δὲ κοινόν ἐστιν Ὁμήρῳ καὶ Ἐμπεδοκλεῖ πλὴν τὸ μέτρον, διὸ τὸν μὲν ποιητὴν δικαιον καλεῖν, τὸν δὲ φυσιολόγον μᾶλλον ἢ ποιητὴν (1447ᵇ).

Koller, too, emphasizes this sentence, but without, however, establishing a connection between *mimesis* and *poiesis*. But at the same time he stresses that in mimesis Aristotle had found the conceptual means of "separating genuine literature from that which merely resembles literature, for, according to the previous custom of using metre as the decisive criterion, didactic poetry would fall under the category of literature even though it is none, whereas prose literature would be excluded. Aristotle's great achievement lies in the recognition of this fact" (Koller, p. 106).

13. αὐτὸν γὰρ δεῖ τὸν ποιητὴν ἐλάχιστα λέγειν. οὐ γάρ ἐστι κατὰ ταῦτα μιμητής (1460ᵃ).

14. Ibid.

15. According to G. Storz, "Über die Wirklichkeit von Dichtung," *Wirkendes Wort*, l. Sonderheft (1952), 94f.

16. It is well known, and yet deserves to be stressed once again in our context that in Hegel's time "poesie" was not restricted to lyric poetry, but was a collective term meaning "literature." For the concept "scientific," cf. n. 21.

17. Georg Wilhelm Friedrich Hegel, *The Philosophy of Fine Art*, trans. F.P.B. Osmaston, 4 vols. (London, 1920), vol. IV, 15 [trans. mine]. [*Vorlesungen über die Ästhetik*, ed. H. G. Hotho, 3 vols. (Bd. 10, 1., 2., 3. Abtheilung, *Hegels Werke*, vollständige Ausgabe, Berlin, 1838), III, 232.]

18. Hegel, III, 21. [*Vorlesungen* . . . , II, 260.]

19. Hegel, IV, 17 [trans. mine.] [*Vorlesungen* . . . , III, 234.]

20. Hegel, IV, 25 [trans. mine]. [*Vorlesungen* . . . , III, 242.]

21. For Hegel (and also for Fichte) scientific thought meant theoretical thought.

22. Hegel, IV, 17 [trans. mine]. [*Vorlesungen* . . . , III, 234.]

23. Hegel, IV, 11 [trans. mine]: "Generally, we can grasp this distinction thus: it is not the mere mental representation as such, but the artistic imagination which renders a given content poetic." [*Vorlesungen* . . . , III, 228.]

24. Benedetto Croce, *Aesthetic as Science of Expression and General Linguistic*, trans. Douglas Ainslie, 2nd ed. (London, 1922), p. 22.

25. Croce, pp. 2f.

26. H. Rickert, *Goethes Faust* (Tübingen, 1932), p. 23.

27. Roman Ingarden, *Das literarische Kunstwerk*, 2. Aufl. (Tübingen, 1960), p. 170.

28. Ingarden, p. 171.

29. Ingarden, p. 178.

30. Ibid.

31. Ingarden, p. 182.

32. Ingarden, p. 180.

33. Ibid.
34. Ingarden, p. 181.
35. Ingarden, pp. 181f.
36. Now, Ingarden, in the new edition of his book, has rejected my criticism of his theory of quasi-judgments (pp. 184–192). This criticism did not refer to the theory or the definition of the concept of the quasi-judgment *per se*, but to its application in the description of literary fiction. Nonetheless, I cannot consider my objections to be refuted by Ingarden's supplementary comments and explanatory remarks. Now as then it seems unconvincing to me to ground the fictionality of a novel's world (which is the principal matter at hand) in the observation that the sentences of which the novel is composed are quasi-judgments (in the sense in which Ingarden defines these in his text). My objection concerning his tautological proof is only confirmed (even though dismissed) by Ingarden when he says: " . . . if we know from the outset that we are dealing with a literary work, then—if I am correct—we also know that we are dealing precisely with quasi-judgments" (p. 189). Ingarden then refers to the assertion signs which Russel introduced into logic in order to differentiate the so-called "theses" of a logical system from mere declarative sentences (which are divested of the function of assertion). Applying this idea to literature, he then names as "those external verbal signs which we avail ourselves of in order to indicate that we are dealing with quasi-judgments . . . a different intonation, which is actually other than the intonation we give to sentences in a scientific context," just as "the title or sub-title informs us that we are dealing with a novel or a drama" (p. 190). The contrast between sentences in a scientific context and quasi-judgments seems to refer specifically to the historical novel, to which Ingarden has recourse in countering my criticisms, whereas that special intonation characterizing sentences in a novel is no doubt meant for all novels in general. Apart from the question of these assumed intonational signs which are supposed to hallmark the quasi-judgment, it appears to me to confirm only once again that we can dispense with the declaration that sentences in a novel or a play are quasi-judgments in order to know that these two forms of literature confront us with a fictional world. For these signs merely *state that* there is a fictive world presented in a novel or a drama; they do not, however, show how this fictivity is produced. Though Ingarden further reproaches me, saying that I have "imputed to him the statement that only the quasi-judgments differentiate a historical novel

from any corresponding authentic work of history" (p. 190), and proceeds to enumerate additional differentiations he has worked out: "another style of language, a different composition, the presence of a variety of schematized aspects, the delineational and representational function of the represented objectivities, the presence of aesthetically valent qualities . . . " (p. 190)—still I must uphold my contention that what with all these characteristics, which are not under debate here, the sole decisive criterion is nonetheless lacking. This is namely that of the fictive persons, i.e., the figures who are formed in their fictive Here and Now, who render the novel a novel, and whose structural significance and function for narration is elaborated in my book. I must furthermore defend myself against Ingarden's obvious opinion that I have included sentences in their specific quality as logical judgments within my theory. My concept of the reality statement does not belong to the logic of judgment, but to the theory of language. That above all it does not mean a statement *about* reality has also been elaborated.

37. I. M. Bocheński, *A History of Formal Logic,* ed., trans. Ivo Thomas (Notre Dame, Indiana, 1961), p. 20. [*Formale Logik* (Freiburg, 1956), p. 24.]

38. Ibid.

39. J. H. von Kirchmann, trans., *Aristoteles' Hermeneutica* (Leipzig, 1876), p. 59.

40. Christoph Sigwart, *Logic,* trans. Helen Dendy (London, New York, 1895), 26 [Trans. mine]. [*Logik,* I, 4. Aufl. (Tübingen, 1921), 31.]

41. Ibid. [Trans. mine.]

42. Sigwart, p. 27 [Trans. mine.] [*Logik,* p. 32.]

43. Edmund Husserl, *Erfahrung und Urteil* (Hamburg, 1948), p. 4.

44. H. Ammann, *Die menschliche Rede,* Band II: Der Satz (Lahr, 1928), 125.

45. Ibid., p. 123.

46. Husserl, *Erfahrung* . . . , p. 9.

47. Ibid., p. 7.

48. Karl Bühler, *Sprachtheorie* (Jena, 1934), p. 90.

49. That there is a problem present here is something which has been repeatedly noted and discussed. If J. Ries (*Was ist ein Satz,* Prague, 1931) resists viewing the other sentence modalities as statement sentences, then H. A. Gardiner, who does classify sentences into statements, questions, requests, and exclamations, stresses their interrelatedness and

would ascribe only slight import to their verbal form. "Exclamation and statement are separated from one another only by a thin border in: How well he sings, and He sings very well." (*The Theory of Speech and Language*, Oxford, 1932, p. 190.) H. Ammann, too, suggests that the use of the term "statement" be extended, and would designate "as statements all those verbal structures which can be understood as modifications of the declarative sentence insofar as the structural elements of the declarative sentence are retained in them when the instance of asserting becomes changed to an element of asking, wishing, assuming" (Ammann, p. 67).

50. It is a terminological shortcoming that within the spheres of logic, grammar, epistemology and psychology the concept of the subject is applied in various meanings and functions. In logic and grammar it has a static quality as the subject of a judgment or that of a sentence; in epistemology, psychology, and also in metaphysics it has a dynamic-activistic aspect. In the former instances it signifies (in terms of meta-language) a concept or a word, and in the latter it signifies (in terms of object-language) a person, or more generally, a personalized instance: the thinking, cognizing subject, in whom the trait of personalization is still inherent when it appears in its abstract form as the subject-pole of the structure of cognition; the conscious subject; the transcendental subject (Fichte), the Kantian "I think," Husserl's notion of consciousness in general, etc. In opposition to Fichte's distinction between the empirical and the absolute subject, Theodor W. Adorno emphasizes that precisely since the latter is an abstraction of the empirical subject it falls under, and is intended concomitantly with, the concept of this empirical subject (*Drei Studien zu Hegel*, Frankfurt am Main, 1964, p. 27).

51. Ingarden, pp. 109f., 114.

52. Alfred North Whitehead, *Science and the Modern World* (New York, 1939), pp. 217f.

53. Nicolai Hartmann, *Zur Grundlegung der Ontologie*, 2. Aufl. (Berlin, 1941), p. 17.

54. Ibid., p. 53

55. Ibid., p. 18.

56. For the concepts "experience" [*Erlebnis*] and "field of experience" [*Erlebnisfeld*], see below, apropos of the lyric experience, p. 277.

57. Wittgenstein, *Tractatus* . . . , 2.063, 4.01, 3.318, 4.021, 4.03.

58. This section is taken from my article "Noch einmal—vom Erzählen," *Euphorion* 59 (1965), 61–64.

59. Theodor Fontane, *Sämtliche Werke,* Bd. XXI (Munich, 1963), 239.
60. Hermann Paul, *Deutsche Grammatik,* Bd. IV (Halle, 1920), 65.
61. Ch. A. Heyse, *Deutsche Grammatik,* 29. Aufl. (Hannover, 1923), p. 314.
62. Karl Brugmann, *Die Demonstrativpronomia der indogermanischen Sprachen* (Leipzig, 1904);—Karl Bühler, pp. 102f.

63. Only in the dialogue system of a novel, as the direct speech of a character, can the sentence occur in this form.

64. Brugmann's interpretation of these relationships again makes it apparent that the distinction between "historical" (i.e. statement) and fictional narration has not been recognized. Brugmann says that "the nature of first-person demonstrative pronouns does not change when they are employed in the narration of past events. Specifically when demonstratives which are spatial or temporal in meaning, and which owe their referential nature to the standpoint of the presence and present-time of the person speaking, appear in narration, this is a dramatic usage similar to the employment of a present instead of a past tense. Thus: He sat there in sadness the whole day, for today (instead of 'on that day') he had received two pieces of bad news" (Brugmann, pp. 41f.). Certainly it is correct that the use of first-person deictic pronouns does not undergo any alterations in a story narrated in the simple past tense. What changes is the function and meaning of the past tense, which even in Brugmann's example does not state anything past; and precisely *because* it does not do so it can occur with the deictics. These relations are obscured if one attributes them to "dramatization." What we have here is a means of fictionalization which precisely the drama does not require.

65. Thus Dagobert Frey states in welcome confirmation of the relations which we have discovered working on the basis of theory of language: "In epic fiction the time and place of the action is of a purely objective nature. They have utterly nothing to do with the spatio-temporal determination of the subject, neither with that of the poet nor with that of the listener; they are not at all to be referred to this. History is also to be differentiated from literary narration in that although it, too, is of a purely objective nature, it is nevertheless temporally and spatially ordered in concrete space and time, as these are given in subjective experience" (*Gotik und Renaissance,* Augsburg, 1929, p. 213). This insight, along with our own exposition, is directed against the widely

spread notion, once given practically along with the theory of past-ness, that the epic narrator, i.e., the poet, stands in a temporal relation, at a "narrative distance" to that which is narrated. The principal advocate of this interpretation is Franz Stanzel, *Narrative Situations in the Novel*, trans. James Pusack, Bloomington, 1971 [*Die typischen Erzählsituationen im Roman*, Wiener Beiträge zur engl. Philologie, Bd. 53 (Vienna, 1955)].

66. The tabular present is described in Brugmann-Delbrück, *Vergleichende Grammatik der indogermanischen Sprachen* IV, 2 (1897), as closely contiguous to the historical present: "Here, too, the event in the past stands before the person speaking like an image, and temporal relativity is disregarded. The tabular present first emerged in the written presentation, through either heiroglyphic pictures or alphabetic characters, of what is mentally represented and spoken" (p. 736).

67. Italics mine.

68. Recall the discussion carried on in the 'twenties among the romance language scholars Charles Bally, Th. Kalepsky, and E. Lerch in GRM V, VI (1912–14) and the presentation of this discussion in E. Lorck, *Die erlebte Rede* (1921), as well as Walzel's contributions made in *Das Wortkunstwerk* (1926). Cf. further G. Storz, "Über den 'monologue intérieur' oder die 'Erlebte Rede,'" *Der Deutschunterricht* (1955), Heft 1, 45ff: For a discussion of the *erlebte Rede* in English-language theories, cf. Dorrit Cohn, "Narrated Monologue, Definition of a Fictional Style," *Comparative Literature*, XIII nr. 2 (1966), 97–112.

69. Susanne Langer, *Feeling and Form* (New York, 1953), p. 269.

70. Ibid., p. 263.

71. Otto Jespersen, *The Philosophy of Grammar* (London, 1924), p. 258.

72. Ch. A. Heyse, *Deutsche Grammatik*, p. 360.

73. Raphael Kühner, *Grammatik der griechischen Sprache*, 2. Teil, Bd. 1 (Leipzig, 1898), p. 132. [For an English translation, not cited here, cf. B. B. Edwards and S. H. Taylor, *Grammar of the Greek Language*, by R. Kühner (Andover, 1844), p. 337.]

74. Wunderlich-Reis, *Der deutsche Satzbau*, I (Stuttgart, 1924), p. 235.

75. For instance, A. T. Rompelman, in his essay "Form und Funktion des Präteritums im Germanischen," *Neophilologus*, 37 (1953), points out that the historical present is quite old, appearing in all Indogermanic languages, and he emphasizes that originally "the convenient switching

back and forth from one form to another . . . was not the consequence of a lack of feeling for style" (p. 80), and that one should not interpret this interchanging as being overly temporal in character, which would be too one-sided. He justifies this by referring to the fact that the historical present originated at a time when even the present tense itself was less a tense than a verbal mode expressing action.

76. Brugmann-Delbrück, *Grundriss der vergleichenden Grammatik der indogermanischen Sprachen*, II, 3, 1 (Strassburg, 1916), 733.

77. This phenomenon has been observed, but not really explained, by J. R. Frey, "The Historical Present in Narrative Literature, particularly in Modern German Fiction," JEGP, vol. 45,1: "It is not going too far to say that in narration the lines dividing the tenses from one another do not have the rigidity of which we are conscious when viewing the tenses just as grammatical forms" (p. 53). But Frey finds no explanation for this because he, too, is of the opinion that at least the reader experiences the action of the novel as past. "To the reader even the writer's present is past" (ibid.).

78. H. Weinrich, in his book entitled *Tempus* (Stuttgart, 1964), denies the temporal meaning-content of the tenses and instead orders them from the linguistic point of view into the categories of narrated and discussed world, with the preterite tenses belonging to the first, and the present tense forms to the second. My opinion, set forth in the essay "Noch einmal—vom Erzählen," on the other hand, maintains against Weinrich's polemics that it is precisely the preterite of the reality statement which is an unequivocal indication of past-ness. I still maintain this opinion despite Weinrich's latest addition to our running discussion, "Tempusprobleme eines Leitartikels," *Euphorion*, vol. 60 (1966), 263–272. Here he correctly assigns the genre represented by the newspaper editorial [*Leitartikel*] to that of historiography, but in establishing his point that here preterite tenses, namely those narrating a "history," mix with the present tense forms of discussion, it seems to me he introduces time—which he wanted to free from tense—back into the tense forms: into the preterite, since it states of the past, and also into the present, insofar as it designates something present, something contemporaneous to the temporal point of the statement-subject. A sentence from a newspaper may again serve as an example: "July 3, 1967. The district attorney's office in Karlsruhe is presently investigating the alleged abduction of. . . ." That furthermore the a-temporal present tense used for commentary appears quite frequently in every written work is something we need not discuss.

79. For a more detailed discussion. cf. Käte Hamburger, *Der Humor bei Thomas Mann, Zum Joseph Roman* (Munich, 1965).

80. The same applies, in however weakly accentuated a form, to the example from Keller's *A Village Romeo and Juliet*, cited by H. Seidler in his polemics against my theory, as proof that the stylistic value of the preterite is one of indicating past-ness. The sentence reads: "Far at its base lies a village, which has many a large farm, and stretched over the gentle hillock years ago there lay three splendid fields." (*Wirkendes Wort*, 1952–53, Heft 5, 271ff.) Cf. also H. Seidler's book *Allgemeine Stilistik* (Göttingen, 1953), 139f., as well as the polemics between Seidler and myself in DVLG, Jg. 29 (1955), Heft 3. It is not the preterite form "lay" following the previous present tense which effects the "opening up of a past spatial order," as Seidler says, but rather the temporal adverb "years ago." The preterite here is already relatively unstressed, and it becomes more and more unstressed as the story becomes increasingly more "presentified," i.e., fictionalized, such that it is by no means experienced as already past, but as taking place here and now. Take for example the sentence: ". . . and so the two plowed peacefully, and it was nice to see, in the quiet, golden, September landscape, as they passed one another thus at the height of the hill." Something past or thought of as past cannot be "nice to see," and such a sentence cannot appear in a historical text, in a reality statement (except in an eye-witness account), where the past tense "was" functions as a genuine preterite. The same conditions are present here in abbreviated form as are in the example from *Hochwald*.

81. For confirmation of our illustrations we may consult what one distinguished novelist has said about his own creative experience: "It is a matter of total indifference, and also a purely technical question, whether the epic writer uses the present, perfect or imperfect tense. He will change modes wherever he thinks it wise to do so. What is decisive, and what is certainly not of merely secondary importance to observe, is that what one often reads pertaining to this question is incorrect: namely that the dramatist renders an action which is going on at present, and the epic writer tells about one which has gone on. This is superficial and ridiculous. For everyone reading an epic work the events being reported are taking place now; he experiences them in a Now regardless of whether a present, perfect or imperfect tense occurs in the text. In epic literature we portray things as being just as present as does the dramatist; and moreover, they are also assimilated

into the reader's experience as such." (Alfred Döblin, "Der Bau des epischen Werkes," *Neue Deutsche Rundschau,* 40, 1929, as cited by Fritz Martini in *Das Wagnis der Sprache, Stuttgart,* 1954, 356.)

82. This assumption is confirmed to a certain degree in E. Lerch's substantiation that the French *Imparfait* occurs so seldom as a tense of vivid representation in Old French because vividly presentified action was usually rendered in the present tense. Later, as this tense became less popular, the *Imparfait* appeared in its place ("Imperfektum als Ausdruck der lebhaften Vorstellung," *Zeitschrift für romanische Philologie,* Bd. 42, 1923, 327).

83. H. Brinkmann, "Zur Sprache der *Wahlverwandtschaften*," *Festschrift Jost Trier,* (Mannheim, 1954).

84. Brinkmann, p. 257. In the same discussion Brinkmann also states that the present tense appears in the text whenever human action falters, where the inanimate is more powerful, and where action-verbs recede: "the boat rocks, the rudder gets away from her." But immediately preceeding this the text, also in the present tense, reads: She "jumps into the boat, takes hold of the rudder and pushes off . . .," where, therefore, Ottilie is active and the action-verb in this sense, then, does not recede.

85. L. Hjelmslev, *Principes de grammaire génerale* (Kopenhagen, 1928).

86. So, for example, we read in Pt. I, Ch. 13 (to quote just one from many such passages which would counter Brinkmann's interpretation): "Her intuitive feeling helped Charlotte through all these trials. She was aware of her serious intention of abandoning so noble and worthy an inclination.—How much did she wish to come to the aid of these two. Separation, she felt sure, will not be sufficient to heal such a disorder. She resolves to discuss the matter with the good child; but she is not able; the memory of her own irresoluteness stands in her way...."

87. Bühler, pp. 137f.

88. Ibid, p. 134.

89. Ibid., pp. 136f.

90. Ibid,. p. 137.

91. On the problem of I-saying, cf. P. Hofmann, *Das Verstehen von Sinn und seine Allgemeingültigkeit* (Berlin, 1929), and *Sinn und Geschichte* (Munich, 1937), especially Ch. I and VII.

92. M. Butor, "Des Gebrauch der Personalpronomen im Roman,"

Repertoire, 2 (Munich, 1965): "When a narrative remains entirely in the third-person (except in dialogue, naturally), when it remains a narrative without narrator, the distance between the narrated events and that moment in which they become narrated has no significance" (p. 97). Butor, in further—and welcome—confirmation of our theory, hereby establishes the connection between the fictional narrative function and the a-temporality of fiction. In still another passage, he continues: "The time in which it (the narrative) takes place, is a matter of indifference with regard to its relation to the present; it is a past which is entirely divorced from any real Today, a past which, however, does not recede farther and farther away from Today, but is rather a mythical aorist, in French the *Passé simple*."

93. K. Friedemann, *Die Rolle des Erzählers in der Epik* (Leipzig, 1910; reprinted 1967), p. 26.

94. Ibid., p. 77.

95. Jürgen Petersen, *Die Wissenschaft von der Dichtung* (Berlin, 1944), pp. 151, 160.

96. "Who describes the world in Balzac's novels? Who is this omniscient, omnipotent narrator, who is all places at once, who at the same time sees both the front and the reverse side of things, . . . and who simultaneously knows the present, past and future of each and every character? That can only be a god," is the opinion offered in all seriousness by A. Robbe-Grillet in " 'Nouveau Roman'—Neuer Roman, Neuer Mensch," *Akzente* (April, 1962), 175.

97. This interpretation, which also appears in Robbe-Grillet (n. 96), is not cancelled out in that he, along with all other modern narrative poets, has rejected it and created new narrative techniques.

98. Petersen, p. 152.

99. *Vorschule der Ästhetik*, § 62.

100. Cf. W. Preisendanz, *Humor als dichterische Einbildungskraft* (Munich, 1963). In reply to his contention that I have absolutized Jean Paul's humoristic narrative technique to an exclusive meaning of humor, let me state that this can scarcely be the case since (apart from the wording of my presentation itself) this narrative technique serves only as illustrative material for the problem under discussion in this particular chapter, namely that of the subjectivity of narration.

101. That a significant first-person intrusion of this kind does not always have humoristic intent I have already demonstrated in the article in *Euphorion*, using the example from "Les Faux Monnayeurs," by A. Gide.

102. In his book *Fiktion und Reflexion, Überlegungen zu Musil und Beckett* (Frankfurt am Main, 1967), Ulf Schramm, in studying such examples of reflective style, has drawn significant conclusions about the character of Musil's novel as one stamped with "thinking in terms of possibilities." What from our perspective is understood as an extreme instance of the fluctuating narrative function, Schramm describes as a "zone of transition, where it remains undecided whether thinking overlaps with fiction or vice versa," with the result that "both devices . . . lose their specificness and . . . can no longer mediate anything with certainty" (p. 160).

103. Spielhagen was not the first to pose this requirement. It was Aristotle, who praised Homer because he spoke as little as possible "himself," i.e., as narrator, and instead had a man or woman appear as soon as possible in the work. After Spielhagen this requirement was also posed by Ortega y Gasset ["Gedanken über den Roman," German version in *Die Aufgabe unserer Zeit* (Stuttgart, 1930)], and by Henry Green ["Verständigung," German version in *Die Neue Rundschau,* 1951].—For a discussion of Spielhagen, cf. the good critical work by W. Hellmann, "Objektivität, Subjektivität und Erzählkunst. Zur Romantheorie Friedrich Spielhagens," *Wesen und Wirklichkeit, Festschrift f. H. Plessner* (Göttingen, 1957).

104. E. Lerch, "Die stilistische Bedeutung des Imperfekts der Rede," GRM, VI (1914), 470ff.

105. W. Günther, *Probleme der Rededarstellung* (Marburg, 1928).

106. Lerch, n.49. D. Cohn distinguishes quite well between ironic mimetic formation and that which is seriously intended (cf. Cohn, p. 111).

107. R. Humphrey, *Stream of Consciousness in the Modern Novel* (Berkeley, 1954).

108. Franz Stanzel's *Narrative Situations in the Novel,* which we have already mentioned, and which contains many subtle observations, is a so to speak unintentional confirmation of the fluctuation of the narrative function and its poetological uniformity. Precisely in that Stanzel makes very sharp distinctions between the "authorial" novel type (where the "narrator" makes his presence noticeable by reporting and giving commentary) and the "figural" type (where the vantage-point is shifted to the persons of the novel, such as through dialogue, narrated monologue, and so forth), he cannot overlook the fact that in every novel both situations appear, even though in varying degrees depending upon both the author's individual style and the general style

of the period. "As in the first-person novel," Stanzel concedes, "we can also note a tendency in the figural novel towards admitting authorial elements into the figural narrative situation" (p. 92), and "conversely, when we read an authorial novel we see that not seldom there emerges a total presentification of the narrated, just as in figural narrative situations. This occurs, for example, in longer dialogue scenes . . ." (p. 93). Cf. also p. 47f. Certainly these things ought not to be taken as mere facts, but are to be observed as symptoms that this matter of an "authorial narrator" is more complex than is often to be inferred directly from the text.

109. When Wolfgang Kayser, in retaining the concept of the narrator, designates him as a "created, fictive figure" who is part of the totality of the work (*Entstehung und Krise des modernen Romans,* Stuttgart, 1954, 17), he does intimate that in fictional narration conditions are other than in the reality statement. But his terminology remains inadequate because he has not recognized in what relation fictional narration stands to the one who is manipulating it, i.e., the narrative poet. It is he who narrates; however, he does not narrate *about* his figures, but he narrates *the figures.*

110. Goethe: "The epic poem presents . . . man functioning outside of himself: in combat, travels, every sort of undertaking which calls for a certain breadth, whereas tragedy presents man from within himself" (December 23, 1797). Hegel: "With action everything is traced back to the inner character; with events, on the other hand, the external aspect retains its undivided right. . . . It is in this sense that I previously said it is the task of epic poesie to present the event of an action, and therefore . . . to also confer . . . to external circumstances the same right which in action as such the internal aspect claims exclusively for itself" (Hegel, IV, 135). [Trans. mine.] [*Vorlesungen über die Ästhetik,* III, 357.]

111. Kayser, *Das sprachliche Kunstwerk* (Berne, 1948), 369.

112. Friedrich von Blanckenburg's excellent theory of the novel (*Versuch über den Roman,* 1774; reprinted 1965), recognizes, with respect to Wieland's *Agathon,* "the man's being," his "inner state" (p. 18) as the theme of the novel, as opposed to the public "deeds, events and acts of the citizen" (p. 17) which the epos portrays.

113. Still in 1938, for example, Th. Spoerri, in his book *Die Formwerdung des Menschen* (Berlin, 1938), espouses similar notions to those of Hegel and Vischer in that he opposes "the world of the every-

day" as the subject-matter of the novel (pp. 6of.), the "Epopaea of
reality arranged into prose," as Hegel characterized it, to the world of
the epos, which is stamped by myth (Hegel, IV, 171 [trans. mine]).
[*Vorlesungen* . . ., III, 395.]

114. Petersen, p. 123.

115. Emil Winkler, *Das dichterische Kunstwerk* (Heidelberg, 1924).

116. Max Kommerell, *Jean Paul* (Frankfurt, 1933), p. 30.

117. Quoted by Fritz Martini, *Das Wagnis der Sprache*, p. 354.

118. If we want to be exact, then certainly we should say that from
the fluctuating narrative function only dialogue remains as the formational medium of dramatic fiction. For, as we have shown above, in
epic fiction dialogue is a form of the narrative function. But such a
determination would not only too strongly blur the distinction between
the epic and the dramatic form of fictional literature; it is also not in
place because dramatic dialogue is of a different structural and stylistic
nature from epic dialogue, having different functions from the latter
simply because in drama it is the sole means of formation. W. Kayser,
too, calls attention to this difference when he notes that epic dialogue
"is narrated and not presented," and for this reason the recitor of an
epic dialogue may not try to "evoke the illusion of entirely different
figures" (*Das sprachliche Kunstwerk*, p. 182).

Cf. further Benno von Wiese: "In the drama dialogue assumes certain functions which are most intimately connected with the problem
of the unfolding of the action" ("Gedanken zum Drama als Gespräch
und Handlung," *Der Deutschunterricht*, 1952, Heft 2, 29).—"The
drama is a mimesis of dialogue," as we read in Northrop Frye (*Anatomy
of Criticism*, Princeton, 1957, p. 269).

119. Hofmannsthal, "Unterhaltung über den 'Tasso' von Goethe,"
Gesammelte Werke, Prosa II (Frankfurt, 1951), 212.

120. Thus Otto Ludwig, too, said that "many fruitful perspectives would be gained if one were to derive all dramatic art from the
problem of giving play-acting a substratum" (*Gesammelte Schriften*,
V, 115).

121. Hegel, *The Phenomenology of Mind*, trans. J. B. Baille, 2nd
ed. (New York, 1931), p. 736. [Translation slightly modified.]
[*Phänomenologie des Geistes*, Ed. Lasson, 3 Aufl. (Leipzig, 1921),
p. 510.]

122. Cf. my earlier article, "Zum Strukturproblem der epischen und
dramatischen Dichtung," DVLG XXV (1951), Heft 1, from which I

have taken only what is essential for the determination of the poetological locus of the drama.

123. Günther Müller, "Über die Seinsweise von Dichtung," DVLG, XVII (1943), Heft 1, 144.

124. Max Dessoir, *Beiträge zur Kunstwissenschaft* (Stuttgart, 1929), p. 137; cf. also F. Junghans, *Zeit im Drama* (Berlin, 1931), p. 37.

125. Analyzed more closely in my article "Zum Strukturproblem . . ." Cf. also Una Ellis-Fermor, *The Frontiers of Drama* (London, 1945). These augmentational techniques are discussed in every theory of the drama, but as seen from our perspective of the drama's poetological locus, they are not relevant. Let us also cite from the experience of one dramatist: "The person of the drama is a speaking person, that is his restriction," F. Dürrenmatt says, thereby espousing in a certain respect the currently more or less tabooed monologue form (*Problems of the Theatre*, tr. Gerhard Nellhaus, New York, 1964, p. 22). [*Theaterprobleme* (Zurich, 1955), 33, 35.]

126. Hofmannsthal, *Gesammelte Werke, Prosa II*, 217.

127. Ibid., 44.

128. Ibid., 43.

129. Thomas Mann, *Reden und Aufsätze* I (Frankfurt an Main, 1965), 79f. [This particular essay has not been translated—Tr.]

130. Günther Müller, "Über das Zeitgerüst des Erzählens," DVLG, XXIV (1951), and: "Erzählzeit und erzählte Zeit," *Festschrift Paul Kluckhohn u. F. Schneider* (Tübingen, 1948).

131. The Italian Renaissance theorist Trissino took note of this, when in his work, "Le sei divisioni della Poetica," he says apropos of the Aristotelian definition of time that this is to be gotten more "de la representazione del senso che da l'arte." (As quoted by D. Frey, *Gotik und Renaissance*, p. 200.)

132. In ancient drama as well as in the medieval mystery plays, as D. Frey demonstrates, the audience experienced itself as a participant in the action, as represented by the chorus in antiquity, and in the Middle Ages as part of the processions. Inherently related to this is the fact that "the time and place of the spectator was directly equated with the fictive place and time of the dramatic action" (p. 213), and the problem of the unity of time and place did not arise.

133. Cf. D. Frey, "Zuschauer und Bühne," *Kunstwissenschaftliche Grundfragen* (Vienna, 1946).

134. P. Corneille, *Oeuvres complètes* (Paris, 1963), p. 844.

135. This fallacy was discovered already by August Wilhelm Schlegel, who said apropos of Corneille's laws of unity: "The only basis for such a rule is that we observe a resemblance which is thought necessary for the theatrical illusion, namely that represented time and real time are one. If we once grant a difference like that between two hours and thirty hours, then rightfully we can go much further. The concept of illusion has occasioned great errors in the theory of art." (*Vorlesungen über dramatische Kunst und Literatur*, Bd. II, ed. E. Lohner, Stuttgart, 1967, 22.)

136. Cf. also Junghans, *Zeit im Drama* (Berlin, 1931), pp. 16f., 51f. This book exhaustively treats the problem of time in the drama (differentiated as extension, conquest of time, and duration) with a wealth of material, and in many respects is a confirmation of the problems which we are treating here from an exclusively epistemological perspective.

137. Theorists who reserve the present for the lyric have claimed the future for drama. Thus Jean Paul says: "the drama [presents] that action which extends toward and into the future" (*Vorschule der Asthetik*, § 75), and in recent times Susanne Langer: "as literature creates a virtual past, drama creates a virtual future" (*Feeling and Form*, pp. 306f.). With justification Wellek and Warren (*The Theory of Literature*, New York, 1949, pp. 237f.) treat with some irony this and other temporal metaphysics in literary theory which attempt to fix the major genres via temporal modes.

138. Goethe to Schiller, December 2, 1797.

139. Hegel, IV, 248 [trans. mine]. [*Vorlesungen* . . . , III, 479.]

140. Thornton Wilder, *The Intent of the Artist*, p. 83 (as quoted from Langer, p. 307).

141. That Goethe himself modified this all too strong a personification of the narrator has already been noted (p. 178).

142. It is possible to draw comparisons in retrospect between the modern abstract stage and the small, bare Shakespearean stage. The Elizabethan literary theorist Philip Sidney's critical statement: "Now come three ladies who are picking flowers, and we must imagine the stage as a garden; then, in the same place, we hear of a shipwreck, and it is our error if we do not visualize the rocks. . . ." (*The Defence of Poesie*, 1595, ed. E. Flügel, 1889, p. 102, as quoted by D. Frey, *Gotik* . . ., p. 194) throws light on the problem of the stage as merely

"signifying" versus actually giving the illusion of reality. Sidney, already disposed toward the Renaissance manner of direct visualization via concrete objects, "is making fun of the medieval tradition of the Shakespearean stage," which was still alive in the sixteenth century. But this tradition was one accustomed to apperceiving the merely signifying, symbolic nature of its dramatic repertory, e.g., to considering the actor —who was indeed present in the play, but who was not intended to be (*qua* actor)—as not present, and to interpreting simultaneous stage decorations merely in their symbolic sense of suggesting spatial relationships (G. Frey, p. 192). With respect to the latter, the abstract stage of Erwin Piscator, for example, follows quite similar procedures.

143. This procedure need not first be compared with the framework story of a first-person narrative, as most likely has been done. Narrative literature offers far more appropriate analogies, for example, how in Thomas Mann's *The Magic Mountain* the depiction of Hans Castorp's childhood in the chapter entitled "Of the Christening Basin, and of Grandfather in his Two-Fold Guise" is simply introduced by the sentence, "Hans Castorp had only dim memories of his parents' home; he had hardly known his father and mother . . .," a chapter in which the perspective of recollection is by no means strictly adhered to, which would have necessitated the use of the pluperfect tense. Instead, the narration of the Then becomes fictionalized—in the past tense— to a Here and Now. In precisely the same manner we experience such flash-backs in the film.

144. In what manner the drama as literature is structured with a view toward its form as a theatrical work has been demonstrated above.

145. Hegel, IV, 195. [*Vorlesungen* . . . III, 422.]

146. Edmund Husserl, *Cartesian Meditations*, trans. Dorion Cairns (The Hague, 1960), p. 2. [Translation slightly modified.] [*Cartesianische Meditationen und Pariser Vorträge* (Haag, 1963), p. 4.]

147. That church hymns belong to or can be classified as prayer is confirmed by Friedrich Heiler: "Much of this artistic devotional poetry issues from personal experiences in prayer and is a source of our knowledge of genuine, personal prayer, as for instance . . . the psalms of the Old Testament . . . and the hymns of the various national churches." (*Prayer, A Study in the History and Psychology of Religion*, trans., ed. Samuel McComb, New York, 1932, p. xxiii.) [*Das Gebet*, 5. Aufl. (Munich, 1923), p. 31.]

148. Thus Ingarden, too, notes that in the philosophical-theoretical analysis of the phenomenology of the "literary work," this term serves

"to designate every single work of so-called 'belles lettres,' without distinction as to whether one is dealing with a genuine work of art or with a worthless piece" (Ingarden, p. 1 n.1).

That undertakings such as that of Ingarden and my own deal with structural phenomena grounded in the theory of language (or also in ontology), and not with aesthetic phenomena (as we have repeatedly emphasized) is something which scholars whose orientation is toward literary history and aesthetics cannot easily see or accept. Thus René Wellek's massive criticism of my genre theory, reproaches me—and in particular the analysis of the lyric I—with precisely this, and even calls it "psychologism" ("Genre Theory, the Lyric, and 'Erlebnis,' " *Festschrift f. R. Alewyn,* Cologne, 1967).

Let me take the present opportunity to make a comprehensive reply to Wellek's accusations (whereby I should also like to mention that before his article appeared the chapter on the lyric had already been re-worked for the second German edition of the present book, and, as I hope, many causes for justified criticism eliminated, i.e., in part corrected, in part entirely stricken). Principally, Wellek's criticism is founded on a misunderstanding of what the concepts *Aussage* and *Aussagesubjekt* mean in my theory. The German concept *Aussage* as it occurs in grammar and in the logic of judgment is to be rendered in English by "statement," which has a general meaning beyond that of "assertion" (*Behauptung*). In the English version of Wittgenstein's *Philosophical Investigations* (trans. G. E. M. Anscombe, 3rd ed., New York, 1968), the term *Aussage*, which occurs occasionally there, is translated by "statement." Likewise, H. Herring's recent German translation of A. T. Ayrer's work *Language, Truth and Logic* (Stuttgart, 1970), renders Ayrer's term "statement" by *Aussage*. Cf. also my article "The Theory of Statement," *Allgemeen Nederlands Tijdschrift vor Wijsbegeerte en Psychologie,* 65 (1964). It is not at all to be rendered by "utterance," and therefore neither is the concept *Wirklichkeitsaussage,* such as I have precisely defined it, to be translated as "real utterance" (p. 393), but as "reality statement." Similarly, the concept of the statement-subject is concerned not with a "speaker," but with the structural element of the statement-system of language.—Permit me also to defend my genre theory against the simplistic formula to which Wellek would reduce it: "The dividing criterion is the speaker: in the lyric the poet himself speaks, in the epic and drama he makes others speak" (p. 393). If this were the case, my book would hardly have provided ground for discussion.

149. In hymnals which have included the fourth stanza—for ex-

ample the *Evangelisches Gesangbuch für Elsass-Lothringen* (1914) and the *Christliches Gesangbuch für evangelische Gemeinden* (Bielefelt, 1854)—lines 3 and 4 read as follows: "and Heaven's bounteous gift/Keeps my glance upward-turned." In the *Gesangbuch für die evangel. reformierte Kirche der deutschen Schweiz* they read: "What He reaps is an eternal gift,/Blessed is he who clings to Him."

150. W. Vortriede, *Novalis und die französischen Symbolisten* (Stuttgart, 1963), p. 103.

151. St. Mallarmé, *Oeuvres complètes*, Bibl. de la Pléiade (Paris, 1956), p. 869.

152. Hugo Friedrich, *Die Struktur der modernen Lyrik*, erw. Neuausgabe (Hamburg, 1967). p. 102.

153. Max Bense, *Experimentelle Schreibweisen*, rot. Text 17 (Stuttgart, no year).

154. Ingrid Strohschneider-Kohrs, "Sprache und Wirklichkeit bei Arno Holz," *Poetica*, Bd. 1 (1967), Heft 1, p. 62.

155. F. Ponge, "My creative method," *Trivium*, VII (1949), Heft 2, 96, 101, 107.

156. Ponge, p. 109.

157. On Ponge, cf. Elisabeth Walther's fundamental presentation entitled *Francis Ponge, eine östhetische Analyse* (Cologne, Berlin, 1965), a study employing the principles of modern semantics. Especially pertinent to our problem are pp. 64ff.

157a. When Herbert Lehnert, in his book *Struktur und Sprachmagie, zur Methode der Lyrikinterpretation* (Stuttgart, 1966), conceives of the lyric I as a process of identification of the author with the reader (or listener) (pp. 47, 57, 67, 120), it seems to me that the process of interpretation, which is the topic of the book, is too strongly construed as a structural element in the poem itself.

158. Paul Stöcklein, "Dichtung vom Dichter gesehen," *Wirkendes Wort*, 1. Sonderheft (1952), 84.

159. Wellek, Warren, *The Theory of Literature* (New York, 1949), p. 15.

160. W. Kayser, *Das sprachliche Kunstwerk*, p. 334.

161. *Rahel. Ein Buch des Andenkens*, Bd. II (Berlin, 1834), 352.

162. Emil Staiger, *Goethe*, I (Zurich, 1952), 56.

163. It should be sufficiently evident from my expositions that these statements made by Rahel, Staiger, and Stöcklein are cited only as evidence for the impossibility of defining the lyric I, or respectively

its identity, as being that of the poet. That is, our reasons for quoting them are exclusively those of defining the lyric structure from within theory of language. For these purposes it matters not whether such statements are "hysterical" and "highflown," as Wellek criticizes, who cites these passages but misunderstands their function for my arguments ("Genre Theory, the Lyric, and Erlebnis," p. 394).

164. Cf. Husserl, *Logical Investigations*, Vol. 2, Investigation V: "On Intentional Experiences and their 'Contents,'" 553–556. [*Logische Untersuchungen*, II, 1 (Halle, 1928), 343f.] As precursory to Husserl's definition of the intentionality of experiences we may consider Dilthey's exposition in the second of his *Studien zur Grundlegung der Geisteswissenschaften* entitled "Der Strukturzusammenhang des Wissens," *Gesammelte Schriften*, VII (Leipzig and Berlin, 1927), where *Erlebnis* is described as "the structural unity between mental attitudes and contents."—For a history of the word and the concept *Erlebnis*, cf. also H. G. Gadamer, *Wahrheit und Methode* (Tübingen, 1960), pp. 56–66.

165. To Eckermann (with reference to *Elective Affinities*), February 17, 1830.

166. H. Henel, "Erlebnisdichtung und Symbolismus," *Zur Lyrik-Diskussion* (Darmstadt, 1966), p. 223.

167. Hilde Domin, *Doppelinterpretationen* (Bonn, 1966), p. 31.

168. On this topic, cf. Paul Neuburger, *Die Verseinlage in der Prosadichtung der Romantik* (Tübingen, 1924).

168a. On the entirely different structure of lyric interpolations in Hermann Broch's *Schlafwandler*, cf. Dorrit Cohn, *The Sleepwalkers* (The Hague, Paris, 1966), pp. 103ff.

169. Hellmut Rosenfeld, *Das deutsche Bildgedicht* (Tübingen, 1935), passim.

170. Rosenfeld, pp. 122, 124ff., where the origin of the Greek representational epigram is traced.

171. The description of pictures and of things, which Rilke cultivated to the point of virtuosity in his *Neue Gedichte*, often proceeds there in reverse fashion, such that something in itself non-pictorial, but an otherwise experienced human reality, is re-formed into a pictorial situation. There are distinct marginal cases here, for example the poem "Bildnis" ["Portrait"]. The title of this poem, which refers to Elenora Duse, can have the import of a spiritual portrait, whereas the "Portrait of a Lady" cited above is such that it does not conceal its inspiration from an actual portrait, possibly a photograph.

172. This perfect tense form does not gainsay the character of the picture poem. The sculpture-poem "Kretische Artemis" ["Cretan Artemis"] also exhibits the past tense, and here it has the effect that behind the plasticity there is projected the mythical "archetype" of the goddess, and in turn mythic time itself. That is, the realm of art is transported into the realm of history.

173. Rosenfeld, p. 252.

174. Ibid., p. 13.

175. Ibid., p. 38.

176. Wolfgang Kayser, *Geschichte der deutschen Ballade* (Berlin, 1936), p. 140.

177. *Goethes Werke* (Hamburger Ausgabe), I, 400.

178. Ibid., II, 187.

179. Kayser, *Das sprachliche Kunstwerk*, p. 356.

180. Ibid.

181. Georg Misch, *A History of Autobiography in Antiquity*, trans. E. W. Dickes, Vol. I (Cambridge, Mass., 1951), 46ff. [*Geschichte der Autobiographie*, Bd. I (Göttingen, 1949), 51.]

182. Misch, I, 56 [trans. mine]. [German edition, p. 60.]

183. A comparison of the two versions reveals that the passage cited above and other similar ones appear unchanged in the second version of the novel, which has the first-person form throughout. That in the first version of the part "Childhood" (III, 4), which is in the first-person, these passages are conspicuous because of their third-person form, is, from a purely literary point of view, a symptom of Keller's initially insecure sense of form in this novel. But it also indicates that the Munich parts of the novel are more oriented toward the world than toward the self.

184. For a further discussion of this problem, cf. my debate with F. Stanzel and W. Rasch in my previously cited article "Noch einmal— vom Erzählen" (pp. 66–70). Stanzel and Rasch also elaborate upon the problem of the "subjectivity" of narration.

INDEX OF NAMES

Index of Names

Novalis (F. v. Hardenberg), 238f., 240, 242–246

Offenbach, J., 194
O'Neill, E., 204
Ortega y Gasset, 356
Orwell, G., 111

Paul, H., 66
Petersen, J., 141, 142f., 196
Pirandello, 287
Piscator, E., 361
Plato, 51, 193, 344f.
Ponge, F., 260ff.
Preisendanz, W., 355
Proust, M., 311, 334
Pushkin, A., 194

Rasch, W., 365
Richardson, 177
Richter, see Jean-Paul
Rickert, H., 18
Ries, J., 348
Rilke, R. M., 43f., 51, 60, 64f., 90, 91, 236f., 258, 283f., 295, 296–300
Robbe-Grillet, A., 123ff., 355
Rompelmann, A., 351f.
Rosenfeld, H., 294, 301, 365
Russell, B., 52, 347

Sachs, N., 263, 267f.
Salinger, J. D., 193
Sarraute, N., 193
Saussure, F. de, 152
Schaeffer, A., 336
Schaper, E., 85, 180ff., 184
Schiller, 57, 65, 91, 96, 109f., 206, 209, 281, 360
Schlegel, A. W., 2, 360
Schneider, F., 344
Schramm, U., 356
Seidler, H., 353
Sengle, F., 102ff., 105, 107
Shakespeare, 223, 224
Sidney, P., 360f.
Sigwart, C., 26, 28f., 31
Spielhagen, 140, 142, 356

Spoerri, T., 357f.
Staiger, E., 4, 198, 274
Stanzel, F., 139, 351, 356f., 365
Stein, G., 256
Sterne, L., 152
Stifter, A., 74–81, 123, 133, 156ff., 311, 312
Stöcklein, P., 272f.
Storm, T., 278f., 338f.
Storz, G., 346, 351
Strindberg, 223, 224
Strohschneider-Kohrs, I., 363

Terborch, 57, 87
Tolstoy, 20, 112, 115, 157
Trakl, G., 249–252, 254, 255, 259, 267
Trissino, 359
Tschaikowsky, 194

Utitz, E., 58

Vaihinger, H., 57, 58
Varnhagen, R., 273, 274
Vischer, F., 358
Vortriede, W., 255

Wackenroder, 301f.
Wagner, R., 194
Walther von der Vogelweide, 280
Walther, E., 363
Walzel, O., 351
Warren, A., 273, 360
Weidlé, W., 345
Weinrich, H., 352
Wellek, R., 273, 360, 362, 363f.
Werfel, F., 121, 314
Whitehead, A., 32
Wieland, C., 102ff., 117, 357
Wiese, B., 358
Wilder, T., 213, 360
Winkler, E., 196
Wittgenstein, L., 2f., 52f., 261
Woolf, V., 72, 85, 172, 209
Wunderlich-Reis, 99

Yourcenar, M., 336f.

Zeuxis, 57